American Panorama

West of the Mississippi

AMERICAN PANORAMA

WEST OF THE MISSISSIPPI

A **HOLIDAY** MAGAZINE BOOK

DOUBLEDAY & COMPANY, INC.
Garden City, New York

The illustrations in this book are the work of the photographers
listed:
Following page 54: Ewing Krainin, Tom Hollyman, Walt Dyke
Following page 150: Ray Atkeson, Emil Schulthess, George Leavens
Following page 246: Josef Muench, John Lewis Stage, Thomas Peter
Lake
Following page 342: Elliott Erwitt, Tom Hollyman, George Leavens

Contents

Introduction

The United States is divided naturally into broad geographical regions—mountains, plains, deserts; the broad coastal areas and the great river basins. The pattern of states that has been overlaid seems puny and artificial in comparison. More often than not the borders are odd and arbitrary, reflecting political connivance or geometrical convenience rather than the plain geographical realities.

But these fifty states are more than mere patches of color on the map. In the crucial moments of American history it has been the states that have assumed the leadership. It was, after all, thirteen of them who brought the nation into existence. Less than a century later those same states and many more engaged in a long and bitter war to defend their individual rights, beliefs and habits.

Now as in the beginning there are differences between the states. For a hundred years the differences have been expressed in pride and achievement rather than in hostility, but they have by no means disappeared.

Over the years Holiday has published portraits of all of the states of the Union including the two newest—portraits which reflected their history, their people and their personalities. This series, written by some of America's most gifted writers, has formed the outline of the magazine's continuing mosaic of America.

This volume is part of that total picture—the twenty-four states west of the Mississippi. It is representative of the whole for at least two reasons. It dramatizes our continual differences—the difference between Wyoming and Louisiana, for example, or Minnesota and New Mexico. It also sounds another and greater theme, the theme of unity which in combination has formed and defined this country.

The Editors

PART I *The New States*

laska

by JAMES WARNER BELLAH

Alaska should be entered slowly, by boat or by road; its vast spread makes it impossible to assimilate in the four easy flying hours from Seattle to Anchorage. Its magnitude is untrammeled; its grandeur grows upon the consciousness, like hunger. It cannot be explained by comparison. It offers no common denominator to past experience. There is no instant Alaska.

By ship from Vancouver to Juneau, the capital, you steam three days between the islanded shores of the Inside Passage, through thick-growing timber, and along that entire eight hundred miles there is no scar of forest-fire damage, no smoke wisp of a campfire. You hear no honk of a car horn, no whistle of a train. No one is there to drop a cigarette, to be careless with firesmolder. No one is there at all. In places, no one has *ever* been there.

The Tongass National Forest, in the southeastern part of the state, says the Forestry Service, alone could provide much of the newsprint for the newspapers of the world. United States Army Engineers estimate that a Yukon River dam at Rampart would form a lake as large as Ontario, that would take nine years to fill; and the resulting water power would produce half as many kilowatt-hours as are produced at present in all the other forty-nine states.

Yet in Nome, on the Bering Sea, a guide, after spotting a polar bear from the air, can telephone a Wall Street broker that if he will hop a plane he can enjoy some fine shooting and be back at his desk a few days later.

Arrived at Juneau, you have barely entered Alaska. You must continue westerly about *thirty-four degrees* of longitude before you reach Little Diomede Island in Bering Strait—a scant two and a half miles from the U.S.S.R. You must travel north more than a thousand miles across the entire northwest shoulder of North America before you reach Point Barrow on the Arctic Ocean. You must go almost to Asia before you reach Adak in the Aleutians. Alaska is a *damn* big land.

Despite Edna Ferber's implication to the contrary, there are many respectably-come-by mink coats in Fairbanks and considerably more in larger Anchorage (although the parka is more suitable winter garb). Lilly Daché hats and Irene gowns are sold in both towns—and to prove that this fringe of luxurious insanity is no latter-day innovation, Klondike Kate wore a Worth gown brought from Paris at Dawson's St. Andrew's Day Ball back in 1900—and every gentleman with her in the extant photograph wore tails, except one who came black tie deliberately or was a waiter. And Dawson, fifty miles or so across the line in Canada's Yukon Territory, is a bare 128 miles south of the Arctic Circle.

Alaska is a solidly, stubbornly, prideful American land. You can live and work there in reasonable comfort the year around—despite the mere two hours of summer darkness and the scant two hours of winter daylight.

There is no Skid Row in any Alaskan town. With seasonal employment a condition of life, some Alaskans plan their living better than others, thus live more comfortably in the slack winter season. Some have more, some less—but there are few bums; it is not an environment in which a bum can survive.

Newcomers have difficulty adjusting to the high costs of food, clothing and rent; but wages are high, too, and it isn't long before a balance is struck. Then life settles into a routine much like that in any small town Stateside. There are Scout troops, Cub packs, the Y.M.C.A., bridge clubs, cocktail parties, lodges, luncheon clubs and country clubs of sorts.

The first winter can be a morale hazard if you make it one. Children go to school in darkness and return in darkness. But again, in compensation, the sun is still shining in summer when you come out of the night picture show.

Alaskans work hard, on a seasonal schedule; they are imbued consciously or unconsciously with the challenge of their vast land. They marry young, raise large families and their children for the most part remain in Alaska.

There is a cheerful get-rich-quick flavor to life that seldom pays off; it probably persists from the gold-rush days which never paid off either. This may be due to the absence of huge corporations to dominate commerce and mold organization men. A young Alaskan will get a local job—but he usually keeps one hand free for himself. He fishes and hunts as a routine of life and, as a further routine, he eternally casts about for an opportunity to go into business for himself —however modestly. He has an extremely self-confident and independent character. You cannot be otherwise in the eternal grandeur of this vast land.

There have long been two schools of thought in Alaska about statehood—for and against. The "Fors" wanted their destiny in their own hands, regardless of the taxes needed to support a state. They wanted to be rid of territorial status, to pass their own laws to govern their living—for there is a Great Dream in Alaska, and it can come true only if the individual is untrammeled by Federal paternalism.

The "Againsts" were acutely conscious that the permanent population of Alaska is small and they believed that the economic health was due in great part to the vast military and naval installations. They wanted no curtailment in the largess of Uncle Sam. They saw financial ruin in statehood.

The "Fors" wanted statehood now. The "Againsts" wanted it too— but after a while. Now that the die has been cast, however, most Alaskans seem gratified. They have attained voting representation at last—as a balance to their taxation. Statehood is American—no matter what it costs.

Now that Alaska is a state, it is experiencing a great influx of visitors. There is no Hilton Hotel yet in Alaska and no Forum of the Twelve Caesars to dine in, but if you write for summer-travel information, you'll get enough material on off-trail sights—natural wonders, totem poles, fish, moose, bear and Mount McKinley—to top seven pounds on the bathroom scales. For to Alaska tourism is an essential industry highly organized by the Alaska Visitors Association.

From June to September you can travel Alaska's tenuous net of paint-shy, neon-lighted towns by your own car, hitchhiker's thumb, bus, boat, train or any of a dozen airlines in a reasonable expectancy

of comfort. In winter, hitchhiking will freeze your thumb stiff, and
the waterways are iced in, but with foresight and respect for
weather, travel is not entirely restricted.

There will be a virile echo of the raw frontier in this Alaskan
junket, a sense perhaps of the latent sacrifice that has always attended the March of Empire, a feeling that the Donner Passes and
the Death Valleys that have been long forgotten Stateside are still
nebulously just around the corner in Alaska, in a grandsire's living
memory.

Before you reach Ketchikan on the Inside Passage, there is the
rusted wreck of the steamer *North Sea* on the easterly shore a few
miles north of the Indian Village of Bella Bella. She went down in
1947—with no loss of life. In Juneau, at the Museum, there are two
water-stained life rings of the *Princess Sophia*. She sank above
Juneau in 1918—and there were no survivors. The North Country
can be a hard country.

Ketchikan is the first port of call on the Inside Passage, and there
the frontier forthrightness strikes you abruptly in a hand-lettered
sign: "No dogs. No drunks allowed." This is not tourist stuff. The
proprietor means it. It bears the indelible mark of anger—of long-
suffering patience exhausted at last. You *feel* for the man who lettered that sign.

The average age of the Alaskan today is twenty-seven, which in
all sports—including the challenging one of making a new country—
is about the peak championship age. Bred in Alaska, in many in-
stances for three generations, his grandfather knew the '98 Gold
Rush. His father knew the lean years after 1918—and his children
find the houses too big when they visit the older States, and the
waters too warm for good swimming. "Outside" for a few weeks,
they want to go home—to the snow-capped mountains, the salmon,
the fast, trout-thick creeks, the bear and moose in the broad and
empty reaches of the Big Land—a land that has already grown its
own vital people.

There is the natural friendliness of youth in the Alaskan. It is in-
nate to his character that he offers himself and accepts you without
guile. He passes you from town to town to his friends and neighbors.
Alaska is the biggest small town in the world. Trump your partner's
ace on Monday in Petersburg and it's known—by mukluk telegraph
—in Kotzebue on Tuesday.

Its Main Street is only four blocks long—Southeast Alaska, the In-

terior, the Arctic and "Westward"—which ends at the tip of the
Aleutian Islands, close against Asia. This Main Street, though, has a
cultural texture that could give a scholar a lifetime of research.

Aboriginally, there are the ancient Indian tribes of Southeast
Alaska and the offshore islands that shelter the Inside Passage. There
are the Eskimos of the northern Arctic rim. There are the Aleuts
(give that three syllables, please), an Eskimo stock differing from
the Arctic Eskimo in head shape and in development of basic language, with their culture adapted to a raw, wet climate rather than
to subzero cold. The islands of the Aleuts curve under Siberia—almost to Kamchatka.

In hill-sprawled, jumbled Juneau—named for Joe Juneau who discovered gold there in 1880—it is easy to go back the first ninety-two
years of American Alaska's culture. You can do it in conversation
with the curator of the Museum—or academically with the records
and exhibits kept under his helpful and scholarly hand. Or you can
climb up to Ruth Allman's house and cover the subject informally
over sourdough waffles and Russian tea. Ruth's house hangs on the
hillside with most of Juneau below, framed by the bow windows in
which Judge James Wickersham's old desk and chair still sit. Her
stepfather, James Wickersham, was a United States District judge in
Alaska from 1900 to 1908—often as not riding circuit by dog team—
and thereafter delegate to Congress from Alaska for fourteen years.
He introduced the first statehood bill in 1916—forty-two years before
final passage. He was the moving spirit in the founding of the University of Alaska. His old house is a pleasant home still and a
repository crammed with mementos of his service to Alaska—including a five-foot shelf of his personal diaries.

In the judge's files, there is a photostat of a document that had
long been mislaid in Washington, and which the judge finally located
when he was a delegate: "To the Treasurer of the United States,
greeting. Pay to Edward de Stoekle, Envoy Extraordinary and Minister Plenipotentiary of His Majesty the Emperor of Russia, or order,
out of the appropriation named in the margin—Seven million, two
hundred thousand dollars, being in consideration of certain territory
ceded by the Emperor of Russia to the United States as described
in treaty of 30th March 1867." That Warrant, Number 9759, made
Alaska a part of the United States at a price of about two cents an
acre. A right smart real-estate deal.

Item—from Ruth Allman's conversation: "To make a 'starter' for sourdough cakes," says Ruth, "you boil a few potatoes pretty much away and put the residue in a jar until it ferments. This you carry with you on the trail for the rest of your life.

"You next stir a pinch of soda in a shot glass of water and you stir it with your left little finger as a matter of tradition because that finger is usually cleaner than the others and there were few spoons in the Yukon in Ninety-eight. Add this to a flour-and-water mix laced from your 'starter' and whop it up fast. As you whop it you can hear the batter thicken, for what you are actually going to eat when sourdough cakes are baked is fifty per cent hot air."

In Juneau the people jump to the fire siren faster than in any other town in the world, for the heterogeneous, closely packed, well-weathered buildings are mostly of wood, and the hill funnel in which the town is built can become a roaring chimney if the wind is right. The engine sirens begin with the first sick-cow bellow of the fire alarm, which faintly echoes the urgency of London air-raid warnings during the blitz.

Behind Juneau are the upper workings of the now-idle Alaska Juneau Mine—at one time the biggest gold-mining operation in the world. You can walk through the entire mountain to the water-hung outer workings you first saw from the steamer. It's possible to take sharp photographs in Juneau at half past nine of a summer's night and play baseball by daylight until almost eleven—and if you want a frontier echo after dark, there is the galloping Red Dog Saloon. You will probably eat your first grilled king-salmon steak in Alaska at Mike's, across the bridge in Douglas, and you will never forget its succulence.

You can drive up to Alaska over the Alaska Highway, once called the Alcan, as you can drive through much of interior Alaska. From Canada the Haines Cut-Off connects over the mountains to Haines, where a car ferry with Florida, New Jersey, Alabama, Colorado and other remote license plates carries your car into Juneau.

The Alaska Highway is not a hard-surface road, and in the dry season it is dusty. It is a long road and, if you are easily bored, monotonous. There are, however, gas stations, repair shops and motels every fifty miles or so—and your face will be exceedingly red if, before you started, you were talked into buying do-it-yourself repair kits, extra fan belts and a spare battery, four spare tires and two five-gallon cans of extra gasoline.

Every hundred miles or so in the Yukon Territory there are camping points with water, cooking facilities, trailer courts and a cottage for emergency shelter. Ambulance, nursing and medical service are supplied by the Canadian Army. The Royal Canadian Mounted Police patrols the highway in Canada. The Alaskan Police patrols it in Alaska. There may be a detour or two, and in the dry season forest fires, but you will see retired couples traveling the highway in expensive sedans, women driving it alone, families with children touring in station wagons, and tourists bussing it by scheduled bus.

From Vancouver to Fairbanks, Alaska, it is about 2300 miles of almost breathlessly beautiful country. It is not U.S. 66, and you won't find heated swimming pools at the motels, but there always will be hot water for a bath, and on occasion excellent food and service—and you will have had a safe adventure the like of which is not offered to you anywhere else in the world at this late date.

In Juneau we have pecked lightly at Alaska's nearly one hundred years of American culture. Let us go farther back. Fifty minutes of bush-pilot flying time, westerly beyond the Inside Passage to the open North Pacific Ocean, will land you in Sitka—the old Imperial Russian capital of Alaska. The first Russian governor was Alexandr Baranov. His castle is gone and so is the Russian fort—all but some miscellaneous smooth-bore artillery—but the line of the palisades can still be traced with the help of the National Park Service. The inscriptions on some of the Russian graves are still legible, and more tangibly, there is no telephone book in the towns of Alaska that does not carry some Russian names to this day, many of them American descendants of the Tsar's traders and military. M. L. "Duke" Mitrovich was the mayor of Sitka when I was there and Mrs. Margaret Federoff his very competent city clerk. If you fancy carved wood and inlay work, you know her husband's bowls, table tops and candle holders—even if you have never been farther west than Madison Avenue, New York.

Sitka was founded in 1799 as New Archangelsk, but it was not until 1816 that Father Alexis Sokoloff arrived with an icon of the Archangel Michael and converted the Russian-Orthodox chapel into a church. St. Michael's Cathedral is the direct descendant of that original chapel. Regular services are still held there. It is a log structure, clapboarded outside and lined inside with painted canvas, and if you make a modest altar donation, you will be permitted to inspect the interior.

Inside, you will see the Chapel of Our Lady of Kazan, the Chapel of St. Michael and the Chapel of St. John the Baptist—each with its painted icons embellished magnificently with silver-gilt *repoussé* work, appliquéd to the iconostas, which is the wall that closes off the sanctuary into which no woman may pass. The book of the four Gospels which is used at St. Michael's only at Easter and Christmas is so heavy with silver decoration that it weighs more than twenty-five pounds.

In the National Military Cemetery, at Sitka, the runner, Captain Charles William Paddock, USMC, is buried, the onetime "fastest human," who died in a plane crash during World War II. Not far from his grave lies Lieutenant B. W. Livermore, 2nd U. S. Artillery, said to have been killed in a duel on June 30, 1868—with a whisper to this day that the cause was a woman—to be more precise, a Russian princess, or in the vernacular of the times, a squaw.

The transfer of Alaska from Russian to United States sovereignty took place in Sitka; the Army withdrew in 1877 and then the United States Navy took over.

A Presbyterian missionary named Fannie Kellogg started a school for Indian children, and a United States Naval officer became the first truant officer. Some time during each school day the officer turned up in Miss Fannie's classroom. If the full quota of children was not present from each house, he imposed a five-blanket fine for each absent child.

How much that was in dollars in 1880 is hard to say, but a Thlinget (pronounced Klinket) blanket today is worth as much as a thousand dollars and more. Truancy, therefore, decelerated to zero. (No one remembers what the Navy did with the blankets.)

Close by the flagpole across from the Federal Building are two stone slabs that bear petroglyphs from the deep mists of antiquity—stones marked by a people of whom the Sitka Thlinget Indians have no knowledge in song or legend. All they know is that the marks were made by people who lived in the Big Land long before they themselves came—and the Thlingets have forgotten how many centuries *they* have been there.

They have not forgotten, however, that on the beach outside Sitka, more than a hundred and fifty years ago, they once beat the caviar out of the Russians (the Sitka National Monument marks the spot)—and if the Russians should come back they will do it again at the drop of a Thlinget ceremonial dance hat.

I cannot leave Sitka without mentioning the eating place that was

run by Bill Shields when I was there. We had a mess of shrimp and a
fillet of grilled sockeye salmon that were so delicious we almost ate
ourselves into a delightful decline. A night's sleep, however, and the
palate was ready for cold, cracked Dungeness crab at the Bills Club
in Haines, which you reach by a fifty-minute bush-pilot flight north.

This country between Juneau and Haines—a mountain-girt land
free from the distractions of the outside world—is as beautiful as any
on earth.

The air is invigorating; you need no tranquilizers. Snow never
leaves these bald mountaintops, nor do the mountain sheep and
goats. There are brown, black and grizzly bear in the timber and a
profusion of moose in the flatlands, and fish swim thick in the waters.

Alaska is in the glacier business. The Mendenhall outside of Juneau is a must for visitors, and near Haines is the equally dramatic
Davidson, and the high-hung Rainbow. Little more than thirty years
ago the Rainbow reached down to the waters of the Chilkat; now it
nestles along the upper slopes, a kaleidoscope of color when the sun
strikes it—and a roar of ice-spewing thunder when it stirs. When
there is an earthquake in this country, the mountains dance to the
glory of God. They smoke from base to summit with the saffron dust
of tumbling rocks and there is an awesome grandeur to the spectacle.

The first permanent Army post in Alaska—Fort William H. Seward,
sometimes called Chilkoot Barracks—was established near Haines, in
1898. At one time it was garrisoned by the Second Battalion of my
old Regiment, the 16th Infantry, and it was commanded around 1912
by an old Army character who appears in special orders merely as
Colonel Gardener. To eke out a much lower pay scale than the Army
enjoys today, Colonel Gardener would make a weekly round of the
Haines bars, ostensibly on duty checks, but actually to empty into
his tobacco pouch the clipped ends from the permanently installed
cigar clippers of the day; they supplied his pipe tobacco for the following week. I rather like that homely touch.

"Fiji" Carl Heinmiller—who left an eye and part of a hand in the
South Pacific when he fought the Japanese War for a shirtful of
medals—and four other World War II veterans purchased Fort
Seward from the War Assets Administration in 1946. It is now the
town of Port Chilkoot, and Carl is the mayor and the activating spirit
of Alaska Youth, Inc. This organization supplies summer jobs for
teen-agers, offers craft and trade instruction and has developed

Chilkat Thlinget Indian dancing—done by Explorer Scouts and Ex-plorettes—into a decidedly worth-while cultural attraction.

Since the older Indians no longer dance and the tribal teen-agers regard ceremonial as distinctly old headdress, Port Chilkoot is now the only place in Alaska where you may regularly see these ancient dances. They are as authentic as the midnight sun, for tribal elders have painstakingly coached the youngsters, in many of whom the tribal blood still flows.

If big-game hunting lures you to Alaska you need base no farther north than Haines or Port Chilkoot; the Chilkat River's upper reaches offer bear, moose and mountain sheep and goat in abundance. It was near here, a few years ago, that Forrest Young was mauled by a giant grizzly—chewed from head to foot, with his lungs exposed, one of his ribs torn completely out and two ripped loose. He survived, and en-joys life today, thoroughly.

If you hunt with a camera, this same Forrest Young will take you to Mosquito Lake in his air boat; you can flush moose in the flats and chase them at twenty-five miles an hour while your camera purrs from thirty yards away—until their not-too-nimble brains prompt them to crash to cover. You need no license for this sport.

Or you can photograph mountain goat from a chartered sport plane. You spot a flock and then bank over and flap down, and, if the wind is right, hover. They start then, with the kids scampering after their rapidly curdling suppers. Then you dive after them, leav-ing the goats with the conviction that the Chilkat eagles suddenly have grown very large and noisy.

Alaska is such a youthfully challenging country that it seems some-how incongruous that the average age of its tourists is around sixty. It would appear that young America should accept this challenge, as it has met the challenge of other frontiers, for this is a young man's land.

At Port Chilkoot, if you are tired of high-priced real estate, you can still buy an Army-built two-family house on a 60-by-170-foot lot for $6000, rent half and hunt and fish for the rest of your life. Or you can buy a barracks building that once housed two infantry companies, if you have a large family, as most Alaskans do. If you like straw-berries, the Haines variety (the Festival is in early July) often grows so large that one will fill a coffee cup—and still maintain its delicate sweetness.

At the Thlinget village of Klukwan, a few miles north of Haines, you can watch old Dan Katzeek, chief of the Killer Whale Fin tribe, work on his dugout canoe. This is no tourist act; Dan needs a new canoe. Two of his adzes are Russian trade goods that date back to the time the Killer Whales helped beat the Russians on the Chilkat— but his axes are strictly Sears Roebuck. It takes him two to three months from the felling of the cottonwood log. Pared to an inch in thickness, baked in the sun in the oldest manner, thinned and soaked, the cottonwood shell stretches almost like hide.

The old legends still prevail around Port Chilkoot and Haines. Martin Madsen was in the gold stampede of '98, and Steve Sheldon —who smokes his after-breakfast pipe on the Hotel Hälsingland's veranda—knew Rex Beach. ("Nice fellow who wrote some pretty far-fetched stuff.") He once met Jack London, and understood he was a pretty nice fellow too. ("Drank a bit, however.")

We have walked the length of the first block of Alaska's Main Street, for even though Skagway—about eighteen miles above Haines —is still a part of Southeast Alaska, it belongs immortally to the Yukon and the Klondike. Skagway and nearby Dyea were the ports of entry for the '98 Gold Rush.

They will tell you that Skagway is a ghost town—but if it is, its ghosts are wonderful. At the Pack Train Inn you can drink a mug of ale with the shades of Alex Pantages, Philadelphia Jack O'Brien, Tex Rickard and (according to the sign) Robert E. Service (although I always thought he was Robert W. because his middle name was William when he was a bank clerk in Dawson), and you can hear the echo of the shot that killed Soapy Smith, the gambler who fleeced the gold stampeders.

Judge Wickersham in his book, *Old Yukon*, says that Frank Reid, the vigilante, fired four shots and Soapy fired four shots; but Mary Pullen Kopanskí—who will show you the old Pullen Hotel where President Harding stopped in Skagway, and her grandmother's museum—tells an eyewitness version of the yarn, because her grandmother, Harriet Pullen, was so close she almost got hit. Frank misfired first, and Soapy shot him. Then Frank, still on his feet, smoked one into Soapy and Soapy was dead before he hit the ground. Frank lived eight days after he fell. One of Soapy's hand guns, with two notches, is in the Pullen Museum, as are his roulette, faro and crap tables. Las Vegas would do well to send up to Mary for the design of that crap table. Kidney-shaped and bowled, it swings the dice around almost 180 degrees for a sweet run.

When a shipload of tourists arrives at the Skagway terminal of the Inside Passage almost the whole town puts on the "Days of Ninety-Eight" show. For a dollar admission you get a hundred dollars in stage money to gamble with. Top winner gets a prize.

Townsfolk play all the old '98 characters; they have acted the parts so long they are almost professionals—especially the cancan girls, theatrically speaking, that is. Dance with the "wrong 'uns" and you are mock-tried by kangaroo court. The show's finale is the "Shooting of Dan McGrew"—acted out in detail—then the whole cast goes down and sees the ship off, with community singing.

In Skagway, at Kirmse's Curio Shop, you can hold Pat Renwick's watch chain in your hand. It is made of huge, linked gold nuggets—the largest nugget watch chain of record—and it weighs more than three pounds. Pat was a gambler and he hocked that chain so many times during the gold rush that H. D. Kirmse, who made the chain, used to keep two thousand in cash in his safe in case Pat came in. In a single day, Pat hocked and redeemed it three times.

A hundred thousand men, along with many women and children, hit the gold trail of '98 (there had been only 200 white men in all of Alaska thirteen years before) and the bulk of them landed at Skagway or nearby Dyea. From Dyea they packed on foot over the murderous Chilkoot Pass into the Yukon. From Skagway they packed over the White Pass.

J. C. (Jack) Hoyt, the superintendent of the narrow-gauge White Pass and Yukon Railroad, had read a book I wrote years ago and because he still remembered it vividly, he gave me the courtesy of his line and a seat in the engineer's cab to go over White Pass.

This, my masters, is a trip; if you haven't made it, you haven't lived. Diesel electrics pull the long train with a "helper" engine midway in the string of cars. Hairpinning up through the high pass, it takes two hours to go the first twenty miles. A grouse sat the tracks until the engine's snow scoop was five feet away, then it walked off in contempt. The day before, they told me, it was a brown bear cub. In places, you can look straight down from the cab window—several hundred feet. In the first twenty-one miles, on grades as steep as 4 per cent, the train climbs 2885 feet up mountains of almost solid rock—paralleling the Trail of '98. Joe Sheleby, an old 7th Cavalryman, was the engineer, which was comforting, for that throttle is no place for a fancy-pants soldier. The train runs almost every day winter and summer, taking supplies in and ore out, and has been derailed a number of times by weather as the marks on the ties attest, but no passenger has been lost in a wreck, though two cars were once actually blown off the track by high winds.

Six hours and a hundred and ten miles later, after passing out of Alaska into British Columbia and out of British Columbia into Canada's Yukon Territory, you are in Whitehorse, on the Alaska Highway—the land of the ptarmigan and the devilish wolverine, of the giant rainbow trout, the Great Northern pike, the lake trout and the twenty-pound arctic char, of the elk, the caribou, the bear and the convolute-horned mountain sheep. (If you want any of these, call Mike Nolan at Marsh Lake Lodge—an ex-R.C.M.P. sergeant turned guide.)

Sam McGee's cabin is in Whitehorse. You are twenty-five miles from "the marge of Lake Labarge" and just a step from tailors, dry cleaners, good inns, taxi stands and a branch of Toronto's Eaton's department store. Whitehorse is Canadian, with the deep monarchic tradition which republican America never seems quite to understand; but it is still linked closely with Alaska, for the Yukon races by the White Pass and Yukon Railroad station to its confluence with the Klondike and both territories were opened by gold. Bill McBride's museum holds the mementos of the gold-rush days and Bill is still around to tell you the story.

From Whitehorse's International Airport you can fly the second block of Main Street—to Fairbanks, in interior Alaska. You do this in a little more than two hours, passing slightly north of the village of Snag, where the lowest temperature ever recorded in North America—minus 81°—was clocked in 1947.

Fairbanks is an authentic deep-Alaska town, for it, too, started with gold—from 1902 until about 1917 every store in town had a scale to weigh gold dust against purchases. Miners' log cabins, still lived in, dot the business streets. The United States Smelting, Refining and Mining Company still mines gold in the Fairbanks area; but it is dug by multimillion-dollar dredges from the frozen ground, sold by law only to the Government, which immediately puts it back underground at Fort Knox.

There is a Mode-O-Day dress shop in Fairbanks and apartments and modern business buildings. There are flower shops and the

Travelers Inn—as comfortable a motel as you would want. Or you can sleep aboard the old stern-wheeler *Nenana*, which used to make the run to Fort Yukon, but is now a boatel.

It is risky to give the population of any Alaskan town, for people come and go continually, but we might guess Fairbanks at between 15,000 and 20,000. There's no guesswork, however, about Fairbanks' having the highest cost of living of any community under the American flag; that's supported by Government figures. When I was there beer cost seventy-five cents a can and a haircut $2.50. Cigarettes were thirty-five cents and Coca-Cola twenty cents. A taxi ride that would be eighty cents outside cost two dollars. There is no greedy attempt at the deep gouge, in any of this. They charge steeply because they must pay steeply. Freight rates to Fairbanks are high because of distance. Labor costs are heavy because there are only 120 outdoor working days a year. They have to make a living but they'll give you their shirts if they like you—and they like everyone who likes them—*and they are extremely likable people.*

Only an hour and six minutes by Russian jet bomber from the nearest Siberian Base, the ladies of Fairbanks do not sleep in terror of invasion, with guns under their pillows, as one opportunist correspondent reported. The attitude of interior Alaskans is expressed by a red card you see in stores: "In the event of atomic attack, be calm, complete your purchase, pay your bill—then run like hell!"

All the short-run, scheduled-airline, small-aircraft pilots in Alaska call themselves bush pilots—and proudly, for their safety record is exemplary. Originally there were three leading bush pilots in the Fairbanks area—Noel Wien, Joe Crosson and Ben Eielson—and to them go the laurels for opening interior Alaska to air travel. They blazed the trails. Eielson Air Force Base and the aeronautical engineering building at the University in which the Alaskan Museum is located are named for Ben. Joe Crosson brought back the bodies of Will Rogers and Wiley Post from their crash at Point Barrow; his memorial stands in Fairbanks. Noel Wien's Airline—with Noel occasionally at the C-46 controls—makes it possible for your Aunt Emma to get to Nome and Kotzebue and Point Barrow on the Arctic almost as easily as she gets downtown to shop.

Arctic Alaska is the comparatively small strip along the Bering Sea and the Arctic Ocean that gave the forty-ninth state its "outside" trade-mark of the igloo. The word means house but the Eskimo's permanent home is not of ice. It is a fairly large skin-and-driftwood shelter tunneled into from beneath. Or it can be a cottage, or a Nissen hut, or an apartment in Fairbanks, depending on his job. He builds small igloos of ice blocks only when hunting far from home. He is a pleasant, round-faced person with the ready, incandescent smile of the Himalayan Gurkha—and a capacity for technical education that, in the opinion of Air Force officers, could eventually qualify him to handle any specialized job on the installations of the D.E.W. Line. He has inherited a flair for tools and engines from his Oriental ancestors who, thousands of years ago, probably helped invent the wheel.

He has been reviled in the past for his "barbarity" in leaving his old folks in provisional ice igloos when hunting was bad. But to him it was not barbarism. It was for the good of the greater number; the handicapped being left so the others could go on and survive. He has been reviled, too, for polygamy; but this again was self-preservation. In mid-June and July he goes after whale. Last year some Point Barrow hunters were caught on rotten shore ice with an offshore wind; they were saved, but in years gone all the men of a village have been lost. So polygamy was a matter of survival too.

Of all the original people of Alaska, the Eskimos cling most tenaciously to their tribal customs and their language—probably because their race memory is deeper. They have held precariously to life along the Arctic and Bering Sea littorals for centuries, sustaining themselves on game, fish, berries and roots, and the transition to modern dietary habits at first caused a high incidence of previously unknown diseases—especially tuberculosis. But medical science came with the change of diet and soon brought things into balance.

There is an unfathomable plasticity to the Eskimo mind that is probably the fundamental ingredient of his survival. He adapts. A product of primitive tribal government since the beginning of known history, he was amenable to the overlay of democratic concepts. Early in territorial history he began to sit in the Legislature, so that his place was firmly established when Alaska became the forty-ninth state. He *is* the Alaska National Guard—organized in Scout Battalions with modern light weapons—and he knows how to handle modern heavy equipment. Eskimo teen-age girls look more at home in sweaters, nylons and high heels than Indian girls do.

At Point Barrow, a two-day or a three-day packaged air tour from Fairbanks in July will give you a chance to witness the Nulikatuk, that celebration of a successful whale hunt which is supposed to appease the whale spirits so that there may be a successful hunt next year. It's a time of laughter and roughhousing. Take a sweater.

The Eskimo from time immemorial has made tools and weapons of walrus-tusk ivory and the whale-bone of long-gone corset days— his only durable materials. Then the traders got after him to turn out tourist catchalls, and today the shops are full of all sorts of ivory gewgaws that the Eskimo himself never uses.

Nome, which is only about 130 miles from the nearest point in the U.S.S.R., and is not connected by road or railroad to the rest of Alaska, boasts the oldest newspaper in Alaska—the Nome *Nugget*. The latest movie hit was showing at the Nomerama, from whose door you can pitch a stone into the Bering Sea. The current crop of TV sagas were on KNOM-TV—canned. At the Polaris Dining Room you can try a charcoal-broiled reindeer steak. To get a cab, call Main 170—a soda, go to the Glue Pot fountain—a Martini, the Bering Sea Club.

Come back from the Arctic to Fairbanks and look in on the University of Alaska. Judge James Wickersham, after years of selling the project to Congress, laid the cornerstone in 1915. It was originally an Agricultural School and a School of Mines, but has expanded its courses into Arts and Letters, Biological Science, Business Administration, Chemical, Civil and Electrical Engineering, Education and Geophysics—with graduate work in most of them. The summer-school students may make an air trip over the North Pole which is almost as painless as going out to Montauk, Long Island, from Columbia University in New York.

In interior Alaska, around Fairbanks and Anchorage—eight hours south of Fairbanks by train—you pick up the huge installations of the Armed Services. Eielson and Ladd Air Force Bases near Fairbanks, Fort Richardson and Elmendorf Air Force Bases near Anchorage. These are huge, self-contained military cities, the nuclei of the outer line of defense for the entire continent. Here the line is held along the entire westerly and northerly front of the Cold War. Daylight or dark, winter and summer, defensive air patrols are maintained. Our pilots see the red-starred planes patrolling their side. A thin line of dynamic alertness lies between the two—vast sinews of retaliation tense and readied.

Anchorage is much larger than Fairbanks—but it started as a camp for the construction of the Alaska Railroad, so the aristocratic gold-grubbing tradition does not cling to it. The frontier feeling does, however. There are forty-four bars on Fourth Street, the main drag.

Anchorage has log cabins that are still lived in and two of them stand in the shadow of the fourteen-story Mount McKinley Building. If you want Jack London texture surge into the Cheechako Bar on Fourth Street, just a short step from the svelte Chart Room of the Westward Hotel.

There are smart dress shops and it is a growing town of new apartment houses and housing developments. Drive through Turn-again-by-the-Sea and you might well be in a new California subdivision, except that the ranch houses are smaller for the $30,000 or $50,000 they bring. Smaller, therefore easier to heat against the deep-freeze of winter.

You can drive from anywhere in the United States to Anchorage, by way of Fairbanks. The road roughly parallels the railroad, through the beautiful Mount McKinley country. The Department of the Interior runs the railroad.

In Anchorage you are two hours by air from Kodiak Island, the United States Navy and those Big Bear. They weigh considerably over half a ton and the pelt cures to more than eleven by ten feet. A hundred and twenty-seven pounds of rug, without the head. Call Alf Madsen—and if he's not home he's at Karluk Lake after bear. Alf is in his thirty-eighth year of guiding with no client hurt beyond a mosquito bite—and fourteen-year-old boys have killed their bears under his competent hand.

Donnelley and Acheson in the town of Kodiak is the oldest store in Alaska. Only the Spanish missions outdate it in point of outlander establishment along the American Pacific littoral. It has been at its present location since 1796. You can buy anything there from a Cadillac to a package of chewing gum.

Up the street is the B and B Bar, the seventeenth-oldest licensed bar in Alaska, which is like holding a low-numbered *Fédération Aeronautique Internationale* flying license, for there are as many bars in Alaska as there are lakes on the Kenai Peninsula—or mosquitoes in summer.

Off Kodiak Island the halibut weigh hundreds of pounds, delectable king crab measure six feet across, salmon are thick in season and the Dolly Varden trout follows them upstream to feed on their eggs. The green of Kodiak is as brightly iridescent as in Ireland and Scotland. It shines wet green even at night.

The Navy's Alaskan Sea Frontier—the utterly last frontier in America—stretches down the Aleutians to hang under Asia. This is the last block on Alaska's Main Street. Here are the tiny fishing towns of the beckoning names—Dutch Harbor and Scotch Cap, Ouzinkie, Halibut Bay, Kanatak, False Pass, Squaw Harbor and Unga—down to Adak, which again is Navy and the only installation west of Kodiak that approaches the dimension of civilization, with good docking, good housing, good food, four-engined strips and the finest harbor in the Aleutians. There is no bear or moose or reindeer at Adak, but the Marines have put a caribou herd out to breed. Lonely and isolated under a not unusual seventy-knot wind, and the williwaw that blows 125 knots on occasion, Adak is the farthest western reach of the tangible sovereign dignity of the United States, but children are born here, men work here and this *is* the United States—under the new 49th star.

A Big Land, my masters, which is what Alaska has been called in the language of its older people since long before Christ. The *Main Land* as opposed to the islands that fringe its coast, hence the *Big Land* as opposed to the smaller land of the islands—for that is what the word Alaska means.

Hawaii

by FRANK J. TAYLOR

It's another Hawaii today—this new state—no longer the drowsing and glamorous tropical haven remembered so nostalgically by travelers of past years; different also from the booming, money-mad military outpost on which a million soldiers, sailors, airmen, Wacs and Waves waste no love. In the years since the end of the war the Islanders have performed a near miracle in removing the shambles —barbed wire on beaches, mountains of military junk, miles of drab barracks. But they have not been able to work the miracle of recapturing the prewar Arcadia of the travel folders, and probably never will be.

"I'm selling out and moving to Samoa or some place where civilization hasn't regimented life," one of Hawaii's unhappy *kamaainas* declared, as we gazed out the plate-glass window of her living room at Honolulu, Pearl Harbor, and the blue Pacific with the pastel peaks of Oahu in the distance, a truly breath-taking scene. "The *malihinis* have ruined the old Hawaii forever."

Kamaainas are the old-timers, "children of the soil," in the mellifluous tongue of the native Hawaiians. *Malihinis* are newcomers, the "strangers."

Throughout the Islands, the *kamaainas* mourn the passing of the white-man's paradise, the Hawaii that faded into memory with the war. But the new conquerors of the Islands—*malihinis* and native workers—want no going back—believe they are going forward to a better, common-people's Hawaii with the fiftieth star in the American flag.

Despite the *kamaainas'* complaint, Hawaii is still much the same physically—a beautiful semitropic archipelago of eight main islands 2400 miles southwest of San Francisco. All together, they're about the size of Connecticut and Rhode Island combined, and they're populated by over a half a million people. Hawaii, called by natives the Big Island, is at the southeastern end of the chain and is larger than all of the other islands together. Maui, second largest of the group and having some of the most important plantations, is northwest of the Big Island and is flanked by three smaller islands: Kahoolawe, on the southwest; Lanai, on the west; and Molokai, on the northwest. Oahu, third largest island, is roughly thirty miles northwest of Molokai, and is the richest and most densely populated, with the city of Honolulu. Kauai, called the Garden Island, is still farther to the northwest, and across a channel from Kauai is the mystery island of Niihau, farthest west of the main Hawaiian Islands. Beyond, for about a thousand miles to the northwest, stretches a chain of uninhabited lava and coral islets which were set apart by President Theodore Roosevelt in 1909 as the Hawaiian Islands Bird Reservation.

To the tourist's eye, the Hawaiian archipelago still looks like an unparalleled spot to spend a vacation or a lifetime. To appreciate the *kamaainas'* lament, you have to consider the violent social upheaval wrought by the war in the Islands. The day before Pearl Harbor, Hawaii was a paternalistic, almost feudal, pastoral realm; the day after, it was a human beehive in state of siege, with all civil rights ignored by the military autocracy. Emerging after V-J Day, the Islanders heaved paternalism out the window, adopted collective bargaining, hiked wages to near-mainland standards regardless of the shade of the worker's color, and saw the pendulum of power swing from the big employers to flushed union leaders. Nurses, clerks, cooks, laundresses and employees of 150 industries pinned on buttons of the International Longshoremen and Warehousemen's Union. Because Hawaii depends upon shipping for food, fuel, clothing and supplies, the CIO-ILWU became the big voice in the Islands. Now the pendulum is swinging back part way.

Hawaiians have been trying to digest in one gulp reforms that normally would take a lifetime. They have economic, social and political stomach-aches, but things may not be so bad as the *kamaainas* fear. There is still a lot of *aloha* awaiting the visitor to these perpetually summertime shores. The eight Hawaiian isles still loll in the same sparkling sunshine, are still cooled by the same soft northeasterly trade winds as before. The white clouds still hitchhike across the Pacific on these same gentle winds and drop their life-giving moisture upon contact with Hawaii's steep peaks. You can still push up through the clouds on the road to Haleakala Crater on the island of Maui and see this rain in the making, or you can watch the fascinating meteorological show on a still grander scale from an inter-island plane.

From these vantage points, a glance will reveal why the larger islands are lush and jungle-clothed on the windward slopes; parched and semidesert on the lee side, which gets only the moisture leavings. On the windward side of the Nuuanu Pali, a startlingly steep pass in Oahu's mountains, where on occasions you may toss a penny to the winds and have it blown back to your hands, these same winds may whip up a cloudburst in ten minutes, while back of you in protected Honolulu seven miles away the sun is burning brightly. Frequently in Honolulu you can cross the street and step from rain to sunbeams, so localized is Hawaii's "liquid sunshine."

The big news for you, if you are holiday-bent, is that, though the man-made geography of the islands has been somewhat transformed with the dredging of airfields, naval bases, terminals and building sites from the ocean, Honolulu's weather is unchanged. The average temperature is still 74.6° F. and there is only 6.5° difference between summer and winter, which adds up to the fact that here is the most equable and enjoyable climate on the globe for avoiding work. It's not too humid, not too dry. The trees and vines still bloom the year around, the lei makers still string flowers by their gas-lighted carts. Every little girl has a hibiscus in her hair, and the little boys still dive for quarters as your ship docks or sails, but let dimes sink to the bottom. The coconut palms still shimmer in the moonlight, you can still dance under the stars, and the sun tan you pick up in January is just as brown as July's.

The isles of the archipelago are just as different from one another as they were before the war, and some of them still offer you chunks of old Hawaii. Somewhere on the Islands the traveler with gumption and sense enough to evade the Honolulu-Waikiki merry-go-round may find almost anything he seeks, from a 13,000-foot ski slide to a fishing village whose easygoing Polynesian inhabitants live almost as primitively as did their ancestors in 1778 when Captain Cook first stumbled upon the Hawaiian group and named it the Sandwich Islands after his patron, the Earl of Sandwich.

You have to go out and find the real Hawaii; it won't come to you at the Royal Hawaiian Hotel. Too many visitors discover this too late. By the time they arrive on Oahu, the *aloha* or welcoming isle, where everyone first sets foot either from plane or steamer, they are tied by the American Plan or other commitments to Waikiki, a Coney Island-like mile-long assembly of littered beach, hotels, restaurants and shops, pathetically less glamorous in reality than in song and story.

Four out of five visitors to Hawaii are sun seekers. If you are an average *malihini,* you have bought your *aloha* shirt and bright beach towel and are out on the sand within an hour after being shown to your room. But after the first day on too-narrow, too-crowded Waikiki you begin to look around and wonder how a group of islands with 956 miles of coastline could have so few top-flight beaches. There is an answer to that: the Islands are merely the projecting peaks of a vast submerged mountain range. They fall off abruptly into the depths, except where sea life has built up protecting coral reefs. Elsewhere, the waves crash against sheer cliffs or pound with fury against lava rocks, sometimes blowing spray out of holes above underwater caves in jets that look like Yellowstone's geysers.

In windward Oahu, for instance, there stretch many miles of white coral beaches on which crash breakers like those of the mainland. These breakers look inviting, but are dangerous for any but the strongest swimmers, because of the undertow. The island of Kauai has bathing beaches protected by coral reefs, but few visitors stop to swim there as they whip past them on sight-seeing excursions. Hawaii, the Big Island, offers the weird phenomenon of coconut-fringed beaches of jet-black sand, churned up out of old lava flows by the waves. Here, as on the other islands, sea swimming is usually *kapu,* as the "Keep Out" signs warn you in the native lingo. Even in the protected coves, it is wise to take along a native surfer who knows the reefs and rocks and holes.

This explains why three fourths of Hawaii's sun seekers are inevitably packed around Waikiki, in the sheltering lee of Diamond Head, right in the city of Honolulu. Waikiki is pretty disappointing because it is so small. But it has always been popular and will probably stay that way. Waikiki is made by the coral reef, a mile out, that protects it from the sea. Inside the reef, the water is so safe and shallow that you can put a foot down after swimming a quarter of a mile and make the astonishing discovery that it is only shoulder deep, after all. The waves that break over the reef are smooth and even, perfect for surfboards and outrigger canoes. Catch a wave as it breaks over the reef and you are off on an exhilarating thirty-mile-an-hour ride ending at the water's edge—if you are skilled enough to stay aboard that long.

Mainlanders are not the only sun seekers who congregate like gony birds on Waikiki. Islanders are there, too, especially on week ends—Caucasians, Hawaiians, Japanese, Filipinos. On Saturday and Sunday the water is alive with surfboards and outriggers. Those pictures you see of boys carrying girls on their shoulders, on surfboards riding dizzily on the crest of the wave, aren't just stunts for the camera. The Hawaiians do it for fun and for free, and you can watch them for hours, riding, spilling and splashing.

You must see Hawaii—all of it—to comprehend the extent of its beauty and the extent of its problems. Nature has scattered Hawaii with extraordinary sights, from snow-covered mountains to black beaches, but what seems lovely to the tourist is often just more trouble to the local folk. Instead of flattening out, once they pushed through the surf, the suboceanic mountains that rose up to make the Hawaiian Islands lifted themselves still higher in precipitous peaks. Hawaii, the Big Island, comprising almost two thirds of the area of all the islands and still growing, is a good example. Its sky-scraping, often snow-covered craters, Mauna Kea (13,784 feet) and Mauna Loa (13,680 feet), burst into eruption every few years, piling cinders still higher and pouring lava down the slopes to the sea in seething caldrons, to make the Big Island still bigger. At Kilauea Crater, if you are lucky in your timing, you can drive up to the rim and see some of this red-hot earth cooking.

Islanders never call Hawaii by its name; it is always "the Big Island." Until recently, geologists considered Hawaii the youngest of the islands to emerge from the sea. Now they are not so sure. Parts of the Big Island, such as the Kohala Peninsula and the moist, verdant Hamakua Coast, may have been pinprick landmarks in the Pacific before the "older" islands—Kauai, Oahu and Maui—emerged.

The Big Island is easily the most fascinating of the group, because it has everything. You drive through tropical jungles, stroll through fern-tree forests, detour to primitive native villages in coconut groves by black-sand beaches. You can fish (swordfish, tuna, dolphin) or hunt (wild pigs, goats, or sheep) or climb snow-capped volcanic peaks. You can lose yourself on roads winding through waving, tasseled cane fields. Orchids and a dozen other flowers, mostly trees and vines, bloom year-round and in wild profusion. Nobody has to plant them. The Big Island offers deserts, cactus, wilderness, and history, but it takes time to track them down. Hawaii is so big it takes two days to drive around the island in a car, and a flight from Honolulu to Hilo, moist and verdant second city of the Islands, isn't a fair sample of the Big Island.

The always sparkling Kona Coast, across the island from Hilo, is just as different from the wet Hamakua Coast as it is possible for two sides of the same island to be. Protected by Hawaii's two monster volcanic peaks, Mauna Loa and Mauna Kea, Kona gets only the leavings of the rainstorms that drench the north coast of the island almost daily. Water is so precious that every house has a galvanized roof feeding the captured raindrops into gutters which in turn empty into tanks. When the Kona ranchers speak of watersheds, they mean just that; acres of galvanized-iron sheds high on the slopes, where the showers are more frequent, catch water, delivering it into tanks, sometimes enough to store a million gallons on one ranch. Kona's volcanic soils are so porous that rain sinks into them as through a sieve.

Yet there are enough passing showers to keep trees, vines, bushes and flowers in bloom year-round and the dry-land taro, the waxy-leafed coffee bushes, the papaya, mango, avocado and *lauhala* (pandanus) trees thriving. Kona has probably the nearest-perfect climate in the Hawaiian group; it is where every Islander is going to retire someday to the little grass shack under a breadfruit tree by a taro patch above a fishing cove at Kealakekua. Life is still simple and easy at Kona, and the *pilikia* (the catchall word for trouble) that complicates existence elsewhere hasn't gained a foothold yet. It may never gain one, because at Kona, Nature provides a living— taro root for *poi*, breadfruit, fish, coffee and fruits—and time to enjoy it.

It has been the same since Kamehameha I, the Conqueror of the Islands, returned to his birthplace at sleepy Kailua, on the Big Island about a century and a half ago, after his strenuous years of battle, to live out his days. At near-by Honaunau, you can picnic on what is left of Kamehameha's City of Refuge, where great mounds of volcanic rock rear on a jutting point. Here the kings held court and subjects found protection from *kapus* and vindictive chieftains. The City and another at Kawaihae are the nearest thing to an engineered town the primitive Hawaiians achieved.

Near by is Kealakekua Bay where a monument marks the spot on which Captain James Cook, after being greeted as a white god, lost his life and the white man's prestige in a sudden and foolish battle with native warriors in 1779. In a later expedition, two English sailors, Isaac Davis and John Young, were seized and spared to shoot captured cannon in local wars. They proved the edge in weapons that enabled the Great Kamehameha to purge Hawaii, Maui and Oahu of rival kings.

Prowling the peaceful coast of the Big Island and Kona's slopes, dotted with tiny farms, you have to flex your imagination to conjure this peaceful scene as the militant hub of Hawaii in Polynesian days, the center from which Kamehameha ran a fleet of 600 outrigger canoes, carved from solid trunks of koa trees grown high on the mountainside, to carry commerce to and from the other islands.

Kauai, at the northwestern extreme of the Hawaiian group, is the antithesis of the Big Island. Small, only 555 square miles in area (fourth in size of the Hawaiian Islands), it is rank jungle or plantations from the Nawiliwili tip to the Barking Sands Airport on the other side. Hence its sobriquet, "the Garden Island." Even Lihue, the county seat, over which wafts a pungent molasses odor from the near-by sugar mill, is only a crossroads in the cane fields, with a traffic cop at the intersection and a huge Kress store rising out of the jungle. The near-by town of Nawiliwili, with the name that intrigues every passer-by, is a sugar port on a sheltered bay, from which put out fishing boats whose Hawaiian skippers guarantee that their passengers will always catch something.

The volcanoes that reared Kauai have long since gone to rest, their lavas have eroded into rich red and black soil, which the constant rains have carved into spectacular canyons and rich valleys. Red-hued, precipitous Waimea Canyon is one of the earth's spectacular exhibits of rain erosion. Rainwater, which falls at over 460 inches a year at the peak of Mt. Waialeale, slowly chiseled this 3000-foot "Little Grand Canyon" and the near-by Napali Cliffs which plunge dramatically into the blue Pacific. Time has given them a vast silence, so quiet you can hear it. At Barking Sands Airport, fifteen miles away as the mynah bird flies, the rainfall often is only some twenty inches a year. This contrast between the rain-soaked windward slopes and the sun-parched leeward side is marked on all the larger Hawaiian Islands. The windward side is invariably rank tropics; the leeward side is parched desert. Only on Kauai is the moisture evenly enough distributed by showers and rivers to keep the entire island verdant. After heavy rains, dozens of streams crash over cliffs in foamy waterfalls.

On the Garden Island you roll through waving cane fields, past pineapple plantations, rice paddies, and miles of flowering trees and vines. At Waimea, a monument marks the spot where Captain Cook first set foot on Hawaiian soil. Here Cook was greeted with characteristic Polynesian hospitality, and sailed away to return and meet his end on the Big Island the following year. On Kauai you ponder over the origin of the rock-hewn irrigation ditches, which according to Hawaiian lore were built by a race of dwarfs, the Menehunes, who preceded the Polynesians. Scientists scoff at the idea, but there are the ditches, lined with rocks square-hewn and neatly fitted with a stone craftsmanship the Hawaiians never mastered. Kauai's Barking Sands are another gee-whiz; the sand makes strange noises when you walk across it, or if you put some of it in a bottle and shake it. Part of the explanation is that the grains of sand, as they dry out after each soaking by sea or rain, pick up a thin film of condensed gases which can vibrate with considerable resonance. The shape and outside surface of each individual grain give the sand its peculiar pitch and volume, which suggest a poodle's bark.

Maui, second largest of the Hawaiian group, is nicknamed the Valley Island, a misnomer that ranks with the best Hawaiian paradoxes. Maui has no valleys to compare with those of Oahu or Kauai. The island's big show is the 9318-foot Haleakala Crater, where, according to native lore, a fire-resistant mythological Polynesian hero trapped the sun and harnessed it to shine overtime for Hawaii. Hence, Haleakala's name, "House of the Sun." Maui was probably two island peaks in prehistoric times, each with its belching volcano. Haleakala, with a crater large enough to gulp Manhattan Island, must have been terrifying when on a rampage. After it stilled, the sea between the two isles filled in and Maui acquired what is called "the Valley," but which is in reality a low plain with coast at each end, an area intensely planted to sugar cane and pineapples.

Maui's sugar-cane belt has fingers that fringe the mountains, which are eroded into jungle-covered peaks and spectacular clefts, such as Iao Canyon, and its inexplicable 1200-foot rock needle resembling Rio's Sugar Loaf. Wailuku, nestling at the Iao's mouth, is a good place to see a sugar plantation at its best—cane fields, mills, company towns, the manager's magnificent residence. Around the mountain is Lahaina, a picturesque town basking around a plaza almost covered by an enormous banyan tree. Rugged windward Maui, a narrow, cliff-bound plateau, is cut by deep gorges, each the boundary of a plantation that is a little world to itself. So, likewise, is Hana, at the easternmost tip of the island.

Maui has three satellite islands, Molokai, Lanai and Kahoolawe. All three were short-changed when Madame Pele's volcanic fires were forging new terra firma. None has high enough cliffs to precipitate adequate rains. On the eastern half of Molokai, rising above the Kalaupapa Valley, is a mountain range that some consider the most beautiful spot in all the Islands. Not many people see it, because here is located the famed leper colony, accessible only from the sea. The other end of Molokai is a sloping semiarid plain, with barely enough moisture for pineapples and cattle ranching.

In the lee of Molokai and Maui hovers Lanai, the Pineapple Island, which offers one of the world's best demonstrations of soil conservation. About a quarter of a century ago, Lanai was slowly blowing into the sea. Mormon pioneers had tried growing sugar there and had failed for want of water. Subsequent owners grazed cattle. The cattle and wild goats wiped out the grass, turning the island into a seagirt dust bowl. In 1922, James D. Dole, founder of the Hawaiian Pineapple Company, bought what was left of the island. Company engineers laid out the rolling central plateau in contours, planted pineapples with mulch paper to keep out the weeds and hold down the soil when the wind blew. They planted thousands of Norfolk pines on the slopes to hold the hills in place, sowed grass seed, developed wells. Today, "Hawaiian Pine" has 14,000 acres in pineapple, rated the largest cultivated farm in one piece in the territory. The rest of Lanai is a cattle ranch on which the company raises beef for the island's population. The Hawaiian Pineapple Company, including its plantations on Oahu and its cannery, is Hawaii's biggest single enterprise, employing at the peak of the season thousands of workers, most of whom wouldn't have been on the pay roll

if Jim Dole hadn't tackled the job of saving the island that was blowing away.

Kahoolawe, only fifteen miles from Lanai, is an island that nobody
saved. It is still blowing out to sea, often in red banners that hang
over the ocean for many miles. Only goats now inhabit the island,
which has too little grass for cattle. Yet Kahoolawe served its purpose. Thousands of Army and Navy bombardiers and pilots sharpened their sights on the island, which became a bombing range for
fliers finishing their training on Oahu, Maui and Hawaii.

In spite of the attractions of the other seven islands, Oahu is still
the hub of Hawaii. It is the "Populous Isle" because at Honolulu
and contiguous Pearl Harbor are the two safest deep-water harbors
in all eight islands. They nestle on the lee side, and escape the
oceanic rollers that sweep down from Alaska to pound the windward
coasts with an occasional tidal fury such as that which made a
shambles of the Big Island's Hilo harbor and Maui's Kahului harbor
some years ago.

Oahu is the Hawaii most visitors know, because they never get
any farther. Oahu is where you see what the restless whites can do
to remake the Polynesians' tropics. When the white men arrived,
the ground on which Honolulu stands was a dry, dusty plain. The
whites drove tunnels into Oahu's mountains to capture underground
waters, which made Honolulu a city of flowering trees, hibiscus,
poinsettias.

They filled the swamps, dredged new land from the sea, built the
harbor and the impressive office buildings which make Honolulu's
Little Wall Street, clustered at Fort and Merchant Streets.

Driving past Pearl Harbor to Wahiawa, through swaying cane
fields and stubby, monotonous pineapple plantations, past experimental gardens of Macadamia nuts, litchi and papaya trees, with
the rugged green peaks on either side, you see how white men's
ideas and natives' industry have turned this gently sloping saddle
from jungle into one of the most productive stretches of earth anywhere. Drive a score of miles on the good highway that skirts the
island, and you slip from unreclaimed jungle and precipitous cliffs
to more plantations, flower-bedecked villages on low stilts, gay beach
homes, rocky foam-swept coast, coconut palms, banana and papaya
farms, open-air homes hidden in planned jungles, Diamond Head
(a long-dead crater)—all this, and more, you see in one morning's
brief drive out of Honolulu.

The varied landscape, so pleasing to the traveler, accounts for much of Hawaii's troubles. The mountains that kept growing and never flattened out left altogether too little land for cultivation. Of Hawaii's 6435 square miles, less than a tenth is suitable for crop agriculture. Another tenth is forage land for cattle and sheep. Eighty per cent is precipitous mountains, uninviting lava flows, semibarren desert. The Islands have no mineral deposits, no other resources than the fish that are found in such abundance in the surrounding sea.

When the Hawaiian Islands were discovered, the white men guessed that they were inhabited by 350,000 natives, a figure that historians later whittled down to 250,000. However many Hawaiians there were in Captain Cook's day, they lived a simple existence, pulling most of their food from the taro patches and from the sea.

Today the productive two tenths of Hawaii is hard-pressed to support the half million population, which is roughly one fifth white, one third Japanese, one sixth Hawaiian and part Hawaiian, the balance being Chinese, Filipino, Korean, Portuguese and Puerto Rican.

The Hawaiian land-tenure system, under which enormous landholdings have been built up, has its roots in a momentous event a century back in the reign of Kamehameha III. This liberal-minded monarch was Hawaii's Franklin D. Roosevelt. His particular New Deal is still known as the Great *Mahele*, which means "the redistribution." Under previous Hawaiian sovereigns, title to all the land was vested in the king, who assigned it to his chiefs, and they in turn were charged with seeing that every Hawaiian family had its taro patch and its fishing hole. Disapproving of this paternalism, Kamehameha divided all Hawaii in three parts, one third for the crown, one third for the chiefs, and one third for the people. The king then cut his slice in two, ceding half to the state and keeping half, an example followed by some of the chiefs.

In the years that followed, this well-meant New Deal went askew. The state clung to its lands until the end of the kingdom, through the limited days of the Hawaiian Republic under a flag that is a curious combination of the Union Jack and the Stars and Stripes, and finally delivered them to the United States Department of the Interior when Hawaii was annexed in 1898.

The natives, never having felt the need of private ownership of land anywhere in Polynesia, soon sold their land for pittances to opportunistic whites. The latter were mostly traders and fortune seekers, and not missionaries, as is popularly believed. The whites experimented with crops and eventually built up, after many failures, the cane and pineapple plantations that now support many Islanders. The few natives who held their lands did well, particularly those daughters of the *alii*, or nobles, who married white husbands wise enough to manage and increase estates.

The Hawaiian Islanders' most persistent *pilikia*, is the land famine. There just isn't enough good earth for enough farms or enough home sites. The tightly held holdings have resulted in land values that would be fantastic for comparable ground on the mainland. The demand for home sites, sold on the square-foot basis, has been so urgent in the Honolulu area that the enterprising Dillinghams, who struck it rich building railroads, dredging harbors and constructing breakwaters, have been using their equipment to dredge new subdivisions out of what was ocean shallows or swamp land a short time ago. Spread with a thin frosting of top soil, these coral beach fronts become fabulously priced building sites overnight.

The restless whites have been wresting land from the sea, the jungle or the desert ever since they arrived on the Islands. To the easygoing Polynesians, this seemed like an unnecessary struggle with Nature. The natives would have none of it. There were fish in the sea and taro root in the swamp. The Hawaiians, at the time the whites arrived, were sprung from a seagoing race, who, when their homelands became too crowded, took off in fleets of outrigger canoes on long sea voyages that still baffle the anthropologists. They brought their children, dogs, plants and foodstuffs, and after multiplying prodigiously in the hospitable Hawaiian Islands, lost their ancient navigating skill.

Before the whites arrived to settle in the Islands, the local kings and chiefs had been purged in a series of bloody invasions by Kamehameha I, the Conqueror, who died in 1819. The Hawaiian Islands were a kingdom, and the king owned everything in feudal totalitarianism. He owned his subjects, men and women alike, if he wanted them. He held his people in constant fear of taboos punishable by death.

When the first New England missionaries reached the Islands in 1820, the old taboos had broken down. The Hawaiians were hungry for a new religion. It was a rugged paradise, in which the missionaries soon found themselves combating not only the Devil but the raucous sailormen of whaling and trading ships. Gradually the missionaries, by their steadfastness and industry, gained the upper hand, only to be cut off by the Mission Board in New England and forced to earn their own living. Some tried the agriculture in which they had attempted unsuccessfully to interest the Hawaiians. They were joined by traders and other white settlers, and from this struggling start grew the sugar industry that is Hawaii's largest source of support.

Before they could grow cane, the pioneers had to clear away the jungle, or turn deserts into gardens by building spectacular canal systems that tapped mountain streams. They had to build mills to crush the cane and refine the juice into sugar. This called for capital, which few of them had. They found it in Honolulu, where other pioneers had established agencies, first to service trading and whaling ships and later the isolated plantations. The agencies, or factoring companies, bought and stocked supplies for the plantations and marketed their crops. They also invested in the plantations and mills.

Statehood for Hawaii was not a matter of economics, for the territory was not only self-supporting but paid more Federal income tax than did any one of a dozen states. The big problem was to convince prejudiced groups that statehood for such a geographically distant area was feasible, and that the national ballot should be given to the Japanese, Chinese, Filipinos and Koreans, as well as the Hawaiians. Statehood supporters point out that there is virtually no race problem in the territory itself, that there is no area under United States jurisdiction where a greater complexity of races lives so harmoniously.

The cosmopolitan complexion of the Islands today stems not so much from this international background as from the fact that the native Hawaiians dislike heavy field labor and repetitious chores. No Hawaiian can see why he should sweat out a living in a cane field or a sugar mill when he can earn his livelihood fishing, sailing a boat, riding a cow pony, holding public office, or blowing a police whistle. After the first futile efforts to make farmers of the Hawaiians, the early plantation operators gave up and imported Chinese.

For a few cents a day, the coolies built the ditches, planted the cane, hoed the weeds, harvested the crops. Their sons and grandsons moved to the towns and cities, became merchants, lawyers, doctors—some of Hawaii's outstanding business and professional men. The planters brought in Portuguese from the Madeira Islands, good workers whose sons likewise preferred the town. Japanese were the next and largest wave. They, too, were industrious, dependable plantation labor; but their sons and daughters, the second largest pure racial block in the Islands, went to town. As a last resort, the plantations brought in Koreans, Puerto Ricans and Filipinos. They too, are migrating off the land, and machines are taking their place.

The younger generation finds no lure in agriculture, and this is one of Hawaii's top problems today. The University of Hawaii, which offers excellent courses in agronomy, can't interest students in the training for the Islands' basic industry. As a substitute for manpower, managements have built ingenious and expensive machines, many of which are operated by whites, among them ex-servicemen who became intrigued with plantation life while on duty in Hawaii. Nearly every plantation is operating with one third fewer employees. The rest have gone to town. These fugitives from agriculture became the work force for the hundreds of postwar enterprises that sprang up almost overnight. They found higher-paying jobs in the 55 new manufacturing establishments turning out garments, jewelry, jam and jelly—these being but a few of the products that were not being made on the island at all when the war ended.

For years a serious lack of good hotel space had hampered Hawaii's tourist trade. More mainlanders wanted to go to Honolulu than Honolulu could accommodate; that is until 1954, when the dynamic Henry J. Kaiser turned a run-down motel into his fabulous Hawaiian Village. Later Mr. Hilton and the Sheraton chain descended on Waikiki. Between them they have bought and reconditioned or are building anew thousands of hotel rooms to handle the jet-boosted tourist trade.

Meantime, the Islanders are organizing their traditional *aloha*, which can mean welcome, hospitality, love and good-by, all rolled into one neat word, to meet the changed conditions. They have revived the Hawaii Visitors Bureau, supported by the community not only to lure travelers but to help them find rooms, food, transportation, souvenirs or toothbrushes.

The Bureau's manager, promises that no visitor will set foot on the Islands or leave them without a lei around his or her neck. The lei makers, mostly Hawaiian women, are lined up again on Fort Street outside the pier on steamer day.

Before the whites came, Hawaiian music consisted of chants to the accompaniment of beating drums and calabashes. The songs and the dances were to propitiate the gods or to extol the prowess of the chiefs. The missionaries turned this love of pagan music to love for hymns. Queen Liliuokalani gave it another turn; inspired by a touching parting of lovers at the palace gate, she retired to her room one night and wrote what is perhaps Hawaii's most haunting melody, *Aloha Oe*. Half Hawaiian and half English, with a refrain from an old hymn, it was the pacesetter for the outpouring of *hapa-haole* songs so popular in the Islands today.

Hapa-haole is a word that means literally "half white," but by usage, "part Hawaiian." Anyone with a few drops of Hawaiian blood is a *hapa-haole*. So is a song with a few Hawaiian words. Many of them sprang spontaneously out of an evening strumming of guitars and ukuleles, the latter being the Portuguese contribution to Hawaii's music lore. Every new song, serious or comic, inspires its own interpretive hula dance, in which gracefully flowing hands speak a language to the rhythm of swaying bodies, a language part pagan, part missionary, part night club.

The Islanders, regardless of ancestry, love the rhythmic symbolism of the hula. They use the slightest pretext—parties, welcomes, farewells, politics—to activate a hula.

***

Not surprisingly, the two faces Hawaii presents to the world— bustling boomland and leisurely tourist paradise—do not always smile at each other. It is one of the problems—more of the *pilikia*— of coming of age. Yet there is a truism that every traveler, Hawaii bound, could well remember:

"If you love Hawaii, Hawaii will surely love you and greet you always with *aloha*."

PART II *The Pacific Coast*

California

by IRVING STONE

So much has been written about California there is little left to be told: except the truth. In a state where the hyperboles are picked green and allowed to ripen en route to the Eastern market, an ounce of astringency is worth a pound of praise.

Northern California is a lean, hard-bitten mountain man, a Jedediah Smith or Joseph Walker fighting his way across the snow-clad Sierras with a hunter's gun slung on his back; male, rugged, disciplined, carrying the indestructible seed of a new civilization. Southern California is a lush, red-lipped, sensual female who came up from Acapulco in the cabin of a well-rigged Spanish ship, and now suns herself in a patio surrounded by bougainvillaea, her gown cut sufficiently low to intimate how abundantly the coming generations may be nourished.

This love affair and marriage have been passionate and prolific, but not always peaceful; there have been quarrels, bills of divorcement; yet the partners have remained in wedlock because of the magic and wealth of the family name.

Intemperate Californians have been heard to say (it's not enough to be on your guard against the natives, the converts are the worst exaggerators) that their state is another Valley of the Nile or Euphrates, cradle of a civilization richer than any the world has ever known; a land of milk and honey and ripe orange groves, green fields, shining streams, sun-drenched ocean beaches: the Promised Land.

Can there be even a smidgen of truth in such outlandish claims?

Everyone knows about our North and South Poles, those two charming geographical concepts. If Moscow is the East Pole, and certainly the Kremlin is calling the tunes for the Orient, then California is the West Pole, the heartland of the new and fresh democracy we feel is being fashioned in the Far West.

What are its components?

It is the life of the individual homeowner, who is not buffeted or mastered by the changes of the economic or political cycle, to whom democracy means neighborliness, getting along with the people next door. It means living with lack of tension, suspicion, hostility, in a largely informal and classless society: for there is food and space, mountains and sea, fertile valleys, cities and villages, sunshine for everyone. We are not a cramped people, in spite of the staggering onslaught of newcomers into the state; neither are we pushed, harried or harassed.

It is living with nature, yet without the constant conflict with the elements, of drought and flood, of ice and sleet. It is the joy of going to work in the daylight and returning in the daylight, with the chance to recoup one's energies in the sun, the surf, the pines, the streams, or just cultivating one's garden.

California fashions have contributed to the nation a picture of the casual life, the gay and informal: the easily cared-for costume, colorful slacks and sports jacket for men, the cotton skirt and thonged shoe for women, the servantless home with the kitchen a part of the living room so that the housewife, in her brightly hued, tapered pants and peasant shirt, can chat with her guests as she tosses a Caesar salad while her husband broils the steaks on the barbecue.

The big houses are being torn down, the grounds subdivided to make room for twenty modern homes. So too with antiquated social distinctions: few Californians try to keep up with the nabob Joneses; now they try to uncomplicate their lives and keep their pretensions down with the democratic Smiths. When each man owns his own garden, his sacred little piece of the good earth, he is anybody's equal.

Be forewarned: when all the facts about California are piled on top of each other, they will constitute a volume thicker and more amazing than Baron Munchausen's book of travels. Along with the Texan, the Californian identifies himself so strongly with his state that he constitutes himself an individual chamber of commerce, sometimes permitting a soupçon of braggadocio to enter his otherwise cool and objective appraisal of his birthright.

The state is almost eight hundred miles long (longer than Italy), embracing within its boundaries staggering contrasts: the stark, barren, primordial rock mountains towering above the sand and creosote-bush wastes of the Mojave Desert to the south; in the north, the dense green forests of redwood and *Sequoia gigantea,* the largest trees in the world, the epitome of long life, of the power of growth and survival.

The Californian offers equally astonishing contrasts: he came during the gold rush in a flash flood of humanity representing almost every race on earth: the Italians in the Sonoma and Napa valleys, the Armenians around Fresno, the Chinese of San Francisco and the Sacramento Valley, the Mexicans of Los Angeles and the Imperial Valley, the Germans around Sunland, the Scandinavians in the lumber towns and around Twin Peaks, the Japanese wherever flowers and vegetables will grow, the Portuguese and Finns of the northern fishing villages, so like the rugged coast of Wales; as well as the thousands of New Englanders, New Yorkers, Pennsylvanians, Southerners. Each group brought its mores, its heritage, the flavor and tone of its state or national character, creating in the Far West a cosmopolitan culture; for the state has the same assimilative powers as the ocean that rolls in from the Sea of Okhotsk and the Tasman Sea.

It was not the billions in gold taken out of the state that enriched California, it was the wealth of humanity that poured in.

Californians see themselves in the large; in their own minds they are all Paul Bunyans who can swing allegorical axes and level forests. Aside from those born here, which requires only modest courage, most of the people who made the long journey to the state were hardy, adventuresome souls. Courage is at the base of California character: the lone coward I've met in all my journeying up and down the state is myself, during the years I had to cross the cemetery on my way home from a night job.

One measure of people is how much they dare, and Californians have dared greatly: Isadora Duncan revolutionized the dance; Frank Norris (we consider any man who has lived here for five years as a true Californian, though of course not with all of the privileges pertaining to the native) liberated the American novel from sentimentality to realism; Jack London blueprinted the coming world of authoritarianism; Gertrude Stein released the American language from its outmoded word-forms; Luther Burbank created edible cactus, plumcots, stoneless prunes; John Muir, the naturalist, saved Yosemite and some hundred million acres of forest reserves for the nation; Upton Sinclair, at sixty, began an eleven-volume historical novel.

We have Chief Justice of the U. S. Supreme Court Earl Warren, who helped bring in a unanimous antisegregation law; writers Saroyan and Steinbeck of Fresno and Salinas origin; Nobel Prize winner Ralph Bunche of the U.N.; Nobel Prize winners Ernest Lawrence, developer of the cyclotron, Glenn T. Seaborg and Edwin M. McMillan, discoverers of plutonium; Jackie Robinson, who pioneered the way for Negro athletes into big-league baseball; Beniamino Bufano, whose vast sculptures have kept San Francisco in an uproar; Richard Neutra, who has carried forward magnificently creative Frank Lloyd Wright's revolution in modern architecture, and says that nowhere else in the entire world could he have had as great an opportunity to experiment in living forms and materials. Many of these men were born elsewhere, but came to California to mature and do their work; did they come because they knew they could find the freedom and strength to accomplish or does being plunged into the inspirited atmosphere of the state increase a man's courage and scope?

On the pediment of the State Office Building in Sacramento is the line: *"Bring Me Men To Match My Mountains."* A tall order: for the Sierras go up to the greatest heights in North America.

How would you like to enter California? From what direction, in what area of time, by what means? By Spanish ship with Cabrillo in 1542, around the Horn in an English ship with Drake in 1579, on foot from Lower California in 1769 with Padre Junípero Serra, by foot and horseback with Captain Juan Bautista de Anza from Mexico in the spring of 1774; down from the Bering Strait in a Russian ship to found Fort Ross in 1812, to remain until 1841 and then sell out just before the discovery of gold; into the harbor of San Diego with Richard Henry Dana (*Two Years Before the Mast*) in 1834, or in the hundreds of ships that sailed through the Golden Gate Strait into San Francisco Bay, true womb of California, with the thousands of gold miners in 1850? Would you prefer to come down from the north, after crossing the Oregon Trail with Parkman, or from the south, across the blazing heat of Death Valley with the Jayhawkers, or over the Sierras with John Bidwell, in covered wagons down the Humboldt with the Chiles-Walker Party in 1843, or with what remained uneaten of the Donner Party in 1847? Would you prefer an automobile on Highway 66, crossing bleak California deserts until you're sure you've been had by the chamber of commerce, and then suddenly come to the top of a bluff and see spread below you a land of ripe orange groves, green meadows and sparkling streams? Or perhaps you want the last word, the jet that leaves New York in midafternoon and reaches California that evening when, replete with Martinis and pheasant under glass, you will circle the phantasmagoria of lights that is San Francisco or Los Angeles, and be taken in a limousine to a swank hotel.

The name California, like so much else in the state, is the invention of a fiction writer, one Ordoñez de Montalvo, who wrote around 1510, "At the right hand of the Indies there is an island called California, very near to the Terrestrial Paradise. This island is inhabited by robust dark women of great strength and great warm hearts; when children are born the females are preserved but the males are killed at once, saving only those required to guard against depopulation . . ." Sounds a little like present-day Hollywood.

The first inhabitants of California found it anything but a terrestrial paradise; the thirty-odd tribes of Indians were the sorriest to stumble onto the North American continent: poverty-stricken, living largely on nuts and berries, without the skill to grow food or make tools or weapons. The only characteristic they shared with their smarter cousins to the east was that they managed to get their squaws to do the work. When the Spanish arrived, the Indians would gladly have closed out the whole state for the same twenty-four dollars that bought Manhattan. Instead, the Spanish put the braves to work building missions, whereupon most of them folded their wretched huts and vanished. The best-known Indians remaining in California today are those who get themselves shot by studio cowboys protecting covered-wagon trains.

Cabrillo, sailing around the Horn in 1542, claimed California for the Spanish and set a four-hundred-year tourist precedent by exclaiming when he saw the coast at Carmel:

"The mountains seem to reach the heavens!"

By 1769, Junípero Serra began to build the missions that became
California's first permanent settlements: San Diego, San Juan Capi-
strano, San Fernando, Santa Barbara, San Luis Obispo near Monterey, Mission Dolores in San Francisco, Sonoma, most of them now
rebuilt. Aside from the missions, and the sparsely manned military
presidios at San Diego, Santa Barbara, Monterey and San Francisco,
the Spanish thought little of California: it was too remote, too undeveloped, without any of the golden wealth they had drained out of
Mexico and Peru.

The Mexicans were barely settled when *americanos* began filter-
ing in from the northern mountains or the southern desert: Jedediah
Smith, a trapper, in 1826; James Pattie, a fur trapper, in 1828; Ewing
Young in 1829, Joseph Walker in 1833, John Frémont and Kit Carson
and John Bidwell in 1841, then American sailors who jumped ship
when their barks anchored in California ports, and those put ashore
sick and left to die. They did not die; of all the multitudes sent to
California by their family doctors back home, not one has been
known (publicly) to succumb. Many of the Americans became *Cali-
fornios:* and why not, with thousands of acres of fertile land for the
taking, and beautiful black-eyed *señoritas* languishing for husbands?

The first revolt of Americans for independence from Mexico was
started by the wrong social set; that's probably why we hear so little
about it. Isaac Graham, their leader, was the owner of a distillery,
described by Hubert Howe Bancroft, our fabulous source historian,
as "a wild and unprincipled man, with no good qualities except personal bravery." Graham and his followers wound up in a flea-infested
jail in San Blas, Mexico.

But six years later there were some seven hundred Americans in
California, owning a great deal of land, restive under Mexican rule.
In 1846, Colonel John C. Frémont, son-in-law of Thomas Hart Benton of Missouri, the most rabid western expansionist in the Congress,
having appeared from over the mountains with a band of well-armed
explorers and cartographers, had a brush with General Castro, the
military commander of California, and raised the American flag on
Gabilan Peak for three days of defiance. Then, moving northward,
he was overtaken by Marine Lieutenant Gillespie, who had confi-
dential dispatches from Secretary of State Buchanan. Frémont
turned south, united the *americanos,* and so began the story of modern California.

Very soon thereafter an excitable young wheelwright by the name of James Marshall, while building a sawmill at Coloma for his Swiss boss, John Sutter, glanced over at the tailrace he had built across a bend in the American River, and noticed a number of flecks of yellow where the water was sluicing through a sandbar. If the Flower of the Pacific was wrested from Mexico through rape, and its birth as an American state must be branded as illegitimate, there was no questioning the legitimacy of that gold; it started a rush that has never slackened, and will not abate until some fifty million people call themselves Californians.

Superlatives are indigestible; let's sample a few, and have done with them.

We have the largest number of owner-occupied dwelling units of any state, the widest diversification of agricultural crops and livestock, bringing the highest cash farm income; the widest diversification of minerals, of recreational facilities; the largest number of automobiles, driven by the wackiest drivers; the largest bank, the lowest land point, Death Valley; the tallest trees, the tallest storytellers, starting with Mark Twain and his *Jumping Frog of Calaveras County*. We spend more money than any other state for public services: education, public welfare, highways. California is the third largest state geographically (alas, we can never become first), embraces 158,693 square miles, bigger than New England with New York and Ohio thrown in for friendly measure; has the second highest per capita income of the major states. . . .

What do these facts and figures mean? What is their true significance? The Himalayas are big, but they have produced no Athens or Florence, while I have yet to meet an elephant who has written *The Brothers Karamazov* or a dinosaur who has painted Van Gogh's *Vegetable Gardens*. Size and wealth are meaningless unless translated into terms of the good life for a whole people.

The best way to know California is from within, by working its veins and arteries, as the original gold miners did, and as this writer did; drive a San Francisco grocery wagon and have the horse fall down in its harness when you attempt to take him down the perpendicular Haight Street hill; dig holes for electric poles across the hot Central Valley; oil dynamos at a Kern River power plant in the mountains above Bakersfield; whitewash the trunks of apricot trees in Hollister, pick peaches in Marysville in the farm belt, wrap meat in a Los Angeles packing plant and watch the hams and bacons dance on the rack when an earthquake rocks the building; or check

vacationers in and out of a swank Lake Tahoe mountain resort as a
desk clerk. Deliver suits for Pauson's and fling a package up a long
dark flight of stairs on Grant Avenue in San Francisco's Chinatown,
fleeing in terror because you've been brought up to believe the stories of Chinese opium dens and white-slave trade; some years later
play *Smiles* and *Margie* for an Italian wedding in a Grant Avenue
hall with your back against a lattice-work partition, on the other side
of which a Chinese orchestra is playing Old Country music for one
of their weddings; blow a saxophone at the Orange Show in the lush
southern citrus land of the San Bernardino Valley for ten days and
nights, or on the back of a truck helping to gather Central California
crowds in Benicia, Vallejo, Napa and Sacramento, so that political
haranguers can tell the people why they should vote for John W.
Davis for president; entertain with a traveling vaudeville troupe
through the mining regions of Angels Camp and Chinese Camp, the
mountain and lumber towns of Jamestown, Sonora, Tuolumne; work
as a stock boy in one of San Francisco's oldest bookstores where you
unpack hundreds of copies of Ibañez' *Four Horsemen of the Apoca-
lypse*, the best seller of the day, and at every opportunity read a
few pages in the storage stacks until the manager tells you to take
a copy home and read it on your own time; be signaled out of an
8 A.M. senior discussion group in economics at the University of
California at Berkeley, unshaven, and be asked by the professor to
take the rostrum and replace the Teaching Fellow whose appendix
had been removed an hour before, thus stumbling into the noble
profession of teaching.

California is actually five different states, with a variety of cultures: the sun worship of the vast southern desert; the semitropical
life of Los Angeles with its hundred-mile aura of influence; the valley
culture of the five-hundred-mile-long, rich agricultural land between
the Coast Range and the Sierras; the fog culture; the mountain and
big-timber culture of the north.

San Francisco is the capital of the fog culture, though its natives
will tell you that it has no fog, or if they are confronted with the
sight of it rolling in from the beach at fourteen miles an hour, that
they find it exhilarating. You will be driving north from Los Angeles,
with the top of your convertible down, baking in the hot sun; you
reach the south end of the suction cup, perhaps five miles down the
peninsula from San Francisco, and find yourself engulfed in raw
penetrating cold. The fog will blanket the whole city as you drive

over the Mission hills, past the ball park, across Market Street, by the Civic Center with the beautiful Opera House, and out automobile row. The waters of the strait will be milk gray, with only the tips of the vast steel girders of the Golden Gate Bridge visible, as though they were hung downward from the sky. Yet once across the bridge, and through the cut in the hills, a matter of a mile or two, and you are again in the hot clear sunshine.

Every man writes a biographical novel with the blood of his spent hours; but if you have freedom of choice, San Francisco is a good town in which to be born.

My first memory of the city is at the age of three, when I stood on top of Twin Peaks with my mother on an April night in 1906, watching San Francisco burn to the ground. My mother said: "We will never live like civilized people again; we'll roam these hills like wild animals, foraging for our food."

On the ashes arose the city in which I grew up, the ugliest city in the world, built of hard wood and harder gray stone, a grim-visaged masculine town with its houses glued together in long, tall, dark, narrow rows, the steps emerging out of the very sidewalks, mounting the hills like the rungs of ladders, with no blade of grass, no tree, no flower, no touch of soft feminine earth. The architecture was haphazard; district after district was plain, austere, heavy, unbeautiful.

But you turned a corner and unexpectedly you found yourself on the crest of a hill. Below lay the bay, with its islands bold and clear in the brilliant sunshine; in the docks along the Embarcadero nestled the dozens of ships being loaded for Oriental ports, and the quaint ferry boats plying the waters; beyond were the green hills of Oakland and Berkeley. And suddenly the irresilience dropped away, the street and the people grew soft and friendly, and you knew that you lived in a city with mood, with tone, with style, with beauty: the most beautiful city in the world.

San Franciscans, like the amazing hills they have climbed these several generations, are a hard, stony people, astonishingly like New Englanders: stubborn, proud, willful, self-contained, tenacious, fiercely independent, rooted in rocky tradition; not the kind of hardness that is mean or uncharitable, but rather the kind that demands so terribly much of itself. Easterners say, "We can always tell a San Franciscan: there is a touch of accent, of Boston thrown into a crude pioneer settlement; a touch of the arrogance of people who can flourish under difficult circumstances; a submerged grimness of purpose, a shortness of humor, cultivated"—we natives like to boast that we had an opera house and a first-rate literary magazine, the *Golden Era*, before we paved our streets—"and yet at the same time curiously insular, almost like an island folk."

Do not gather the impression that San Francisco is a cold city; actually it is one of the warmest communities in the world, with the old Spanish tradition of the latchstring always being on the outside still predominant. San Francisco is warm and hospitable to strangers, trusts newcomers and takes them at face value. When you have done raving about the tiny tart shrimp at Fisherman's Wharf, the cable cars clanging up Powell and California streets, the view of the Golden Gate Strait from Pacific Heights with tramp steamers coming through the narrows, the Bay Bridge seen from Coit Tower or the Top of the Mark, the soignée San Francisco women, among the best groomed in the world, the breath-taking panorama of Market Street extending from the foot of Twin Peaks all the way down to the now obsolete Ferry Building; when all of this has been recounted, it still does not disclose the secret of why San Francisco is one of the world's most beloved cities: the incredible fact that after an hour you feel that you belong, that this city which embodies and projects a quality of delight, could be your home forever.

A lot of folks did. They came originally to find gold, but when they grew bored with digging, or the gold did not pan out, they resumed the trades they had practiced at home: carpentering, farming, doctoring, trading, bookkeeping, schoolteaching, the law.

Few came with any great wealth, and whatever social position they may have enjoyed at home they necessarily left behind them. San Francisco created its own wealth, its own society, its own erudition. Class lines never had much chance to solidify, for the great lady in the mansion up on Washington Street was probably as newly arrived as the mining, sugar, railroad-shipping or real-estate money with which her husband built the ornate forty-room house.

When I told my mother, who had read from cover to cover but one book in her life, Mary Antin's *Promised Land*, that I was determined to become a writer, she wept with fear for her only son: for in one of my Aunt Julia's flats lived a writer with his wife and three daughters. They had no furniture except two beds, a kitchen table and chairs, no carpets on the floor. When the writer ran out of food money he would pick up a tray of toilet waters and peddle them to the wives of chicken farmers around Petaluma. To my mother's objection I replied:

"San Francisco is a good place for writers to be born." What more can any city give its children than the unshatterable faith that they can accomplish whatever they may set their minds and hearts to?

In 1923, when I was an economics instructor at the University of Southern California in Los Angeles, sharing an office with three other instructors, two handsomely dressed young men from the Janss Investment Corporation made us an offer: they would give each of us a large lot free, in something that was to be called Westwood Village, where a southern branch of the University of California was purportedly to be built, if we would contract to erect a $10,000 business building within three years. Though the four of us could not have collected ten thousand jelly beans, we piled into my Model T, drove through the miles of open plains on either side of Wilshire Boulevard, then trudged over the sand dunes wondering why these slick operators did not confine their confidence games to wildcat oil wells.

Today Westwood Village is one of the most sparklingly beautiful and prosperous communities in the state; you can't buy a lot there with money, let alone jelly beans, and the faculty complains that it is the only university town in America where the rentals are too high for the professors to live.

I, for one, should have known better: as a child I stood on a high sand dune in San Francisco overlooking the Pacific with my grandfather telling me how, in 1870, he had stood on this very dune waiting for sight of the ship, reported lost, coming from around the Horn with his wife and children. To my question of whether there ever would be houses on these miles and miles of lonely dunes, my grandfather replied:

"Never. There aren't enough people in the world to fill them up."

The only sand you can find today is on the beach south of the Cliff House.

Not long ago I drove through Los Angeles to the International airport, out Sepulveda Boulevard past open fields and dunes where I had been horseback riding the day before. I flew to New York and remained long enough to send a book to press, three months at the most; when I returned I found the same countryside occupied by several thousand bungalows, with the streets in, trees planted, lawns and flowers already up, kids playing under the sprinklers.

Why do they come? Why are they willing to give up home, family, friends, jobs, clientele, roots? Why do so few become disappointed and return to the place of their birth?

The climate is one of the two commanding factors: in Southern California, the weather is a friend with whom you can have a delightful time the year around. People say, "If I'm going to have to work for a living I might as well do it where it is warm and pleasant all year." There are other reasons: most of our cities are new, clean and sun-drenched; our buildings rarely go over two to four stories and those coming from skyscraper cities can see their world horizontally instead of vertically, surrounded by a huge bowl of sky instead of cement walls. There is no snow to be shoveled, coal and oil to be burned, soot to be fought; men don't have to wear heavy overcoats and rubbers, women don't have to bundle up the children in wools and ear muffs. Folks live in their own homes, with flowers in front and a back yard where the kids can play in safety all year round. Many middle-cost builders are replacing the rumpus room or extra bedroom with a small swimming pool.

The second motivation is exemplified by my own family: my mother and stepfather moved down to Los Angeles from San Francisco in 1919 because Los Angeles, then a sleepy village, was just beginning to offer fresh business opportunities. With expanding aviation, automobile, steel, oil, motion-picture, real-estate and a hundred other industries there is work for all, and opportunity aplenty.

Some years ago, when some friends moved to Los Angeles from New York and I asked their sons what they were majoring in at school, they replied disdainfully, "Recess. Every time we turn around we have to go outside and play," to which their mother added, "Apparently you Southern Californians are trying to develop a race of seven-foot dopes." This is no longer true: in a leisurely two-hour drive from the beautiful U.C.L.A. campus in Westwood one can circle past Los Angeles City College, U.S.C., and go east through the San Bernardino Valley past Occidental, California Institute of Technology, Whittier, Scripps, Pomona, Redlands and now the new liberal-arts branch of the University of California at Riverside, all fine educational institutions.

Los Angeles was once the capital of bad taste in America, with all manner of vulgar architecture, restaurants in the shape of hot dogs and tamales, with bastard Spanish or Moorish monstrosities for residences. In towns like Beverly Hills the original builders built thick-walled, narrow-windowed Spanish houses, black dungeons which are being ripped out and converted to moderns to make way for the sun and light. The intellectual tone of the community, totally insular and isolationist, was dictated by senior citizens retired from the rigors of the Midwest farm states, who came because living was cheap.

Though Los Angeles still has to borrow San Francisco's opera company for two weeks out of the year, it now has its own symphony orchestra, growing art museums, many little theaters, vigorous bookstores, superb private collections of paintings and sculpture available for local showings. The motion-picture industry has helped to make the change, bringing in creative artists from all over the world.

Even in California, the democratic West Pole of the world, we have our dissenters and defeatists and crackpots. In spite of the maturing of our arts and education, Los Angeles still remains one of the most powerful anti-intellectual centers in the country.

Yet there is a vitality abroad that is building new schools, libraries, whole outlying communities: a vitality that says make way for life, the California life.

The country for 120 miles south of Los Angeles to the Mexican border, the first half dominated by the oil derricks of Culver City, Signal Hill and Huntington Beach and the wells out in the ocean, is a narrow strip with houses hugging the mountains overlooking the sea. Behind this wall of mountain there are tremendous valleys where only a few cattle graze. In South Laguna you can have your own private beach and catch fish from the rocks; in La Jolla you can skin-dive for abalone and put out your lobster traps. San Diego has beautiful views of the ocean and bay wherever you turn and the most exciting zoo in the world.

The most beautiful and cultivated trio of towns in the Los Angeles area are Santa Barbara, Pasadena and La Jolla, generically alike and formerly known as the "Three R's": rich, Republican and reactionary. This canard can no longer be charged; the cities are extremely prosperous, but many of the great Eastern and Midwest fortunes that founded them have gone to their rewards: the Treasury Department. Pasadena's big estates are being broken up for handsome two-story modern apartment houses, while whole suburbs of precision-instrument workers are moving in to man the new plants. La Jolla is being settled by the overflow of middle-class families from San Diego,

while Santa Barbara is becoming an important college center with
its new University of California campus.

A hundred miles of magnificent beaches are a half hour's drive
from anywhere in the Los Angeles area; so are the mountains with
good fishing in summer and skiing in winter. Except for Old Los
Angeles, Southern California is sparkling new, with the gleaming
whiteness of house and market and street, a constant joy to the new-
comer.

The word "slum" has dropped out of the language in California;
even the rundown sections have a bit of lawn, shrubs, a few flowers
in front of the houses.

Southern California families live as much outdoors as they do in;
modern architecture includes the out-of-doors as part of the interior
decoration. This willingness to experiment, to try the new and different has helped to lessen the tightness and the tensions of a more
rigid world. *California's greatest difference is that we are on the way
to creating an anxiety-free people.*

And in Southern California there is Hollywood.

California has always been a romantic area and concept, from the
beginning romance of its name, through the discovery of romanti-
cally free gold, the romance of its semitropical flowers and brilliant
sunshine, its golden oranges and golden poppies, its Mediterranean-
date crop around Indio in the Coachella Valley, and finally that great
romance breeder which has made the name of Hollywood famous
in the remotest villages of Afghanistan.

The proper way to describe Hollywood is in terms of the motion-
picture industry: the various companies are only ostensibly in competition. Actors, producers, directors, writers shift from M-G-M to
Fox to Warners to Paramount to Columbia to Universal-International
and back to M-G-M without changing a picture on their desks or
knowing that they have actually moved. The steady and secure core
of the industry are the technicians, the engineers, sound men, elec-
tricians, property men, all well but not exorbitantly paid, and enjoying almost full security. These are the gentle folk, the soft-spoken,
the totally decent and reliable.

Do the movie big shots have a more amoral set of values than the
leaders of other industries? If you were playing poker with twenty
dollars in the pot and saw an opportunity to cut a corner in order to
win, you probably would not be tempted to take advantage; but if

there were two hundred thousand dollars in the pot, and you saw a chance to cheat. . . . Only in Hollywood can a man who is earning five thousand dollars a week be unemployed the following Monday, the man who is broke and cannot meet the payment on his home suddenly get a contract or sell a property to the movies and have a hundred and fifty thousand dollars in the bank.

Only in the motion-picture industry are millions spent each year on promoting individual personalities, until actors and actresses believe their own press notices and come to regard themselves as kings and queens with the divine right of royalty. Imagine what this does to the integrity of human beings; imagine what these men and women will not do to remain at the heart of the greatest romance creator of our age, and to reap its fabulous harvest—even though in their hearts they know they really earn but the smallest portion.

What is the effect of living in Southern California, through whose communities are spread the thousands of people engaged in the motion-picture industry? It is a pleasant one; at the sneak preview at your nearby movie house you will see the entire cast of big pictures as well as the director, producer and cameraman of the film which will be splashed across the newspapers three months hence. Not even the gala international world *premières*, with the lights and the stars and the special stands, can make any shattering change in your life; but all these things are fun, they are gay, they lend color and character to Southern California.

Picture to yourself two high walls of mountains, the Coast Range and the Sierra Nevada, going up over 14,000 feet at Mount Whitney; and between the two a mammoth valley some five hundred miles long and forty wide—roughly half the size of England.

Two thirds of the state's agricultural lands are here, irrigated by the Central Valley Water Project, which stores water high on the Sacramento and San Joaquin rivers and carries it five hundred miles south to the once desert lands around Bakersfield. Every species of temperate-zone and subtropical fruit, vegetable or field crop is produced: pears, asparagus, celery, beans, onions, rice, lettuce, grapes, prunes, peaches, apricots, plums, olives, cotton (we produce more cotton than any state in the South, except Texas), oranges, lemons, pomegranates, figs, avocados, loquats, guavas, almonds, walnuts, dates, artichokes, cherries, honeydew melons, cantaloupes, tomatoes, cauliflower, spinach, dry beans, garlic, alfalfa, apples, sugar beets, grapefruit, barley.

In this earthly paradise have grown prosperous, modern communities whose millions of people live free of insecurity and want. The three most important towns of the Central Valley are Sacramento, about a hundred miles northeast of San Francisco, which grew up around Sutter's Fort, with orange and magnolia trees shading the streets, architecturally half old, half new, with hundreds of suburban ranch-style houses; Stockton, an inland port, important as a trading post long before the gold rush; and Fresno, center of the billion-dollars-a-year trade of the San Joaquin Valley, halfway between San Francisco and Los Angeles, a young, vigorous, almost completely new city.

In towns like San Jose, forty miles south of San Francisco, a center of canning, dried fruits and wineries, three quarters of the families own their own homes, as they do in Sacramento and such prosperous southern towns as Pomona, with its colleges, Redlands, Riverside and San Bernardino. Millions of Californians want no part of the life in the world-known cities of San Francisco and Los Angeles; they like the intimacy and camaraderie of the coastal towns or the hot, small communities of the Central Valley: Marysville, Lodi, Stockton, Modesto, Merced, Fresno, Visalia, Salinas, San Louis Obispo and a hundred others, many of them with a single shopping center and conventional neon signs which are slowly draining their individuality. In towns like these you can know nearly everyone of your own generation; you need never live among strangers. You can, and do, marry young, frequently out of high school. Friendship is strong because it underlies almost every social activity. There is a homogeneity, not merely of ideas and values, but of income levels as well. No one need get lost. The weekly poker game you start during the last year of high school will still be going twenty years later with the same fellows, and probably the same gags. You won't enjoy much privacy; the other women will know exactly how much your wife spends on clothes and when you and she last quarreled. And you will also know everything about them.

Without this Central Valley, this modern-day Valley of the Nile, California would be a magnificent front, able to support less than half its population, hollow at its economic core.

The newest culture in the state, and perhaps the most exciting, is the life of the desert. The desert can be cruel; to many newcomers it appears hostile, fruitless. But the desert is also intensely alive, mysterious, masterful. Palm Springs is the center of the vacation area; no hospitals or sanitariums or industrial plants or farms are permitted in this particular mountain-enclosed valley. Palm Springs is attracting more devotees each year by what they like to call its optimum climate: the greatest amount of beneficent clear sunlight and the least humidity in the United States; but what is not generally known is that thousands of families are exchanging the business-suit-and-necktie life of formal cities for the open-sport-shirt-and-sandal life of the Coachella Valley, which includes Indio, heart of the date palm.

You drive through the eye-burning smog of Los Angeles, then climb up the San Gorgonio Pass, through Beaumont and Banning into the desert itself, with its towering wall of sheer brown rock; and suddenly you can breathe deeper, suddenly you are in a world of brilliant sunlight and color, the openness of vast areas where no person or object can fence in your body or your thinking. No matter how tired or ill you may be, or possessed by *Weltschmerz,* your troubles and complaints fall away: for there is little tension on the desert, pressures dissolve in the hot sun, as do the nervous confusions of a competitive world.

The recuperative power of the desert, its ability to bring one closer to the eternalities of nature, the ever-shifting forms of the sand, and the shadows on the mountains, with the sun on your back during the day, the warm silk-soft air of the night on your face, have caused thousands of people to move into the area around Palm Springs and make it their permanent home. There will be hundreds of thousands more in the balance of the Coachella and Imperial valleys, now that they are watered from the Colorado River through the new All-American Canal.

The desert is one vast *Kaffeeklatsch;* everyone is friendly and helpful because everyone is himself a new arrival, remembering how it felt to be lonely. When you live with the vastness of sky and sun and mountain, with the magnificent panorama of changing pastel colors, vivid purple sunsets, skies so thick with stars you can reach up and pick them like bunches of grapes, you stop worrying about Russians, hydrogen bombs, income taxes; you become, instead, in your own simple way, a philosopher. The products of philosophy, alas, cannot be boxed and shipped like the superb Coachella grapefruit and dates or the Imperial Valley melons; but by breeding an anxiety-free man, the desert is adding a new dimension and a new health-drenched culture to the complex geographical and mystical entity of California.

Northern California, the third of the state that lies north of San Francisco, is as different from Southern California as New Hampshire is from Florida. The mountains and stands of pine, redwood, Douglas fir, incense cedar, western yew, mountain birch and white oak are majestic, the towns and people few. There is privacy and solitude, great hunting, fishing, camping for a hardy stock that can take thirty-five below zero in winter, ninety-eight above in summer, and will not hesitate to brave the worst of these extremes to bag a fine mule buck or catch a large brown trout, or be averse to taking a wee drop now and then. The people living in the far north conceive of themselves as still living in an almost-frontier country; they enjoy the romantic conception of the hardy, robust, difficult life.

Northern Californians, too, live close to nature; it is an outdoor interest that explains the presence of most of the residents, particularly among the professional classes, yet the rugged four-season life is the exact opposite of that led by the new desert dwellers. They are never more than a few minutes away from upland meadows, mountain torrents, rock gorges through which the Kings and Kern rivers have cut their beds, high Sierra peaks and passes often snow-laden, nearly impenetrable forests carpeted with swordfern, huckleberries, buckthorn, elderberry, teeming with bear, antelope, mountain sheep and mountain lions, fox, beaver and muskrat.

The towns of Northern California are old and so inbred that if you have an argument with a merchant or city clerk in Alturas you find that you have offended half the families of Modoc County. The people here are harder, sterner, more ruggedly set than the soft, easygoing, fast-changing but slower-moving and slower-talking Southern Californians.

The social life is exhausting: bridge parties, community concerts, baseball, bowling and rifleshoot competitions, an endless round of luncheons, cocktail parties, dinners, dances and picnic suppers. In a town like Ukiah, a hundred miles north of San Francisco, the community life of the churches, P.T.A., fraternal, scouting, political organizations and volunteer government committees is so highly organized that there is almost never a free hour; while the most often repeated line in Alturas is, "I got a meeting tonight." There are few book or music shops in these northern towns; however, the book clubs do a flourishing business and many middle-class families maintain credit accounts at San Francisco and Oakland bookstores.

The people of Northern California are a little like their redwoods: lean in temperament, resentful of intruders though exhaustingly hospitable to friends; opposed to change, to the new or different, disdaining the Southern California backyard-barbecue and swimming-pool set. To the Southern Californian, anything that is not built tomorrow is old-fashioned; to North Californians that which smells of paint, the most cherished of all perfumes in the south, is parvenu.

Around Lake Tahoe, where California and Nevada make an elbow bend, the rings on the *Sequoia gigantea* add up to four thousand years, probably the oldest inhabitants of the state; the northern people have somewhat the same solidity of tradition, priding themselves on being an "old" culture. This is true all the way down to Fresno, about midway in the state, after which the pride comes in being spanking-new.

California is not Utopia, yet it is a land to dream on; seventeen co-operative colonies, from the religious Fountain Grove near Santa Rosa in Northern California to Madame Modjeska's agricultural colony near Anaheim in Southern California, have been essayed in the past hundred years. When you drive through the gold-rush regions, pass abandoned mines and the high piles of rock displaced by hydraulic mining, and the river beds where millions in golden dust were taken out, it's all you can do to restrain yourself from jumping out of the car, grabbing a shovel and commencing to dig.

The state is changing: subdividers are ripping out walnut orchards and orange groves in the south for residential tracts, prune orchards and vineyards in the north for drive-in theaters or hardboard factories. The old-timers in Mendocino County don't want to be industrialized any more than the original settlers of San Diego want their two-lane roads expanded to superhighways.

Sentiment in the East used to be, "You can live cheaply in California, but you can't earn a living there." Today there is work for all, but the cost of living is high.

When I grew up in San Francisco a human being was a precious commodity, there were so few of them on Market Street or Powell. When I moved to New York in 1926 I was stunned by the hordes of humanity jammed on Fifth Avenue or 42nd Street during the day and on Broadway at night. If there are so many people in the world, I thought, can any one of them be truly valuable?

A Californian moving to New York today would not be so stunned by the difference: for we are fast acquiring people. By the year 2000 we should have a population of 50,000,000, outnumbering most of the countries of Europe.

To this writer, who has spent his summers in the north since he was six, the Sonoma and Napa valleys, and Jack London's Valley of the Moon, are the most beautiful parts of California, surpassed only by the view of the Lombardy plain from the top of Assisi. The immigrating Italians, back in the seventies and eighties, searching all over America for their native Italy, found it in these valleys, cleared the mountainsides of first stand redwood and pine, manzanita and madroña, planted their vineyards and made some of the world's finest wines, enriching the country with the best of their native character, particularly gastronomically. But the third generation no longer wants to plow the fields or cultivate the grapes; they've become Americanized and prefer to work in factories. The superb little wineries, with some exceptions, have been sold to the larger distilleries.

What is the character of the state today?

Californians are by nature a tender and gentle people somehow given to violence, doubtless a vestige of the pioneer days when folks had to take care of their own hangings. If you feel the urge to blow up your parents on their yacht, or poison the milk of your best friend because you're in love with his wife, California is far and away your best bet: true-blooded Californians are too close to the pioneer days to convict anyone for a crime of passion.

Politically, it is clean; it would be after fifteen years of Earl Warren as attorney general and governor; yet we are not too aseptic to elect an occasional hack politician to high office, and have him celebrate his victory on election night by getting falling-down drunk in one of the swankier night clubs.

In the early part of the century, California was so predominantly Republican that we hardly knew there was a two-party system. I was first introduced at the age of nine to the Democrats by a gang of Mission district boys who grabbed me and shouted, "Who are you for?" I was for Teddy Roosevelt, but since it appeared obvious that they would not have grabbed me had I been for the right candidate I answered, "Taft!" Their leader bulked his fist in front of my face and cried, "You be for Woodrow Wilson, or I'll punch your nose in."

While the strike was in progress, a gang broke into the room of Frank W. Little, an IWW organizer suffering from a broken leg, and hanged him to a trestle, pinning on him the old Vigilante number, 3-7-77, meaning three feet by seven feet by seventy-seven inches, the dimensions of a grave. The strike ended in about six months, but martial law remained in effect for more than a year.

More blood was shed three years later, when gunmen fired into a picket line near the Butte city limits, killing two men and wounding nineteen. The most recent disturbance occurred in the spring of 1946. During the course of a ten-day strike, houses were stoned, windows broken, furniture moved from homes, families threatened. The mob outbreak lasted sixty hours, amid outraged cries of communism and unanswered demands for martial law. The union disavowed responsibility, denounced the destroyers of property and offered its help. One hundred of its men were sworn in as special deputies. Property damage was considerable, but personal injuries few and slight unless counted among them was the fatal injury of a boy by a stray bullet.

Twelve years before that time, after the inauguration of the National Recovery Administration, Butte returned to the closed shop and again became a union stronghold. Earlier than that, following reports of the Bureau of Mines and the Public Health Service, the operators agreed to spend millions of dollars in equipment and practices to reduce the incidence of pneumonia, tuberculosis and silicosis.

Violence in Butte seems pretty far away today. So does the old wholesale corruption, if you except the sportiness that still prevails, if less extravagantly. You could conclude that more amicable relationships were likely to prevail. The Anaconda Copper Mining Company, divorced from Standard Oil through Teddy Roosevelt's trust-busting, has announced an interest, aside from copper, in the community of Butte. It has projected long-range plans that contrast with the philosophy and practice of the mere exploiter. It has established for employees a clubhouse, complete with theater, bowling lanes, library and game rooms, that comparatively few men could afford to belong to anywhere.

But Butte, in spite of change, remains Butte, more cosmopolitan, more outlandish, different in make-up and temperament from other cities in the state. It is an immensely interesting, hearty, friendly place; but it isn't Montana.

Neither is the western slope quite the genuine article. It belongs more to Idaho and Oregon. Men are known to raise cherries there, and apples, which may be the finest in the land but still aren't wheat or beef or mutton. It is hard to think of a Montanan as a cherry picker or an apple knocker. He needs to have wheat straw in his hair and cottonseed cake in his whiskers. He needs to have the print of wind in his face and the mark of the saddle on his pants or the smell of sheep in his Mackinaw.

Most of Montana, more than four fifths of it, I'd estimate, lies east of the Continental Divide. And it is here that you get the feel and color and smell of Montana. It is here that the west wind blows and the sky is high, where you know that space is something no one can understand, not even Albert Einstein. It's here, too, that you keep your directions straight, provided you live within sight of the front range of the Rockies, for west always are the mountains, stony and blue and beautiful against the arch of sky.

Great Falls is both more flourishing and more Montanaish than Butte. So is Billings. Geography and people have the more nearly typical stamp. Here you see and remember the men who wear outdoors indoors.

Great Falls lies in a bend of the Missouri, close to the mouth of Sun River. The main range of the Rockies rears to the west. East and southeast are other ranges, the Highwoods and the Little Belts.

On a flat above the town lies East Base, selected and installed by the military for the special training of flyers because so many days are clear.

Great Falls didn't start as a mushroom town, generated by gold or copper. It started slowly, planned by a man who saw its industrial possibilities. The man was Paris Gibson. In 1883, three years after he had looked at the site, he came back from Minneapolis with a surveyor and an attorney and plotted the townsite. It wasn't long until a hydroelectric plant—the first of the present-day four—was installed at one of the numerous falls that break the nearby Missouri. Before then a flour mill, planing mill, lumberyard, school, bank and newspaper had started operations. Here, in what a few years before had been the heartland of the savage Blackfeet, white institutions took root.

The greatest institution, though, is not dams or refineries or industries of any sort. It is the memory of a man—of Charlie Russell, cowboy artist, sculptor, author, wit and hearty liver, who combined in one personality the characteristics Montanans most admire. His paintings command big figures now. So does his sculpture. His books have entertained thousands and thousands. But it isn't his work that the Montanan particularly likes to talk about. It is Charlie, dead since 1926—Charlie with his easy conviviality, his store of stories, his love for the old Montana, his Will Rogerish ability to point up a situation with a crack.

A rancher who was a friend of Charlie's leased his place to a character reputed to be an honest prohibition farmer. In the course of a couple of years the farmer made off with nearly all the equipment on the ranch.

Charlie commented: "It looks like the only thing that honest prohibition farmer won't take is a drink."

High on the rimrock above Billings, bronze Bill Hart sits his bronze cayuse while airplanes drone in and out of the airport nearby. Let them ride the sky. He is the Range Rider of the Yellowstone, overlooking the great reaches that cowpunchers used to work. Four hundred feet down, on the bank of the Yellowstone, rests the town, prosperous in a valley that a reporter of 1874 termed "valuable for neither agriculture, grazing, nor minerals. . . ." The reporter was wrong about grazing, and he didn't reckon with irrigation. Billings is cow country and sugar-beet country and alfalfa country and wool country. And it is Montana country. Here again you see the marks of horse and hayrack.

In a state like Montana, where population is small and space great, human affairs are immediate and personal. Welfare legislation is not an imponderable, written in answer to statistics. The man who draws unemployment money, the oldster who receives assistance—these are known to their communities, not always favorably. The Montanan, especially the old-timer, is apt to sniff and ask what things are coming to. Physically his world is large; population-wise it is small. He gets a look at things. Both the largeness and the smallness affect him. He finds it hard to imagine a crowded world, difficult to think of humanity en masse. And so, I might add, would you. This is a different world from the Midwest and East. Different circumstances bear on judgment. You feel isolated, happily isolated, free of the frets of our time. Let the world go hang. It is at this point that you need to remind yourself that we tried to let it go hang before.

Part of the citizenry is glad that the ratio of space to population is high. They don't want a lot of outlanders to people the unpeopled places, to fish out the trout streams and spoil the hunting. Another part wants to promote the state, but even the promoters, like the Montana Chamber of Commerce, speak rather cautiously of small, home-owned industry that would help to solve the seasonal unemployment problem. With syndicate operations and mechanization growing both on farms and in lumber areas, they foresee even fewer seasonal jobs.

In part, it is perhaps space and climate that give the Montana resident his humor, his readiness to accept, his disinclination to exaggerate the importance of self. Montana, the fourth-largest state in the Union, is a various and mighty country—146,997 square miles of badlands, high plains, foothills, mountain spurs, glaciered mountains, valleys. The tourist finds the drive from border to border, north and south, a fair day's wheeling. The Great Northern's crack Empire Builder, toiling east across the mountains by way of Marias Pass and dropping to the endless plain, takes just ten minutes short of twelve hours getting from Troy, on the western edge, to Glasgow, which is still one hundred and twenty crow-flight miles from the North Dakota border. The state is rugged. It possesses a grim beauty. Any way the eye looks, it is filled—with nothing, said an Easterner who couldn't see. The grandeur of the place makes self-concern incongruous.

Weather does too. You never can tell what will happen to your prospects in a country in which the temperature ranges from 50° below zero to 110° above. What you do come to realize is that nature isn't overly concerned with you. Montanans take the climate without even due complaint. Cold? Hell, the eastern sloper will tell you, there isn't a month in Montana without at least one day in which a man will be comfortable in his shirt sleeves. Ever feel a chinook? he asks. Chinook? It's a warm wind from the west. Last time it started up, a rancher who'd come to town by sled just managed, going home, to keep his front bobs on the snow. Like to killed his horses doing it.

The exaggeration isn't so extreme. Balmy days do come in midwinter. Snow doesn't often stay on the ground very long except at high altitudes.

Another element helps to mould the Montanan. It is the element of peril—peril from climate, animals, geography, seclusion. In nearly any graveyard can be found markers to sheepherders who died in blizzards with their bands. One July night a Dupuyer sheepman named Broadhurst Smith left his summer-range camp to relieve the night herder. He took a .30-.30 carbine with him. He had settled down for the night when he heard a disturbance in the band. Two grizzly bears were there. He ran at them, shouting, and scared one away. The other began to circle him. As it reared, he shot it down, worked the lever of his rifle and advanced to administer the *coup de grâce.* The hammer clicked on an empty chamber. The sound brought the bear up. It charged Smith and mauled him badly. When it had left him, Smith started, too soon, to crawl away, fearful that if he waited he'd die from loss of blood. The bear came back, fiercer than before. It tore his scalp away. It bit him, bone-deep, on arms and legs and shoulders. It clawed his face. Afterward Smith somehow got to camp and climbed a horse and rode for help. He survived the horseback ride, survived an eighty-mile automobile trip to a Great Falls hospital, survived wounds and shock and loss of blood. The last I heard, he was back on his ranch.

The frontier is so close that social stratification hardly exists in Montana. The man of money and command plays poker with his barber. There's no worship of ancestors, of landholders, little kowtowing to money, not much regard for the dubious bases that snobbery rests on.

There are exceptions. The Indian, for instance, the mixed-blood. No absolute cleavage exists here; the aborigine may win to brotherhood; but some Montanans are likely to feel, without assessing causes, that Indians and "breeds" are thieves and no-goods, for whom nothing can or need be done. Too bad, they'll say, the way the South treats Negroes.

The Montanan has escaped the evangelical religions. He allows his neighbor the right to believe and the right to live in his belief—unless the neighbor happens to be a Hutterite.

The Hutterites are a sect, agrarian and socialistic. They won't bear arms. They live apart, in barracks, refusing to participate in the lives of the communities in which they've settled. And more and more of them have been entering Montana as a consequence of restrictive legislation in Canada.

Montanans don't like them, don't like their whiskers, their dowdy, uniform dress, their seclusion, their socialism. They say they spoil a country. They say there ought to be a law.

If religious convictions, with this exception, are respected, if snobbery scarcely exists, there remains a rigidity in political and economic opinions, a tendency to damn a man if he dares differ from the bunch, a kind of intellectual Vigilanteism. The defender of the Hutterites, for whom something certainly can be said, is likely to be regarded as a crackpot or a rascal. Up to a point you can be free and have friends. Beyond that point you have to pay a price. People haven't time or temper for fool ideas.

Not until recent years did Montana begin to pay real attention to its past, perhaps for the reason that history just walked out the door. People still living can remember when Paris Gibson founded Great Falls. Within the lifetimes of others occurred the massacre on the Marias River, where a band of friendly Piegans were savagely and senselessly slaughtered. It isn't so far back to General Custer and the Battle of the Little Big Horn, nor so far from there to gold strikes on Grasshopper Creek and in Alder and Last Chance gulches. History? It had hardly happened yet.

Along came a man named Bob Fletcher, though, with both interest in and knowledge of the state's past. Then on the staff of the highway department, he had an idea. He wanted to put signs—big ones—along the roads to tell tourists about the country they were passing through. Now, on road signs widely copied elsewhere, motorists, pulling up at convenient driveouts, get pieces of information written humorously and accurately by Fletcher himself.

Along came another man, out of St. Paul, to raise wheat in Cascade County. Charlie Bovey got interested in history, too, so interested that at Great Falls he established Old Town, a re-creation of the Montana settlement of the 1880's or 1890's, complete with barbershop, saloon, smithy, general merchandising establishment and the outmoded goods and fittings that went with them. Not content with that, he revived Virginia City, a moldering mining camp where road agents and Vigilantes once raised Ned. The old spots there have been restored, the furniture and trappings rounded up and put in place. The town swarms now with tourists. Plays are put on; family nights are held at the old brewery. One bartender wears a mustache like a longhorn's points. Hurdy-gurdies and music boxes play. Peepshow machines hold pictures that, from this point in time, are more comic than risqué. Quite a place.

A passionate expatriate Montanan like me asks himself what binds him to the state. Is it just my interest in a time and activity, in the mind-heard echoes of old trappers on the beavered streams, in the imagined grind of prairie schooners? Is it the rise of a trout to a royal coachman? Is it a buck's antlers showing through the quaking asp? Is it scenery, space, the opportunity for solitude? Is it friends? Is it old and rich associations with places and with people?

It is these: It is mountain water over shining rock. It is stars like campfires in the sky. It is the riffle of the west wind in the redtop. It is clouds among the peaks of Glacier Park. It is a cottontail at the edge of a thicket. It is a pack trail to the Chinese Wall and the Continental Divide. It is a horseman and a bronc. It is the Blackfoot Big Lake's grave on the benchland. It is limpid fishing streams like the Madison and the Flathead and Sun River and the Teton. It is a round of ditchwaters with old-timers who by and by will get to reminiscing. It is the aching roll of badlands. It is Lewis and Clark and the things they saw that I see now. It is the girls, the lithe young girls, goldened by the blood of Scandinavia, coppered by the touch of *voyageur* and Indian. It is a bar of song remembered from some long-ago country-schoolhouse dance. It is the wild geese V-ing before a storm. It is the cool summer nights with the coyotes crying.

It is the informal cordiality that a man encounters from border to border. It is the grease monkey and the hasher saying "You betcha" to a request. It is the unknown rancher in a pickup who stops to ask if he can help you with a flat.

It is all these, and it is more than these. It is something else, something that makes others love the state though they recognize its shortcomings, that gives to visitors the sense of living in a different, a less fretful, and a better world. It is, as I think I've already indicated, that here one feels an individual superiority to event, a be-damned attitude toward mischance, a freedom from or ascendancy over the anxieties that press so hard elsewhere. Montanans somehow stay on top of life.

A rancher I know lived in town. He had a great wheat-crop prospect one year—six hundred acres standing thick, almost ready for the combine and the elevator. Wheat was high, almost three dollars a bushel. The ranch foreman came to the house early one morning. He roused the rancher, to tell him hail had felled every straw during the night.

"Oscar," the rancher said, "why'd you want to wake me up to tell me this? There's plenty of time to worry when I'm ready to get up." With that he turned over and went back to sleep.

I know the man. I know he'd do it. He's pure Montana, out of Norway.

Wyoming

by HAMILTON BASSO

James Runningwater is a Crow Indian. He is somewhat heavier than the average run, stands close to six feet, and looks considerably older than his twenty-nine years. An infantryman in the last war, he lives on the Crow Agency in Montana. He has a mother, a wife, two children, four horses, and a battered, rheumatic, 1937 sedan. Every year, in the third week in July, he piles his family into his car, along with as many extra passengers as he can squeeze into it, and heads south for the three-day rodeo in Sheridan, Wyoming. The rodeo is known as the Bots Sots Stampede; Bots Sots is Crow for "very best."

My impression is that the Sheridan rodeo is the year's most exciting occasion for many of the Crows. Several hundreds of them come down from Montana and pitch a tepee village just outside the rodeo grounds. They do a moderately brisk trade in beaded moccasins, leatherwork and other Indian crafts, cheer those of their number who participate in the various events, and, strictly for tourists, perform some of their tribal dances at night.

I first met Runningwater at the rodeo while hunting for a bathroom for a ten-year-old boy. He gave me the directions I needed. Later, while admiring a particularly handsome buckskin pony that was part of the string the Crows had brought down to run in the bareback relay race—one of the high spots of the program—I saw him again. Thanks to Runningwater, I became a Crow man. We exchanged congratulations when their jockey came in first. The following afternoon I set out for a late ride from the ranch where I was staying. After an hour or so of cross-country ambling, I made my way back along a dirt road that forms one boundary of the ranch. It was just before sunset. The huge outcroppings of rock that rib the slopes of the Big Horn Mountains shone in the slanting light, that immense solitude so characteristic of the West hung over everything, and except for the clopping of my horse's hoofs and the distant chatter of a magpie there wasn't a sound. I was startled to find a battered, dusty automobile parked ahead of me as I rounded a curve in the road where it mounted the crest of a hill.

A man was standing beside the car, absolutely motionless. He was dressed in the ordinary, workaday costume of the American West—the blue jeans, blue shirt, plow boots, and moderately big hat that used to be common from the Mexican border to both Dakotas before the corrupting influence of Hopalong Cassidy.

As I approached and he turned in my direction, I saw that it was James Runningwater. I also saw that the car was stuffed with Indians. I noticed three youngish men dressed as Runningwater was, an old brave with braided hair, and a woman and two children.

Staring across the hills, they gave me hardly a glance. Runningwater recognized me and we greeted each other. He apparently guessed what was on my mind. "We are looking," he said, "at the grass."

I suppose there are those—especially those who put signs in their shop windows saying "No Indian Or Mexican Trade Solicited"—who will find this incident another example, even a "perfect example," of loco Indian behavior. I don't think so. As I see it, Runningwater and his friends were looking at the most important thing in the whole state of Wyoming. So far as its character and personality are concerned, there isn't anything in its 97,548 square miles nearly as significant as grass.

In relation to Wyoming, the usual batch of statistics are only of moderate value. It is helpful to know that it lies midway between the Mississippi River and the Pacific Ocean, and that it ranks ninth among the fifty states in size. Nor does it do any harm to remember that three great river systems—the Columbia, the Colorado, and the Missouri—have their sources in its mountains, or that it is one of the most sparsely populated areas in the country. The most vital fact about it, however, is that in some sections it is overspread by more than 150 kinds of grass. Because of their scarcity, small size, and inaccessibility, most of these are unimportant. But the blue grasses, the wheat grasses, the fescues and the redtops—these are enough to make an Indian's heart stand still. Or a white man's heart, too, for that matter, provided grass has ever meant more to him than the cheerful greenery that brightens front lawns.

The whole of Wyoming's history, until very recent times, can be told in terms of grass. First the original nomads, then the Indians, and finally the latter-day white men—grass is what brought them to Wyoming and grass is what kept them there. The story of the trek into Wyoming is too large and complicated to be told here, but its outlines are simple enough: the buffalo followed the grass, the Indians followed the buffalo, and the cattlemen followed the Indians. That tattered, worn-out term, "grass roots," has consequently a very special meaning in Wyoming. It is from these roots that the state has sprung.

Compared with certain other states that have been completely transformed during the past fifty years—Texas and California, for instance—Wyoming cannot be said to have sprung very far. In the entire state, which is seventy-eight times the size of Rhode Island, there are only slightly over 200 settlements. Less than 100 of these are lived in by more than one hundred people, and only three towns in the state, Cheyenne, Laramie and Casper, have a population of more than 15,000. Nearly all of its settlements, moreover, are from thirty to fifty miles apart. I have driven more than one hundred miles in Wyoming without seeing a single habitation—or, indeed, a single living thing—and I know of no place where man's passage has left so little imprint on the earth. Everywhere his footprints are lost in the grass. And where there is no grass—in the badlands of the northeastern part of the state; in certain sections near the even yet not completely explored Wind River Mountains; in those big, semiarid reaches where the cover is so sparse that it requires forty to fifty acres to support a horse or cow—there is no sign or indication that man has ever been. It is hard to escape the feeling that were Wyoming's first aboriginal inhabitants to return today, along with the Indians who came after them—the Crow, the Blackfeet, the Sioux, the Cheyennes and others—they would find the country much as they left it.

Yet, in common with the rest of the West, Wyoming has had a

vivid history. Furthermore, many chapters of its history are a part of living memory. There are wrinkled braves still living who rode on the buffalo hunts. There are others, younger, who remember the gathering of the tribes for the Battle of the Little Big Horn. There are men and women who saw the first Union Pacific train arrive in Cheyenne in 1867, and there are still a handful of grizzled veterans who drove the longhorns up the Texas Trail in the days of the open range.

So the feeling of emptiness one gets in Wyoming—the ache of vastness and of solitude—is not because it has no past. It is rather because the signs and monuments of the past are so meager and so few. The characters in its cavalcade—the Indians, the trappers, the miners, the scouts, the bullwhackers, the mule skinners, and the cowboys—left hardly a trace in their passing. They came, they did, and they went. The decaying logs of an old fur press, rotting sluice boxes, the stone abutments of an old railroad trestle, a rusty beaver trap lying in the weeds along a river, a broken arrowhead kicked up in a field—these are the relics of Wyoming's history. Nearly everything else is scenery, emptiness, and the ever-enduring grass.

The history of Wyoming divides itself, schoolbook fashion, into four convenient parts—exploration and fur trading; emigration along the Oregon-California and Overland trails; Indian campaigns; territorial days and statehood.

Nobody knows the name or identity of the first white man who got to what is now Wyoming; the chances are that nobody ever will know. Two French-Canadian fur traders, François Vérendrye and Louis Joseph Vérendrye, may have made their way to the central part of the state in the winter of 1742–43. It seems more likely, however, that their wanderings did not take them any farther west than the Black Hills of South Dakota—which, it might be added, was pretty far west. After them, in the early part of the 19th Century, came other trappers and traders—great doers and great talkers like John Colter, Jacques La Ramie, Jim Bridger, and various others. They made the first maps and opened up the first trails; they went where no others had been before.

Back in St. Louis—the center of the fur trade, the warehouse and arsenal and jumping-off place—the news of an untapped, virgin, beaver-rich country began to get around. Bald-headed Benjamin Bonneville—Benjamin Louis Eulalie de Bonneville: the son of a French refugee who went to West Point, graduated in 1815, and worked his way up to Captain of the Seventh Infantry, U.S.A.—knew a good thing when he heard of it. The years he had spent on frontier duty hadn't gone for nothing. Taking two years' leave from the Army in 1832, Bonneville, backed by one of John Jacob Astor's partners, led a fur-trading expedition of 110 men into the Wyoming region. He also made a radical, farsighted, notable experiment—he took twenty wagons along. He had trouble along the way, the same kind of trouble that was later to dog the fortunes of thousands of emigrants, but he got his vehicles to and over the Continental Divide. The tracks they made ran straight across history; once again the impossible had been done; a new era was in the making.

By 1840, with Martin Van Buren in the White House and the war with Mexico six years off, the Federal Government began to think of looking into the region. Officially, that is. Then, as today, the machinery of government moved with something less than startling speed. It was not until 1842 that an exploration party was sent into Wyoming. At its head was a young, good-looking Southern-reared lieutenant named John Frémont. It marked the beginning of the career and reputation that was to cause Frémont eventually to aspire to the presidency and signaled Wyoming's entry into the second phase of its history—emigration along the Oregon-California and Overland trails.

Those who went westward along these trails, however, were restless, far-seeking people. Wyoming was merely a stretch of country they had to pass through. The land of heart's desire, along with the gold fields of California, lay farther to the west. The first permanent settlers in Wyoming were a party of Mormons who established themselves at Fort Bridger in 1853. Even they did not stay long. Pursued by the bitterness that met them at every turn, and also by a small U. S. Army, they burned their homes in 1857 and fled elsewhere. Other transcontinental migrants—those who were tired of the heartache and backbreak of travel and who might be tempted to homestake in Wyoming—were daunted by the Indians. A few of the tribes had more or less gone over to the white man, but the Sioux—the wild-riding, relentless, implacable Sioux—were still on the warpath.

The climax of Indian fighting in the Northwest came in 1876, with the Battle of the Little Big Horn and the names that once had the sound of silver trumpets to little boys—Custer, Crook, Mackenzie, Sitting Bull, Dull Knife, Red Cloud. Their biggest victory, the Battle of the Little Big Horn, was also the Indians' biggest defeat;

after that descent into humiliation the white man would no longer be denied. By 1880 the Sioux had taken their last scalp; Wyoming enjoyed comparative security from then on.

In the relatively short time between then and now, a state twice the size of New York has had to get itself organized, settled, and built up. Some of the difficulties attendant upon those tasks, moreover, could not be remedied simply by the passage of time. Time could bring railroads, telegraph and telephone lines, paved roads, and all the other appurtenances of modern civilization. What it could not do was to change the basic character of the state. Wyoming has oil (including Teapot Dome); it has coal (the most extensive coal reserves in the United States); and it has a large number of different minerals (most of which are buried so far beneath the earth's surface that no way has been found of mining them in quantity). But even with its coal and oil and minerals, Wyoming is what it has always been—a grazing state pure and simple. The fact that there are nearly twenty times more domestic animals in the state than human beings pretty much sums up the story; it is simply not the sort of place that attracts people in large numbers.

Most of the people who live in Wyoming are native-born, although in the mining town of Rock Springs some fifty-odd nationalities are said to be represented—Greeks, Russians, Italians, Finns, Irish, Welsh, Chinese, and others. Rock Springs, however, is an exception.

Of the native-born, a considerable proportion are the sons and daughters, the grandsons and granddaughters, of the original settlers. There is a large strain of Texas ancestry in the state—brought up along the Texas Trail—and a similarly large strain of Midwest derivation. It strikes me that the Texas drawl is rapidly going down under the Midwestern twang; the speech of Wyoming appears to be getting closer and closer to the Ohio River and farther and farther away from the Rio Grande. But whatever its individual accent happens to be, it is a common language.

With a population of less than three individuals to the square mile, with the past so close to the present, with a network of personal associations crisscrossing the state, nearly everybody in Wyoming knows nearly everybody else. There are indeed times, as often has been said, when the place seems to come closer to being a secret society than a state.

Membership in the society, however, is fairly easy to come by— no initiation fees, no board of governors, no dues.

"All a man has to do," I was told by a rancher acquaintance, "is to move on in. The more the merrier. There's room for all. *Ain't* there room, though! Just look at all the room!"

"But what is there to do in Wyoming?" I have been frequently asked. "What is there to see?" The question has both a ready answer and one that is not so ready. The what-to-do part is simple—you can fish, you can ride, you can participate in the entertainment that is provided by any of the various dude ranches, or, if you are so minded, you can simply sit in the silence and invite your soul.

The what-to-see part is rather more complicated. First and foremost, of course, there is the scenery—all the scenery you can take in. But the state occupies such a lot of room that even its scenery is sometimes hard to come by. It is even possible to cross the southern part of Wyoming without being made to realize it has any. Geologically, Wyoming is a big, high mesa—the average altitude is 6000 feet. Its mountains—the Big Horns, the Tetons, the Wind Rivers, and the Absarokas—are simply the outthrusting peaks of the mesa. And they are all in the north and west, somewhat out of the beaten path. As Struthers Burt has said, in a highly readable book about Wyoming called *Powder River,* they go and hide themselves. And as an old-timer acquaintance of mine said more recently, "They ain't hankering after company."

To see Wyoming properly I would say that three things are necessary—an automobile, a willingness to make long hops, and a certain amount of interest in the American past. Given these—and time out for a few long horseback rides, to see the country close up—it is hard to imagine anyone's not finding it worth the while. What follows is one man's Baedeker; I know that I will be quarreled with for leaving this place or that place out. It should be said, too, that I have made no effort to arrange anything so ambitious as a "tour." What I have tried to do, instead, is to follow the itinerary of history—to begin at the beginning, before even the Indians came, and to trace the story of Wyoming up to the present.

The monuments left by primitive men are extremely few—the great slabs of Stonehenge, the huge statues on Easter Island, and the terraced pyramids found in some of the South Sea islands are those that come immediately to mind. Yet in the northern tip of the Big Horn Mountains in Wyoming—the Big Horns being in the north-central part of the state—there is one of the most arresting of them all. Everything we know about it (or rather everything that has been surmised about it) can be contained in a brief paragraph, but there is no question that it is one of the oldest works of man, if not the very oldest, on the North American continent. It is called the Medicine Wheel and outside the borders of Wyoming it is virtually unknown. Few visitors take the trouble to get to it, for it takes a certain amount of getting to, and I have been unable to find any reference to it in those books that deal with the prehistoric era in North America. In nearly every other country, the Medicine Wheel would be a national treasure; here we don't even know we have it.

Our family expedition started out for it early one morning from a ranch near Sheridan. The excellently paved road soon began the steep ascent of the Big Horns by means of switchbacks, more switchbacks, and a continuous series of hairpin curves—it is not a trip I would recommend to anyone troubled by high places. There is one place about thirty miles from Sheridan where on clear days it is possible to see the Black Hills, 200 miles to the east, and further along, still climbing, you come to a great jumble of huge boulders of all shapes and sizes that were deposited by a prehistoric glacier on the hill-like slope of one of the peaks. Known as "The Fallen City," the predominantly oblong blocks of stone do indeed suggest the scattered ruins—houses, temples, forums, villas—of an ancient, forgotten city leveled by some mysterious disaster. Then, a mile or so along, you reach a tremendous outcropping of rock, eight or ten stories high and having the shape of a V, that has been christened "Steamboat Rock." Though I grew up a Mississippi River man, I have never been able to find anything steamboaty about it. I am more reminded of the Winged Victory—the lofty spread of the V, massive though it is, strikes me as having the same kind of airy lightness, the same soaring quality, and the same feeling of momentarily arrested flight.

Shortly past "Steamboat Rock" the highway levels out and runs across a level plateau that is one of the saddles of the Big Horn range. You are now over 8000 feet high; the clean, high air, crisp and heady even in July, puts needles in your lungs. The road becomes a narrow passage through one of the heaviest stands of timber in Wyoming—pine, spruce, cedar, and fir—broken here and there by mountain meadows covered with wildflowers. We took time out to walk around in one; we found Indian paintbrush, gentians, harebells, touch-me-nots, lupines, and big tangles of wild rose. I have never seen such wildflowers anywhere.

But the real excitement of the trip to the Medicine Wheel comes after you leave the main highway and branch off on a state road. Immediately you start climbing again, and immediately the solitude swallows you up—except for three deer, a big hawk, and a grinning coyote that bounded out of nowhere, we passed not a living thing. Branching due west, the constantly twisting road rises to the summit of the Big Horn Range near a peak known as Bald Mountain (10,030 feet altitude) and then, some twenty-three miles from the highway, meets up with a dirt lane that is just barely wide enough for a car to travel on—the Medicine Wheel, it says on a sign, is three miles away.

It seemed more like three hundred—not in distance but in time. I thought I knew something about hazardous roads, but this one was the prize. Had I known what we were getting into—the foot-deep ruts, the slithery mud, the litter of rocks, the big patch of glassy ice (yes, ice in July) at a particularly abrupt curve where there is nothing between you and a sheer, precipitous drop of several hundred feet except some particularly thin air—had I known about all this, as I was about to say, we would have forsaken the advantages of the combustion engine and gone by foot. What would have happened had we met a car coming from the opposite direction I hate to think. It is not my habit to give advice, but I do believe that the Wyoming authorities in charge of such matters would be well advised to set aside certain hours for getting to the Medicine Wheel and certain other hours for getting back. That road just isn't a two-way street.

We got there, however. The road finally gave up the ghost and petered out and we had to walk the rest of the way. That mile-long climb is one of the things I will always remember. For when at last you gain the summit of the mountain, on which the Medicine Wheel lies, nearly 10,000 feet high, you have the feeling, in those pure, clean reaches of the upper air, that you have made your way to the moral top of the world. You understand why the Indians held this place in reverence as Big Medicine; some atavistic stirring tells you that it is Big Medicine still.

On top of the mountain, which levels off into a kind of small plateau and from which you can see for miles, there is an almost perfect circle made of rough, unhewed stones laid side by side. None of the stones is particularly large and no effort was made to fit them together. They were just laid there, one after the other, apparently as they came to hand. The circle, or wheel, is seventy feet in diameter and 245 feet in circumference. In its center is a mound of stones like a hub, three feet high, and twelve feet around, from which twenty-eight spokes radiate to the rim of the wheel. These spokes are also made of stones of varying shapes and sizes. Around the rim of the wheel, at irregular distances, are six stone mounds that are somewhat smaller than the one in the center. They now look like piles of rock that children at play might have heaped up, but when first discovered by the white man they were built up on three sides with the fourth side left open, after the fashion of an armchair. Five of them had the open side facing inward toward the center of the wheel, and the sixth, which is the one on the east point of the compass, faced outward toward the rising sun. The mound in the center for many years supported a bleached buffalo skull, the eye sockets of which also looked to the east, but it disappeared some years ago. The general suspicion is that some tourist made off with it.

All that is known for certain about the Medicine Wheel is that it is ages old—so old that even the Indians have no legends about it. The Crows say that the wheel was there when their people first came to the Big Horns. The old men of the tribe say they do not know who built it; they say that the wheel was there "before the light came" or "before the people had iron."

Archaeologists are no more help than the Indians. Some find a resemblance to the calendar stone of Mexico; others detect a link with Egypt and Babylon; still others surmise a kinship to Stonehenge. But all this is guess and speculation. Nothing has been proved. There is no question, however, that the wheel was used for some sacred purpose.

If few visitors to Wyoming ever get to the Medicine Wheel, practically everybody gets to Jackson Hole. And for good reason. Known as one of the scenic attractions of the United States, it is everything it is said to be—even more. Lying in the northwestern part of the state, not far from the Idaho line, it is in the Grand Teton country—some of the most wonderful country in the world.

A green, fertile valley watered by the Snake River and containing two indescribably beautiful lakes—Jackson and Jenny—Jackson Hole is some 400 square miles in area and is bounded by mountains on all sides. Naturally, the best way to see it is from one of these eminences. This involves a real climb, however, and those who haven't the time, wind, or energy can get a fine panoramic view by motoring to the top of nearby Signal Mountain. The towering sky line is dominated by ten major peaks. Grand Teton, the highest, is 13,766 feet; Mount St. John, the lowest, stops at 11,412 feet. All are part of the Teton Range, a massive barrier forty miles long. The range is tipped slightly toward the east, and the east face, exposed by uplift and erosion, is one of the steepest fault escarpments in the world —Grand Teton wasn't scaled until 1898. The name "The Tetons," bestowed by French trappers who penetrated the area in the early 1800's, was originally attached to but three mountains—Grand, Middle, and South Teton. The Frenchmen knew them as *les trois Tetons;* the blunt, forthright translation is "the three teats." An even earlier explorer, Wilson Price Hunt, called them the Pilot Knobs. An intrepid man, Hunt, but, in this instance at least, probably a little too genteel. *Les trois Tetons* won out over the Pilot Knobs.

They were first seen, however, by a fellow who didn't bother to do much christening, John Colter, the first white American to set foot in Wyoming. He got there in 1806.

An enlisted man under Lewis and Clark, he made his way with the expedition to the Pacific Coast, followed it back on the return journey to St. Louis as far as the mouth of the Yellowstone River, and then, meeting up with two trappers, he asked for and received his discharge. That was in August, 1806. Within a year, having tired of his partnership with the two other trappers and going it alone, he had rung up a long list of "firsts"—first explorer of the Big Horn River and the country of the Big Horns; the first white man to cross Union and Teton passes; the first white man to see the headwaters of the Wind, the Snake, and the Green rivers; the first white man to pass through what is now Yellowstone Park; and the first white American to see the Teton Mountains, the Teton Basin, and Jackson Hole.

Where Colter led, others followed. Jackson Hole, now a national monument, became a favorite rendezvous for the mountain men— it is named, incidentally, after one of them. So far as Colter's memory is concerned, there isn't a place in Wyoming that bears his name. And all he did was to discover it practically singlehanded.

After Colter and the other mountain men, history moved with the rush of a mountain river when the snows begin to melt. By 1840, the push to the West was on. By 1850, Wyoming was familiar territory to the restless thousands who made the long trek from Missouri to the Pacific Coast by way of the Oregon Trail.

More landmarks of the Oregon Trail are to be found in Wyoming than any place else along its two-thousand-mile route. Over in the Wind River mountain country in the western part of the state there is one spot where, in a ledge of soft limestone that lies flush with the surface of the ground, you can still see the deep ruts worn in the rock by the wagon wheels—seven pairs of ruts in all. And all along the way across the state, as you follow the course of the Sweetwater, you pass landmark after landmark noted in the diaries of the pioneers—Split Rock, Devil's Gate, Three Crossings, and many others.

But of all the names that are associated with our first transcontinental highway, the most famous are Fort Laramie and Independence Rock. Honesty compels me to say that I'm afraid that only the historical-minded will find them worth going out of the way for. Independence Rock is a rather unusual geological specimen, but the state is full of other geological specimens that can give it cards and spades. Actually, the Rock is a tremendous granite boulder; all in all, measured around its circumference, it covers an acre or more. It stands in the middle of nowhere, with sagebrush and buffalo grass stretching for miles, and unless you remember the things that it once stood for—a pause on the way; friends and fresh water; great distances conquered; a time of rest before another major effort—it is apt to strike you, prosaically, as nothing but a big old rock. Once known as the Register of the Desert, it used to be covered by thousands of names—50,000 is the figure usually given. You can still make out a number; some are chiseled in the stone.

The emigrants who followed the Oregon Trail got to Fort Laramie some two hundred miles before they got to Independence Rock. You drive to it, today, from the town of Torrington in the southeastern part of the state. And once there, after you have crossed the North Platte River, you are faced with some of the saddest, most melancholy ruins in the U.S.A.

Founded as an advanced outpost in 1834 by one of the fur companies, Fort Laramie was bought and garrisoned by the United States Government in 1849. It remained an active Army post until 1890, when it was sold. The state of Wyoming later obtained the property and transferred it to the National Park Service, which now looks after it as a national monument. It would be hard to think of any one place that bulks more dramatically in our history than Fort Laramie. Indians, fur trappers, the hell-for-leather boys of the Pony Express, stagecoach drivers, Forty-Niners, Brigham Young and his followers, gamblers, traders, prospectors, homeseekers, cowpunchers who brought in the first herds of cattle—Fort Laramie knew and sheltered them all.

But the fort today, like so many others, is rather a disappointment. Most of the old buildings have fallen into ruin and the ones still standing are in a bad state of disrepair. To me, however, the place had a kind of magic nonetheless—it was one of the places I had long wanted to see, and now I had. It was a warm, bright day when we were there and the grounds were completely deserted except for a little, fair-haired girl playing in the tall grass with an Indian doll dressed in the costume of the Sioux. There it was, I thought, the whole history of the American West—a blue-eyed child of the blue-eyed invaders, playing happily in unthinking possession, and those who were once among the fiercest enemies of her fathers reduced to nothing more dangerous than a toy.

A cowboy and a cow—here, I suppose, is the symbol of Wyoming in the average imagination. What has to be remembered is that it took the forces of history some time to whip the symbol into shape. The wealth that lies in the native grasses of Wyoming was discovered in 1864, when a Government trader with a string of cattle was caught on the plains in a December blizzard. There was nothing for him to do but turn the cattle loose and accept their loss. But in the spring, miles from where the animals had been set free, the trader came across his herd again—whole, fat, healthy, and in much better condition than when he saw it last.

That sort of news was bound to get around. By 1870 tales of the wonders of the Wyoming grasslands were general throughout the West. Up came the cows and cowboys on the long drive from Texas, heading for the open range—fifty million big unfenced acres of it. For more than a decade afterwards, the cattle barons were lords as far as they could see. They built their ranch houses, turned the Cheyenne Club in Cheyenne into one of the glittering social centers of the new world, incorporated their companies, turned loose their cattle on the open range, and organized the Wyoming Stock Growers Association, which, until very recent times, had something in the nature of a double nelson on the politics of the state.

They had it too good for it to last. The sheepmen wanted in, and so did the "nester," and finally, after something close to civil war broke out, and blizzard and drought and speculation took their toll, the free, spacious, untrammeled world of the big cattlemen went the way of the free, spacious, untrammeled world of the Indians they had dispossessed. Many of the early ranches, however, are still operating, although some have changed hands. Wyoming is not one of the big beef-producing states. But it does have, in the Wyoming Hereford Ranch just outside Cheyenne (visitors welcome), one of the most famous outfits in the West. Founded in the 1870's, it takes in 6000 acres that provide elbowroom for some 3000 head of whiteface cattle who can trace their distinguished lineage back to 500 ancestors brought over from Herefordshire, England, as breeding stock. The stock did its job so well that in 1945 the manager of the ranch turned down an offer of $100,000 for one of his bulls—a refusal that has already incorporated him in the folklore of the West.

But of all the ranches in Wyoming the most famous of all is one that has only incidentally to do with cattle. Known all over the U.S. simply as "Eaton's," it specializes in dudes. Sprawled out over some 7000 acres in and about the Big Horns, it has its own town, its own post office, its own telephone system, and its own mythology. It also has a place among the minor footnotes of American history in that the three Eaton brothers—Howard, Alden, and Willis—were the ones who started the whole dude-ranch business.

Howard, born, like his brothers, in Pittsburgh, headed west in 1880 and started the Custer Trail Ranch near Medora, North Dakota. Alden and Willis soon joined him. Their enthusiastic letters back East caused so many friends to come and visit them that the three brothers found themselves using up a substantial portion of their income for entertainment. One of their more perceptive guests, comprehending the situation, made a suggestion—why not charge something for board and lodging? The suggestion was adopted and that's how dude ranching was born. Looking through some old account books at Eaton's, I came across the name of their first paying guest—the first dude that ever was. He came from Buffalo, his name was Bert Ramsey, and he spent the summer of 1882 in the wilds of North Dakota. Two years later, in 1884, a less obscure dude went out to enjoy a few weeks with the Eatons—man by the name of Theodore Roosevelt.

The three brothers moved their seat of operations from Dakota to Wyoming in 1904 when they bought the property now occupied by the ranch. All three are now dead, but the ranch and the business are still in the family. With the old stone ranch house as its center, a whole community has grown up to take care of the requirements of the one hundred and twenty-five guests that the ranch can accommodate at one time.

To go to Wyoming and not visit Yellowstone Park is a little like going to New York City and not visiting Times Square. Be careful, though, that you are not trampled in the rush; over a million tourists now make their way to the park each year. That Yellowstone Park should be our Number One, four-star, seven-alarm tourist attraction is thoroughly in keeping with our national character. Here is the sort of thing we Americans seem to like best— one excitement popping loose after the other; a vast, 3472-square-mile Believe-It-Or-Not; Mother Nature putting on her biggest, best, most extravagant show. Consider some of the entertainments on the bill. Great travertine terraces. Spectacular waterfalls. The grand canyon of the Yellowstone River. Fossil forests. Mud volcanoes. A towering cliff of pure obsidian. Hot springs of all shapes, sizes, and colors. Yellowstone Lake, twenty miles long and nearly a mile and a half above sea level. More geysers, including one known as Old Faithful, than are to be found in all the rest of the world put together. Buffalo herds, elk, moose and deer. One of the nesting places of the rapidly vanishing trumpeter swan, and hundreds of lazy, shiftless, ingratiating panhandlers disguised as bears. With all that to choose from, you can hardly go wrong.

All the same, you can't help wishing that you'd been lucky enough to have been tagging after John Colter when he got to it for the first time. Not that Colter ever got any thanks for discovering it. All it did for him was to get him the reputation of being the biggest liar since Munchausen. His trouble, it seems, was that he played it straight; he came back and tried to give a factual report of what he had seen. Jim Bridger, another trapper who figures large in the early history of Wyoming and who also explored the Yellowstone Park area, fared much better. Beginning with the same batch of wonders as Colter, Bridger took the truth and then deliberately distorted it into a tall tale—consequently, instead of being put down as a chronic prevaricator, he is remembered as one of our great storytellers.

For instance: Bridger told how one day he sighted a magnificent elk, took aim, and fired. Instead of dropping, the elk seemed not even to have heard the report of the rifle. Drawing a second and more deliberate bead on the animal, Jim fired again—and still the elk went on grazing peacefully. Completely out of patience, Jim seized the rifle and rushed forward to club the elk into submission. Then, as he ran, he crashed into something hard and immovable that turned out to be a mountain of pure, transparent glass. But there was something stranger still. Not only was the mountain of glass, on the other side of which the elk continued to munch in peaceful security, but the glass had a telescopic effect—that elk was twenty-five miles away!

Then there was Jim's alarm-clock story. He said that across from one of his camping sites there was the bald, flat face of a mountain that had such a peculiar acoustical arrangement that any sound originating in camp was not echoed back for six hours. He said that upon retiring for the night he would call out "Time to get up! Time to get up!" and that six hours later the echo would wake him. And in telling of the fossil forests in the Yellowstone Park region Jim went on like this: "There was one place where petrified leaves and branches still clung to petrified trees and among them sat petrified birds singing petrified songs." All tall tales, of course. But in Yellowstone Park there *is* Obsidian Cliff, a huge outcropping of volcanic glass; there *are* places that take a moderately long time to return an echo; and there *are* petrified leaves, petrified branches and petrified trees.

It was not until 1870, when a full-fledged scientific expedition was sent by the Government into the wilds of the upper Yellowstone country, that the stories told by Colter and Bridger found sober, accurate corroboration. In 1872, Congress voted to set aside the area as a national park. One doesn't like to think of what would have happened to the place if it hadn't—hot-dog and hamburger stands everywhere, ten cents for a chip off Obsidian Cliff, a half dollar to see Old Faithful, a quarter to watch each of the other geysers, steam baths at the hot spring, beauty packs at the mud volcano, and who can say what else!

Here and there, as you travel about Wyoming, you come across places where people have gathered to live—the most important of these, in point of numbers, are Cheyenne, Casper, Laramie and Sheridan.

Sheridan (3737 altitude) is the largest town in Northern Wyoming. With the possible exception of Dubois, in the Wind River country, it has always struck me as being the most "western" of all

Wyoming's more sizable communities. The commercial establishments, in good cow-town fashion, are strung out along Main Street and there are always a few Crows and Cheyennes about. Along with the ranch hands, who now go in for cowboy garb that a sophisticated fifth-grader would look down upon as kindergarten stuff, the Indians have been brought up to date—instead of wearing buckskin and hand-tanned robes, they now go around in bright blankets of modern design milled in New England. The first building in Sheridan was erected in 1878 by a trapper named Jim Mason. The town itself was staked out on a forty-acre plot on May 10, 1882, and named in honor of the Civil War hero, General Philip H. Sheridan. Unlike Cheyenne, which had a way of blowing the roof off, Sheridan was always a rather sober community. It had a smithy and two general stores before it had a saloon—a state of affairs practically unheard of in the West—and only one person was arrested during its first two years. A case, I believe, of disturbing the peace.

Sheridan, however, has had its share of excitement. As late as 1939 a number of Sheridan residents, dissatisfied with Wyoming's political setup, called upon Northern Wyoming to secede from the rest of the state and form a separate, forty-ninth state of its own. The new state was to be called Absaroka and was to include Yellowstone Park and most of Wyoming north of the Platte. Sheridan's street commissioner appointed himself governor and named a small staff. The new state got no further than that, but residents of North Wyoming, when displeased with the action of the state government, appealed for redress to the "Governor of Absaroka." Interestingly enough, it worked—most of the matters in dispute were settled to the satisfaction of the "Absarokians."

Laramie (7145 altitude), the seat of the University of Wyoming, lies in the southeastern part of the state on the east bank of the Laramie River. One of Wyoming's oldest cities, it is also the state's intellectual center. Things were not always thus, however. Named for the French-Canadian trapper, Jack La Ramie, the town began as a tent settlement several weeks before the tracks of the Union Pacific Railroad reached it in the spring of 1868. A few months later 500 shacks had been built, and on May 9, 1868, the first train screeched and rattled into town.

That's when hell popped loose. A provisional government was formed, but by that time the outlaw element had taken over. The government was forced to resign and there then followed months of what can only be described as premeditated anarchy. In the established pattern of the American West, strict as a Hollywood scenario, civil war broke out. An army of 500 vigilantes laid plans for simultaneous raids on several outlaw hangouts on the night of October 29, 1868. Target Number One was a saloon and dance hall known as "Belle of the West." In the siege that followed, with most of the town pitching in, five men were killed, fifteen were wounded, and four outlaws were strung up on telegraph poles. Laramie, after that, began gradually to settle down—so much so that, by 1880, Edgar Wilson (Bill) Nye, one of this country's gentlest humorists, was able to be both its postmaster and justice of the peace at the same time. Nye left Laramie in 1883 to go to work for the *New York World*. In resigning his postmastership he wrote in part as follows:

> Post Office Divan
> Laramie City, W. T.
> Oct. 1, 1883.

To the President of the United States:

Sir: I beg leave at this time to officially tender my resignation as postmaster of this place, and in due form to deliver the great seal and key to the front door of this office. The safe combination is set on the number 33, 66, and 99, though I do not remember at this moment which comes first, or how many times you revolve the knob. . . .

You will find the postal cards that have not been used under the distributing table, and the coal down in the cellar. If the stove draws too hard, close the damper in the pipe and shut the general delivery window. . . .

You will find the key under the door-mat and you had better turn the cat out at night when you close the office. . . . If Deacon Hayford does not pay his box rent, you might as well put his mail in the general delivery, and when Bob Head gets drunk and insists on a letter from one of his wives every day in the week, you can salute him through the box delivery with an Old Queen Ann tomahawk, which you will find near the Etruscan water pail. . . .

Mr. President, as an official of this government, I now retire. . . .

> BILL NYE.

Casper (5123 altitude) is the second largest city in Wyoming. Situated in the central part of the state, it lies on the south side of the North Platte. The most industrialized community in Wyoming, specializing in oil, Casper's location at the crossroads of four national highways and two railroads has made it the distribution point for a wide trade area.

The Oregon Trail ran through the townsite of Casper some forty years before it was staked out in 1888. An estimated 300,000 people passed through before wagon traffic was rerouted in the 1860's to the more southerly Overland Trail.

Casper, like Laramie, was the child of a railroad—the Chicago and North Western. When the first passenger train arrived in June, 1888, nearly one hundred persons had located on the townsite. Since the Chicago and North Western was not then a main line, Casper's growth was considerably less rapid than that of the Union Pacific terminals. When the town was incorporated in 1899, the population was less than 400. An ordinance adopted at the first meeting of the city fathers made it unlawful to discharge firearms within the town's limits—which didn't keep the mayor from beating an enemy to the draw on Main Street a few months later—and another decree made it unlawful for any woman to "use any vile, profane, or indecent language . . . or to smoke any cigar, cigarette, or pipe" on the streets.

Casper had a brief attack of gold-rush fever in the early 1890's, which lasted until the "rich" veins turned out to be asbestos, and also went through a much more important boom when the first oil well in the neighborhood was brought in. The initial strike was made in 1889. By 1896 six wells were brought in and shortly thereafter the first pipe line was laid to the Casper refineries.

The boom transformed Casper from a crossroads settlement into a city larger than it is today. A local census in 1925 showed 32,000 people within the city and its neighboring refinery camps. The boom ended in the late 1920's. Several hundred miles of pipe line connected the fields with the Casper refineries, the rigs were dismantled, and the need for extensive field equipment was over. The big bust of 1929 completed the retrenchment and Casper's population fell to a little more than half its total during the boom years.

Cheyenne, pronounced *shy-ann* (6062 altitude), is Wyoming's capital and largest city. Founded in 1867 as another terminal of the Union Pacific, Cheyenne is old enough to have a few tenement dis-

UTAH The primitive rainbow trail, with a rider leading his pack through a sandstone gorge 2,000 feet deep.

IDAHO (*center spread*) A farm near Moscow, Idaho, radiates contentment from its nest of green, its fruitful work underway.

COLORADO Garden of the Gods: a wonderland of stone. In the distance rears much-loved, much-climbed Pikes Peak.

tricts, but its new streets, new lawns, new hotels and new houses give it the general appearance of having been settled not later than day before yesterday.

Generally regarded as one of the roughest, toughest, six-shooting-est communities of the West—second perhaps only to Tombstone—Cheyenne's early reputation fitted it like a glove. The Union Pacific rails came in on November 13, 1867, and by 1868 its noisy career was in full blast. Cheyenne inherited all the lawlessness of those who trailed along behind the Union Pacific rails, in addition to its own flotsam and jetsam. Liquor was cheap, pay was good, ammunition was plentiful and stakes were high.

By the middle 1870's, however, though still quick on the trigger, Cheyenne was no longer so pronounced a wild-west cycle of Dante's Inferno. By 1869 cattle were coming north from Texas, in 1870 the first Wyoming-finished cattle were loaded at Cheyenne for the European market, and by 1877 the Cheyenne Plains were stocked. The town then became the social and financial capital of a vast cattle-ranching area, with the famous Cheyenne Club as its center. Population increased from 3456 in 1880 to approximately 10,000 in 1897, and it has shown a steady, though moderate, increase ever since. Cheyenne, with its cattle industry, three railroads, transcontinental airline and highways, plus its state, county, and Federal offices, is still the most important city in Wyoming.

One shouldn't be misled by those creameries, however—it still runs more to redeye than butterfat. And once a year, just to prove that it has kept its hand in, it stages a celebration called "Frontier Days" that rocks the surrounding territory like an earthquake.

Cheyenne's Frontier Days is fairly indicative of Wyoming's basic character. It's still cow country; in other words, still a place where a man on a horse is regarded as being rather more important in the scheme of things than a man on foot. I'm not so sure, however, that the white man, on horse or on foot, isn't still in the position of being an intruder. The notion keeps growing on me that in order to know Wyoming—to know it as a New Yorker knows New York or a Parisian knows Paris—you have to be an Indian. It may be the enormous silence, it may be the vast, unbroken emptiness, or it may be the endless reaches of the sky—in any case, it seems to me that you have to see it through the eyes of James Runningwater; you have to be able to stand by a broken-down automobile and look at the grass and see beyond the grass. Not being an Indian, that I cannot do. I can only fall back on what James Runningwater told me. "It is almost as it was," he said. "You can hear the land." That, to me, is Wyoming; it's where you can hear the land.

Nevada

by LUCIUS BEEBE

In the introduction to an anthology of Western folklore, the late Bernard De Voto, indisputably the ranking historian of the region, remarked that foremost among its blessings San Francisco counts the fact that it is West. "It is thinking accurately," says the Sage of Harvard Square. "For, stranger, San Francisco is West as all hell."

This signal favor of Providence is one which Nevada, and particularly the northwestern portion of the state lying just across the Sierra from California's most golden precincts, shares in generous measure. Indeed, in the days of the bonanzas, when the wealth of the Comstock was making almost every man in the Palace lobby a millionaire, San Francisco considered itself a sort of suburb of Virginia City, then the scene of the wealthiest tumults on earth. With the years things have changed, and it is more probable that San Francisco now considers Reno a suburb, just as Las Vegas is a winter resort for Los Angeles. But the bond between the cities of California and the Silver State is strong and enduring and it is founded on nothing so much as their joint participation in being, as Mr. De Voto put it, West as hell.

Nevada is still so very West, even in mid-20th Century, and so vast in its Westness that passengers on the Southern Pacific's overland trains crossing the seemingly illimitable desert between Salt Lake and Reno are sometimes terrified by its desolate prospect. For hundreds of miles at a stretch no habitation is visible save the occasional shacks of track gangs, and no life save the dust plume marking the distant passage of a lonely rancher's car through the alkali. On either side are gloomy mountain ranges, and the train crew will tell you that beyond these, both to the north and south, are other, apparently unending ranges, unimaginable desolations of desert over whose thousands of miles of dusty roads no vehicle may pass for months on end, and once-populous cities now crumbling and deserted. The informed trainman can recount that there are fewer than two and one half inhabitants for each of Nevada's 110,540 square miles.

The scenery of Nevada and its at times plutonian landscape—rivers that run to no sea, endless sage, geologic formations that would have interested Dante—are a far cry from the pretty pastorals of New England, the garden vistas of the Deep South or the conventional snow-capped peaks of the mountain states. To the first settlers who forged their way westward over uncharted trails toward California the Golden, Nevada was all a part of the "Great American Desert," implacably grim, hostile, a land of death and of legends of death.

To the Eastern city dweller, Nevada still may partake of these aspects on first sight, but automatic drive and the assurance of an air-cooled motor court, swimming pool and liberal Martinis at the day's end have robbed the desert of its terrors. Claustrophobia is an ailment unknown in the Nevada lexicon. There is space to swing a cat, to fall down in if one wishes. There is no fatigue implicit in driving 450 miles a day over its matchless highways. Its desert atmosphere makes it hang-over proof. The native Nevadan will tell you that the moon rises in more incredible fullness over the Great Salt Lake Desert or Toiyabe National Forest or the Washoe Hills, as the case may be, than anywhere else on earth. The sunset shadows creeping across the chocolate-ice-cream hills form shapes of history instantly discernible to the perceptive eye. The past is very close indeed in Nevada, and to the ear attuned to the vibrations of the Western continent the sound of stagecoaches on the night wind and the rattle of gunfire are reality and not illusion.

If there are fewer lyrics written about "Nevada the Beautiful," it is because the Nevada theme song has already been written. It is hard to improve on *Oh! Susanna* and *Oh, My Darling Clementine*.

Against the background of Archean geology and decay of empire it is possible to understand Nevada's tolerance of social nipups frowned upon by other states, the vehemence of its demands for booze-and-branch at all hours of day and night, its easy attitude toward divorce and its approval of legal gambling as one of the mainstays of the state's economic being.

Nevada is heir to the great tradition of the West and so far has escaped the density of industrial population which elsewhere beyond the wide Missouri has spelled the end of that tradition. It has never been an agricultural state with the usual inhibitions of sod busters. Its first settlement was based on mining, an occupation whose morals are known for tolerance. An important industry continues to be ranching—never conducive to a narrow philosophy of living—and its major source of revenue today, dwarfing all others almost to insignificance, is tourism.

Some of Nevada's allurements for visitors are shared by other states. Elsewhere there are fine weather, historic landmarks, hunting, fishing, winter sports, superb highways, luxury resorts and scenic vistas of lake and mountain. T-bone steaks are universal in the West. So are supermotels with swimming pools, valet service, room telephones, all-night coffee shops. Almost everywhere there are splendid bars—magnificent oases running the atmospheric gamut from frontier décor to the *moderne* of neon lighting and chrome. The visitor who follows the wagon tracks of the pioneers lives in upholstered ease, as the Union Pacific slogan has it, Everywhere West.

One thing he enjoys in Nevada alone—legally and in unabashed splendor—and that is gambling. The tourist trade comes to Nevada in search of fun and games and, again in the words of Mr. De Voto, the tourist trade is thinking accurately. Step right over yonder, stranger, to that long mahogany board where the gentlefolk are rejoicing, and the band is playing *Dixie!* Handy to the bar you will see gentlemen in green eye shades presiding over games of chance. You are welcome at either or both, twenty-four hours a day, and should you run out of the ready, an extension of credit may be arranged. Bartender, see to the stranger's pleasure!

The folklore, mores, economic and social backgrounds of Nevada originated in the mining of precious metals. Until the discovery late in 1858 of the surface bonanzas of the Comstock Lode at Virginia City the largest community in the Territory of Western Utah (as it was first designated) had been Mormon Station, a staging depot at the very base of the High Sierra. It had a population of 200.

The discovery of fantastic silver deposits in the Washoe Hills twenty-odd miles south of today's Reno started the greatest gold rush of history, backtracking across the Sierra from the already failing placers of the Mother Lode in California. At times the traffic eastward was so dense in Donner Pass and Echo Summit that westward-bound travel of any sort—even the valiant Pony Express—cooled its heels for days at a time in Carson Valley.

Overnight the world became Nevada-conscious through the silver riches of Virginia City. The surface diggings progressed downward into deep quartz operations to become the most famous silver mines in history. Virginia City flowered as the swaggering metropolis of the West. Its millionaires—James Flood, Jim Fair, Adolph Sutro, George Hearst and William Sharon—commenced altering the San Francisco sky line with vast rococo mansions. The wife of Nevada's richest man, John Mackay, popped the eyes of Paris and London with entertainments such as never before had been given by a private citizen. Marcus Daly departed the Comstock for Montana, there to make a few more fortunes in copper. Virginia City's date line ranked in the press of the world with that of Washington, Berlin, Rome and Boston. San Francisco went through a dementia of speculation in Comstock mining shares that enriched housemaids, beggared millionaires, finally wrecked the mighty Bank of California and drove its president, William Ralston, to probable suicide.

The name Virginia City was synonymous with unbelievable wealth. The discovery of the staggering deposit of silver and gold in the depths of the Consolidated Virginia mine, ever since capitalized as The Big Bonanza, caused Bismarck to order Germany off the silver standard. The Central Pacific Railroad, today the great Southern Pacific, was at first conceived as a feeder from Sacramento to tap the riches of the Comstock. Virginia City became the most important outpost of the powerful banking and express firm of Wells, Fargo & Co. The city had a railroad, opera house, oceans of champagne, balls with evening dress *de rigueur* and was the best theatrical road town in the entire United States. It also had violence as a commonplace and it had the *Territorial Enterprise*, prototype of frontier newspapers everywhere.

The consciousness of its Comstock beginnings has never entirely left Nevada. Other minor bonanzas followed at Austin, Eureka, Hamilton, Tonopah, Goldfield and Rhyolite—the last three after the turn of the 20th Century—and all served to keep alive faith in hard money and a mining economy, vestigial traces of which are Nevada's preference today for silver dollars and its scorn for "California cabbage." That the mining economy has disappeared (except in copper in the eastern part of the state) and been supplanted by tourism is not even now unanimously accepted. To doubt that gold and silver production will come back is regarded as a sort of breach of faith.

The fact that Nevada's yesterdays were not the yesterdays of Texas or Wyoming or New Mexico is not always understood by the rest of the United States. It never was a beef state. Even today, hair pants and bowed legs are indigenous only to Elko County in the center of Nevada. It was a place of urban life set down in the desert. Its horses were not tethered to the hitch rack in Main Street; they were harnessed to the shiny rigs of city dwellers. Its attire was the frock coat and top hat of banker, merchant, gambler or mine superintendent—or the garb of deep mine worker; rarely was it the florid attire of the cowpoke. There are probably more horses on dude ranches in Nevada today than there ever were in the bonanza years.

Reno and Las Vegas, Nevada's two principal cities, and almost the only date lines in the state known to the rest of the world today, both had their inception through the agency of the railroad—Reno as a division point on the Southern Pacific; and Las Vegas as a railroad land development conceived to sell lots in the southern desert by the acquisitive Sen. William A. Clark, of Montana's San Pedro, Los Angeles & Salt Lake Railroad, now the Union Pacific's Los Angeles Division.

The transition from a mining state to one dominated by tourism was practically painless to Reno where the substantial commerce of the state was already concentrated. But the mining communities simply fell apart at the seams, some, like Rhyolite, becoming ghost towns overnight; others, like Austin and Eureka, drawing out twilight existences based on motels and filling stations and memories of the glorious past. The eight short-line railroads, built for hauling ore and mining machinery, were torn up one by one. A certain amount of sporadic mine activity is centered at Tonopah, but this once populous boom city makes a living largely from the fact that it is just halfway between Reno and Vegas—a convenient overnight stopping spot. Virginia City saw that oblivion was at hand if it didn't do something about it, and quickly. Today it is one of the tourist meccas of the West, with as many as 10,000 people a day in summertime passing through its faded saloons and lingering in its once glittering mansions.

It may be pertinent to examine one more aspect of Nevada's social economy. Little of the great wealth produced by the Comstock remained in Nevada, in contrast with Colorado, where the great fortunes made from the mines of Leadville, Central City and Cripple Creek found their way to Denver and Colorado Springs, where they remain to the present time.

With the sole exception of John Mackay, the nabobs of Virginia City looted and left. Their monuments are mostly in San Francisco, where the Palace Hotel, the Hearst newspaper, the Fairmont, the Flood and Sharon buildings, Roos Brothers department store, the Wells Fargo Bank & Union Trust Company, all bear witness to the wealth removed from the deep mines of the Comstock.

Little stayed in Nevada save Mackay's endowments of St. Mary's in the Mountains Church in Virginia City, and the Mackay School of Mines which is a part of the University of Nevada at Reno.

No other single Nevada institution, no hospital, museum, historical society, school or public foundation is richly endowed with wealth originating in Nevada. The sole foundation of consequence for benefit of Nevada charities and public works, that of the late Major Max Fleischmann, is endowed with money made in yeast—elsewhere. Nevada sinks or swims on its own economy; it's root hog, or die, because no rich men have ever cared.

Throughout all the West of the Wells Fargo years, the properties of the frontier included—in addition to the thorough-braced Concord coach and Colt's Navy equalizer—the keno goose, the roulette wheel and the poker deck. A willingness to wager anything and everything on the turn of a card was the hallmark of life beyond the Missouri.

But with the taming of the frontier and the gradual decline of the old uninhibited West, professional and legalized gambling came into disrepute. It declined steadily, along with gun fighting, vigilante law and open prostitution, in the once-wild towns of Arizona and New Mexico, in the Black Hills, Colorado and Montana, although morality could hardly be said to have achieved any very drastic hold on these localities until around 1917.

Only in Nevada did gambling flourish with all the untrammeled hoorah, high stakes and picturesque characters of the bonanza years. All sorts of speculation and games of chance were given renewed vitality by the tremendous "excitements" in precious metals at Tonopah, Goldfield, Rawhide, Manhattan and Rhyolite. The presence of such financial notables as Charlie Schwab and a younger

Bernard Baruch in these tumultuous diggings did nothing to abate the gambling fever which overflowed from the mining exchanges to the saloons of Tex Rickard and Tom Kendall. In the Tonopah Club, George Wingfield, a cow hand from Oregon who later went on to own Reno's de luxe Riverside Hotel, made his first stake of $2200 from Frank Golden, later proprietor of Reno's Golden Hotel. Zeb Kendall, Tom's brother, made and lost seven substantial fortunes at the turn of the century; made them in mining properties and lost them at roulette, faro bank and the race track.

It can be said accurately that gambling in Nevada has enjoyed practically unbroken continuity from the state's earliest times until today, when Las Vegas is the world's most concentrated, not to say bedizened, capital of chance. In 1910, to be sure, a state law was passed outlawing roulette, dice and card games—with almost the same effect, locally, of national prohibition a decade later. Gambling, unabated and unregulated, went on with little attempt at conceal-ment, and the familiar philosophy was that risking a dollar on an illegal card or throw of the dice was striking a blow for personal liberty.

By 1912 the farce of prohibited gambling was obvious, and Ne-vadans realistically modified the law to allow "social" games of chance, a regulation which, altered now and then, signified nothing until 1931, when the entire unworkable bundle of legislation passed into the limbo of noble experiments. The lifting of the ban on open gaming was celebrated with a statewide carnival which lasted nearly a fortnight.

Nevada's social and economic structure today might well be rep-resented by an animated montage of craps, roulette, slot machines, twenty-one, keno and, in a few rare cases, by the now declining faro bank and big six wheel, all spinning, clicking, snapping, slapping and clattering twenty-four hours a day from Elko to Las Vegas and from Harolds Club in Reno to Honest Uncle Len Haffey's tables in the Delta in Virginia City. In such placid appearing crossroads as the tiny community of Beatty, whose country exterior masks Saturday night revelry of Babylonian proportions—in Minden, the state's dairy center—in Tonopah, Ely, Winnemucca, Carson City and Eureka— Nevada presents a solid front of ornate slot machines paying the cus-tomer approximately eighty cents of his every invested dollar. In larger communities there are attended games of craps, dice and roulette.

Obviously, the implications of an economy such as Nevada's are enormous. They range from such modest boons as all-night buffets embracing Maine lobster in aspic and truffled *foie gras* for an over-all dollar to the complete nonexistence of any state income, inheritance, or sales tax. Hotel apartments which elsewhere would be forty dollars a day for two are available in the upholstered magnificence of the Las Vegas "strip" for around eight dollars. A free one on the house is taken for granted in Nevada every third round. So are thousands of miles of magnificent state highways reaching from horizon to horizon. The house take of 12 per cent on twenty-one, 17 per cent on craps and their allied averages pays in Nevada for an uncommonly spacious and uninhibited way of life.

Nevadans themselves are entirely aware of the existence of such amiable desert-surrounded communities as Elko with its vast cattle ranges and dusty cowpokes shouldering their Saturday night way into the bar at Newt Crumley's remarkable urbane Stockman's Hotel; or of Carson City, the smallest state capital, where the chief executive may be seen reading his evening newspaper on the porch of the Governor's Mansion. They know the legend of Virginia City's great years when San Francisco's Montgomery Street was populated with Comstock millionaires in the same numbers as today crowd the lobby of the Shamrock in Houston. They recall the romantic youth of Austin, where the future Madame Emma Nevada sang for pennies outside the bar of the International Hotel. They know that the world's finest butter is produced amidst the lush meadows of Minden, where icy Carson Water flows in abundance from the adjacent Sierra.

But to the outer world, Nevada means just two places: Reno and Las Vegas. And these two communities in turn mean just one thing in the common awareness: de luxe gambling for practically unlimited stakes.

Nevada's two most notable communities fall into the social and economic pattern of the two California cities closest to them, and from which a major portion of their patronage derives. Reno, 235 railroad miles from San Francisco, reflects the character of that town as a mature, easygoing but conservative-minded metropolis in microcosm. Its architecture is more vertical than horizontal, its financial and professional life geared to the stable occupations of banking, insurance and lumber. The façade of Reno's gambling industry, as might be expected of a community so closely linked to San Francisco, is conservative, decorous, opulent and aware of the historic past. Ostentatious displays of wealth are infrequent and considered in bad taste.

Las Vegas, a free-wheeling luxury resort that suddenly blossomed in a desolation of sagebrush and alkali, mirrors the sports-coat and convertible-motor-car philosophy of life in Southern California. Its ranch-style architecture flows in terraced symmetry along U.S. 91 some 225 miles from Los Angeles. The guest lists of its super motels, which combine the functions of residence and casino, are generously recruited from top names in the film industry. Its night-club head-liners playing to capacity audiences in sports shirts along the Las Vegas Strip are the same who please night-club audiences in hardly more formal attire along the County Strip in Hollywood. Las Vegas sprawls, both figuratively and literally, beside splendid swimming pools set amid landscapes planted to rare and exotic shrubs and flow-ers. It drinks tall, cool drinks of gin and lime rather than the Bourbon-and-branch of the old frontier, and it plays games of chance for vast sums tossed on the green-covered tables in ostentatious grandeur. Las Vegas is very young, very affluent, and sometimes very brash— as it will cheerfully admit.

Easily the capital of chance of the known universe, Las Vegas is a phenomenon that has to be seen, touched, tasted, smelled and heard to be believed, for the evidence of a single sense alone might be doubted. Its wonder and glory is The Strip, the glitter mile of de luxe resorts along U.S. 91 which rivals Hollywood in the dimensions of its publicization. Here is where the big names and big bankrolls as-semble, where the sports cars are the gleamingest, the swimming pools the most photographed, the breakfasttime reports of losses and winnings the most fabulous. The big names on The Strip are the Desert Inn; El Rancho Vegas, pioneer of them all; the Last Frontier, which in addition to the conventional properties of a hotel-casino maintains a whole Western township complete with saloons, barber shops and a jail; the Thunderbird; the Flamingo; the Sands; and the Sahara.

While architecture differs—most of the exteriors are what is gen-erally known as ranch-style-Californian with interior décors ranging from French Moroccan at the Sands to Texas-cattle-ranch at the Last Frontier—the basic pattern of The Strip is universal: rooms and meals at tariffs well below comparable accommodations elsewhere, living apartments handy to the gaming rooms, landscaped grounds with almost limitless resources of parking space, theater restaurants starring top Broadway and Hollywood names and round-the-clock operation of everything in sight.

Just to give you an idea of the implications of wealth involved in its operations and the hold on the public imagination it has achieved in recent years, it is interesting to note that during one month the manager of the Desert Inn received begging letters requesting that, for no visible reason, he shower down the sum of $950,000 upon importunate correspondents.

Life in Reno is characterized by less hysterical urgency around the gaming tables, but the city's yearly total of more than 4,000,000 out-of-town visitors, many of them conservatively well-to-do who shun Las Vegas' brassy flamboyance, assures it of something better than mere municipal solvency.

Reno's two luxury hotels, the Mapes and the Riverside (the latter the fourth of that name to stand on the banks of the Truckee) maintain floor shows only slightly less costly than those of the Vegas Strip, while its monstrous department stores of gambling—Harolds Club, the Golden-Bank, Nevada Club and Cal-Neva—almost always are in process of enlargement, usually a sign of economic health.

In the old days of less impetuous schedules, the Southern Pacific's Overland Limited, westbound, used to stop for as long as three-quarters of an hour to load mail and baggage in Reno at the convenient hour of ten in the evening, after having already dallied a half hour or so in Sparks on the outskirts of town to change engines. Informed transcontinental travelers, aware of the bonus of more than an hour's time in a city famed for fun, used to get off at Sparks and taxi to the Bank Club handily adjacent to the tracks in Reno. One could win or lose a tidy sum and hoist several nutritious drinks in an hour and, just before departing, the engineer was accustomed to give a long blast on his whistle and casino attendants shouted "Overland leaving" much as theater ushers call "curtain going up" at the end of intermission. Now, the train stops a bare three minutes in Reno, and the lagniappe of gaming enjoyed by travelers in the old days is just a memory.

Reno's dubious fame as a citadel of divorce and burial ground for broken hearts is so firmly established in the national credo that statistics are needed to combat it. For the record, Washoe County (in which Reno is located) yearly issues marriage licenses in a ratio of better than 4 to 1, as compared to the divorces granted. And that ratio has remained virtually constant for more than a decade.

Dude ranching—and all out-of-state residents here for divorce are classed as dudes—is undeniably a factor in the economy. The valley resorts south of Reno—Washoe Pines, Emmie Wood's Flying M-E Ranch and other de luxe dude ranches—charge more than $100 a week in summer and only slightly less out of season, and most of them are booked well in advance. Since a very large proportion of their clientele is patently well-to-do, this basic $100 per capita per week is by no means the entire financial story of the divorce picture.

Reno also has the University of Nevada. The university has better than 3,000 students, mostly native Nevadans, many of whom are supported by scholarships financed by Harolds Club, the Reno department store of gambling. Every year Harolds presents a scholarship to an outstanding student in each of the state's thirty-five high schools. The only requirement, aside from scholastic achievement, is that, during the four years in which he attends the university, he shall never enter the portals or play the devices of chance at Harolds Club.

Best known of the technical schools at N.U. is the Mackay School of Mines, endowed by the family of John Mackay, the silver king of Comstock times, for more than $3,000,000 at the turn of the century. It is one of the ranking institutions in its field in the country, the peer of those at Columbia, Missouri and the University of Colorado.

Another N.U. school that gets a lot of attention is its school of journalism. Whatever one's estimate of the worth of journalism schools, and the matter will get you an argument in any city room, N.U. has had a remarkable record for placement of graduates on Western newspapers.

Nevada life outside Reno and Las Vegas is less influenced by the economy of gambling and, with certain exceptions, more or less resembles small-town life elsewhere in the West. The old spacious violence characteristic of the frontier has, of course, largely disappeared, but now and then there is a reversion to type. Such was the case with the shooting outside the Senator Saloon directly across the street from the State Capitol in Carson City some years ago. Two cowpokes from Minden, meeting on the sidewalk, opened fire in the best Culver City tradition, scattering the citizenry and grievously ventilating each other. What fascinated Nevadans was not the shooting itself— to which they are acclimatized by tradition if not contemporary practice—but the fact that a number of stray slugs penetrated the contents of a delivery wagon full of laundry. The community rocked with merriment over what a local wit described as the first legitimate excuse for the condition in which laundries frequently return shirts to their customers.

The other communities of Nevada resemble nothing so much as rare and infrequent jewels strung along some of the finest highways in the world, where the natives consider eighty-five the normal cruising speed on their way to Lake Mead or Salt Lake. So splendid are Nevada's roads that the state is fast becoming a paradise for sports-car drivers, thousands of whom tool up from California every summer to make safari. The Nevada Horseless Carriage Club, largely sponsored by Harrah's Club of Reno, possesses one of the finest collections of antique and classic motorcars in the world.

Carson City, Nevada's tiny capital, is one of the few state capitals in the Union without a railroad, and save for its neon lights and cement sidewalks is a page right out of the Old West. The principal employers of its inhabitants are the state and Federal governments, whose ranking officers are available to callers to a degree that is unheard of in Washington or Albany. At noontime, when it is in session, the Nevada Senate rises for lunch in a body and occupies counter stools across the street, at the Senator Restaurant founded by State Senator Kenneth Johnson.

Nevada politics are a triumph of simplicity and democratic practice and, at election times, of almost intolerable bad feeling. Until the death, practically in harness, of that noble old war horse, Senator Pat McCarran, the state's politicians looked largely to him for guidance. Whatever other Americans may have felt about Mr. McCarran's foreign policies, Nevadans revered him as a personal senator and a deliverer of instant and effective service. The microscopic population of the state made it possible for him to give his personal attention to almost everyone.

In the days when the United States Senate was regarded as the world's most exclusive club, Nevada contributed a long succession of "silver senators" including the peerless William Morris Stewart, "father of American mining law"; John Percival Jones, hero of the great fire in Crown Point mine; William Sharon, satrap of the Bank of California on the Comstock; Francis G. Newlands, Sharon's son-in-law; and finally in our own generation, Key Pittman.

Nevada's towns extend north and south on the extreme Western edge of the state along the valleys and arable meadows which receive water from the Sierra: Reno, Carson City, Gardnerville and Minden; and east and west along the routes of the Southern Pacific and Western Pacific Railroads, where in the 19th Century came into being such communities as Wells, Elko, Palisade, Battle Mountain and Winnemucca, variously sustaining life as ranching centers, warehouses to remoter hamlets and as stopping places on U.S. Route 40.

If the traveler is amazed to discover such once flourishing communities as Eureka and Austin, he must remember that both of these towns once knew great mining activities and both formerly had railroads of their own connecting with the life-giving main line of the Southern Pacific.

The life of today's average Nevadan is uncomplicated by the urgency of existence in the East or elsewhere in an industrial age. He probably makes a living as proprietor of a motel, an ever-increasing industry everywhere in the state; as an employee of an eminently leisurely commonwealth; as a banker or insurance man in Reno, a city characterized by something less than the frenetic tensions of Wall Street; as a rancher in the agricultural communities of Yerington, Dayton, Fallon or Minden, or as a dealer or other employee in one of the many houses of chance.

One thing Nevadans share in common: when the fishing or deer hunting season opens, they will turn the locks on their places of business—barbershop or bar, bank or bagnio—for the duration. Other outdoor attractions, aimed at the evergrowing tourist trade, are increasingly occupying the Nevada mind. Lake Mead, for example, above Hoover Dam, has become perhaps the most improbably situated yachting center in the entire world. Reno Ski Bowl with its spectacular lifts is helping to make the town a year-'round instead of a seasonal resort. Desert explorers and rock collectors regard Nevada's southern deserts as a paradise of buttes productive of agate and other semiprecious stones.

Life in Virginia City, where the author makes his residence among the dusty but romantic souvenirs of the Comstock bonanzas, strives valiantly to maintain itself as a tattered page from the life of the authentic Old West. Since its only source of income is from tourists, it has to. It glories in its twenty saloons for 950-odd permanent residents, perhaps the greatest density of oases in the world; in Piper's Opera House where the mighty once assembled in claw-hammer coats to hear the celebrated of their generation perform *Hamlet* or

Mazeppa; and in the still functioning outrages of the *Territorial Enterprise.* Virginia City was delighted with the witticism attributed to Charlie Addis, C Street's foremost character and seventy-seven-year-old newsboy for the *Territorial Enterprise.*

Encountering another ancient who was carrying three loaves of bread under one arm and six bottles of Old Reprehensible under the other, Charlie incredulously asked, "What in hell are you going to do with all that bread?"

Perhaps the key to Nevada's feeling of superiority to and independence from the rest of the Union lies in the circumstance that it has more about it of the 19th Century and less of the 20th than any other part of the nation.

The one link with the immediate present, and the atomic future—the selection of Frenchman's Flat near Las Vegas as the proving ground for many tests of atomic armament—is viewed with distaste by Nevadans. Nor do they particularly admire the jet noises, the strange sights and sounds, the trailing vapors in the night skies that connote the jet age. Philosophically, however, they accept these things on the basis of the state's own highly explosive and pyrotechnic past. Any community, they reflect, that could survive the gunfire and the tumults of Nevada's pioneers can take the atomic age in its stride. A hydrogen bomb, did you say, stranger? You should have been in Carson City in the sixties when Senator William Morris Stewart tried cases before the Supreme Court with a Colt's Navy revolver in each hand! We're used to that sort of thing.

Utah

by SAMUEL W. TAYLOR

You get your suit pressed at a While-U-Wait shop, and when paying for it automatically slide a dime tip across the counter. The proprietor pushes the dime back. "I make a profit from my business," he says. "I don't want anything extra."

You pocket the dime, wondering if you've been away too long. You should have known better than to affront the dignity of a Mormon businessman.

You're on a tour of Utah, to see the state as a tourist might. You're talking with motel owners, gas-pump jockeys and hash slingers, and you're interested in what makes it Utah—things typical or peculiar, like the rainbow cliffs, the "hope" houses, and Salt Lake City during a Latter-day Saints Conference.

Often you'll carry away and remember the little things. You'll forget that, at Bingham, the biggest open-cut copper mine in North America has forty-two power shovels scooping up 200,000 tons a day, but you'll remember the hairbreadth approach to the mine through the town's single street, so narrow that the dogs proverbially wag their tails up and down. Everyone knows that a swimmer can't sink in the brine of Great Salt Lake, but what impresses you is that the granite boulders of the railroad embankment weigh so little in the dense water they literally float away during storms.

You are impressed with the primitive wildness of much of Utah, but what drives it home is the news that the only doctor of Blanding was drafted into the Army. Blanding, with 1178 people, is the largest city of San Juan County, into which could be dropped Delaware, Connecticut and Rhode Island. You ask a waitress if Blanding is a Mormon town. "Well, no, it isn't," she says. "There are six Gentiles here."

In any small town, the integration of Church affairs and daily life is complete; the Gentile either joins or cuts himself off from all social and recreational life. So he pitches in, and sometimes finds himself appointed to an office and a title in the Church.

You get to Blanding (from Salt Lake City, of course—everything begins and ends there) south and east on U. S. Highway 50. At Wellington, a few miles beyond Price, you stop for a snapshot of the tiny city hall and the "hope" house adjoining, and you have your only interview with a mayor. When he sees your camera, he breaks away from a customer and dashes across the street from his service station to tell you that Wellington is really going places, now that they've got water and a sewer system. The hope house, the mayor explains, is the Legion Hall, and he's a bit annoyed because the Legion doesn't clear away the weeds. Right here on the main drag too.

Nothing better illustrates the Mormon horror of going into debt than the hope house. It consists of a concrete basement roofed over and used for living quarters—or, as in this case, the Legion Hall. By largely doing the work himself, the canny native can get a roof over his head; and when he has saved the cash he'll build himself a house atop the basement—so he hopes, hence the name. You count hundreds of hope houses throughout the state, many with TV antennas sticking from the low roofs, or with brand-new cars alongside.

You continue southeast on U. S. 50 through big country, where nothing stops the eye and you can see forever, country so big it seems the rim of the world, but after you turn south at Crescent Junction you go over the rim and enter a new world. It's something from the moon. It's a stage set. It's fairyland. You accept it as you do Mickey Mouse, as fantasy.

You take the first branch road to the right, rough going over sand and slickrock, one-way road, thirty miles down and thirty back, and your destination has the enticing name of Dead Horse Point. But as you drink in the vista of the Colorado gorge, tier upon tier of rainbow cliffs to the end of vision, watching the living color of the stone bloom and fade and change with the time of day, you forget the name and the road and even that the natives unconsciously damn it with assertions it beats the Grand Canyon view. (Is a rose more beautiful than an Easter lily?) Now you're within gunshot range of Monument Canyon (not to be confused with Monument Valley), the Needles, Chesler Park, and other Technicolor fantasies, though you'll see them by Jeep, packhorse or airplane—not passenger car.

You think natural bridges are something, so you turn east to Arches National Monument. Here, at last count, were eighty-eight natural arches, or bridges—there is a technical difference between an arch and a bridge, though whatever it's called, Landscape Arch is the longest natural *span* in the world, at this writing. When you stand below this tremendous arch you wonder if it will be there tomorrow, for its time is running out and any day can be its last. It spans 291 feet and the enormous weight of this almost flat arch is supported by a ribbon of soft sandstone shaved by the cutting wind to barely six feet thick. Other spans have fallen in; you see their skeletons. Of those that remain there are double ones side by side and one atop the other, and twins that look like the ruins of an enormous pair of eyeglasses. The same erosive forces of wind and rain and frost that enlarge and eventually destroy an old arch are at work creating new ones. Natives watched the birth of the youngest arch here just fifteen years ago. Natural forces are one thing, vandalism another. The Goblet of Venus, down near Blanding, is now nothing but a picture on a post card. As a joke, a deer hunter shot its slender base away and it was a big laugh when it toppled.

You've thought of uranium as rare and exotic, a fearful thing from far reaches, and it seems a matter of course that in this fairyland uranium is the biggest industry. The towns of Moab, Monticello and Blanding are booming, mining uranium, trucking it, processing it, building roads to get it out. You watch the blasting at the painted cliffs high on the rim of a breathless canyon as a road is carved where no road could possibly be, except for uranium. There's oil down here, too, in country so wild they had to float sketchy drilling equipment down the deep gorge of the treacherous Colorado, and then cap off the oil because they had no equipment for getting it out. With roads going in they'll get the oil now, but eventually they'll dig more gold from the tourists, because of those roads, than from either oil or uranium.

There is no east-west road across Southern Utah, and by now nobody has to tell you why not. You leave the blacktop at Monticello, and from Blanding you continue south over slickrock and quicksand. You stop for a watermelon at Bluff, a ghost town of decaying sandstone mansions haunted by strangers; the Mormon founders moved on when the San Juan ate away their farmland and the Government gave their rangeland to the Indians. "Take your pick, four bits apiece, any size," says the old codger selling them. You ask if he's L.D.S. "No," he says, "you see, we raise melons; we don't have no time for religion." As you stagger to the car with the watermelon (the map says "Carry Water" doesn't it?) he calls, "Seen the Goosenecks? Well, you're seeing the sights, ain't you? Then, by God, see the Goosenecks!"

So you see the Goosenecks, the great convolutions of the San Juan, fifteen hundred feet below where you stand. And then, despite the big sign which warns against it, you fight the sand traps and the bottomless holes left by the last cloudburst and head south through Monument Valley, where the huge stone sentinels rise from the floor of the terrible plain one after another into the violet haze, impossible, unforgettable; you grow smaller and more puny by the mile.

Now you've crossed into Arizona, and you have to make a 250-mile triangle—west and north—to get back into Utah. You come north over the ridge in the Kaibab Forest on U. S. 89 and the trees fall away to the desert floor below, and ahead is the border of Utah. *Now, wait a minute,* you think, *this can't be.* For the boundary between Arizona and Utah is an arbitrary line ruled on the map by politicians in Washington. Yet ahead, running right along that accidental line, are tiers of the great painted cliffs.

You enter the cliffs and the state at Kanab, just a hop, skip and jump from the two best-known scenic attractions, Zion Park and Bryce Canyon. They're all you expected—Zion's Great White Throne rising a sheer 3000 feet out of the red cliffs, and the living kaleidoscope of Bryce's fiery city of stone. You can take in Cedar Breaks the same afternoon. This is your dish, if you want your scenery laid out for you on a platter. But if you want to fight for it a little, to see something not *every* tourist does, you detour from the main drag and head out State 24, southeast through Loa and Bicknell to the Wayne Wonderland, with its natural bridges, its weird sculpture and its Great Organ, a symphony of color. Here is Capitol Reef, with Chimney Rock rising blood red from the cream-plastic slopes. And from here, if you really want to earn your scenery, you make trips to the cream-and-yellow buttresses of Cathedral Valley or nature's gargoyles in the grotesque Valley of the Goblins.

You schedule your tour to be in Salt Lake City for the semi-annual Conference of the Church of Jesus Christ of Latter-day Saints, for then it is the city the Mormons themselves know and the city the average tourist never sees. Conference comes in April and October, not in the tourist season. During Conference week the faithful flood in from all over the world, coming "home"—whether you're born in Utah or not, it's home to all L.D.S.—back to Conference. Local residents stay at home during Conference week, turning their city over to the visitors. A tourist can still get a room at a hotel, for Conference visitors traditionally stay with friends.

A stream of 20,000 people flows into Temple Square for the afternoon session. At an eddy in the stream are two men wearing oilcloth vests lettered with anti-Mormon texts in two colors, passing out literature in the literal shadow of the wall. "Any converts?" you ask one. He just smiles, refusing to be baited, and hands you a tract, *How I Was Saved Out of Mormonism.*

Anyone can attend Conference. You don't have to show credentials or give any signs or passwords; there are no tickets; just walk in. But go early. Those who really want to sit down arrive hours before the morning session, with lunch in hand, prepared to homestead their seats all day long. "All seats taken!" newsboys shout at the south gate. "Get your paper here to sit on the grass!"

The front center section of the Tabernacle is reserved for those holding the office of bishop or better, and these officials can afford the luxury of arriving merely on time. They file in, well-fed, well-barbered, well-scrubbed, gregarious, alert and aggressive, and the double-breasted gray suit is almost a uniform. This is the amateur clergy—unsalaried, untrained, part-time officials who make their living as business and professional men—who run the Church at the local level. Above them, on the stand facing the audience, are the General Authorities, aloof in blue serge.

Everyone arises, and in the hush a man appears on the stand. He moves along the leather bench, his mane of silver hair gleaming in the TV lights. This is the Prophet, Seer and Revelator, David O. McKay, President of the Church. He takes his seat and the great audience sits, and in the air is a tangible feel of warmth and reverence. Conference is in session.

Practically all male Mormons hold the Priesthood and are eligible for office; there are enough offices in the Church to give a title and position to more than half the population, both men and women, from the age of twelve. You are, in effect, rubbing shoulders with an entire population of ministers.

In Utah, you have a curious feeling of isolation. This is a mountain island, and within its mental wall all is always officially well. In Utah bookcases you find on display the "approved" books—standard Church works and those written in the same style—*i.e.*, religious tracts. If Mormons read anything about Utah not "approved" they won't admit it. "When the Brodie book came out," you're told at the Salt Lake Library (reference is to *No Man Knows My History*, by Fawn M. Brodie, a biography of Joseph Smith, blacklisted in Utah), "people called for it with their own dust jackets, so that apparently they were carrying away *The Five Little Peppers*, or *Tom Swift and His Captive Gas-Filled Balloon*." You ask a Mormon his opinion of a new Utah book, just released, too new to have had the word passed. "I don't know whether I like it or not," he says. "I haven't been told yet."

A strange island, this Utah, populated by ministers who are passionately interested in their history—but only (to use their phrase regarding the Bible) as it is translated correctly.

During Conference the Hotel Utah is the place to eat, dance, hold a convention or meet somebody. Second choice is the Temple Square Hotel, also Church-owned. You're surprised to see smoking in the coffee shop of the Temple Square, and ask the cashier when the ban was lifted. "The 'No Smoking' signs are still up," she says. "But you've got to do business. So we leave up the signs and put out the ash trays." Officially, all Mormons are perfect; actually, some of them have a struggle. You're told the sale of chlorophyl tablets, presumably to kill tobacco breath, is sensational. The amazing thing is not that the stern demand of 100 per cent is broken, but that so few give up trying to meet it.

You will see more of Salt Lake City on a rubberneck bus than do many people who have lived there a lifetime. There are various tours offered, and the Grade AA Super DeLuxe model gives you the well-known city high spots, the canyons, the Tabernacle concert, Great Salt Lake and the Bingham mine in time for the blasting, in a one-day package.

The rubberneck tour makes you realize that Salt Lake City isn't all Mormon. It's only 60 per cent L.D.S., and the other 40 per cent is in there pitching. Competing churches have erected tremendous buildings to show there's somebody else on deck. You realize that everything in Utah is either Mormon or a reaction to it.

Then there's the small bungalow with red shutters which has, your driver announces, seven kitchens. After an intent silence a rubber-neck asks, "Why?" and the driver says, "I don't know. I never asked Mr. Kitchen."

For some curious reason, outsiders cannot fathom the method of numbering streets, which is so simple that any native can walk into a strange town in Utah and go directly to any given address without asking directions. Your driver makes it all clear: "We are going west toward Sixth East on Ninth South. At the corner of Sixth East and Ninth South we will turn north on Sixth East. Then instead of going west on Ninth South toward Sixth East we will be going north on Sixth East from Ninth South."

This explains it perfectly.

A devout Saint, on his first visit to the Mormon Mecca, is startled at the way such words as Zion, Deseret, Mutual, L.D.S. and Temple are applied to business enterprises. He is appalled at the sign, "Temple Café, Drink Coca-Cola," for Coke is against the Word of Wisdom too. But what really curls his hair is the "Temple Wrecking Company."

As far back as you can remember, there have been oil booms, timed by coincidence to hit the papers at Conference. You have suspected promotion, but now they seem to be getting actual oil, so you decide to see what the boom looks like in the Uintah Basin, over in the northeastern corner of the state.

You go east along Daniels Canyon from Heber, on U. S. 40, and the aspen leaves shimmer butter-yellow against the deep green conifers. Daniels is just one of a dozen canyons that could be promoted as tourist attractions, except that Utah has so much scenery. Where the country opens up near Strawberry Reservoir a line of double-decked trucks comes barreling out of the mountains on a yellow dirt road. Here is the reason you've missed what used to be one of the characteristic features of Utah travel, the sheep herds trailing the highways. The trucks are packed with sheep, transporting an entire herd from mountain range onto winter range in the desert.

The trucks jam to a stop at a little café and the truckers swarm out of the cabs. First they get the sheep up; a sheep that goes down can smother within a few minutes. The truckers jab them with hot shots—rods with sharp points and electric coils—and they come up fast. Then the truckers stomp into the café and order coffee. One gets a can of beer. None of them smokes. You notice such things in Utah. The boss trucker tells you he hauls sheep spring and fall, coal between times. "Hauled 70,000 sheep last spring off the desert into the mountains, and only lost one head." He drains his coffee. "Ready, boys? Let's top it."

You climb up through the "World's Largest Piñon and Cedar Forest," the sign says, into the big country of the Uintah Basin, and you wonder if you'll really get the courage someday to leave California for someplace like this, where you can have a hundred miles of front yard. At Myton, you stop for honey, the best in the world, because nothing blooms in the Basin that makes bad honey. There are no fruit trees, not even much sage; it's clover honey.

When you stop for lunch there is watery imitation-maple sirup for your waffles. You wonder why they don't serve local honey, why you see French-fried shrimp, oysters and halibut steak featured on this inland desert and rarely the beef, mutton, turkey and chicken that Utah exports.

The Basin is another area where a few sketchy roads peter off into nowhere. U. S. 40 runs along the north rim of the wild tangle of plateaus and canyons and mesas that extends south the entire length of the state and into Arizona, country so broken that just one all-weather highway crosses its expanse (U. S. 50, which you traveled on the way to Blanding). This enormous wasteland, one quarter of the entire state, is drained sterile by the deep gorges of the Green and the Colorado.

To the north of U. S. 40 are the Uinta Mountains, claimed to be the only range running east-and-west in the nation. Here are Utah's highest mountains, rising from the immense desert, cradling dense timber and a thousand lakes. This is the proverbial sportsmen's paradise; at least 100 of the lakes have never been fished. The high Uintas have been preserved in their original state as a wilderness area without roads or houses. Here is the great watershed of Utah, the source of its best rivers. Ironically, much of the water of this desert state is wasted, running from the slopes of the Uintas into the sterile trap of the Green River gorge. Utah is 96 per cent scenery— only 4 per cent of its land can be cultivated—yet so determined is the state to keep the high Uintas primeval that the Central Utah Project, which would reclaim 200,000 acres from the desert by using some of the Uinta water, is opposed because it would injure the scenery.

At Roosevelt you find the Indians eating T-bones and the whites ordering hamburgers. The Utes not only nicked the Great White Father for thirty-two million bucks on an old land claim but they've got oil on the reservation besides. The whites gnaw their hamburgers and really pity those poor Utes, getting all this jack and not knowing how to spend it. They tell of Indians buying refrigerators and vacuum cleaners and washing machines without having electricity to run them, about big new cars. With a wink they point out squaws with permanents, walking down the street in evening dress at high noon. "The Government shouldn't give them money until they've been taught how to spend it," you're told. You hear of Indians driving blind drunk, and that they can't handle liquor, which is something the whites could give lessons on.

And you hear the oil stories, the ones you've heard about every oil field in the world. The one you like best is about the Watkins Man. He had a barren farm and a fertile wife and a battered car for selling his Watkins products, and then one day they struck oil on his farm. He took one look at the black stuff spurting from the ground and rushed into town for the one thing he always had yearned for, a gleaming new Lincoln. Soon the Watkins Man was rich, but unhappy. He had nothing to do. So he loaded up his Lincoln with Watkins products and returned to his route, selling the stuff at cost because he didn't need the money.

At Vernal, you find the town on the upbeat after a local recession, and you learn that an oil boom comes during drilling operations. Once wells are down and flowing, your drilling crews move away and the bottom drops out of your boom. Vernal is an isolated metropolis. In the old days the distance from markets made the going tough. You remember as a kid when relatives called from Vernal and your mother said what a blessing it would be when the railroad went through. "Blessing?" came the appalled reaction. "We never hope to live to see the day!" The old-timers had an unholy fear of Gentiles coming with the railroad. The railroad never did come, but oil and hardtop road brought Gentiles and strangers.

Dinosaur National Monument spraddles the Utah-Colorado line next door to Vernal, and after peering at a barren ledge containing vague outlines of what once were bones and now are rock like the rest of the ledge, you sympathize with the lady tourist alongside you. "Did we," she asks bleakly, "come 350 miles to see *this?*" For once Utah doesn't live up to its billing. But if it's scenery you want, Split Mountain, right next door, can make you forget the so-called bones. Split Mountain is exactly what its name implies. The gorge of the Green cuts through its middle from peak to base. And here you're in color again.

Vernal is like Blanding—the only surfaced road is back the way you came. But you can "earn" your scenery north on State 44 over the Uintas to Manila. Red Canyon and Horseshoe Canyon, on the way, make you feel it was effort well spent. And you wonder if the Utah genius for prosaic names for breath-taking scenes might have a sly system behind it. Perhaps Dinosaur Monument fell on its face for you because its name had fired your imagination. No amount of previous build-up can spoil a spectacle named Goosenecks, Dead Horse Point, or Horseshoe Canyon; these take you completely and delightfully by surprise.

At Manila, you're smack up against the Wyoming line, and you have to leave Utah again to get back into it, cutting across the southwest corner of Wyoming to Evanston. Here at a café the inevitable rack of picture post cards displays two scenes of native Wyoming, two dozen of Utah. There could be no greater tribute to Utah's scenic attractions.

There are two routes into Utah from Evanston. One takes you north alongside Crawford Mountain to Bear Lake, lying across the Utah-Idaho line. Bear Lake has the unreal, picture-post-card, blue-green intensity of Canada's famed Lake Louise, and from it you go over the hump and down Logan Canyon, a gem among the state's many canyons. (Incidentally, there is a Mormon Temple at Logan, one at Manti, in central Utah, and one down in the southwest corner of the state at St. George. Rumor has it that here, away from the tourist crush, interested Gentiles occasionally get a peek inside the doors, which doesn't happen at Salt Lake City.) The other route from Evanston is down Echo Canyon, with its red cliffs and weird erosions; and then, in the afternoon, you come into Weber Canyon and into another typical Utah scene—cars parked along the stream and fishermen casting across the waters. Most Utah men live minutes from a trout stream rippling among unsurpassed scenery, and to look at the number of fishermen, practically everybody takes advantage of it. But there are still fish for those who know how. And it goes deeper than that. "When things go wrong, when I get in a fight with the wife, when the kids are impossible and the world goes to hell," a fisherman tells you, "there's nothing an hour on the river can't cure."

As you travel the state you see everywhere the great new Church houses—ward chapels for local congregations, stake houses for groups of wards. This is the current passion in this land of high fevers. Throughout the tour you hear stories of wards overextending themselves, of faithful Saints mortgaging their homes in the furious competition to equal or better the neighboring ward chapel.

You stop one late afternoon for ice cream at a stand just across the street from a great new ward chapel. The lady at the counter tells you it has just been dedicated. That means paid for. The Mormons don't dedicate a debt to the Lord.

"Frankly, we didn't want to start it," the good sister says. "Some of us were bitterly opposed. But the stake presidency pushed it through. The ones who decide are the ones who can afford it. Once it was approved there was nothing to do but do it.

"The assessment for us was $1500. That's cash, and it wasn't easy to scrape it up. We also raised a ward calf; everybody raised something, a calf or a sheep or chickens or grain to sell for the building fund. Women took over extra duties so the men would be free to work on the ward house. The men went into the mountains and cut timber and sawed it, so the rough lumber didn't cost any cash. Everybody worked on the construction and finish and decoration. But even so, it cost $150,000. The Church puts up half of that. It was a struggle. We had our regular tithing on top of it all, and they're always dollaring you for something.

"Then came the big push, to finish it and be out of debt so it could be dedicated for Stake Conference." She sighs. "I don't know how we did it—somehow we did."

Then she smiles, and her face softens as she looks across the street. "Isn't it beautiful?" she whispers. "Isn't it lovely? I'm so fortunate, right here all day long where I can look at it. I just love that steeple, and the way the roof slants, and—oh, everything about it is just perfect! And now it's over with I'm so glad we made the sacrifice! Don't you think it's wonderful?"

Yes, you agree, you think it's wonderful, and you drive on in the twilight feeling warm from her warmth, knowing it is wonderful and she is wonderful and the other seventy-nine families of the ward are wonderful.

Utah is a rich field for research into the birth of new religions, and you spend an evening with each of four founders and prophets of new sects, as well as an entertaining afternoon with a gentleman who has his own private model which he figured out and proved strictly by mathematics. But you learn not to discuss this type of research at random. One of the great intellectual hobbies of Utah is research into the origins of Mormonism but this is a secret pursuit, discussed in strict confidence.

You find, on all levels, a blanket intolerance for contrary belief, peculiar among the people who have suffered so violent a history because of intolerance. "Let's not go to seed on tolerance," a university professor tells you. "Let's maintain a little healthy bigotry." This candor and lack of hypocrisy is refreshing, at least. Religion is based more on faith, after all, than on intellectual proof, and if you believe your brand is right, then that makes all the others wrong.

Mixed in with the co-operative tradition in Utah you find rugged individualism that really has knobs on. You can lead the Peculiar People, but don't try to shove them.

"The creamery penalized me ninety dollars a month because my milk was too rich," a Utah Valley man tells you. "Said people didn't want cream in their milk any more. Maybe they're afraid to let people get a taste of good Jersey milk." And, rather than reduce the quality of his milk, he sold out and got a job.

"Salt Lake is the worst city in the world to do business in," you're told by an individualist who moved to Ogden. "Rebates, kickbacks, discounts—my hell, practically everybody in Salt Lake can get it wholesale. Here I make twice the money for half the work."

You learn that Utah gained tremendously in population in the last few years as people poured into the Wasatch Oasis, the narrow strip of fertile land that runs down the center of the state from above Ogden to below Provo. Here in north-central Utah there's an industrial boom, and if you were born in Provo it's a shock to return to the country town of memory to find it such a bustling industrial city that there's a smog problem.

The old home, where your mother still lives, is now next door to an apartment house. Ernie Hansen's neighborhood grocery is gone and with it the houses of an entire block, to make room for the big

Sears store. The old Roylance orchard is a subdivision, the First Ward pasture a golf course, the city dump on East Center a city park.

Cities traditionally grow westward, the east sides degenerating into slums. Just to be different, all Utah cities grow eastward, and on the east foothills of Provo where there was nothing but sagebrush are now the showplaces of Snob Hill.

The mountains rise so abruptly into the morning sky that strangers in town tell you of an uneasy feeling that the peaks might topple over on them. And with autumn these overwhelming slopes are huge crazy quilts of raw color. Beyond the end of University Avenue to the north is Timpanogos, majestic and alone, 12,008 feet. Timp is a local institution, featured in publicity, held in deep reverence. There is a community hike up its slopes each summer, people swarming to its summit by the hundreds; and in July a ski meet is held on its high snows.

You make the fifty-mile Alpine Loop that circles Timp, seeing the convoluted cliffs of Provo Canyon, and Bridal Veil Falls, the prodigal autumn color of the woods and the power of sheer rock towering into the eternal snow above timberline. You walk into the viscera of the mountain at Timpanogos Cave National Monument, and find deep inside the cave the great heart-shaped stalactite, moist and blood-red. There are strict rules against touching any of the formations, and you wonder what would happen if you did; would the mountain tremble if you put out a hand to touch its heart? You go down American Fork Canyon to complete the Loop, and return to Provo.

When you feel a bit pensive about the passing of a country town you're told, "My hell, it's gone anyhow now; let's look ahead."

You find a curious rivalry between industry and education. Until the early 1940's Provo was The University City. Then with the arrival of Geneva Steel it became The Steel City, and the Brigham Young University was relegated to a seat far in the rear, behind a post. Then the brethren reached out and plucked a Mormon lawyer from Washington, D.C., to be president of the Church university, and things began happening. Ernest L. Wilkinson is an executive, a hard worker, a driver, a man who gets things done, rather than a lofty intellectual. He represented the Utes in putting the bite on the Great White Father for thirty-two million. Utah natives stand in awe of success like this; by now the story's grown, it was sixty-five million and his fee the largest in history. "When he wants a new building for the campus he just goes to Salt Lake and comes back with the money," you're told. "He knows where the bear sleeps."

You go up on the hill to see what is happening and are absolutely lost on the campus of your Alma Mater. The new buildings have dwarfed and misplaced the old ones. There are no landmarks left. The biggest and most prominent building on the campus in your day was the library, and now you can't find it; an undergrad (a mere boy; they sure go to college *young* these days) has to show you the way. The throb of jackhammers fills the academic air as workmen swarm over three and a quarter million dollars of additional construction.

When you attended these hallowed halls there were about 1500 students and a chilling rumor that the Church was going to turn the school over to the state or back to the Indians. Now they enroll a freshman class of about 3000. You pick up a campus paper and admire an ad for gals' underwear, featuring a photograph of a fetching young thing wearing a bra and Pantie Girdle P-17. Yes, things have changed at dear old BYU since your day.

The BYU admits students of all faiths, on condition they observe the Mormon moral code and take a two-hour class in religion each quarter. The base of religious instruction is broad, and a student can select courses in psychology of religion, religious philosophy, the Old Testament, history of religion and kindred subjects without being exposed to Mormon doctrine. Thus any Gentile may, at his own risk, enroll if he meets the academic standards. But the risk is real, for some 25 per cent of the Gentile students are baptized as converts before graduation, and there is the added hazard of marrying a Mormon gal met at school and joining the Church eventually. The Y is one of the most marryin' schools in the world. One year every member of the student body executive council got married—in fact they all married each other.

Along with the frank recognition that gals do wear bras and Pantie Girdle P-17's, you find more evidence of religious consciousness than there was back in the cynical 30's. The athletic teams now pray before each contest, a custom initiated by the players, not their elders. Students used to attend Church, if at all, in town. Now the school has two branches of religious services, and 1200 devout undergrads crowd into Campus Branch, their desire to bear testimony so great that the procedure has been put on an assembly-line basis. All those who feel impelled to tell of their personal conviction of the Gospel's truth and the Divine agency of its Prophet are asked to stand, and from the young army that arises are selected a lucky two dozen who receive numbered cards. There are two traveling microphones, and as holder of card No. 1 bears his testimony the holder of card No. 2 gets ready at the other mike, every moment being utilized, bearing testimony by the numbers.

You leave the campus with one more evidence of size and change. They now have campus police, who have given you a parking ticket. And as you complete your tour of the state you notice that education has vanquished industry. The new signs urge tourists to visit "Provo, The University City."

You head west to leave the state, through Grantsville and past the corner of stone wall sticking from the sagebrush that once was the house where your mother grew up in a plural family during the brief flowering of the Principle in Utah. You look back for a last glimpse of the trade mark of the old Mormon towns, the Lombardy poplars, and then you head west over the salt flats, the great and bitter barrier upon which for thousands of square miles there is no bush nor twig nor weed nor blade of grass nor living thing (but have you seen it bloom pink at the sunset and violet at the dawn?). The salt flats isolate the state on the west as do the Uinta Mountains and Great Salt Lake on the north, the broken canyon and mesa country on the east, and the Grand Canyon on the south. You are leaving this physical island with its strange mental wall, in which a peculiar people live their religion as a way of life.

You've put 5000 miles and four new tires on your car, you've been to the end of every major road in Utah and several minor ones. You've got enough material for a book, but what is the essence of it? What story would you tell that would typify Utah?

Would it be about the rainmaker?

The irrigation ditches were running dry and the crops were burning up, so the county supervisors agreed to hire a rainmaker to end the drought—for a fee reported at $100,000. The local Stake Presidency became incensed. This was throwing money down a rathole. Had people lost their faith? The way to get rain was to pray for it. So some prayed, and some paid, and some to make sure both prayed and paid. For three weeks nothing happened. Then one day some clouds drifted over. The faithful put on a big burst of prayer and the rainmaker put his machines into high gear. And down came the glorious rain, and that delicious moist smell arose from the parched earth. And then the rain quit. It had hardly dampened the surface. That was several years ago, but a violent argument is still raging in the county—what brought the rain, the machines or the prayer?

Or would it be about the Priesthood meeting?

A faithful Saint, a relative of yours, was coming to the end of a long and devout life, but was determined to climb out of his sickbed to go to Priesthood meeting. He hadn't missed Priesthood in forty years and he wasn't going to now—especially now. When the bishop phoned, as he did each day to find out how the good brother was, the wife said she didn't know what to do. "I don't think he should miss Priesthood meeting," the bishop said. "It means so much to him." And so as the good Saint lay upon his deathbed the Priesthood Quorum gathered at his house rather than in Church, and his bedroom became, for this once, a holy place of worship. He had gone to Church all his life; now the Church had come to him.

Maybe neither of these. Maybe it's impossible to roll Utah into a capsule. Why try?

On either side as you cross the salt flats you see the mirage of the floating mountains sailing on their peaks. At Bonneville, where the fastest things on wheels have sped, you turn onto the blinding surface and open your car up. It's rough up to fifty, then it begins smoothing out and then you're floating over the vast table of salt and it's just a question of time and nerve and gasoline. You head back to the highway dismayed that you couldn't crack ninety, and soon you're in Wendover, the state line, and spraddling the line is the biggest mannikin in the world, greeting your entrance into Nevada with the sign, "Where the West Begins."

At first this seems strange, but after you get into Nevada you realize how right it is. You haven't been in the West. In physical layout the villages of Utah are New England. You haven't found Western clothes, customs, language or mental attitude. You have been in an island fairyland of enormous beauty, peopled by a unique brand of tightly-knit Puritans.

olorado

by DEBS MYERS

In the old mining town of Fairplay, almost two miles high in the Colorado Rockies, stands a monument built to a burro named Prunes. Prunes, the townspeople say, was cussed and headstrong, but he was also a good-luck burro who brought fortune to every prospector who owned him.

When Prunes died, the people of Fairplay put a marker on his grave—"Prunes, a burro, 1867–1930"—and sent him off in style.

On the day I was at Fairplay an old man sat on a wooden box near the monument squinting through the sun at the mountains beyond the town. The old man said that his name was Frank Mayer, that he was 102 years old—"in this climate the only way for a man to die is for 'em to hang him"—and that he had been soldier, Indian scout and prospector. "Me and Prunes," he said, "belong to an ornery breed that's about gone. Maybe it's a good thing; we don't fit any more. But I don't worry about it because I've had fun and never in my whole life did I deliberately do one bad thing to any person." He sighed and added thoughtfully: "Except, of course, to a few rascals I had to kill."

The old man at the grave of the burro, living in the past in defiance of time, symbolizes an important transition in Colorado history—a transition that is certain to shape its future. The old-timers who built the state in their own image and wanted it to stay that way are about gone and their influence is dying. Colorado is no longer content to live in the shadow of its roaring legends.

There are still plenty of reminders of the past, but the typical Coloradan is too busy to tell you just how grandpop stood alone in the mine shaft, cut off and surrounded, with the claim jumpers charging across the gulch.

This does not mean that Colorado is losing its customary flamboyance. You are likely, as I did, to enter the office of a chamber-of-commerce manager and find seated behind the desk a young man wearing a ten-gallon hat, frontier pants and a purple shirt. Probably, if he could grow them, he would have purple whiskers.

And there are, inevitably, tourist traps aplenty, some of them ferociously picturesque and full of what Coloradans apologetically call atmosphere, but these are the natural hazards to be expected in a state that attracts more than 3,000,000 visitors a year.

No one has explained why Colorado needs phony atmosphere. It has the most awesome scenery in America: 600 mountain peaks more than 12,000 feet high, 300 peaks more than 13,000 feet high, and fifty-two mountains that stretch above 14,000 feet; it has brawling rivers racing across glacial canyons, lakes on the flat tops of mountains, tiny streams that make the kind of rippling noises that streams are supposed to make; it has uranium, oil and coal, silver and gold, and even a desert created from the sands of a long-vanished inland sea. When nature made Colorado, it was on a show-off bender.

Colorado isn't all mountainous. The eastern third of the state is as smooth as a tidal flat, which is what it was in the distant past. I had visited Colorado many times before (it is doubtful there's a better place anywhere for a summer vacation), but this trip was different; instead of settling down at a resort and taking it easy, I planned a leisurely trip by car across the state. Anyone who expects cool temperatures immediately upon crossing the state line is in for a disappointment. I came into Colorado by car at the eastern boundary on U. S. 40. The thermometer, in a gas station at Cheyenne Wells, just across the Colorado line from Kansas, recorded 102°.

The attendant in the gasoline station gave me two pieces of advice. "When you get up in the mountains," he said, "and your car starts knocking [which it did] just turn on the radio—loud. And don't worry about getting hurt falling into the canyons. You'd starve to death before you ever hit bottom."

Driving across this flat stretch of Colorado, I passed through Firstview, Kit Carson and Wildhorse—all prosaic farm communities. It's easy to guess how Firstview got its name; from here, on a clear day, you can see the Rocky Mountains, more than 150 miles away.

From far away the mountains are humped shadows; as you get closer, forty or fifty miles off, they have a theatrical, almost artificial, look, a little too dramatic to be authentic, like a cardboard television prop. Once you get to Denver you are close enough to know they're real; only twelve miles beyond Denver are the brown-and-green foothills and beyond the foothills towers the snow-capped Front Range.

In the old days Denver was a capering alley cat of a town. Today it understandably has quieted down. It isn't sedate or stuffy, you understand, far from it—merely mature enough to want to go to bed at night.

Denver is justifiably proud of its mountains and its climate. Residents insist that the sun, even during the winter, is strong enough to keep them tanned the year around, and that winter days often are mild enough for picnicking. And—as Coloradans are fond of pointing out—one of the nicest ways to start a day is to eat breakfast watching the sun strike a snow-capped mountain.

Denver has thirty-five parks within the city limits. The most elaborate, probably the finest owned by any city anywhere, is the Mountain Park System, which stretches over almost 25,000 acres of the Front Range. This area, within an hour's drive of Denver, includes lakes, trout streams, mountains, canyons, barbecue pits, picnic grounds and some of the world's most impressive scenery. It is doubtful if any other city has a back yard to match it.

This area also covers Red Rocks Park, where Denver residents sit in the summer to listen to their symphony play under the stars in an amphitheater made out of red sandstone; Lookout Mountain, where Buffalo Bill is buried, and 14,260-foot Mt. Evans, where some of the nation's leading physicists study cosmic rays in a laboratory jutting from the granite top of the mountain.

I left Denver and drove northwest; constantly, the peaks became clearer and sharper. By the time I reached Boulder, thirty miles from Denver, the mountains were rising from Boulder's back yard. Boulder is the home of the University of Colorado, and the only town in the United States that owns a glacier, from which it gets its water supply. This particular glacier is a mile long, nearly a mile wide and 500 feet deep, the largest in the Rocky Mountains.

The day I arrived in Boulder a group had just returned from a day-long climb to the glacier summit. The climbers included Jim Yeager, former University of Colorado football coach; this was his first venture at mountain climbing, and, he added, his last.

"I have two pieces of advice for mountain climbers," he said. "In the first place, don't go; if you must go, ride a horse."

It is relevant to point out here that in Colorado mountain climbing is more than a sport; it is a fetish. Local mountain climbers talk about the statistics of ridges, crevasses and peaks with the hot-eyed enthusiasm of a baseball fan discussing batting averages. This is likely to be a little startling to more sedentary visitors, who can't see the sense of risking their necks just to get to the top of a mountain, which probably would be uncomfortable once they got there.

Taking off from Boulder on the same northwest course, on a climbing road toward the mountain country, I stopped at Estes Park, only seventy miles from Denver. I came into the village of Estes late in the evening, when long shadows were slanting across the forested mountains rimming the town. Estes Park has only one industry— tourists. Townspeople say that during the summer a million and a quarter tourists travel along Elkhorn Avenue, the principal street. On a summer night, the village is a combination of Coney Island and a county fair. There are square dances, shooting galleries, hot-dog stands, a dozen kinds of games in which barkers challenge you to win an Indian blanket or a kewpie doll.

Estes Park has its quota of characters. One of these I met was a sixty-three-year-old painter named Dave Sterling, who has been painting the mountains, glaciers, lakes and trees of Colorado for more than thirty-five years. In his studio six miles west of Estes village, he delivers impromptu art lectures to prospective customers and other visitors who are merely curious.

On the day I entered the studio, Sterling was exhibiting picture after picture, and maintaining a running spiel before an audience of a dozen persons, several of them middle-aged women, who, it developed, were schoolteachers from Iowa. One of the teachers started to rise from her chair . . . "We better be going," she murmured. Sterling reached into his desk and confronted the schoolteacher with what appeared to be a .22 target pistol. "Hell's almighty, woman," he shouted, "I'm not through yet. If you're getting tired of this, just say shut up and see if I shut up." (The pistol later proved to be a toy reproduction.)

Now that his audience was quiet, not to mention spellbound, Sterling continued: "Art is winding up in the gutter and manure piles. The modern boys paint to scare you to death. I belong to the old school, me and Michelangelo. Any damn fool can dab paint on hard, but to handle paint, so that you see air instead of paint, you have to be the world's greatest artist, which conceivably I am. Though my worldly acquisitions are few, I am the richest man in the United States. Millionaires cry on my shoulder because I'm happy and they're not.

"Why is this? The answer is easy. If I had all the money in the world, where would I live, what would I do? Why, I would live right here, in this same cabin, and I would paint pictures of these dad-blamed mountains."

Estes Park is one of the entrances to Rocky Mountain National Park. I entered the park and drove to Grand Lake across Trail Ridge Road, which offers some of the most dramatic scenery in Colorado. The road, which partially follows an old trail used by the Utes and Arapahoes, rises from 7500 feet at Estes Park to a summit of 12,183 feet. High on the road the air has the tangy smell of a million Christmas trees; you can, if you're lucky, see deer, elk and perhaps mountain sheep; have your picture taken throwing a snowball; feed peanuts to chipmunks (by this time word must have spread among the chipmunks that all the chumps in the world pass along Trail Ridge Road); study the enduring imprint of glaciers, and overlook timbered canyons with lakes and rivers thousands of feet below.

High on Trail Ridge Road at Iceberg Lake, which is fed by melting snowbanks and is never entirely free from ice, someone overladen with civic spirit and red cells, or perhaps a headier stimulant, had crawled down a steep ledge and spelled out in the snow in huge letters, "Athol, Kansas." Later, I looked it up; there is such a town. It must breed a dedicated type of citizen.

There seems to be something about mountains that makes people want to leave the record of their passing, perhaps because the mountains seem so permanent. The inscription I liked best was scrawled on a rock on Trail Ridge Road overlooking Forest Canyon and the Gorge Lakes. It read: "This View Approved by Kilroy."

Grand Lake Village, at the western end of Trail Ridge Road, has a quiet, restful atmosphere that belies its gaudy past. More than seventy years ago, gold, silver and lead were discovered on the western slope of the Never Summer Mountains and Grand Lake became a mining town, filled with clamor and violence.

After five years of boom Grand Lake went bust and almost vanished when the gold gave out. The mining camps became ghost towns. Today Grand Lake is a thriving resort center, with hotels, lodges, cabins and dude ranches and even a yacht club, perhaps the only one in the world that holds annual regattas a mile and a half above sea level.

Some of the old-timers, like Jake Spitzmiller, have trouble realizing this is the same town they knew half a century ago. He made his first trip to Grand Lake in 1907 in a wagon across the mountain trails. He came to Grand Lake in those days to hunt, fish and prospect for gold. I asked him how he liked Grand Lake today, with all its tourists, boat races and modern gadgets. He contemplated; obviously he didn't want to make a snap judgment. "I think I'm going to like it," he said, "though I must admit the winters get very monotonous."

The ladies bow and the gents bow under,
Hold your holts and swing like thunder.

On the day I came across Rabbit Ears Pass—named because two rocks poke up high above the countryside—and into Steamboat Springs, the sidewalks were thronged and dozens of square dancers were cutting their fanciest didoes in the streets. The town seemed pleasantly daft and proud of it.

Steamboat Springs, a winding four-hour drive northwest of Grand Lake, is the most dance-happy town in the country. Two women named Portia Mansfield and Charlotte Perry are responsible for this. For more than thirty years, they have conducted a girls' camp and a coeducational theater-dance workshop for adults. Several years ago, to supplement an annual series of recitals, musicals and plays, they persuaded the town to sponsor a square-dance competition. Today this big summer festival is the world series of the square dance. Anyone who thinks he can "do-si-do and allemande left" is invited, regardless of how far away he lives, but he'd better be good. The competition is terrific.

As many as fifty square-dance sets dip and swirl at one time; the girls wear hoop skirts, pantalets and poke bonnets, the men fancy shirts, cowboy boots and frontier pants; judges prance from contestant to contestant, and the callers cry out, "When the birdie flies out and the crow hops in, that is the time for fun to begin." There is even a clinic for callers.

Steamboat Springs' reputation is not confined to the square dance. It is also one of the few towns where skiing is a regular part of the public-school curriculum. An instructor holds classes each afternoon for different grades of skiers, and children become adept at the simpler turns about the time they're in the second grade.

Perhaps you've wondered how a cow-and-farm town in the Rockies got the name of Steamboat Springs. Unlike some Colorado place names, this one makes sense. There used to be a spring in the vicinity; as it gushed from the ground it made a chugging noise like a side-wheeler steamboat.

Wherever I went in Colorado, people said, "You should go to Georgetown and see the Hotel de Paris," so I retraced my course across Rabbit Ears Pass, heading southeast, crossed Berthoud Pass, 11,314 feet high but comfortably wide for driving, past the tiny community of Empire into Georgetown. Georgetown was once the most important silver camp in Colorado; now it's a tired little town with little trace of its one-time opulence. The Hotel de Paris, fifty years ago the gathering place of celebrities like Sarah Bernhardt and Jay Gould, is shuttered and closed to customers, an ugly two-story brick building hemmed in by mountains.

The hotel became a landmark because its owner, a Frenchman named Louis Du Puy, was one of the most perverse, unpredictable and explosive characters ever to come to Colorado. After squandering his fortune, Du Puy deserted both the French and the American armies and wound up in Georgetown, where he was injured in a mine accident. Local citizens took up a collection and set him up in the hotel business.

Du Puy prided himself on his skill at sizing up a prospective boor; he ordered away those guests whose looks he didn't like. He hated women, and seldom permitted them in the hotel, even when his best friends tried to bring their wives to dinner. How much of this was temperament, and how much hard business sense, no one knows. At any rate, the Hotel de Paris attracted world celebrities, who would argue art, politics and romance with Du Puy, and eat the excellent food he cooked.

From Georgetown I set out for Central City, Colorado's most publicized mountain village. For some obscure whim, later regretted, I decided against the more conventional route through Idaho Springs in favor of a road leading across Virginia Canyon. There are people, it seems, who like to gape at the glories of nature while manipulating an automobile around hairpin turns on a narrow two-car road with nothing between them and the jagged rocks below but several thousand feet of invigorating mountain air. I'm not one of them. Nor was the man in the car immediately behind me. As soon as he arrived at Central City, he went into the Teller House, and gulped down a double bourbon. "That road," he said, "should be traveled only by Jeeps and jackasses."

Central City, known as the richest square mile on earth during its heyday as a mining town, is famous now for a summer festival which features opera and drama. The festival hires stars from the Metropolitan Opera and the Broadway stage, who like to come to Central City to combine a few weeks' pay with a mountain vacation. These celebrities, in turn, attract other celebrities, not to mention intellectuals, socialites and thousands of ordinary tourists who come to Central City merely to ogle and have a good time.

From the beginning Central City has done things with a flourish, even to building its houses, many of which dangle precariously from the side of a mountain. When President Grant visited the town in 1873, he walked from the stagecoach to the Teller House on a path of silver bricks. Today the Teller House, though ancient, is still ornate, a favorite gathering place for visitors who admire its Victorian ostentation. Many of them are impressed with the palpable antiquity of "the face on the barroom floor," a drawing which is preserved under glass on the wooden floor of the Teller House bar.

It's sad to spoil a good story, but the picture was drawn, not in the roistering old days but in 1936, by a Denver artist who did it on impulse before dawn one morning when the bar was deserted. At first the owners were indignant; it wasn't until some time later that they realized they had a good thing.

From Central City I headed west, back through Georgetown (carefully avoiding Virginia Canyon this time) over the Continental Divide on Loveland Pass (11,992 feet), and across Vail Pass (10,603 feet). (The Continental Divide is a giant ridgepole winding through the middle of Colorado, splitting it into two roughly equal sections, the eastern and the western slopes.) Heading west along

an excellent highway merging U. S. 6 and U. S. 24, I came through
Glenwood Canyon, where sheer walls rise 1000 feet above the
foaming Colorado River as it gathers snows from the Continental
Divide and cascades toward the Gulf of California. At the western
edge of Glenwood Canyon is the town of Glenwood Springs, an
attractive resort, mineral bath and ranch town. One of the show
places of the town is the Colorado Hotel, which has kept intact
through the years a suite formerly used by President Theodore Roosevelt when he came here on hunting trips. The suite is now occupied with equal comfort by both Democrats and Republicans.

An hour's drive southeast of Glenwood Springs is the town of
Aspen. Imagine, if you can, a hard-bitten old sourdough, leathery
and seamed with the years, who suddenly has taken to effete ways,
hobnobbing with musicians, professors and other high domes, up to
his hairy ears in good thoughts, good books and good deeds, wondering just what the hell has happened to him, and there you have
a picture of Aspen.

Aspen is a mining town that has gone in for culture. Between
1879 and 1898 a silver boom made Aspen a town of more than
15,000 population, with two railroads and a sizable weekly payroll.
Then the silver market collapsed and so did Aspen. Today it is
booming again as a year-round resort and cultural center, with
skiing, an opera group, summer study groups headed by leading
educators, and a summer repertory theater.

Some of Aspen's unreconstructed old-timers take a jaundiced view
of what they call Aspen's "culchaw." They long for the old days when
mill and smelter smoke made a haze over Aspen's skies; and they
insist that they'd walk a mile over broken glass to avoid hearing a
symphony orchestra.

Most Aspen citizens, however, have learned to relax and like it.
They realize that the old days are gone forever and are grateful
that Aspen is a year-round resort, which means they can be soothed
by the tourist dollar in December as well as in June. A lot of them
even have developed a liking for the visitors, who, over all, are
unpretentious people trying to have some quiet fun.

I met Frank Gimlet, a white-whiskered old man who used to be
a hermit. Finally he gave it up. "Only one flaw to hermiting," he
said, "too lonely, nobody to talk with." I encountered him sitting
in a battered old automobile at the summit of Monarch Pass, more
than two miles high in the Colorado Rockies. He motioned toward

the cars traveling along the highway. "Look at the people in those cars," he said, "wearing skimpy clothes and burned as black as tobaccy, gadding about in their automobiles, thinking they're seeing Colorado. All they're seeing are the white and yellow lines on the highway. There's only one way to see Colorado, the way I used to do it. Just put a pick and provisions on the back of a jackass, go out into the hills and hunt for a glory hole."

Most Colorado visitors would agree with the old man on one point: there's an awful lot to see. This country is big, lavish, contradictory and sometimes frightening. The average visitor can see enough in a day to be overwhelmed; after traveling about Colorado for several weeks he learns he has just tapped the surface. To really see all the things in Colorado worth seeing—that's a lifetime job.

A few hours after I had driven into Grand Junction, the biggest town on the western slope, I overheard an old man say: "I still can't believe I'd ever see the day when that stuff meant money. Shucks, I've thrown a bushel of it away while I was hunting gold." He was talking about uranium.

To many people uranium is something precious and more than a little mysterious; to the miners of Western Colorado who have been mining it off-and-on for more than forty years, there isn't anything mysterious about it—it's just a yellow rock that has a pesky habit of petering out when you least expect it.

Uranium is mined on the red cliffs of the Colorado plateau, in the four-corners region of Colorado, New Mexico, Utah and Arizona. As almost everyone knows by now, uranium is the radioactive mineral that generates nuclear fission, and nuclear fission is the process by which atoms are split. It wasn't until the atom bomb that uranium took on a terrible, new significance. Up to that time, sometimes it was worth mining; sometimes it wasn't. Most miners tell you that mining uranium is a lot harder than mining gold. Whereas gold usually appears in veins, uranium appears in pods. The pods may be a foot long, or 100 feet long or longer, and it may be necessary to dig through fifty feet or more of worthless rock to reach a paying pod.

Even though a boom has developed in uranium, it would be wrong to believe that Grand Junction is a rowdy mining town. It is primarily a market and trade center. I was in Grand Junction on a Saturday night and there were more farmers than miners. The people still seem a little puzzled by what the uranium boom will do to their community; it's adding to the payrolls and increasing the population, that's sure, but to the people of Grand Junction it seems a tricky, undependable kind of metal. They can remember during the war when the uranium operations became secret, how the big trucks came lumbering up from the canyons carrying loads of the stuff, and then came Hiroshima. Some of the people in Grand Junction shake their heads and say they would just as soon that it were mined somewhere else.

Only thirty minutes by automobile from Grand Junction is the Colorado National Monument, 18,061 fantastic acres of odd-shaped monoliths, box canyons, precipitous cliffs, caves, petrified wood and prehistoric remains.

Dinosaur beds extend more than 100 miles along the banks of the Colorado River, and this has created in the Grand Junction area a group of amateur bone hunters who spend many of their week ends climbing over unsurveyed trails and bleak rock outcroppings in the hope of being able to sink a pick in the undug grave of an animal which died about 160 million years ago.

From Grand Junction, I headed southeast on U. S. 50, an excellent road, toward Gunnison. This is an easy half-a-day drive passing through the towns of Delta and Montrose. On the first part of the trip the scenery is reminiscent of those Western movies featuring wagon trains and Indian ambushes (the only danger these days is ambush by real-estate agents); gradually you enter the high-plateau country which has produced some of the best cattle in the world. Gunnison is an authentic Western town without much regard for the fripperies of the resort centers on the eastern slope. This isn't a place where people come to exhibit sun tans, play golf or lounge around in fancy sports clothes; the people who come to Gunnison come to fish.

It's the conversation you hear at breakfast, lunch and dinner, in hotels, lodges and on the street corners: Craig Goodwin pulled out a five-pounder yesterday while fishing from horseback; Pete Eastman's boy got four dandies yesterday just above 10-Mile Bridge; did you know that Bob Hope, the radio fellow, went fishing on the Gunnison River in a kayak and got dunked in four feet of water?

I went fishing with the Gunnison navy, known also as the sage-brush sailors. Because there are in the Gunnison River many inviting spots beyond the reach of the most expert fly-caster or wader, some of the citizens fish while floating down the river in kayaks, which combine the features of the Eskimo's covered kayak and the duck hunter's flat-bottomed skiff.

About sixty miles west of Gunnison just off U. S. 50 is the Black Canyon of the Gunnison, the deepest gorge in Colorado, with walls rising almost vertically above the narrow bed of the river. It is what the name implies, a black canyon.

I took a good long look and headed southwest to Ouray, which with justification calls itself the Gem City of the Rockies. The town nestles in a pear-shaped valley at the very edge of three towering mountains, White House Mountain (13,493 feet) on the west, Hayden Mountain (13,100 feet) on the south, and Cascade Mountain (12,100 feet) to the northwest. To the east is a huge natural amphitheater which is part of a game refuge.

I left Ouray in a lashing rain and started the sharp ascent up Uncompahgre Canyon. This road, which directly overlooks Ouray at the outset, is twisting and narrow in places and it didn't help my morale to recall a story about a truck which had lost a wheel here, plunging down the mountainside and crashing through the roof of an Ouray home. About this time the windshield wipers quit working, and I was high up the climbing highway, into the clouds and swirling vapor, with the rain still falling. I saw a sign nailed to a tree and wanting to be certain I was on the right road I got out of the car and walked through the rain to the sign. It stated: "Vote for Jack Evans for Congress."

I know nothing about Jack Evans or his qualifications; I do know that at the precise moment I would not have voted for him. As it turned out, I was on the right road—U. S. 550, otherwise known as the Million-Dollar Highway. One story has it that it cost $1,000,000 to build the road; another that the road was so named because of the gold-bearing gravels with which it is surfaced. This much is certain: it furnishes a view of the most awesome scenery in Colorado. Here on Red Mountain Pass, words like "beautiful" and "magnificent" don't apply; this scenery is raw, elemental. The Red Mountains are saw-toothed masses of stone, colored an orange-red by iron pyrites in the rock, and they seem to split the sky.

In tortuous turns, the road leads sharply upward past mine shafts, old mills and tumbled houses, past curiously colored rock outcroppings once melted by volcanic fire, and great glacial chasms where creeping masses of ice gouged into the granite of the mountains. From the summit (11,018 feet) the highway leads downward through the San Juan National Forest to the town of Silverton, which, according to legend, got its name from the remark of a miner: "We may not have gold here, but we have silver by the ton." In the old days, Silverton had a population of 2153 people, 35 saloons, two breweries and a gaudy reputation. Today it is a pleasant, quiet town with only a few reminders of its lush and skittish days.

The people of Silverton claim a strange distinction; they say that in San Juan County, of which Silverton is the county seat, there is not an acre of tilled ground. When I asked an old man what the people did, he looked at me as though I were a little touched. "Why," he said, "we do a little mining, we look at the scenery and go fishing. What the hell else would anybody want to do?"

Two hours from Durango by automobile, in a corner of Colorado overlooking Arizona, New Mexico and Utah, is a forested, flat-topped mountain known as Mesa Verde—the green tableland. Here, amidst 50,275 acres of canyons and mesa lands, are the excavated ruins and cliff dwellings of ancient Indians who built a culture long since vanished.

Archaeologists have pieced together a partial history of these people—who they were, where they came from, where they went; yet much of it is still a mystery and probably will remain so. That, perhaps, is a basic reason why it exerts so powerful an attraction for tourists; approximately 100,000 of them come each summer to this out-of-the-way corner of Colorado, to inspect the ruins and conjecture among themselves about the riddles of the cliff dwellers' existence.

About 800 years ago the cliff dwellers deserted their homes and vanished. There have been varied theories as to why this happened: plague, superstition, or a surprise attack that resulted in annihilation. The archaeologists shake their heads to this; they attribute this mass exodus to a great drought which they believe afflicted the Southwest from 1276 to 1299; year after year the crops withered until the cliff dwellers lost heart and moved out of Mesa Verde.

Before they left, probably heading deeper into the west, they built on the mesa top a curious walled structure known as the Sun Temple. The accepted theory is that this ancient temple, built around intricate passageways and kivas (underground ceremonial rooms) was intended to placate the Sun God and to bring a merciful end to the drought. The temple was never completed. Why? No one knows, of course; perhaps because the people lost faith in the promises of their medicine men.

That is only one of the riddles. Where did the cliff dwellers finally find refuge when they made the long journey in search of water, what is the significance of the peculiar structure of the Sun Temple, what strange rituals took place in the underground ceremonial chambers? The answers—well, one guess is as good as another.

Leaving Mesa Verde, heading toward the town of Salida, I left the main highway to drive through an eerie desert of twisting sand known as the Great Sand Dunes National Monument. Here in South-Central Colorado close to the town of Alamosa, nature has played one of its most paradoxical tricks; in the middle of a state that is noted for its mountains and lakes is a vast expanse of barren sand, stretching to the edge of the Sangre de Cristo Range.

These shifting dunes, rising 100 feet and higher, are believed to have been formed from the bed of a huge inland sea that dried up ages ago. The color of the dunes changes with the light. In the glare of the sun, they are dazzling white; late in the afternoon, the sun tinges them with purple and red, and by moonlight the ridges are pale and bleak, making a plaintive whispering noise as the wind riffles through the sand.

This is a place of legends. There are stories of men and women found mysteriously dead, families which have disappeared, sheep-herders and their flocks who have gone into the wastes and never come back. There is a legend, also, of horses seen on the horizon at sunrise racing across the sand with webbed feet.

From Salida I made a side trip to the Royal Gorge, the Grand Canyon of the Arkansas, a walled gash in the mountains, 1000 feet deep, from rim to river bed. In addition to the Gorge itself, there are two chief items of interest: the 45-degree-angle railroad by which you can descend to the bottom of the canyon, and the 1260-foot-long suspension bridge across the chasm, the highest automobile bridge in the world.

I drove out on the slightly swaying bridge, looked straight down into the gorge and came back to Salida. From there I headed for Colorado Springs. Colorado Springs is a town where a lot of people come planning to spend a day before they push on deeper into the mountains; once they arrive and look over the place they're likely not to budge for the remainder of their vacations. How, they inquire, can any place be better than this?

There is some merit to this reasoning. This is a city more than a mile high, located where the plains end and the Rockies begin; it has broad streets, handsome homes, good hotels and restaurants, plenty of trees and shrubbery, a fine climate and a sprawling forested landscape that includes Pikes Peak. It also has numerous other scenic attractions including Garden of the Gods, Seven Falls and Cave of the Winds.

The townspeople take pride in their history, which is understandable; matter of fact, it's easier to understand Colorado Springs once you know how it got that way.

From the beginning it was inevitable that a city should be built where Colorado Springs now stands. It is at the foot of Ute Pass, which is one of the convenient ways in and out of the mountains, and, further, it was the center of mineral springs which purportedly had healing qualities. (It may be that all mineral springs everywhere in the world are purported to have healing qualities, just as all chorus girls are supposedly beautiful, all fat men jolly, all itchy old loafers on park benches wise.)

The two show places of Colorado Springs are, of course, Pikes Peak and the Broadmoor Hotel, both of which are large and almost equally scenic. The Broadmoor was conceived by an implausible character named Spencer (Spec) Penrose, who came west as a young fellow out of Harvard, tried his luck in the Cripple Creek gold field, found it was good, not to mention incredible, and wound up with a large number of fancy suits, the pockets of which were stashed with gold.

Penrose was a prodigious builder. He built a road up 9200-foot Cheyenne Mountain, just back of the hotel, and climaxed this by building a highway up Pikes Peak.

There are thousands of visitors who wouldn't think of coming to Colorado Springs without taking a trip up Pikes Peak. I went up, not on the highway built by Penrose but on the cog railway. The conductor kept up a stream of comment as we moved upward, and this is a capsuled version of what he said: "There never has been a passenger accident on any of these trains through the years, so sit back and enjoy yourselves. . . . The railroad is eight and nine-tenths miles long; it climbs from an initial elevation of 6571 feet to 14,110 feet above sea level at the summit. . . . The maximum grade is 25 per cent. . . . The black spot you see on the plains to your left is the Black Forest, a crest of Yellow Pine, sixteen miles northeast of Colorado Springs and more than forty air miles from here. . . . On clear days it is possible to see the wheat fields of Kansas more than 200 miles away. . . . We have now reached Windy Point, more than 12,000 feet high; the flowers you see are the same you would find approaching the North Pole. . . . On the left where you see the light-colored spots on the mountain is Cripple Creek. . . . Eight thousand feet below and more than sixteen miles away you see the city of Colorado Springs. . . . Before us is the Summit House, built on a foundation of ice. The top of Pikes Peak is a mass of small boulders filled with ice which thaws in the summer to a depth of five or six feet, but below this depth is a perpetual mass of rock and ice."

Sitting on the train in front of me were an old man and woman. The man obviously liked it all, the precipitous cliffs, the far look across the mountains, the thin air. When he pointed out the sights to his wife, she nervously shrugged him away, keeping her eyes trained on the floor of the railway car, away from the chasms. Once at the summit, she straightened her shoulders, grabbed the old man by the arm, and assumed command.

"All right, pa," she said grimly, "you've seen your passel of rock. Time's come to go home and put some corn in the bin."

My last stop in Colorado was Pueblo, an hour's drive south of Colorado Springs. Pueblo is Colorado's second largest city. Though it is a gateway and departure point for the tourist country, Pueblo, save for the week when the state fair is in operation, is too busy to fool around with frontier atmosphere. In Pueblo, the workingman wears overalls, not ranch clothes.

In contrast with most Colorado cities, Pueblo has an atmosphere of bustle and urgency; it is an industrial island in the midst of the plains country, with steel as its prime industry. At night, the red glare from the furnaces of the Colorado Fuel and Iron Corporation can be seen far across the countryside, a reminder that this is the largest steel mill west of the Mississippi.

That day driving back through the flatlands of eastern Colorado the brassy sun was baking the ground and the hot winds came across the fields with a whimpering noise. In the bludgeoning heat the countryside seemed lifeless, parched for water. Inevitably, the traveler contrasts this with the mountains, with the sprawling lakes on the flat mesa tops and the streams racing along the sides of canyons.

I thought back on Frank Mayer, the old man sitting at the grave of Prunes, the burro, in the little town of Fairplay and remembered what he had said about mountains.

"I reckon," he said, "there isn't a man in the whole world who, in his own heart, isn't a little humbled by a mountain. In my younger days, I used to climb on top of an old mountain called Silverheels, named after a dance-hall girl, and I used to wish they could bring all the big statesmen and the diplomats and the nabobs in the world right there to the summit of old Silverheels and say to 'em: 'You're kind of little and not very important, aren't you, compared to what you see on every side, so quit your fussing and act like gentlemen.'"

I recalled, too, an inscription on the walls of the Statehouse at Denver, and wondered if this was a prophecy of Colorado's future:

And men shall fashion glaciers into greenness
And harvest April rivers in the autumn.

PART IV *The Southwest*

rizona

by DEBS MYERS

Arizona considers its winter climate to be among the most re-warding blessings the Almighty has seen fit to bestow upon man—not as important as breathing but a passably close second. This viewpoint has merit. When I boarded the train at New York City in midwinter, bound for Arizona, the sky was the color of warmed-over gravy and a bitter wind pounded the skyscrapers. At Chicago, rain had turned to sleet and the temperature was two below zero. Thirty-five hours later, 1887 miles beyond Chicago, when the train reached Phoenix, the temperature was 72 and a brilliant sun made it seem late spring.

Men on the street were in shirt sleeves, and girls wore summer dresses. The car that took me from the station to the hotel was a convertible, with the top down. The streets were lined with orange and palm trees; at the city's edges were orange, grapefruit, lemon and lime groves bearing fruit. In the hotel restaurant a man was drinking a rum collins while his wife sipped iced tea. The man unfolded a copy of the *Milwaukee Journal* and showed his wife the headline: "Sub-zero Blizzard Hits." "Really going through hell back home," he said, with snug satisfaction.

It wasn't many years ago that the word Arizona conjured up visions of Geronimo, Wyatt Earp, Billy the Kid and an implausibly stacked rancher's daughter, all galloping hell-bent for nowhere, like the jacket on a Zane Grey novel. Today millions of Americans have found out what Arizona is really like. In few places has so much happened so fast. In the lifetime of men and women who made their own laws and built Arizona into a state, cities with gleaming buildings and sprawling green lawns have grown where there were only sand, cacti and mesquite.

The desert itself—once a wasteland where only the tough or lucky could survive—is now a winter playground, occupied by travelers from October to May. Those who can afford it keep coming back. Thousands of others, fed up with snow, furnaces and virus cures that won't work, find or create a job and settle down to stay. (This isn't always easy. Typical of resort areas, prices aren't low, salaries aren't high, and jobs are often hard to find. In other words, living is simple, but it isn't always simple to make a living.)

Arizona claims to have more sun—more mellow, pleasant sun— than any other place in the world. Somehow, the sun seems to set the hormones of the visitors vibrating. Quiet, mild-appearing men emerge in gaudy cowboy clothes which afford equal freedom to their shirttails and inhibitions. Many women, following the same pattern, take on the appearance of Calamity Jane as processed by Elizabeth Arden; others, scorning Western styles, become antiseptically tweedy, as though they expected a fashion photographer to pop out of the mesquite and snap them with their favorite water spaniel.

A Phoenix newspaper columnist named Bert Fireman told me: "There are more cowboy clothes worn in Arizona now than during the peak of the cowboy days. In the old days when a cowboy came to town, he usually dressed in a blue serge suit from Sears Roebuck." It isn't easy, except for the experts, to distinguish the visitors from the genuine Westerners. Not all cowboys, alas, are bowlegged, or squint their eyes like William S. Hart.

When Arizonans talk about their climate—which, understandably, is a prime conversation piece—it is best to inquire which climate, because Arizona has a sumptuous variety. In midwinter, you can play golf in a T-shirt in the afternoon, but you'll need a jacket once the sun sets behind the mountains. There isn't much twilight in Arizona, just a soft blue sky overhead, then a sunset so incredible it appears painted by a daft surrealist. You can swim in Phoenix and a little more than an hour later, traveling by airplane, you can ski at Flagstaff. One day at the Grand Canyon, during a driving snow storm, I inquired about the weather at Phoenix and Tucson.

"Sun's out," I was told. "Temperature about 70." Further, while Phoenix and Tucson are sweltering during the summer, the people in the mountainous northern part of the state are likely to be sleeping under blankets. As an illustration, a ski meet is held at Flagstaff every Fourth of July.

To understand Arizona's climate, you need to know that this is a land of distance and geographical contrast. Arizona is spread over 113,956 square miles, which means, according to those statisticians who get excited about such things, that Arizona is as big as Illinois and Wisconsin put together, with room enough left over to graze a few hundred head of broad-beamed Hereford cattle. Arizona is far from flat; it has plenty of mountains, many of them in the midst of the desert. Nor does the desert itself fit the popular misconception of a bleak and tortured expanse of yellow-white sand, lifeless except for rattlesnakes, Gila monsters and itchy old prospectors willing to share the last swig out of their canteens with their faithful burros. (In Arizona, I saw only one prospector; he was methodically kicking his burro in the hindquarters in an effort to make the animal move.) Actually, the desert is full of life, both plant and animal; the year around there are cacti and green shrubbery, and in the spring when the flowers bloom it is a tapestry in Technicolor.

At first many visitors dislike the desert; intuitively, they feel it isn't to be trusted. But the desert has a way of creeping inside you. First thing you know, you're falling in love with the place, not wanting to live anywhere else. It happens to a lot of people, though few of them ever really get to know the desert. The desert is a place of moods, with the whims and guile of a range mustang. It is usually cozening, always contrary, and sometimes cruel.

In the mornings, the desert earth has the clean, fresh smell of herbs and shrubbery, and the wind makes a whispering noise like a random lullaby. During the full sun there is a hush over the land, the rocks glisten with fool's gold, and the mountains in the distance are silent reminders that this was once a brooding emptiness. At night, the desert comes into its own; from beyond the steel and stone of the cities it seems to move forward swiftly with the dusk. The towering pillars of saguaro cactus take on gnarled, primitive shapes, like crouching sentries left forever at their posts; the black silence breaks with the night cries of animals seeking food, and you know that the desert, for all its appearance of lulling peace, is a muted battleground where the struggle for survival goes on always.

A trip to the desert botanical garden outside Phoenix is rewarding for those interested in desert plant life. Most desert lore is based on whoppers grown respectable with the years. For instance, the purple sage celebrated in a book written by Zane Grey is gray; from a distance, it looks purple. The century plant blooms at intervals not greater than twenty-two years, then dies. The fluid in the barrel cactus, which reputedly has saved the lives of countless prospectors dying of thirst, isn't drinkable and if anyone is fool enough to try it, the fluid will coagulate in his stomach with agonizing results.

The bane of the desert is neither the summer heat nor the lack of rain, but the horde of jack rabbits which raid the gardens. Tomcats and gopher snakes are kept to kill the rabbits. However, a tomcat has to be unusually big and ornery to tackle a full-grown jack rabbit; the rabbit is likely to haul off, mule fashion, and kick the tomcat from here to there.

The gopher snakes hide behind plants and ambush the rabbits, in the style of miniature pythons, squeezing them to death.

Probably the desert has affected Arizona's character as a state; certainly, both are contradictory. Arizona is both frontier and metropolitan, ghost town and plush resort, cowboy and Indian, dowager and business big shot; it is a king-sized colorful Kansas with cactus and climate, and a fledgling Texas with less horn-tooting. The essential reason for these contradictions can be traced to the state's booming population. In 1920, Arizona had 334,162 people; in 1960 more than a million. This means the population more than tripled in forty years. It means also, inevitably, that Arizona's tempers, moods, whims and inclinations are changing almost as fast. The typical Arizonan—if there is one—is casual, not much given to guff or gabble, hard to hurry, harder to stampede; independent as a yearling bull in knee-high clover and just as fidgety if someone tries to shove him. (This independence applies to everything from politics to poker; he likes to play both by ear.) He's inclined to place a high premium on comfort—the climate isn't calculated to make a fellow want to get himself into a swivet—but, despite this he's willing to go along with the tourists and act picturesque, though there are times when he feels like a fool doing it. If he has lived in Arizona as long as five years, he considers himself something of an old-timer and feels qualified to cuss the summers authoritatively, though you would have to prod him with a blowtorch to get him to move anywhere else.

Contributing to the complexity of the Arizona character is the state's sizable Indian population. There are about 60,000 Indians in fifteen separate nations living on seventeen reservations. Like Indians in other states, many of them seem confused, apprehensive over the future, often resentful of the white man's careless way with promises and weary of his pretensions.

In Flagstaff, while talking with a young Navaho named Virgil Tiyo, I noticed an Indian and his wife, both blanketed, walking along the street with a portable radio, listening to Arthur Godfrey. A portly Eastern visitor, wearing boots, tight-fitting cowboy pants, purple shirt and big white hat, motioned for the Indians to halt, and took their picture. The visitor was laughing so hard he had trouble focusing the camera.

Tiyo turned to me, shaking his head. "I wish I had the money," he said, "to take the pictures of some of these people who consider us so comical. It would make an interesting album. At nights before I went to sleep I would get out the album and look at it. It might be that other Indians also would consider the pictures of these white men amusing. It might help us to sleep better."

A capsuled index to Arizona's character can be found in the city of Phoenix, which reflects much of the best in the state and probably a little of the worst. As befits the capital city of a state proud of its scenery, Phoenix is a lush green oasis rising dramatically from the treeless desert. Rimming the city on every side are gaunt mountains —Camelback, the Superstition, the Four Peaks—silently emphasizing that this was a barren nothingness before men created a farm empire by means of canals carved through the desert.

Some of these irrigation ditches follow the pattern established hundreds of years ago by Indians who built a primitive civilization, then vanished. According to legend, Phoenix was named by an early-day canal builder, Darrell Duppa—variously considered a scholar or stewbum, take your choice—who was impressed with the idea of a town rising on the ruins of a departed civilization.

Today Phoenix is in the heart of the Salt River Valley, an oval bowl twenty miles wide and forty miles long, where farmers raise lettuce, cotton and other crops the year around. The Salt River, in the Phoenix area, incidentally, has all the requisites of a river save one: no water. Except in unusual flood time, it's as dry as Carry Nation's cupboard.

The mountain snow water which rolls in the upper stretches of the Salt River is impounded by a series of dams forty to ninety miles away. This water, routed to the arid soil of the valley through canals, is the reason Phoenix has grown so rapidly.

Phoenix civic leaders predict a Phoenix population of a million by the year 2000, which illustrates how the buoyant desert air enables a man to look over the mesquite clumps to the mountaintops. "All you have to do," one said, "is to spit on the desert and something will grow. It isn't the old families, though, who have built this city. It's the newcomers. They see two things they like: climate and opportunity. If the old families had their way, this would still be a one-horse town."

In Phoenix the visitor soon learns to adjust himself to surprise. When I first walked into the high-ceilinged lobby of the Adams Hotel, a city landmark and rendezvous for cattlemen and politicians, I blinked and looked again. I had been conditioned to many types of wildlife in hotels, but this was the first time I ever had seen a bull in a hotel lobby, not a large bull, perhaps, by Arizona standards, but large enough to look moderately odd amidst the leather furnishings. It developed the bull was an ad for a livestock show.

From atop the Adams, where there is a swimming pool on the sun patio, or the fourteen-story Westward Ho, another excellent hotel, it is possible to see, stretching around the perimeter of the valley, the luxurious resorts and the lush private estates of such gentry as P. K. Wrigley and Fowler McCormick. Much of the capital that built these establishments comes from Midwestern and Eastern businessmen who came to Arizona to soak up the winter sunshine and decided to take partial root in the desert soil.

George Borg, a Midwestern industrialist, arrived in Phoenix in 1944 to negotiate for a research plant. He reserved rooms at Jokake Inn for four days. The deal failed to materialize but four months later Borg was still there. To his business associates who pressed him to return home, he wired, "If you want to see me, you'll have to come here." For a while, he reserved accommodations for the visiting executives at a guest ranch. Two years later he built Casa Blanca, one of the outstanding resorts of the countryside.

There are accommodations in and around Phoenix for every kind of visitor, from pleasant quarters in a motel, to the gold-plated resorts. The more noteworthy of these resorts include the Arizona Biltmore, one of the truly magnificent resort hotels of the country, the Castle Hot Springs Hotel, the San Marcos, El Chorro, the Wigwam, the Arizona Ambassador, the Arizona Manor, Camelback Inn, Jokake Inn, Paradise Inn, the Royal Palms and the Casa Blanca at Scottsdale.

Scottsdale is a little community which calls itself the West's most Western town and prides itself on being picturesque. With its store fronts of knotty pine, peeled pine porticoes and hitching rails, Scottsdale resembles a Western movie set in which the director decided to replace horses with station wagons. The town is the post-office address of many artists, writers and craftsmen.

Wickenburg, fifty miles northwest of Phoenix, is the capital of the dude-ranch country, proclaiming that it has every kind of ranch for every kind of dude. One of the best-known is the Remuda, started in 1925 by Jack Burden and Bob White, a couple of young fellows from the East. Burden and White were in Wickenburg on a week end discussing the idea of starting a dude ranch when a young woman named Sophie Fletcher asked them to recommend a place where she and a party of friends could relax and ride horses. They told her they knew the exact place, signed up the party, rented a ranch and horses the same afternoon and called their place the Remuda. Today the Remuda is operated by Mrs. Sophie Burden, who married her host, now dead, shortly thereafter.

"There's an extra man here. Is there an extra woman in the house?" A woman stepped into the group of square dancers. The caller clapped his hands to the boisterous rhythm of the phonograph music and set the dancers capering with:

> *Duck for an oyster, dive for a clam.*
> *Dive for your home in the happy land.*

The scene was a square dance at the Triple H resort ranch, eight miles east of Tucson. The caller was a rangy man in his shirt sleeves, an oversize Western tie loose at his neck. The dancers spun about the ranch-house floor, the people on the side lines tapped their feet in time with the music and the caller jigged a little as he cried out his commands:

> *When you meet your partner, what do you do?*
> *You swing your partner and she swings you.*

Square dances are common across the country, and this one was nothing unusual except for one thing: the caller was United States Supreme Court Justice William O. Douglas. If, by chance, you had last seen the Justice in his black robes grouped austerely with his colleagues in the marble Supreme Court building in Washington, the effect was—well, it was a little startling.

The people at the dance took it casually; Justice Douglas, it seems, comes to Arizona whenever he can and, if possible, attends a square dance. Earlier in the evening, when he had first entered the ranch house, several of the dancers greeted him as an old acquaintance.

"Doggone it, Judge," a man said, "for years I've been wanting to see you get off the bench and back into politics, but you've been ducking it."

The judge chuckled. "I'm still ducking," he said.

"Do you think, Judge," a woman inquired, "that you'll fall off a horse this trip?"

"I guess a man has to do a thing only once," Douglas said, "and he gets a reputation for it."

Later, leaving while the dance was still going on, I saw the swirling figures of the dancers outlined against the window and heard a man's voice—a little hoarse now—shouting:

I got a gal at the head of the holler.
She won't lead and I won't foller.

"That Judge Douglas," said an elderly man, standing in the doorway with his wife, "he's a pistol."

Matter of fact, it takes more than a Supreme Court Justice calling a square dance to surprise Tucson. For a sprightly city still suffering from growing pains, Tucson is curiously reminiscent of a wise old man who has seen too much to get into a dither about anything. Few cities combine so much of the old and new. Tucson has been under the flags of three countries: Spain, Mexico, America. During the Civil War, the town changed hands twice, both times without a battle. In 1861, the Union garrison abandoned the settlement and six months later the Confederates moved in. Later the Confederates retreated before the California volunteers, and on May 20, 1862, Tucson became Union territory again. In the old days it was a walled garrison town defending itself against raiding Apaches. In those days it was as tough a town as could be found in the West.

An early-day historian summarized the situation thus: "If the world were searched over I suppose there could not be found so degraded a set of villains as then formed the principal society of Tucson."

Today it is one of the fastest-growing, most vital and most colorful cities to be found anywhere. It isn't preciously Western, mind you, but naturally colorful. A street scene on a typical day is likely to include ranchers, cowboys, Indians from the nearby Papago Reservation, Mexicans, artists, writers, sculptors, soldiers from the Davis-Monthan Air Force Base, Eastern dudes, convalescents fleeing Eastern winters, university professors and students, and perhaps a professor with Geiger counter and burro, though the professor is likely to have sold his burro and bought a Jeep by this time.

A lot of visitors coming into Arizona by train stop first at Tucson, 121 miles southeast of Phoenix, and having stopped there, see no use in going farther. What, they ask, can be better than this? Tucson, like Phoenix, is a winter resort that lives up to the name: sunshine during eighty-four out of every hundred daylight hours during the year, an average humidity of 34 per cent and an altitude of 2400 feet. This adds up to a climate that is warm, sunny and dry.

In the past two decades Tucson has had a tremendous growth. Many of the newcomers have come because the climate is good for what ails them, whether it is rheumatism, asthma, arthritis or a plain dislike of cold weather.

The Tucson area receives an average of only 12.5 inches of rain a year and the city pumps its water out of deep wells which tap both the basic water table and the dry Santa Cruz River. This is causing a disturbing decline in the underground water level, but Tucson does not engage in public lamentation; it is too busy counting up its assets which include—in addition to its climate and the acquisition of new industry—copper, cattle, cotton and culture. Much of the culture is concentrated at the University of Arizona, which is located in the middle of the city on an attractive forty-acre tract (presented to the city in the 1890's by three public-spirited gamblers who evidently had a penchant for higher education).

The university represents a major victory over rival Phoenix. Many years ago, so the story goes, there were two pieces of political pie to be awarded, a state university and a state hospital. Phoenix, being the capital, had first choice and took the hospital, which appeared a more rewarding proposition than an infant college. Today the university has around 10,000 students and a good academic rating. Phoenix wryly wonders how it could have been so wrong.

Ultimately, though, Tucson's well-being rests on its climate. It has been only during recent years—since the organization of a promotional group known as the Sunshine Climate Club—that Tucson really has bragged about its advantages. Now thousands of persons are finding out every year that Tucson is not merely a place with a pleasant climate, but a place where they can live as relaxed, casual and carefree as they want, dependent only upon their ambitions and the state of their pocketbooks.

Like Phoenix, Tucson has tourist facilities designed to meet varying budgets—motels, ornate lodges, and hotels like the Santa Rita, the Pioneer and the Westerner. The elaborate resorts outside the city include El Conquistador, the Arizona Inn, Caravan Inn, El Dorado Lodge, Hacienda del Sol, Pepper Tree Inn, Sierra Vista Lodge and The Lodge on the Desert.

An illustration of what can happen to people who pull up stakes and move to Tucson is furnished by a young man named H. W. (Bill) Taylor and his wife, Susan. He originally lived in Detroit, where he owned an insurance brokerage business; she lived in Cincinnati. During the war they met while he was recovering from wounds suffered when a Jeep hit a mine, promptly fell in love and got married. Somehow, the brokerage business wasn't fun any more, so they sold out and headed for the West, hoping they would find a place they would like.

A couple of weeks later, they drove into Tucson, lounged in their convertible in the bright sunshine, breathed deeply of the clean desert air, looked at the distant mountains, wreathed in purple, and looked at each other.

"Honey," he said, "what do you think?"

"Uh-huh," she said.

They took the money from the sale of the brokerage firm and bought a 6o-acre tract with 6ooo trees bearing grapefruit, limes, lemons, oranges, dates and figs. The grove was beautiful, so was the house that went with it; there was, however, one trivial handicap. Neither knew anything about raising fruit.

The deal became effective on December 31, 1945. They spent New Year's eve in their new home, in the midst of the grove. The next morning Bill awakened first. "Susan," he said, "I'll pull up the blind so we can look out at all those oranges and grapefruit." He pulled up the blind. They looked and neither said anything. The impossible had happened—there was half an inch of snow on the ground.

Understandably, they didn't have it too good at first. It was mostly work and learning, with little money coming in. They experimented with new products. They canned dates, spiced dates, coated dates with brandy; they pickled figs, distilled an amber liquid called Passion Fruit Juice, candied citrus peel and made pecans into patties. Finally it began to pay off.

They were over the financial hump. They could relax at night, sit on their front lawn, watch the spread of stars overhead, and listen to the night noises of the desert—the deep hoot of the horned owl, the high-pitched bark of the fox, the howl of the coyote singing to the moon or perhaps to his missus.

The pretty girl, dressed in a bright sweater and slacks, stepped on the running board of her automobile, shielded the sun from her face with a road map and said, exasperated, "Will someone *please* tell me how to get to the Petrified Forest?"

A Forest Ranger, standing nearby, grinned. "Lady," he said, "you're smack-dab in it right now."

I had come up from Tucson and Phoenix across the Apache trail and through some of the most impressive scenery to be found anywhere. Now I was in the upper part of Arizona. The girl, on the running board, had expected—in common with many people—to find trees turned to stone and standing upright. Actually, the Petrified Forest is a 92,000-acre National Monument including five so-called forests of petrified logs.

It is doubtful, according to naturalists, that many of the trees even grew in this particular vicinity. They were probably swept into the area by flood waters and buried in the semitropical marshes which covered this land millions of years ago.

A few miles beyond the Petrified Forest is the Painted Desert, a 300-mile stretch of desert badlands tinted fantastic shades of orange, blue, red, yellow and brown by iron and other minerals in the soil.

Following Highway 66, to the west, I came to the Barringer Meteorite Crater, located between Winslow and Flagstaff, six miles off the main highway. The crater itself is a gaping hole in the mesa land; it is the story behind the crater which makes it fascinating.

About 50,000 years ago, a tremendous cluster of meteorites, believed to weigh between a million and ten million tons, plunged from outer space at a speed of many miles a second and gouged out a crater which today, after thousands of years of erosion, is nearly a mile in diameter and, measured from the tip of its elevated rim, 570 feet deep.

Within a few miles of the crater is the American Meteorite Museum, presided over when I was last there by a small, wiry man named Dr. Harvey H. Nininger who had spent more than twenty-five years studying and collecting meteorites. He had in his museum workshop more than 5000 stones and lumps of iron, which plunged from the sky and landed on the earth's surface. He shopped for meteorites like a housewife for a good loin of pork, paying a dollar a pound and up for any meteorite that struck his fancy. One of the meteorites, when found by Nininger, was being used as an anvil by a Mexican blacksmith. Another was being used as a weight on a sauerkraut barrel.

What happened when the cluster of meteorites smashed into what is now Arizona? "A scene of violence impossible to re-create," says Nininger. "A column of fire pierced the atmosphere. The earth quivered and rocked. Rock fragments fell in a mighty shower. The land throbbed again and again as though struck with a mighty hammer."

Flagstaff is a town with a genuine frontier flavor. It never had a boom, never had a bust, believes in comfortable living and is content with its lot. During the winter, the snow is likely to get a couple of feet deep, and for a long time the civic leaders seemed ashamed of it, what with Phoenix and Tucson frolicking in the sun. Then along came a man named Al Grasmoen and his wife, Ven, and demonstrated that the snow was really an asset. On a mountain fourteen miles north of Flagstaff, the Grasmoens opened a ski resort called the Snow Bowl. The first customers showed up wearing cowboy boots and hats. Today, on a week end, the slopes are thronged by hundreds of skiers. The senior classes of high schools in southern Arizona sometimes are given a trip to the Snow Bowl as a graduation present; for many it is their first experience with snow.

A two hours' drive north from Flagstaff—and the road is open throughout the winter—is the Grand Canyon, one of the great sights of the world. People many times have tried to describe it or paint it and few have succeeded; it has too many moods, too many shifting colors. Upon first looking at this chasm, a mile deep and ten miles across, most people are awed, overtaken with what—for lack of a better expression—I'll call cosmic intimidation.

Most visitors arriving at the Canyon ask two questions: "What caused it?" and "When did it happen?" The answers to the questions are: The brawling Colorado River; over a period of millions of years.

The Canyon isn't easy to visualize. You look at this massive cleft in the earth stretching for miles on every side and the thread of river down below. (At close range, you can see this isn't a thread of river but a giant with tremendous power.) It's hard enough for your imagination to bridge 10,000 years or even 1000 years; as for bridging millions of years—well, let's say that Nature has been doing nip-ups on this planet a lot longer than man; it isn't reassuring to contemplate, but it could be that man is overmatched.

There are numerous stories, some of them true, about the first comments of visitors looking into the Canyon. There was the little boy who wrote in his diary, "Today I spit a mile"; the Vassar co-ed who cooed, "Gee, isn't it cute"; the movie director who observed, "O.K., we've seen it, let's get on to L.A."

A favorite story of the Rangers deals with the Englishman who came all the way from London to see the Canyon. While looking through the binoculars at the Yavapai observation point, he was interrupted again and again by a loud-mouthed man who was determined to share his enthusiasm for the Canyon not only with his wife but with the Englishman as well.

Finally, the man slapped his wife and the Englishman on the shoulders simultaneously and boomed:

"By golly, folks, it sure does beat hell, doesn't it?"

For the first time the Englishman removed his attention from the binoculars. "My word," he said, "you've been everywhere, haven't you?"

The Canyon, from top to bottom, is filled with animal and plant life. Deer walk along the highways, and if a car stops, they're likely to stick their heads through an open window to beg for food. There are mountain lions who prey on the deer. It has the smack of a tall story, but Rangers insist that a few years ago two elderly sisters from Philadelphia saw a mountain lion sitting alongside a canyon road, figured it was tame like the deer, got out of the car and offered the lion titbits. The lion, understandably startled, backed away. The sisters moved closer. The lion retreated again, and when the sisters approached for the third time, he bounded off into the timber. The sisters, curiously, weren't in much danger—a mountain lion, the Rangers say, won't attack a human unless it is wounded or suffering from rabies. (This story is not guaranteed to convince a mountain lion.)

In the Canyon there also are mules. Except in the worst weather, visitors ride mules down the Canyon walls, a sixteen-mile round trip. (The south rim of the Canyon is open the year around, with excellent accommodations at El Tovar Hotel.) The mules are especially trained for the Canyon trip. Kickers and buckers get special attention. Trainers hitch an automobile tire to the hind leg of a kicker; no matter how hard he kicks, the tire comes back and whacks him. If he is a bucker, the tire is attached to his saddle; when the mule bucks, the tire jounces around, slapping him just about everyplace a mule can be slapped. Unless he is a fool—and most mules are wise when their own comfort is involved—he gives up in disgust.

At the Canyon I met one of the world's most profound students of mule psychology. He was a stubby man with white whiskers and he bore the improbable name of Colonel Custer Yarberry. He was about eighty, give or take a few years, and since the age of ten he had been currying mules, coaxing mules, cussing mules. He had been a mule trainer and handler at the Canyon for more than thirty years. His views on mules were pointed. "The only gentle mule," he observed, "is the one whose ornery bones have been bleaching in the sun for a quarter of a century."

I left the Canyon remembering Yarberry's final counsel: "A mule is a good deal like a woman. You can be scratching her between the ears and she can be nuzzling you and the next thing you know she's likely to kick you clean over Gabriel's left shoulder."

Heading back toward southern Arizona, I passed through the domed, brilliantly colored rocks of Oak Cliff Canyon and stopped in the little town of Sedona, the home of Max Ernst, dean of American surrealist painters. With his wife, Dorothea Tanning, also an artist, Ernst moved in 1947 from Paris to Sedona, where he set about building his own house by hand. (He decorated the walls, incidentally, before he got around to roofing the living room.) When I asked why he had come to Sedona, he gestured toward the red cliffs towering above his home. "That's the reason," he said.

After the arrival of Ernst and his wife other artists moved in and the sleepy trading center of Sedona is showing signs of becoming an art colony. This influx of arty newcomers is looked upon with skepticism by some of the old-timers. I spoke with an old man named Bill Fredericks, who had lived in Arizona, and the Arizona territory, for more than sixty years, trapping wild horses, now and then doing a little prospecting. For thirty years he had lived in a cabin, deep in the Canyon country outside Sedona, alone except for his dogs, the jack rabbits and an occasional mountain lion.

The day I saw him he tugged at the one suspender holding up his droopy pants, spat carefully over the front stoop of his cabin and said: "I liked it better in the old days when a man could be left alone. Arizona is changing too fast—too many dudes and gadgets." The old man snorted grumpily and looked at the surrounding cliffs. "Time's finally come when this country ain't safe. A few years back I decided to take a trip; I was out on my horse, minding my own business, thinking hard the way a man can on horseback, when all of a sudden there was an awful screeching and yowling and the next thing I knew I woke up in a hospital with a broken leg and a nurse standing beside my bed.

"'What happened?' I asked her, and she peers at me like maybe I'm a mite touched and says, 'Man, you got hit by a train,' and sure enough I had."

He hitched a thumb in his suspender and sighed. "Yep, Arizona's changing so fast, old-timers like me can't keep up with her. Reckon the time's coming when I'll have to clear out of here. Just too blamed much traffic."

New Mexico

by OLIVER LA FARGE

Not so long ago a merchant in the town of Española, New Mexico—which lies some twenty-five miles north of Santa Fe at the junction of U. S. Routes 64, 84, and 285—requested an Eastern manufacturer for an estimate on a sizable order of his product. The manufacturer sent back an estimate in pesos, with instructions as to the type of international bank draft he would require. The Española man had a lot of fun answering that letter.

A New Mexican never ceases to be surprised to hear visitors—standing within sight of a Chevron filling station, a clearly labeled United States post office, and a Coke-advertising drugstore, with a movie theater right down the street—ask the tariff on a purchase they are contemplating "when we take it back to the States." Often the tourists are distinctly sorry to be disillusioned, and offer considerable resistance.

Nevertheless, New Mexico belongs to the United States family, species *Western*, subspecies *Southwestern;* it's un-American only in its thoroughly American insistence on being its own kind of place. If you ask a New Mexican what constitutes the Southwest, he will name New Mexico and Arizona; after hesitation, he may add the adjacent portions of Colorado, Utah and Nevada. California, Texas, and Oklahoma he rejects, for reasons which will appear later.

The state partakes of the nature of all its species. It is large, the fifth largest in the Union, 122,634 square miles—but we don't think of ourselves as being so big, it's just that so many of the other states are smaller. The population is increasing fairly rapidly, but by Eastern standards it remains sparse. Its lowest portion, in the southeast, dips below 3000 feet—which to a New Mexican is virtually sea level—is intolerably hot in summer, and achieves subtropical flora and fauna where there is sufficient moisture. In the north, its mountains climb high; two of its highest peaks, Truchas and Wheeler, reach above 13,000 feet. There we have ski runs, and at the highest levels you might encounter even white ptarmigan, if you are very lucky and your lungs hold out.

Between those extremes the variety is great. You can be camping up in the northern mountains, and in the morning break up your camp under blue spruce and fir, wrangling your horses out of the lush grass and the columbines in the meadow where you caught your breakfast trout. By noon you can take your break under cottonwoods in an irrigated section of orchards and corn and chili fields, and camp that night in desert where you are lucky, and distinctly relieved, when you find the water hole. You could, alternatively, stay in the mountains until the heavy winter snows close you in.

The state has flat, drab, repulsive, strangely fascinating desert by the mile, dramatic, colorful canyon country, and vast spaces of open, sparse, yet productive range land. It has little Spanish villages of adobe houses, as close-clustered as medieval towns around their miniature plazas and churches.

You can fish for trout in clear streams and mountain lakes, and you can camp by arroyos which, if you dig down a few feet under their dry sands, may or may not yield up that seep of water which will sustain life—and down which the roaring waters of a cloudburst that happened fifty miles away can come at sixty miles an hour in a wall ten feet high, with a haze of dust hovering over the rushing wall and whole trees revolving in its mass.

We have certain conventional expectations of beauty, in mountains, in combinations of green land and water, in gaily painted cliffs or bright desert, but the perceptive eye learns to see beauty in less obvious forms. Much of New Mexico's real estate seems barren and monotonous on first sight; with a little time, as with the sea, those who live with it before their eyes learn to follow the constantly shifting moods, the delicate and incessant changes of light from day to day and from hour to hour, which give that empty-seeming country a life of its own.

Like most Western states, to a usually beautiful landscape New Mexico adds qualities of spaciousness, grandeur and drama. It also achieves softness. Its mountains, very old, lying at the southern end of the chain of the Rockies, do not rise to the line of eternal snow; relatively few peaks reach above timber line. They are not jagged but worn round by aeons of time. One might say that, like so much in this new-old state, they are older and mellower than the mountains of its neighbors.

Most Western states have, and exploit, Indians. New Mexico, next to Arizona, has by far the largest proportion of full bloods and of Indians living a basically Indian life. The presence of this picturesque element is one of the reasons why it is a great tourist state, to the profit of the Indians and of the community as a whole.

The Indians can be listed among the state's natural resources. Others are oil, gas, potash, pumice, and a scattering of other metals and minerals, to the list of which vanadium is the latest addition. These assets, and the lumber of its forests, have made wealth here and there, but they are not enough to make New Mexico rich. It is a ranching state, with cattle predominant in the center, south and east, sheep more to the north and west. Although your self-respecting cowpuncher still hates a lamb, the old, deadly sheep-and-cattle wars are over; the choice of which to run on a given range is made according to the nature of the feed and the terrain.

The average visitor, who wonders how animals can live on its sparse grazing lands, finds it hard to believe that New Mexico is also agricultural. Where there is water, it is.

Where there is water—that's the point. So seldom is there water, never is there enough water. In the richest parts of the mountains rainfall reaches thirty inches a year, but along the Rio Grande Valley the *average* is ten inches, which means that one dry year means hardship, several dry years in succession mean privation and ruin for men, crops and beasts. Of those few inches, much falls in storms so violent, in such masses, that the ground cannot absorb it and it runs off in flash floods. The dryest, most desert country is seamed, scarred and excavated by the violence of floodwaters. These waters are caught in the main rivers, but bring with them tons of silt, raising the river beds, so that another paradox of this hard land is the loss of tons of water and miles of good land through the development of marshes.

The life of the state, of the crops, of the grass which feeds the cattle and sheep, depends upon the winter snows and the chancy advent of gentle rains, what the Indians call she-rains, in July. A good snowfall in the highlands means steady water in the little creeks, which means in turn a flow in the irrigation ditches all through the growing season. Then the ribbons of fertile land above the watercourses will be richly green, there will be corn, wheat, apples, apricots, and alfalfa, the horses will be sleek, and in the fall fat lambs and calves will go to market and the drying strings of chili will make masses of scarlet against the warm brown walls of the adobe farmhouses.

Water is life, and the theft of water may be punished, extralegally, as one would punish the taking of life—which is one of the reasons why men are meticulous about closing their water gates the moment their time for irrigation is up. The last fight I know of occurred in one of the mountain villages in the dark. Epifanio Tal, as we may call him (the case did not come to court, so I don't want to use real names), had the water from midnight till two, Amadeo Fulano got it at two. Their watches did not agree. Epifanio still had the water running on his place when Amadeo went to open his gate, so he came storming across the field with his lantern in his hand. Both men were irritable from lack of sleep. Finally, Amadeo reached to turn off his neighbor's water, and Epifanio poked him in the stomach with his hoe handle, knocking him down. Epifanio picked up a stone and threw it, knocking Amadeo out cold. No one was seriously hurt and, both men being devout members of the cult known as *Penitentes,* the Elder Brother who was head of that order in their village stepped in and got them to patch up their quarrel.

Men may take the law in their own hands; there is also a special body of law dealing with water. As English common law never embraced irrigation, this body is based upon the ancient water laws of Spain.

The importance of water is personified in the famous Rio Grande. Take a look at it; it is a poor-seeming body of water, often no more than a muddy trickle, sometimes only a dry river bed, hardly worthy, anyone would say, of its high-sounding name or its place in the American mind. This meager stream is the subject of interstate disputes, of hearings in Congress, the occupation of special boards and committees. It is the subject of compacts between states and of treaties between the United States and Mexico; the construction of a dam near its headwaters may be a subject of international concern. The prosperity or reversion to desert of thousands of miles of land in both republics, from Colorado to the Gulf of Mexico, depends upon the vagaries of this unpromising-looking stream, and upon man's use and abuse of it and its tributaries.

The volume of water that moves in it is, in fact, considerable, but at every point along its length most of the constant flow is drawn off into the ditches, which is why it, and many other New Mexico rivers, seem so pitifully inadequate. The water may be flowing miles from the river bed, used to the last drop, and even so there is never enough.

In an acute form, then, New Mexico has the Western characteristic of too little water, which is one of the standard Western gripes. Another is that it is economically a colony, a producer of raw materials, much of the profits from which, including a considerable part of the profits of the cattle industry, are siphoned off to the East and West Coasts. The ultimate development of the state is to an alarming degree dependent upon the decisions of people to whom it is not home, is not essential, but merely an investment to be held only so long as it yields a good return.

In all of these things I have been describing a typical Western state with a few local peculiarities; New Mexico differs from all of her forty-nine sisters in far more than those. We are, for instance, a state which has the East on both sides of it, and much of the West to the east of it. The presence of California on the other side, with only our close sister, Arizona, between, is what puts us in the position of having the East on both sides; for Californians, in outlook, speech, habits, and in their less effulgent forms of raiment, are definitely Easterners. They form one of the two largest bodies of our tourists, and on the whole they are intelligent, appreciative visitors, even though it must be admitted that they do drive like madmen.

As to a large part of the West being to the east of us, I have reference to the sovereign (and don't forget it) state of Texas, and what seems to be its colony, Oklahoma. Texas claims above all to be The West, yet a New Mexican thinks of a Texan as being from, if not of, the East, and a New Mexican, Indian or non-Indian, will automatically speak of members of such Oklahoma tribes as Kiowas, Cheyennes or Osages as "eastern Indians."

Texas bulks large in our consciousness. For years, being a claiming sort of state, it claimed half of New Mexico, clear to the Rio Grande. It once even launched an invasion to annex the area. Latterly, the Texans have gone in for more peaceful conquest. Towards the Mexican border, in the area of the big cattle ranches, a large portion of the population derives from our neighbor to the south, while the eastern part of New Mexico, where it marches with the Lone Star State, is known as "the Texas Strip," because of the Texan dominance.

New Mexicans look down upon their great neighbor. Why shouldn't they? If they looked levelly towards the east, all they would see is sky. Any New Mexican can, and if given the opportunity will, tell you that New Mexico could be bigger than Texas if she chose to spread herself thin and flat, as her neighbor does. Texans, who comprise the other principal group of our tourists, condescend right back at us with vigor and often with charm.

An amiable sort of running feud goes on between the people of the two states, keeping both on their toes. When a Texan told me one time that he was a *real* old-timer, and that he personally had dug out the bed of the Pecos River, the Lord gave it to me to answer that, while he was doing that, I was up in the Sangre de Cristos melting snow to run in his ditch.

This exchange left us both happy and led to an agreeable acquaintance.

The Texan settlers form one of the elements in the endless diversity that is New Mexico. If they give the tone to the east and south, the north and west are colored and dominated by the Spanish-Americans.

The ancestors of these Spanish-Americans settled this country before Virginia or the Bay Colony existed, and have lived here ever since. They have been citizens of the United States for over a century, fought in the Civil War and in every major war since; they are devotedly patriotic, and as a regular thing send more than their share of men into the nation's battles.

New Mexico is the one place where the question of the hyphen is approached logically, although the logic leads to a beautiful illogic. All Americans except Indians are considered hyphenated; we are divided into two groups, Spanish-Americans and Anglo-Americans, and, just as in Salt Lake City even Jews are Gentiles, so here all but the Spanish are Anglo-American regardless of national origins.

One of the leading "Anglos" of Santa Fe is Chinese. About fifty years ago the *New Mexican,* the Santa Fe paper, mentioned that "a Chinaman" had arrived in town to open a laundry. He did. He brought his family. From the laundry he graduated to a restaurant which became, and remains, the most popular simple eating place in town.

The waitresses, Anglos and Spanish, work under the supervision of his wife, whom they address as "mother." I remember when his son, who later served with distinction in the Army Air Force, won the soap-box derby. The reception he gave at the leading hotel in town after his daughter's marriage, and the housewarming when the family, extended by marriages and grandchildren, moved into the houses they now occupy, are considered as among the largest and most chic Santa Fe has ever known. For some years he was chairman of the local Restaurateurs' Association. In this town, there is nothing surprising in all this, to him or to anyone else.

The Spanish settlers and conquerors, bringing with them old Spanish ways and an ancient faith, came from distant Mexico over deserts fiercer than any ocean, to conquer and convert a yet more ancient land. The Pueblo Indians had been planting their corn for centuries, and for centuries evolving their elaborate religion, the public manifestations of which, the great summer dances, are one of America's finest spectacles. For at least 2000 years men had farmed the little valleys; the art of irrigation was old and well established. Two dry-country farming peoples met. The native ones were conquered, revolted and drove out the conquerors; the Spaniards came back. In the end Indian and Spaniard settled down together to a harmonious pattern of social and cultural exchange and no little intermarriage, a pattern into which the Anglo-American newcomers are steadily merging.

These Spaniards were cut off from the world. A trip to the vice-regal capital in Mexico was an adventure not to be lightly undertaken until, in recent days, the railroad and later the motor roads spanned the wastes, and the wild tribes that haunted them had been broken. North and east the mountains and prairies offered little attraction to the settler, and they, too, were thronged by wild tribes; to the west, the worst deserts of all cut the colony off from the West Coast. In speech and in customs the people kept and still keep much of 17th and 18th Century Spain, although in the last generation the language has decayed rapidly, soaking up English words and losing structure.

In the rural districts, old ways hold fast. The *velorio*, the lamenting wake for the dead, the wedding receptions with their great formality, vast eating and drinking, their dances led off by the bride in her wedding dress—and occasionally their fights—go on as they did 300 years ago. The people are still, by preference, wine drinkers, sweetish, heady wines, after the manner of Spain, and *cabrito*, a three-month-old kid roasted whole, remains, deservedly, a prime delicacy.

In some of the villages the *Penitentes*, a lay order with special ritual centering around Good Friday and Easter, maintain their practices. Because of excessive flagellation their rites were banned by the Catholic Church for a time, but the people refused to give them up. The present archbishop has wisely brought them under control by removing the ban and bringing the organization under the Church and into the open. Even in Santa Fe the religious processions are still maintained and the *alabados*, the traditional hymns, many of which were brought from Spain, are still sung.

West, north, and south of the Pueblo country, which was and is the main farming area, lay the various tribes of Apaches, the warriors, the raiders. They still hold to sections of their ancient range. On the Colorado border are the Jicarilla Apaches; in the southeastern part of the state, the Mescalero Apaches occupy the green, rich mountains which were once their ancient stronghold. In the northwestern corner some of the greatest of all the Apache tribes, the Navajos, are to this day trying to make a success of sheep ranching in a desert.

The Mescaleros and Jicarillas live in good grazing and timber country. They are prosperous, hard-working, and progressive. From the tourist point of view they don't offer much, as their old culture is almost gone. Some of the older Jicarilla men still wear their hair in braids, and a fair number of the women keep to the full-skirted, calico costume which became established among many tribes in the latter part of the last century. The Mescaleros offer less to the eye than that, but on the Fourth of July, if you can take hours of driving through very hot, bleak range country and rugged camping conditions, it is worth going to their celebration to see their renowned Crown Dance, a masked dance unlike any other, portraying the mountain spirits. The Jicarillas also have a masked ceremony, in which I have been allowed to participate in a very small way, but one should not try to attend uninvited.

Most people who know Apaches like them enormously and are enthusiastic about them. They are good friends and delightful companions. In the Southwest, at least, it is the common observation that Indians have a delightful sense of humor, and of all the tribes, the Apaches have the keenest and quickest. People sometimes ask me for examples, and then I am stumped, for it is not a humor of the formal joke; the things that made me laugh so hard became merely flat when repeated out of context. It is a sense of the ridiculous, kidding which is never malicious, a constant, pleased awareness that the funny side of life is also always with us and a readiness to indicate it by a quick, unexpected phrase. A form of it is in the roar of laughter that shook the medicine lodge when old Maipi, showing the young men how a certain song should be sung, lifted his voice so well that his upper plate jumped out and fell on the drum—and above all in the fact that he laughed as hard as the rest. It is in a thousand lesser, less obvious moments.

Apaches, including Navajos, are something else again when they are angry; you want to stay away from them. I remember when an Apache leader decided to put me off the reservation. Things were really sticky for a while, but fortunately there was a division of opinion, and he dropped the project. Later we became friends. When the women get angry, you want to get clear out of the country. I have seen Navajo women, in their velveteen blouses and their full, calico skirts and their jewelry, rising up one by one from where they sat behind their men in council and shouting at them to start fighting, and have watched the men's uneasy response and mounting tension. It was then that I understood why Navajo women are given such names as War Encircling, War in the Mountains, Followed to War, and Dancing for War. It was a profound relief when some influential leaders talked them down. I wasn't involved in what had made them so angry, but once they got going, I thought they might include me on principle.

By comparison with the tribes now known as Apache, the Navajos live in deep poverty on their ash heap of a desert, ever vainly presenting to the Great White Stepfather a dreadful bill of broken promises. Nonetheless, they have kept their old spirit and many of their old ways. Their big ceremonies are dances lasting all night for several nights, and most of them are held late in the fall. Attending them means driving over bad roads, rough camping, and sitting in the cold night on hard, cold ground. For those hardy enough, it is worth while. The dances, masked or unmasked, seen by the light of bonfires, the gatherings in themselves, the strange, hypnotic music— all these add up to a genuinely moving experience.

It is the Pueblos whom the tourists visit most, and with reason. Their villages are on or within easy reach of the paved highways; most conveniently, many of their dances occur annually on fixed dates. The villages, of warm, earth-colored adobe houses, are charming in themselves. The people are friendly by habit, and from long experience know how to deal with strangers. Almost all of them engage in some form of craftwork. The variety of their dances is bewildering. It is almost impossible to judge between them, but the most famous, and among the finest, are the Corn Dances of San Felipe, Cochití and Santo Domingo, in May, July and August. These are performed by lines of fifty or more men and women accompanied by drums and a powerful chorus.

When you attend one, you will be at first a trifle bewildered by the sheer mass, then fascinated by the costumes, the color, the music. Shortly after this you will find the performance monotonous, the sun hot, the ground hard, the dust annoying. This is the point at which many people leave. If you stay on, *and if you keep quiet,* the rhythms of drum, song and dance, the endlessly changing formations of the lines of dancers, the very heat and dust, unite and take hold. You will realize slowly that what looked simple is complex, disciplined, sophisticated. You will forget yourself. The chances are then that you will go away with that same odd, empty, satisfied feeling which comes after absorbing any great work of art.

Simply to complete the list of the assorted elements that make up the population of the state, we should note that its northwest corner touches the southeast corner of Utah. That point is inside the Navajo Reservation, but the Mormons have filtered down into the San Juan River Valley just to the east of it. To New Mexicans, Mormons are a variety of Anglo, however they may classify themselves. Their settlements are characterized by the planting of poplars and roses; the people by industry, temperance, hospitality, and great kindness towards strangers.

The most famous and most visited part of New Mexico is the central valley, the strip along the Rio Grande from Albuquerque north past Santa Fe to Taos, guarded on the south by the Sandia, on the west by the Jémez, on the east by the Sangre de Cristo Mountains. It is an area about a hundred and fifty miles long by about sixty miles wide, possessing a special magic. Here for thousands of years people have been drawn and have stayed in the slow, sunlit peace between the mountains.

Here, as many thousands of years ago as your imagination desires, men hunted, and here they acquired the art of planting corn, squash, and beans. Other men, other tribes, joined them in one millennium or another, from the north, the east, and the west, to form the chain of settled, semicivilized villages and towns, some of them almost cities, which the Spaniards found here.

In this same area the Spaniards settled and stayed. They, too, like the Pueblos, were isolated from the ever-changing, corroding, restless currents of time. The Mountain Men, dropping down into Taos for a spree, married, built houses, became one with the country. Currents from the main stream of the Anglos' westward migration flowed in between the mountains. The valley absorbed them all.

Latterly, in the last thirty years or so, there has occurred a curious, mixed immigration of artists and anthropologists who, like so many others, came to exploit and stayed to participate. Their influence has been profound. Art and science formed a firm alliance and the two made the earlier comers aware of the riches that lay in these many times and cultures, not superimposed, but existing and interchanging side by side. It was they who stopped and reversed the existing trend to replace the native adobe architecture as rapidly as possible with commonplace brick and frame houses.

The old Mountain Men dressed in a mixture of Indian and Spanish styles because that was the kind of clothing available. The artists and their surrounding group are likely to turn up in Indian moccasins, sombreros from Old Mexico, and any combination one can imagine in between. Out of an original, Western informality they have developed an atmosphere in which everyone, of either sex, dresses as he pleases, while adaptations of Spanish and Navajo women's dresses have ceased to be merely local and have spread throughout the country.

They are a picturesque group, these latecomers, ranging from what, since Dorothy Thomas' story on the subject, is known as the "fainting robin," the starveling poet without paper or typewriter, to the—shall I call her "expatriate"?—of wealth who may become the fainting robin's patron. They include artists and scientists of national and international standing. They will join a party, go to Mexico, or take off for the Navajo country at the drop of a sombrero, are active in local politics, have fifth columns in most of the newspapers, and by and large are steady, respectable workers. The kick which they, and the Indians, get out of observing the appearance and antics of the tourists is no greater than the kick the tourists get, legitimately, out of them.

I remember, in particular, John Sloan. Since the 1920's he had been the dean of Santa Fe painters, an indestructible man, everyone thought, and a leader in every imaginable interest from renovating the annual fiesta, which had become a shabby affair, to winning the Indians their rights. The news of his death came as many of his associates, painters such as Randall Davey, Josef Bakos, and Will Shuster, were on their way to a musicale given by a woman who had been one of his good friends and patrons. The musicale went off all right, but around the drinks afterward there was a sort of silent wake, remembering the landmarks of his old, faded velveteen Navajo shirt and his silver concho belt, remembering the unconventional stunts he used to start, sometimes in that very house, and looking at his magnificent portrait of the owner. There will never be anyone else like him, but the young ones keep coming up; new movements, new art centers, new rebellions are organized annually. The art colony that stretches loosely from Albuquerque to Taos is made up of extreme individualists, but its strength is collective, and it is continuously self-renewing.

To this rich mélange the last war brought the strangest addition of all, the atomic complex. On the eastern slope of the Jémez Mountains, where the adolescents of Los Alamos Ranch School used to study their books and ride their ponies, the great center of Los Alamos was established. It has brought into the valley an increment of people, mostly young and energetic, of far higher than average intelligence, education, and artistic sensitivity.

Just outside Albuquerque are Kirtland Air Force Base and Sandia Army Base, both concerned with the new weapons. In these installations is to be found one of the highest concentrations of intellectual commissioned officers anywhere in our armed services; Army colonels and Navy commanders with Ph.D. degrees are commonplace there. Considerably farther south, in the arid, open-range cattle country, are the White Sands Proving Grounds, where they shoot off the big rockets.

It gives us a queer feeling to have these activities in New Mexico, and to have their nerve center nestled cozily in the soft grandeur of the Jémez, overlooking the heart of our timeless valley. One has a feeling of some sort of violation, yet that feeling is based upon a dream, for out of this valley, as I have said, the young men keep going to war. There has been no greater violation than that a whole regiment of New Mexico men, out of the Spanish-speaking hill villages, from the country of the drawling cowhands, from the deserts and mountains of the Indians, a whole regiment of them, should have been lost on Bataan.

All of these elements give the state its character and give it, also, its quality of being at once rawly new and richly old, the home of peaceful farmers and craftsmen when Europe was at the bottom of the Dark Ages . . . and one of the newest states, full of hope and vinegar.

It is unfortunate that an honest description cannot stop at this point. It should be enough that on a Sunday a Pueblo Indian, having spent the preceding week cultivating his red, blue, and yellow corn in his ancestral field, will put on his Indian clothes to sing in the chorus of a dance in which his daughter, who during the week works at Los Alamos, will take the part of the Buffalo Maiden, that during the performance Spanish-American neighbors will kneel in the bower at one side of the pueblo's plaza to sing *alabados* before the image of its patron saint, while artists, scientists (both anthropologists and nuclear physicists), tourists and plain businessmen watch the performance with appreciation and respect. It should be enough, but it is not.

As in old melodramas, the lovely maiden, the happy home, are threatened by villains, of which here there are two principal ones. The first of these is a dwindling land base. In arid country, unirrigable land is used generally for grazing, and if the grazing is not carefully controlled, the grasses are eaten up, what shoots appear are consumed before seed can form, and the grass dies away. Then the hard rains carry off the soil, until the fertility has literally been mined out of the ground. This is happening over altogether too much of New Mexico.

The second villain is race hatred. In a community such as New Mexico the opportunity to demonstrate a real melting pot is priceless, and there are sections where that demonstration is being made. There are also sections, large ones, where the reverse is true. This is particularly the case where the Texas influence is strong, but it is not confined to those areas. An Indian may or may not be Jim Crowed, according to where he happens to land, regardless of whether or not that particular town makes a big noise about its Indians for the tourist trade.

The Spanish-Americans are politically powerful and sophisticated; nonetheless they, too, encounter race hatred. In parts of the state they are truly equals, and Spanish-Anglo marriages are common; in others, notably in the south and east, they, too, encounter a frank Jim Crow system.

Neither of these villains has as yet actually obtained a mortgage on the old homestead or tied the heroine across the railroad track. They are still more threat than imminent danger; and powerful groups in the state are working to defeat them.

What is New Mexico, then? How sum it up? It is a vast, harsh, poverty-stricken, varied, and beautiful land, a breeder of artists and warriors. It is the home, by birth or by passionate adoption, of a wildly assorted population which has shown itself capable of achieving homogeneity without sacrificing its diversity. It is primitive, undeveloped, overused, new, raw, rich with tradition, old and mellow. It is a land full of the essence of peace, although its history is one of invasions and conflicts. It is itself, an entity, at times infuriating, at times utterly delightful to its lovers, a land that draws and holds men and women with ties that cannot be explained or submitted to reason.

Texas

by SEAN O'FAOLAIN

What does the average traveler expect of Texas? Not much in the way of joys and pleasures, if I may judge by the slightly astonished headline I once achieved in a Waco newspaper. It said: IRISHMAN HERE FOR PLEASURE! All I can say is that if tourists, native or foreign, do often visit Texas for any other reason than pleasure, it is very foolish of them.

Still, I find it hard to blame them. Texas, in one way and another, has had a poor press, chiefly along the lines of:

> *My grandfather lived in Texas,*
> *He couldn't write his name.*
> *He signed his checks with x's*
> *But they were worth a helluvalot just the same.*

And we all know that Texans boast and brag from dawn to dark. I prefer to call it the Texan Flourish. Every yarn about Texas has to be taller than the last. Only yesterday a friend assured me on his Bible Belt oath that he once bought a bottle of whisky in Laredo marked *Guaranteed Not More Than 6 Weeks Old.*

If the average stranger expects anything at all of Texas he expects little more than emptiness, fat cattle, lean men, flat-chested women, oil derricks as thickly sown as pine plantations, and oil millionaires with more money than taste. He probably comes into the state from the east, from Shreveport, along Route 80. He plans a quick look at Dallas, chiefly because his wife wants to see the Neiman-Marcus store, and then drives as rapidly as he can through Amarillo for an ungratefully rapid exit to Santa Fe. And we have to admit that as he races northwestward from Dallas and Fort Worth, over that level-to-barely-rolling treeless, birdless, sun-scorched, wind-torn, dusty land called the Panhandle, he is not likely to find in nature a great deal to satisfy his eye or mind, unless he happens to be a man who loves expansive spaces of earth and air, stars at eye level and endless processions of little cloudlets which are not worth a damn to farmers longing for rain; or unless he is interested in such earthy treasures as fat stock, or green belts of wheat or oil or natural gas. No, this is not an exciting route; and those long, level, empty roads lure one on and on—out of Texas altogether. I am afraid most of us who have gone this way cheer with relief at the sight of the first New Mexican mesa. I confess that this was the sum of my own experience the first time I came here many years ago.

It is not the best way (nor the right frame of mind) for an entry into Texas, or an exit out of it. I think we should come in from the extreme southeast, through the shadowy pines and rice fields behind the Gulf—come in, perhaps, across Town Bluff Lake, under the longleaf, the shortleaf and the loblolly pines, beside the Alabama-Coushatta Indian reservation and that weird region called the Big Thicket, where wild grape and vines have made an almost impassable jungle, and so on down into Houston through the Sam Houston National Forest. Or we could take Route 87 by the woods and salt-marsh grasses of the coastal prairies of Jefferson and Chambers counties. Or, and this may be the best entry of all, we could drive due south for 350 miles through Dallas, Waco, Austin and San Antonio, more or less following the old Shawnee cattle trail.

Then, at San Antone, as they call it (some say S'Antone), we might take a wide sweep through Corpus Christi on the Gulf, to see the great cattle ranches of the southern tip—the King Ranch is down here, a million acres of it. Then north and west up the Rio Grande, with its citrus orchards and green farmlands, and, higher up, its isolated, poorer, brush-covered Spanish-speaking regions like Zapata County, until the country begins to be cut by gorge and canyon and covered with mesquite, stunted oak, huisache, chaparral, and that pretty, silvery-gray shrub called cenizo, and scores more that I

cannot name; until at last the land grows quite wild and mountainous beyond Big Bend National Park; and from there we go on
to El Paso and out to the inevitable Santa Fe.

Here we become aware of one of the main frustrations of Texas—
its size. For if we have followed this last route we shall have left
out Houston, missed two thirds of the coast, ignored the whole east,
and the whole of the vast region northwest of the *balcones* or
balconies, as they call the great semicircular escarpment west of
Waco, Austin and San Antonio. Yet immediately behind the *balcones*
lies one of the most picturesque parts in the whole state, all of it
simply crawling with the ghosts of cowboy tradition and early
ranch history. I remember how poignantly this hill country came to
haunt Frank Dobie when he was teaching American history at
Cambridge University during the war. As he looked out over the
fens at evening, and watched the Lincolnshires being herded into
their stalls, he saw again the mirages, as it were, of tens of thousands of Longhorns striding out of the south, every spring, on their
way up the long, long trail to Kansas and Montana, their spurred
and jingling riders screwing up their already sun-buttoned eyes to
peer through the dusted glare at far horizons.

What *can* any traveler hope to do with a state of such ridiculously
dropsical proportions? The place is bigger than France. It is nearly
three times the size of Scotland, Wales and England put together.
It has the supreme impertinence to be eight times the size of Ireland.
Indeed, I wonder whether it isn't, after all, something of a frustra-
tion for Texans themselves to live cooped up inside 170,000,000 acres
of state; a prison composed of 254 counties, of which nobody can
ever hope to know intimately more than half a dozen? For vastness,
also, can be a prison.

A mayor of Dallas once said to me, "This isn't a state—it's an
empire," and the flourish of it was magnificently Texan; but I gathered that it must be very bothersome to feel that you are living in
an empire when you are actually living in one-fiftieth part of a
nation—and when, damn it, nothing would satisfy the nation but to
add as the forty-ninth state a chunk of land even bigger than Texas.
People sometimes say, irritably, that Texans are too big for their
boots; perhaps the truth is that they are? I swear that this alleged
Texan bragging—in so far as it has any real existence outside of joke
books—is nothing but a sob for the lost lone star, a psychological
compensation for lost national glory. As a member of a race which

is not incapable of an occasional flourish, I know the disease very
well.

Still, vastness is not without its virtues, such as widespread
variety, dramatic contrasts, strange contradictions. In climate, for
instance. Within thirty-six hours one could fly to Dallas from the
hot sun of Los Angeles to find that bitter sleet, snow and rain,
driving before a savage northwester, have shrouded the city in
whiteness, covered every twig with hoarfrost, bent every birch into
a grounded hoop; and then go on to find Waco wrapped in a low-
lying fog from the Gulf; then come down through drizzling rain
into a shivering Houston, and there, the next morning, have to fling
open the windows and switch on the Oriental *punkah* in the ceiling
to kill the exhausting heat crawling in from the sea at a humid 70°.
Brownsville, at the mouth of the Rio Grande, can be subtropical; El
Paso, dry as a bone; and I remember Lev Aronson, that excellent
first cellist of the Dallas Symphony, telling me that the orchestra
once had to play with their jackets off in Beaumont, east of Houston,
in the merry month of March. The ideal months to travel here are
April and May, and again in October and November.

Do Texans realize this vast variety of their state? I have a suspicion
that they do not. I recall that impressive little chat I had one dull
morning at Waco airport:

Me: (*With Old World pessimism*) That ceiling looks pretty low.
Think we'll take off on time?

He: (*With New World optimism*) Of course we'll take off on
time!

Me: You never know. Planes don't always.

He: Planes *always* take off on time from Waco. This is one of the
safest and surest airports in the state of Texas.

What impressed me about this brief snatch was that it never
occurred to this good citizen that before a plane can take off from
one part of Texas it has to come in from some other part. In fact
we had to wait an hour for our connection. It is a common jibe at
Texans that they do not recognize the rest of the Union; in my
observation Texans often don't recognize the rest of Texas. It is just
too big.

So big, indeed, that changes in its landscape seem to occur
insidiously. When, for instance, we drive west across the state we
hardly notice the flatness beginning to acquire a faint roll like a
swelling sea; that what was the green of the corn is now the green

of ricefields (Texas and Louisiana are the two greatest rice states in the United States); that the tall trees are now not pines but oaks; that the oaks grow more small and stunted as the tall gums and the myrtles fade behind. Bit by bit we become aware of mesquite or cactus. Then that pallid grass, so affectingly pensive in the evening light of summer, or when winter mists it lightly, blends into coffee-colored, into sun-browned, into hard, black knobbly land where the little trees look like tethered black ponies. There is less cotton and more cattle—from the university tower at Austin one can see cotton to the east and cattle to the west. There are fewer fans, goatees, Negroes in old straw hats, louvered doors, fewer hotels with marble floors, fewer cloves in the hams or lobsters on the menu, more high-heeled boots, more white hats, more dust, more rodeos.

West of San Antone we are in game country among accumulating hills, all cedar-darkened and laurel-sheened. The creeks grow dry. White stones glare. The sky grows more merciless as the land grows more arid. But now we can bear it better because we breathe more easily as the land rises. Whereas at Austin we were only 650 feet above sea level, we find at Amarillo that we are 3600 feet up. Guadalupe Peak, if we should go that way, soars 8000 feet above the waters of the Gulf. All these changes develop slowly in an 800-mile drive.

Nature here is endlessly inventive. Even if one has no special interest in farming or folklore, bird life or plant life, Texas instantaneously evokes one's curiosity about such things and keeps it on the alert: as when we discover, for example, that the political, social and even military history of Texas has grown with the very grass—the food of the bison on whose flesh the original nomad Comanches and Apaches lived—and that in the end the Indians were beaten out of their sheltering plains and hills not by rifles turned against them but against the wandering buffalo. It was with the decimation of the buffalo that the Indian menace began to wilt and old strong points like Fort Griffin became ghost towns, their work done. But empires fade and grass still grows. It went on nourishing those later ruminants of the prairies, the Longhorns of the great ranches.

Underground in Texas there is great wealth; underfoot there is also great wealth. The Agricultural and Mechanical College of Texas has estimated that the state's grasslands carry some 7,500,000 range cattle, 6,500,000 sheep and 2,500,000 goats.

I am a complete dilettante in plant lore, but in Texas I found myself fascinated by the subject, especially by the cacti. They are at their best across the Pecos River—its crescent encloses the rough country between Big Bend and El Paso. Some of the plants rise to six feet; some, the so-called globose type, spread three feet. All blossom tenderly—a rare sight for us Europeans—though some briefly and pathetically, dying, after so hard a life, so long a labor, within three short hours. I was delighted to lay eyes at last on the maguey. I could have drawn the maguey for you (and so could many inhabitants of northern Europe) at the age of seven: you find it all over our seaside parks—in green-painted cast iron! It is a sort of agave, something like the aloe, and of remarkable beauty. But, as for color, there must be several thousands of native flowers in this state whose dun soil, in its proper seasons, blossoms in acres upon acres of radiant hues. So much for the travelers who suppose Texas to be just one vast, blank, gray, dusty, monotonous state of uniformity.

The human surprises are just as varied. I recall my visit to Waco, where I had gone to look at Paul Baker's brilliant experimental theater (is there another like it in the United States, or even in Europe outside of Paris?). Within two hours on the campus I was informed that this daring venture is part of a Baptist-controlled university so conservative that it conferred an honorary degree on Harry Truman *in absentia* because he was known to take a drink occasionally; that no alcoholic drink could be bought openly in the town, other than watery beer; that to get hard liquor all one has to do is to drive a couple of miles into the next county; that any doctor could, in any case, prescribe a half dozen highballs for me if I really wanted them; that gambling is outlawed, as everywhere else in Texas, but that about twenty miles away first-class cockfights are held regularly, and I am sure that nobody imagines that nobody bets at cockfighting; that up to a little time ago, girl students on the University campus were not allowed to smoke or use make-up; and that I could buy the most sexy magazines at any drugstore. I may add that in this same Waco one may find 122 churches representing twenty-two different sects—a higher proportion between pastors and population than in Roman Catholic Ireland.

How can any place be so liberal in some things (most Baptist clergymen are against segregation) and so narrow-minded in others? I asked this question a score of times in Texas, and the nearest to a sensible answer came to me one night in talk with a wealthy oilman from San Patricio county—he was of Irish descent and a Roman Catholic. He said, "It all depends on the way you look at the world. In the Bible Belt the great idea is to prove to the good Lord by your strict behavior in this wicked world that you are worthy of enjoying the next. But this is God's good world. After all, He made it! Why can't we go ahead and enjoy the fruits of it? Within reason, of course. Another glass?" I am happy to say that distilled spirits are legal in Saint Patrick's county.

In Texas I find that it is wiser to measure matters by years rather than by miles. To give a simple instance, Fort Worth and Dallas are only thirty-two miles apart; each has its own meed of modernity, but essentially Dallas is much more modern, and far less traditional in the Texan sense, chiefly because it is a big mercantile and banking center, whereas Fort Worth is essentially the headquarters for the West Texas cattle industy. The one is as self-consciously culture-minded as the other is proudly cattle-minded—famous for the splendid Holsteins and Jerseys that have made Tarrant county one of the best dairy counties in Texas. If these two cities were not divided by many generations in their outlook, one would not find in Dallas one of the best symphonies west of the Mississippi; one of the best newspapers, the Dallas *News;* a lively theater; a fine periodical, *The Southwest Review;* first-rate bookshops; and, most surprising and welcome of all, a wonderful restaurant, La Vieille Varsovie, which truly ranks among the best in the United States; and every woman in America knows that one corner of Dallas, Neiman-Marcus's famous store, is forever Fifth Avenue.

The distance between Houston and San Antonio divides them by a bare two hundred miles; there is an age of difference between them in temperament. San Antonio *is* far older, of course—it was first visited by the Spanish in 1691—but it is also the nearest large city to the Mexican border, and hence more cosmopolitan, with a soothing Latin tempo. My own first impression of this charming city was that it was too good to be true; which meant that I feared I was being delighted by charms that, as they were the more familiar to me as a European, were thereby the less Texan—and after all I was in search of Texas. My lasting impression of San Antonio is a blend of envy and happy recollection; I leave it to Texans to decide how Texan they consider a city which offered me Italian grand opera, a symphony, affecting and sometimes lovely 18th-Century

Spanish missions; and another welcome restaurant, La Louisiane, allegedly French but more inclined, I thought, to serve Creole and Mexican food.

I still feel the general *ambiance* of San Antonio's picturesque Southern detail; see the rotting, green, sunshot, semitranslucent banana leaves, the light, delicate greenery trailing over old iron-work balconies, the tall palms, the large, cool, dim lobbies with marble floors like Italian houses, the magnolia, redbud, persimmon, *lluvia d' oro*. I respond again to their colors, their scent, their tropical suggestion. I feel the dark skins, hear the foreign words, taste the foreign food, remember the blend of Southern feeling and Northern conscience, as evident in the Church festivals, as in the double feature I saw at a neighborhood cinema in the Latin Quarter— *The Blood of Jesus* and *The Last of the Desperadoes*. I relax in the memory of the slow, sleepy, sun-drowsed tempo broken suddenly by noisy fiesta gaiety. I could go on and on, nostalgically. This is, to me, the most affecting town in Texas.

Drive on from there to Houston. What a leap in time! Houston is now the second-ranking port in the United States in point of movement of tonnage, rich in industries of every kind; busy, noisy, grinding away down by the ship channel and the turnabout like some dockside corner of Marseilles; inhabited by a great many people of wealth ("The residential part of Houston," says a folder, "now has over *One Thousand* millionaires"); and inhabited also by many people of taste. It possesses one of the most gracious residential suburbs in America; it has an excellent symphony; fine bookshops; a lavishly endowed Museum of Fine Arts; a passable restaurant or two; good clubs—the Petroleum, the Coronado, the Tejas.

Yet Houston is so very raw and recent, and in such a hurry, that while most of it has outrun its own past, much of it has not yet caught up with its own future. Its taxis are musty. Its hotels are un-admirable. Its press is away back. Its business center looks as if some superbillionaire had mail-ordered a dozen blocks of Manhattan C.O.D., to be dumped down among the old tin cans and slithering water rats of what once was Buffalo Bayou and now is the ship channel—where one sees masts and funnels teeming day and night. To say, then, that San Antonio and Houston are two hundred miles apart is to say nothing. They are two hundred years divided, at the very least.

Not, I hasten to say, that Houston is not an enormously exciting town with its own bizarre beauty. I remember vividly its brief streets of skyscrapers, so often crowned by clouds, ending as abruptly as if cut off by an ax. They gave me the sensation that this is a rapidly built and still unfinished city, and therefore a city gambling with time. I watched the evening skies from one of those high rooftops—the Gulf's gay sunset pink, ebbing faster and faster into a deeper blush and then into a sullen, sultry, stormy, dusky sea that suddenly vanishes completely, and one's eyes are drawn to the Manhattan lights of the city twinkling at one's feet. I remember those dramatic skies because they seemed to me to match this drama of the city's growth, and even of the growth of the whole state.

Houston is the natural dynamo and powerhouse of Texas. One cannot miss, immediately one arrives here, a sense of drive and competition that one gets nowhere else in the state. People move faster. You get a feeling that everybody is at least vicariously involved in the breakneck speed of the city's success, getting a kick by proxy out of the pervasive atmosphere of a gold-rush gamble.

I remember how entertained I was by the old taxi driver who acted as my native guide down to Galveston. He rolled out names to me as if they were dice, not men, assuming that every stranger must know all about the Cullens and the Joneses. I would say, "Do you mean Jesse Jones?" Or, "What was the history of this Cullen you are speaking about?" In his wonderful Texas drawl, like an expiring concertina with a hole in it, my driver would merely say, "Jesse Jones started working for eight bucks a month and made six hundred million"; or, "Cullen signed a check for fifty million for the University of Texas," just as if he were saying, "And then Aladdin got hold of an old magic lamp and——" Or he would point to some store, or factory and say, "Schlumberger's! That's a big outfit! What do they do? I dunno! But, hell, ain't it *big?*" And so on to more true fairy tales about this last get-rich-quick corner of America outside the uranium fields of Utah.

The things that gave me most pleasure here were to find that from as near as Eagle Lake, sixty-five miles away, you can bring into the streets of Houston quails, pheasants, pigeons, ducks; or to hear a youth of about twenty saying, as we looked at a dirty, built-around bit of bayou not three minutes from my hotel, "I used to swim here when I was a kid," as if he were an ancient-of-days remembering woodland ponds fifty miles out of town some seventy years ago; or, driving out past wonderful homes—pillared, snow-white, old Spanish, colonial style or *modernissimo*—set among mossed trees and well-watered lawns, hearing a friend driver saying, "So-and-so lives there; so-and-so lives here," just as in Beverly Hills one is shown the *palazzi* of movie stars. The whole place is as intimate as a country town crackling and sputtering with the latest gossip, though built to the proportions and with the amenities of a metropolis.

I recall the chat I had one evening about this with an elderly gentleman smoking a cigarillo in the lobby of my hotel; and especially his reply when I asked, "Austin, San Antone, Dallas, Houston—which would you live in if you had to choose?"

"Here—if I could make a couple of little changes."

"Such as?"

"Well, I'd put Houston where San Antone is, for the sake of the climate. I think I'd move the capital down from Austin. I'd like to see the Neiman-Marcus store transferred from Dallas, and there's a mighty good restaurant up there that I'd like to have near at hand. I'd install a good theater, a livelier newspaper, a few first-class hotels, a bigger airport, more public parks, a race track and a couple of drinking night clubs with gals. Otherwise Houston's perfect."

I still do not know if he meant it. Texas humor is as dry as most of Texas.

No stereotyped Texan, then. No monolithic Texas. Rather, a Texas full of variety, contradictions, idiosyncrasies. But we also find ourselves aware of change inside tradition. There are plenty of Texans who fear that their state is developing too fast, outrunning itself, losing touch more and more every year with its own traditional values. To those Texans, represented by long-memoried men like Bill Kittrell of Dallas or Dobie of Austin, the symbol of the old true Texan tradition is the remote cowboy and *vaquero* with his lonely, passionate, arrogant rejection of the ways of the busy world. The frontier, the ranches, the prairies, the dusty trails, the wide spaces under the lofty stars, the unending struggle between man and nature have here bred a stubborn individualism, an admiration for every kind of personal skill, self-reliance, independence and unconventionality—bred their own tempo, their own humor, their own heroism. They have bred a real culture in T. S. Eliot's definition of the word—i.e., a complete life mode; not something to be hung on the wall like a picture or an antique, but life as it is lived, fully and skillfully.

Within that old frontier way of life men could enjoy the luxury of being persons; they could be different; they did not have to be buttons out of a button mold. They were sometimes interesting, sometimes what we call colorful, sometimes gaudy, and on special occasions they could perform gestures splendid enough for an old saga. To return to this old matter of the Texan Flourish, I should like to recall my favorite instance. During the wartime landings in Sicily a rangy Texan stood in the prow of a landing craft watching his first European beach come nearer and nearer. As the boat grounded he lifted his fist and flung out on the beach a lump of earth he had brought with him all the way from America, shouting, "Come on, boys! That's a fistful of Texas!" It takes a hundred years of frontier tradition to produce that kind of heroic gesture.

The main enemy of the old ways is urbanization and industrialization. For over a generation now, the big ranches have been disintegrating. There must be many reasons for this, but one all-too-obvious reason is the old lure of the city's lights. Few of the famous big ranches of the northwest now remain intact. The Pitchfork, the Waggoner, and the 6666 are still there, but it is characteristic that in 1951 the Matador, originally founded in 1878, was sold by its Scottish owners and has since been broken up. Old Bob Thornton, as traditional a figure as one could hope to find, ranch-born in 1884, once said it all to me in two sentences: "The country around here has now lost twenty-five per cent of its population to the city"; and he groaned, almost in the same breath: "My boyhood is *fiction* to my boys!" He was saying, in effect, that the more American Texas becomes, the less Texan it remains.

But Texas isn't just an old clock crunching away on a log-cabin wall. It is a living organism. It has to grow and develop and adapt itself. Unhappily, adaptability is not one of the strong points of Texans. They look on innovations with a highly suspicious eye. A slight illustration of this appeared not long ago in the Dallas *News*, anent a meeting of the Confrérie des Chevaliers du Tastevin in Stan Slawik's Vieille Varsovie restaurant. The writer sadly recalled the time when such foreign whimsies as wine tasters and chevaliers and Caviar de Beluga would have frightened the lives out of the brave boys who rode the caboose to Kansas City with the cattle cars, for whom beef was beef and food just something that stuck to a man's ribs. It was all said in good fun, but there was, between the lines, a hint that Texas was going to hell hand over fist and that if people did not take care, cowboys would soon be starting every meal with

caviar and ending it with vintage port; together with a little suggestion, too, that all this wine-tasting stuff was an un-Texan, not to say
an un-American, activity.

A more serious illustration of Texan conservatism is the way in
which the liquor laws are handled. The state is dry or wet by local
option. Most of it, by area, is bone dry. But most of its population
lives in wet or anyway in damp areas. There is neither rhyme, reason,
system nor understanding about this wet-and-dry map of Texas.

The basic thing behind this peculiar behavior is, no doubt, the
tussle between the churches and liberal opinion. We are in the
Bible Belt down here. I have mentioned the town of Waco and its
high proportion between pastors and population. This can only mean
that practically all its people—including women, children, babies
and the infirm—go regularly to church and are well attended to by
churchmen between Sunday and Sunday. This is why, in this same
Waco, in one of those cafés where one may have a beer with food,
I noticed that my beer always came in the glass; and why, on looking around one night, I saw that every other client drinking beer
had his drink brought without the bottle. A trivial detail? It is a
tribute to the power of the dominant church in Texas. It means that
it pays economically as well as spiritually to be orthodox in Texas.
As a lawyer in Austin said to me, "One is easily corrupted into
conformity."

But surely the old frontier-pioneer values were not shaped in this
way? They were humane and humanist values, fashioned by men
and women giving simple, perhaps even crude, but always positive
answers to the positive challenges of the frontier way of life. No
church can replace positive responses by negative interdictions.
What bids fair to replace the old ways, in practice, is what one can
only call civic spirit. So, not too long ago, I noted that 152 churches
of the Baptist Association were organizing to work with the law-
enforcement agencies on the problem of juvenile delinquency. The
Baptist Church can be dynamic in other ways, too—creating a liberal
atmosphere of opinion on the Negro problem, or sending young
missioners off to places like Burma and Africa to work for God, or
organizing charities on a big scale, or, as we saw in Waco, founding
great educational institutions. All this strikes home as a more creative
approach to goodness than the old-fashioned hot-gospeling, drum-
beating, squeezebox-and-banjo-playing, nostrum-selling revivalist
campaigns (*From Dixieland to Canaan's Land*) that one still sees

marching across the state, offering noisily to "deliver all from sin, sickness, disease, poverty, doubt and fear." As Josephine Pinckney drily said—and we have to admit that she said it quite a while ago now—"Victorian ways have survived somewhat beyond their appointed time in the Bible Belt."

The future of Texas is with the larger cities. How strange and difficult and exciting their role is struck me forcibly one night in Dallas. I was at the symphony, for the *Magic Flute* overture, a *Scherzo* by Mendelssohn and Schubert's *Fifth Symphony*. It was a bitter night, wet, sleety, uncomfortable, so that the auditorium was half empty. The conductor, Walter Hendl, sensing that the atmosphere was more intimate than usual, dropped all formality and chatted with us from the podium after each item, reminiscing about his student days in Vienna and that city's close associations with Mozart and Mendelssohn. He was so informal that after the lively *Scherzo* he said: "Let's do it again for fun in double-quick time!"

It was a charming idea but as I relaxed, like everybody else, to enjoy the lovely, skittering music, I could not help thinking of the wind blowing across the Panhandle, down the cold, high, treeless plains, the drying creeks, the deep canyons, down over the rolling prairies. Every wire fence, I thought, would be netted with icicles in the morning, and if there were cattle out, their rumps would be to the wind and their fur blown rough. Certainly Mendelssohn never dreamed of so sophisticated a setting for his *Scherzo* as this auditorium. I wondered if there had been anything like it since Sarah Bernhardt played in *L'Aiglon* in a Texan tent for far-riding cowboys.

But when I came out from the symphony I found I could not buy me a hot toddy in the bars of proper Dallas, where the customer must provide his own liquor, and in the bar where I consoled myself with beer there was a young man blind drunk—from, I presumed, raw whisky. He was one of those lean young men, beautifully without hips, not a waste shred of flesh on his bones, in jeans, high-heeled boots, a cowboy hat on his poll—there was a rodeo at Fort Worth that week. For a boring while he kept appealing amorously to the girl behind the bar. Then—and I know it sounds too hackneyed to be true, but it is what happened—he began to part croon, part groan, in a rather fine tenor voice, the cowboy ballad that all the world knows, *Home on the Range:*

Where the graceful white swan
Goes gliding along
Like a maid in a heavenly dream. . . .

Outside, the rain went skittering against the windows, like the Mendelssohn *Scherzo*. The wind from the prairies blew it down the street.

"So?" I said to myself, as I got up and walked out, head down against the wind. "So *this* is Texas."

I might have had more sense. What snap judgment is ever worth its own breath? This tussle between past and present, tradition and innovation, the old and the new, is not confined to Texas. I know now that "this" is not Texas. But it is America. Has Texas at last joined the Union?

Oklahoma

by DEBS MYERS

Oklahoma is cattle and crops, oil and politics. It is the Pioneer Woman and a woman bandit named Belle Starr; prohibition and rambunctious individualism; Jacksonian democracy and Jim Crow; land rushes, rattlesnake roundups, cities born out of the red clay overnight, a writer named Marquis James, an artist named Acee Blue Eagle, a baseball pitcher named Carl Hubbell.

It is the sprawling plains, with flat heat over the flat land; it is also mountains, in the Kiamichi country, where at night the wind makes a grieving noise as though it were trying to say something that no one can understand. It is a farmer looking at the brassy sun, well-off now with money in the bank, but a little fearful always that the day will come again when his acres yield only bitterness and dust.

It is an illiterate Cherokee artist named Sequoyah who invented an Indian alphabet; Geronimo, proud and unconquered, in the stockade at Fort Sill; Jim Thorpe, warming up before a football game by standing on the 50-yard line and casually kicking goals at both ends of the field.

It is an Indian death march known as the Trail of Tears, and the biggest cowpath in history, the Chisholm Trail.

It is palomino horses prancing in a show ring, marcelled bulls selling for a fortune and, deep in the hills, razorback hogs not worth butchering.

It is Alfalfa Bill Murray, a governor with an iron whim, using the state militia as a police force and defying the legislature to impeach him: "Don't try to tell me what's in the state constitution—hell, I wrote it."

It is an oilman named Frank Phillips paying off the debt of every church in the city of Bartlesville; a town marshal named Oscar Morgan killing a bandit in a gun fight and declaring: "I'm alive because the good Lord was at my side, but for a minute we was both in an awful fix," or Will Rogers capsuling the truth in easy doses and packaging it with a rope.

Oklahoma is also a Choctaw Indian named Joe Oklahombi whom I met in the Kiamichi Mountains. He is known to his neighbors as a mild, agreeable man who likes to hunt and fish and be left alone. As far as anyone knows, he never let his temper get the best of him but once in his life; that was more than thirty years ago and it is still the talk of the countryside. It goes back to the time when he was an infantryman in France during World War I; he awakened one morning feeling mean-tempered and miserable, not like himself at all, and before the day was over he had captured 171 Germans and killed more than he wanted to count. For this he received a flock of medals, a couple of generals made a fuss over him, and he was promoted to private first class.

Now, well-padded and comfortable, Joe Oklahombi likes to sit with a fishing pole on the banks of Horsehead Creek outside his home at Wright City. When I asked him about the time he became a hero, he scratched his head and said he didn't know for sure what got into him. "I reckon for once in my life," he said, "I got the itch to be a bear. And, growing up in Oklahoma, a man learns fast that anytime he wants to be a bear, he better be a grizzly."

Oklahoma was born with a strain of grizzly; in the early days it knew drought, flood, tornadoes, guerrilla warfare and Indian rebellion. During the territorial days, before statehood, it was a stamping ground of gamblers and gunmen. Violence became so common that the nearest Federal judge, Isaac C. Parker, of Fort Smith, Arkansas —known as the "hanging judge"—installed a specially built gallows so that he could drop prisoners through the trap in simultaneous batches.

Today Oklahoma is prosperous, though not nearly so rich as it hopes to be, and respectable, though still a little seamy at the edges. Understandably, the people take pride in the state's colorful beginning, but they learned a long time ago that they can't live on legends. They are not much interested in how Grandpa and Uncle Clem shot it out with the Cheyennes; they prefer to talk about the new Turner Turnpike, a stretch of highway linking Oklahoma City and Tulsa; the new industry coming to the state; or the bull that a rancher named W. H. Delaney sold for $51,000.

Perhaps because Oklahoma underwent such a turbulent period of gestation and has taken such lusty strides in so short a time—statehood was not granted until 1907—it has been from the beginning a breeding ground of legends, misconceptions and exaggerations. One of these deals with the Indians; according to this stereotyped nonsense, most of them are rich, they drive about in hearses for pleasure cars and have console radios in their tepees. There are rich Indians (the Osages at one time were probably the wealthiest single group of people in the world), but, unhappily, most Indians aren't rich. There have been Indians who spent their money foolishly, which seems to be largely their own business, but I never have seen one driving a hearse or living in barbaric splendor in a radio-equipped tepee.

There are in Oklahoma approximately 110,000 persons of Indian descent, most of them half-bloods or over; this is almost one third of all the Indians in the United States. In most cases, of course, they're no different from any other Oklahomans. Many of them play important roles in state and civic affairs.

Another misconception deals with Oklahoma's climate, topography and people. There has been considerable writing to the effect that Oklahoma is flat, bleak and arid, tortured by heat, cold and its own inhibitions. In some of this, there is a little truth—not much. The summers usually are hot, the winters moderate. Spring comes early; autumn is a mellow season that starts in September and lasts through Christmas.

The topography includes almost everything: long stretches of prairie, hills, mountains, gulches, timbered valleys, game preserves, meandering streams and, surprisingly, almost half a million acres of land devoted to man-made lakes.

The people—well, they're contradictory, hard to peg. For years they voted dry, but bought bootleg whisky in prodigious amounts. They pride themselves on being defiantly independent—primed to

ARIZONA Desert saguaro blossoms open in tenuous glory amid the cactus of Organ Pipe National Monument.

TEXAS (*center spread*) A lone cowboy comes round one of the Monahans Sandhills. The shifting sands stretch for 100 miles in Texas and New Mexico.

LOUISIANA Oak Valley, at Vacherie, is a pink Doric Temple with 28 columns·matching in number the double row of 90-foot oaks which form the archway.

haul off and kick the moon clean over the Red River—but reflect in a hundred ways a wistful desire for outside approval.

At their worst, they are astringently narrow-minded, prejudiced and reactionary; at their best they are spontaneously generous, progressive in a horse-sense prairie way and willing to experiment for the future good—a throwback probably to their restless forebears who were always looking for a better route over the ridge.

One of the best ways to get an insight into Oklahoma is to travel in the southern section of the state, amidst the rolling pasture land known as Hereford Heaven. This, as you can guess, is grazing country for those broad-beamed, white-faced cattle called Herefords. (It is pronounced either "hur-ferd" or "her-i-ford.") One of the better-known ranches in Hereford Heaven is owned by a former Oklahoma governor named Roy Turner. The ranch, near the town of Sulphur, sprawls over 10,000 acres of bluestem pasture grass, which by midspring is belly high to a Hereford bull. These cattle have it good; their barns are equipped with shower baths and fans, they are bathed once a week and curried, combed and curled. When Turner's most famous bull, "Old 81," was put to death in his rheumatic old age, he was buried on the ranch in a tile-lined vault with a concrete-and-stone marker at the head of his grave. Turner's sorrow was understandable; the bull had sired more than a million dollars' worth of sons and daughters.

Turner himself reflects a big slice of Oklahoma life. He has combined oil, ranching and politics into one career and made himself one of the dominant figures of the state. Like a lot of Oklahomans, he was born in Oklahoma and born poor. As a boy he worked in his father's livery stable in the little town of Kendrick. One day a stranger rented a rig and a team of horses and later, coming back from the ride, gave Turner a silver dollar for unhitching the horses.

Awed by this display of wealth, the boy asked his father if he knew the stranger's name. "Yep, young fellow trying to get ahead in the oil business," the elder Turner said, "name of Tom Slick." That was the last Roy Turner ever saw of Tom Slick—later to become one of the fabulous figures of the oil industry—but, then and there, amid the straw and red dirt of the livery stable, Turner decided to become an oilman.

Many years later, after working as a bookkeeper and salesman, he went into oil, branched into ranching as a sideline and ultimately ran for governor and was elected. The governorship of Oklahoma usually is a springboard to nowhere; in Oklahoma's short history two of its governors have been impeached and many of the others threatened with it. But Turner's record as governor was so impressive that President Truman offered him a Cabinet job as Secretary of Agriculture. Turner turned it down. He takes more pride in breeding livestock than in producing votes; his cattle have won a roomful of trophies and ribbons. There is a saying in Oklahoma that if Turner ever really put his mind to it he could breed a billy goat to a secondhand cultivator and come up with a mare that would win the Kentucky Derby.

With Turner and his general manager, Jim McClellan, I made a tour of the ranch. It wasn't hard to tell that Turner had got his start as an oilman. Discarded oil casing and oil pipe had been converted into stalls, and old storage tanks had been made into grain bins. The ranch represents an investment of $250,000 in land alone; including cattle, its value is said to be more than $1,000,000.

Turner and McClellan demonstrated for me how a bull is beautified before appearing in a show ring. First, the animal is soaped and lathered, his coat is combed and curried to bring out the natural curl, his tail is brushed to make it fluffy and his horns are scraped and polished. Then he is shoved into a wooden stand and strapped tightly while his hooves are filed and chiseled until they shine.

The bull represents a big investment and he couldn't be more coddled if he were a sultan, which, after all, is about what he is. It seems, however, that not even the experts can always tell about a bull. An animal that Turner once sold for $35,000 proved to be impotent and Turner refunded the money and took back the bull. Hormone shots were tried without success, and finally the bull was carved into steaks; reportedly fine steaks, too, which seems not unlikely at those prices.

We paused before a fence enclosing a bull named TP Zato Heir, the current pride of the Turner ranch. Turner specified the points that make this bull a champion: "short legs, deep body, which is uniformly well developed, with the top line and the bottom line of his body comparatively straight; a broad, placid face and a wide beam packed with solid meat." Without the horns he would have been reminiscent of one of the more intelligent-looking wrestlers you see on television. I asked McClellan how much the bull would bring if the ranch ever decided to sell him. "Maybe as much as a hundred thousand dollars," McClellan said. "How much on the butcher's block?" I asked. McClellan, pained by the thought, shrugged and said, "Not much—a few hundred dollars."

On the way back to the ranchhouse McClellan pointed to a cow with two calves grazing in the pasture. "She strutted in from the range a while back with a new calf, acting real proud," McClellan said. "But one of the boys got an idea she was up to something and followed her. Sure enough, she had hidden a twin calf in the tall grass and was sneaking back now and then to feed it." I asked why she did this. McClellan spat thoughtfully. "Just plain contrary," he said, "an Oklahoma cow."

From the Turner ranch I traveled south and east past Lake Murray, which is becoming a resort center of several states, and into Durant, at the edge of 93,000-acre Lake Texoma. So many artificial lakes have been established in such a few years in Oklahoma—where they used to say that even the frogs couldn't swim—it is little wonder that certain confusions have developed. As evidence of this, Bennett Story, editor of the Durant newspaper, told me of an incident which —well, make up your own mind. It seems that with the construction of the lake, gulls swarmed into the area for the first time. The countless crows, which had been making a lean living pestering farmers, watched the gulls swoop across the water, dive down and come up with fish; before long the crows were doing it too. It worked both ways, though: now the gulls follow behind the farmers as they plow their fields, battling with the crows for the worms.

From Durant I went deep into the southeastern part of the state to the town of Broken Bow, at the gateway to the Kiamichi Mountains. This is the country Will Rogers was talking about when he said: "There are old guys down there who have an old squirrel rifle laying up over the door on some deer horns and if they shoot at you and don't hit you in the eye—why, they call it a miss."

This is a rugged country of forested mountains, hidden meadows, and creeks flowing across rocky beds. The towns are small, built on lumbering, and the farm houses are mostly log cabins, surrounded by fences of hand-split palings. Lean cattle and razorback hogs run in the woods; farmers say there is only one way to tell whether a razorback hog is ready to butcher—hold him up by the ears, and if the body overbalances the snout, get out the knife. In the woods there are also squirrel, wild turkey and deer. I asked an old man who lives far back in the mountains if he shot many deer during season. "Hell, no," he said, "that's the only time I don't shoot 'em—too blamed many city fools around likely to kill you."

In Broken Bow I stayed at the Charles Wesley Hotel. Meals were served family style, with the guests sitting at long tables passing the food back and forth. Usually, there were two kinds of meats, four kinds of vegetables, cornbread, biscuits, plain bread, stacks of fresh butter, pickles, preserves, jelly and dessert. Second and third helpings were not only permissible—you were urged to take them. The price for all this was as implausible as the variety of the food: 85¢ weekdays, a dollar on Sunday.

After dinner the guests sat in rocking chairs on the front porch, smoking and making small talk. There is a story of the Kiamichis you've heard; whether it ever happened is doubtful, but it's the lore of the countryside.

It concerns an eighteen-year-old mountain boy who showed exceptional promise as a pitcher. A big-league baseball scout found the boy sitting on a fence rail and together they went for a walk in the woods. Suddenly the boy reached down with his left hand, picked up a rock and knocked down a squirrel perched in a tree 150 feet away. "Hey," the scout said, "I thought you were right-handed." "What the heck, mister," the boy answered. "You want I should squash him?"

This mountain country is steeped in Indian tradition; the Choctaws long ago built a civilization here, with their own capital, their own courts, their own laws; a primitive wilderness dominion that finally yielded to the white man's inroads. It goes back more than a hundred years to the grim migration which the Indians called the Trail of Tears, when the Federal Government uprooted the Five Civilized Tribes—the Cherokees, Choctaws, Chickasaws, Creeks and Seminoles —from their homes in the Southeastern states and forced them into the then-unoccupied lands of Oklahoma. Thousands died on the way. These Indians had lived in close contact with the whites for many years; among the Indians were farmers, stockmen, teachers and plantation owners, who had large estates and Negro slaves. In Oklahoma, each tribe established its own government, with tight hold over the lands allotted it by Federal authorities.

Many Choctaws still live in the Kiamichi country. In the community of Eagletown, I talked with an old Indian named John Tonekai, who likes to lean against the buildings on the main street, puff reflectively at a pipe and piece together from memory and legend an account of the old days when Choctaw word was law.

He tells of days when eagles roosted in the Kiamichi forests; of hunts through the snow for wolves, bear and panthers; of tribal ceremonies around flaming campfires; of fiery denunciations of the white men delivered by Choctaw statesmen in the council house at Tuskahoma; of funeral rites in the wilderness where friends would meet on an appointed day, long after the person they mourned had been buried, and wail and feast for days.

"In those times there were no prisons," John Tonekai says. "When a man did something wrong and the judge fined him or sentenced him to be whipped or executed he would go home until the day the judge told him to appear for punishment. If he was to be whipped, he would take off his shirt, put his arms around a tree and hold tight while a Choctaw official used the lash.

"If the man was sentenced to death, he bared his chest, a mark was drawn over his heart and he sat on a blanket facing the executioner. A man on each side would hold the prisoner's arms apart, and the prisoner would look straight into the gun while the shot was fired."

John Tonekai shakes his head. "Finally, though," he says, "we had to build jails. That was after the white men came."

Through the years the Indians and their white neighbors in the Kiamichi country have learned to get along together. There is one rule which visitors learn quickly: the Indians, understandably, resent being patronized. A state forester named W. H. (Bill) Mitchell, who has lived and worked in the mountains for more than twenty-five years, found this out when he first came to the Kiamichis. He got lost one night while fighting a fire deep in the woods and couldn't find his way back to his car, which he had left by a railroad track. Finally he came to a cabin in a clearing and was met at the door by an Indian man about his own age.

Mitchell, by sign language and mimicry, punctuated with "ugh, find 'em car, railroad track, choo-choo," tried to make clear that he was lost. The Indian listened impassively, saying nothing. Mitchell, getting desperate, churned around the clearing, pumping his arms and legs like pistons, occasionally throwing back his head to make a noise like a train whistle. The Indian watched with interest for a few minutes, then spoke for the first time. "If you're looking for the railroad track, it's a mile to your left."

Mitchell gasped. "You speak English?"

"I should," the Indian said. "I went to Cornell for four years."

Oklahoma is a great deal more than cattle and ranches, Indians and mountains. It is also towns and cities; the cities are dominated, of course, by Oklahoma City and Tulsa. It seems curious they both came out of the same pod, pretty much the same environment, for they look different, act differently and, much of the time, think differently. Oklahoma City is as convivial, casual and bouncy as a wet Airedale. Tulsa is more sophisticated, a little reminiscent of an oil field roughneck turned businessman, mature now, with a touch of gray at the temples, and less inclined toward skylarking.

Tulsa is a city built by oil. Oil butters Tulsa's bread, buys its groceries, pays its rent and builds the glistening office buildings that give Tulsa a dramatic sky line. Few cities have come so far so fast. In 1905, it was a roistering frontier settlement known as Tulsey Town, with a population of about 5000 including the customary quota of scalawags. Hogs, cows and goats roamed the streets; there were no sidewalks, no sewers or street lights.

In 1906 came the break that shaped Tulsa's future. The Glenn Oil Pool was discovered near Tulsa—the greatest high-grade petroleum strike up to that time. Realizing that the pool ultimately would play out, and that production would move elsewhere, Tulsa underwent a quick face-lifting with the idea of selling itself to the oilmen as their permanent home.

"You can't constantly move your families across the country, following oil discoveries," Tulsa told the oilmen; "you need a base of operations. This is it." The oilmen liked the idea; before long Tulsa was calling itself the oil capital of the world and it has been living up to the title ever since.

Today Tulsa is the headquarters of more than 700 companies dealing in oil directly or indirectly, a business that supports close to seventy per cent of the city's population.

Perhaps all cities which grow fast and get rich fast acquire a variety of wealthy screwballs dedicated to finding new ways to squander their money. Tulsa has had a few odd characters, but most of its wealthy men have devoted a substantial chunk of their time and money to improving the town. Foremost among the men responsible for Tulsa's growth and affluence is a former mule-skinner named W. G. (Bill) Skelly, president of the Skelly Oil Company. The newspapers frequently refer to him as Mr. Tulsa.

He learned the fundamentals of the oil business in Pennsylvania, came to Tulsa in 1913, organized his own company six years later and is now one of the most respected figures in the industry. He owns a radio station, is president of the International Petroleum Exposition and put up the money for the construction of the football stadium at the University of Tulsa.

Skelly is a blunt, aggressive man, with a robust sense of humor, and it was inevitable that stories and legends would be built about him; curiously in his case, most of them seem to be true. The story most Tulsans appear to like best—perhaps because of a deep-rooted skepticism concerning eastern financiers—concerns a time years ago when Skelly applied to a New York banker for a loan. The banker engaged in a pompous analysis of economic conditions, winding up: "I am convinced the future of the oil business is bleak."

"Tell me," Skelly said, "on your way to work this morning did you see any evidence that horses had been grazing on Fifth Avenue?"

"No, of course not," said the banker, startled.

"O.K.," Skelly said, "anytime you see horses pasturing on Fifth Avenue—you'll know the oil industry has gone to hell. Not until then."

Skelly got the loan.

Tulsa's pride is not limited to its business achievements; it goes in big for culture. Most cities the size of Tulsa are lucky to have one art museum—often the result of years of civic scrounging. Tulsa has two, both of them excellent—the Philbrook Art Center and the Gilcrease Foundation. Each was handed to the city on a silver platter.

Philbrook, located in one of the city's plushiest residential sections, was formerly the home of an oilman named Waite Phillips and his wife. They turned Philbrook over to the city, first providing funds for remodeling and endowment.

The Gilcrease Foundation, located three miles north of the city, is unique among art galleries; it houses what is probably the world's finest collection of modern Indian paintings. In addition to many of the better works of contemporary Indian artists, the collection includes the art of forty-five Indian tribes, dating back to 300 A.D., along with 62,000 letters, books and manuscripts. One of the letters, written by General George Custer, ends: "You will next hear from me . . . not from the plains of Philippi . . . but from those of Dakota, the home of S.B." The initials referred to Sitting Bull, the Sioux chief who later was Custer's conqueror.

Thomas Gilcrease, who established the foundation, is of Indian heritage; his grandmother was a Creek and he grew up in Indian territory. He got rich—you guessed it—in oil. For forty years he has been hoarding books and pictures that deal with Indian life, many of which he picked up during his travels in France and Italy. Hundreds of the pictures were done by white artists like Charles M. Russell and Frederic Remington, who painted Indians as part of the scene in their studies of the American West, but the solid core of the gallery is built around the work of Indian artists, who painted their own tribal ceremonies and customs. In establishing the gallery, Gilcrease made his intentions clear: "I just want to present the facts about the conquest of the West and the way the Indian was treated —maybe that will help people to think about it and draw their own conclusions."

Tulsa's cultural assets are not confined to art; there is the Tulsa Little Theater, which has the longest continuous history of any similar movement in Oklahoma. It was started in 1922, was located at intervals in a tent, a storeroom and a beer parlor and is now a vital force in the community with a professional director and draws excellent crowds.

Incidentally, it was the Tulsa Little Theater which first recognized the talent of a young fellow named Lynn Riggs, who used to come to Tulsa from the nearby town of Claremore and watch rehearsals of his play *Big Lake*, dealing with the days of the Indian Territory. It was during this time that he received word of the Guggenheim Fellowship award sending him to France, where he wrote *Green Grow the Lilacs*. As you may recall, this was something of a success on Broadway—especially after they made it into a musical and changed the title to *Oklahoma!*

Also, lest it be forgot, Tulsa is the birthplace of no less an organization than the SPEBSQSA, which, in the event you want to know, is the Society for the Preservation and Encouragement of Barber Shop Quartet Singing in America. It must have been a popular idea, albeit an uproarious one, for the organization now has over 300 chapters in the United States and foreign countries. And—hang on gamely— the women of Tulsa have now formed a national organization of Sweet Adelines.

For all its suave and elegant appearance, with its towering, compact business district, its gleaming stores and handsome homes, Tulsa isn't much of a night-club town. The upper crust centers much of its social activity around the city's night clubs. Other Tulsans rely on their own initiative for entertainment, and much of it goes on in their own homes. As a result, most of the catnips are on the quiet side, the way a town like Tulsa wants it.

It is inevitable that a town so long dominated by a small group of rich men would be staid and conservative and Tulsa is both. As evidence of this, the building on the University of Tulsa campus that ordinarily would be called the Student Union Building is known as the Student Activities Building. It seems that some of the downtown oilmen who make contributions to the university get a little queasy at the mention of the word union.

Probably Tulsa, at its best, reflects most of the qualities Oklahoma has tried to acquire; Oklahoma City reflects the qualities, good and bad, which are instinctive with the state. Oklahoma City is restless, beset with mighty longings; it is contrary, a maverick that refuses to fit a pattern; it is typically Oklahoman in that if it likes something, it likes it. If it doesn't, duck!

Almost everyone knows by now that Oklahoma City has the only state capitol that sits on top of an oil field, with oil derricks towering over the domeless statehouse; that it was created overnight during a land rush; that during the years it has had a ringside seat at some of the most incredible political shenanigans ever foisted upon a community, with knives and guns flourished in the legislative halls. To a large part of Oklahoma it is known as "The City," and people from outlying areas travel back and forth in their cars, almost like metropolitan commuters.

An Oklahoma City product whom the people watch from afar with interest is Perle Skirvin Mesta, former United States minister to Luxembourg. She is considered twice as lucky as even the luckier Oklahomans; she inherited not one fortune but two—one from her father, William B. Skirvin, an oilman who built the Skirvin Hotel, and the other from her late husband, who was the president of a tool company in Pittsburgh. On a visit to Oklahoma City in 1951 Mrs. Mesta, one of the most prolific party-givers of our time, found the tables turned, she was given the full treatment with gifts, receptions and speeches.

Dan James, owner of the Skirvin Hotel and Skirvin Tower, put her in what used to be the family suite at the hotel and put a bronze nameplate on the door. "For sentiment's sake," he explained. The townspeople seemed to like her fine. An old man who once had been a crony of her father's summed her up this way: "She inherited a hell of a lot of money and she's kept it. That's the kind of diplomat we need—someone who knows how to keep from losing their shirt."

In every section of Oklahoma, from Oklahoma City and Tulsa to the smallest village, the oil companies have wielded a powerful influence on the people, their livelihood and progress. An example of this is the Phillips Petroleum Company of Bartlesville, founded by a one-time barber named Frank Phillips. He started with nothing much but an idea and upon his death in 1950 he had built a 660-million-dollar oil empire reaching into more than half of the states of the nation. It is a story that probably couldn't have happened anywhere but in Oklahoma and then only to a bet-the-sky character like Frank Phillips.

It is illustrative of Phillips' character that he never quit being proud of his days as a barber. A reporter once approached him in a hotel lobby and asked, apologetically: "Is it true, Mr. Phillips, that you used to be a barber?"

"You're damned right," said Phillips, "and if you can latch onto a pair of shears and come up to my room, I'll give you a better haircut than you got right now."

Phillips was born in Nebraska and became a barber in the town of Creston, Iowa; this decision to make a living as a barber was prompted by the fact that as a boy he had seen a barber wearing a pair of striped pants and wanted a pair like them. From a Methodist missionary he heard about oil fortunes being made in Oklahoma. He saved his money—including some commissions he had picked up as a spare-time salesman—talked his brother L.E. into going with him and went to Oklahoma, settling in Bartlesville. This was in 1904. "I think people are going to buy quite a passel of these gasoline buggies," Frank Phillips told his brother, "and they need gasoline to make 'em go. It may be this thing has a future."

Three months later the first Phillips well spouted oil on the grounds of what once had been an outlaw hideout on the banks of Caney Creek. Then they drilled three dry holes in a row. Their money was almost exhausted, and the brothers contemplated quitting. Instead they pinched pennies, moved the rig onto unproved ground, and struck a producer. During the next five years, when another dry hole wouldn't have caused undue worry, they struck eighty producers without a miss.

When the Phillips brothers learned that Bartlesville banks would lend money on horses, mules, farm lands and crops, but not on oil production, they started a bank of their own. One of their first customers was a quiet young man who wanted to borrow $500. Frank Phillips asked the young man his name.

"Henry Starr."

"What do you do?"

"I operate a little, here and there."

"Do you have any collateral?"

"Never heard of it."

Phillips advanced the young man the money. Later, he learned that Henry Starr was one of the most notorious bank robbers in the Southwest. Starr paid the note on the day it was due. This was during an era when an average of one bank robbery occurred each day in that part of the country. The Phillips bank was never robbed. There was a saying that the bandits held up other banks and put their money in the vaults of Frank Phillips.

Frank and L. E. Phillips then summoned a third brother, Waite—the same man who later gave the Philbrook Art Center to Tulsa—and the three decided to open a chain of banks. "Hell, men," said Frank Phillips, "we're not oilmen, we're bankers." They sold most of their properties. Then, as the First World War swept Europe, the price of oil rose to four dollars a barrel. Frank Phillips surveyed the situation. "Hell, men," he said to his brothers, "we're not bankers, we're oilmen."

With the remnants of their oil property they went back into the oil business and once more built up their holdings. They were producers of crude oil and had no intention of going into retail operations. "We're back in the oil business," Frank Phillips said, "but we'll never run a filling station."

Then the oil business underwent an important change. Refiners became big producers, the market became saturated and the Phillips Company couldn't go on as a producer only. Frank Phillips called his executive committee into session. "Gentlemen," he said, "I move that we build the damnedest string of filling stations anybody ever saw. I move further, if it's all right with you, that we make it unanimous." The committee agreed.

Today the Phillips Company sells its products at nearly 16,000 retail stations in twenty-eight states; it has pioneered in petroleum research and its activities reach into more than a dozen allied fields.

In Bartlesville the company even owns a luxurious apartment hotel.

The company emphasizes employee recreation, from bowling to basketball. The Phillips "66" basketball team has won so many championships it is likened to the Yankees.

Fourteen miles southwest of Bartlesville in the Osage Hills, Phillips built an elaborate ranch and museum which he called Woolaroc (a contraction of the words woods, lakes and rocks). At first the ranch was a personal plaything for Phillips; later he made it into one of the authentic show places of Oklahoma.

Phillips built dams and pumped water upstream. "I'm the only man in the world fool enough to pump water uphill, just so I can watch it flow back," he said. He stocked his ranch with an implausible variety of wild animals—llamas, yaks, gnus, buffalo, long-horned steers, red deer, peacock—just about every animal he thought anybody might want to see. Today, except for a few of the ornerier beasts, these animals graze wild in the preserve.

The museum emphasizes Southwestern history and includes one of the finest Western art collections in existence. There is also a frontier buckboard, the saddle of Buffalo Bill, guns, rugs, hides, knives, ancient Indian pottery and the single-engine airplane *Woolaroc I,* which Arthur Goebel, a Hollywood stunt flier, hired by Phillips to promote the sale of gasoline, flew to victory in a race to Honolulu in 1927.

Essentially, Oklahoma is a state of small cities and towns. One of these is Lawton, located in the picturesque Wichita Mountains at the edge of Fort Sill, one of the country's best-known Army posts. The annual Lawton Easter Pageant draws crowds estimated as high as 200,000. There is a story that an early-day marshal, Heck Thomas, once arrested a photographer named Lon Chaney for speeding—on horseback. The same Lon Chaney later turned out to be quite an actor. Other towns include Enid, increasingly important as a wheat-growing, processing and marketing center; Ponca City, which produced two of Oklahoma's most fabulous oil figures, Lew Wentz and E. W. Marland; Ardmore, which calls itself the capital of South Central Oklahoma; Muskogee, a quiet business town at the gateway to much of historic Indian Oklahoma; Okmulgee, former capital of the Creek Indian Nation and the home town of the late General Hugh (Iron Pants) Johnson; and Shawnee, which has suffered more than its share during the years from violent phenomena, such as flood and storm, but manages to remain one of the most prosperous of the smaller cities.

Oklahomans have a built-in genius for letting off steam, and this is particularly true of the town of Norman, home of the University of Oklahoma.

The University of Oklahoma isn't by any means exclusively an assembly line for producing muscular young men. For instance, its schools of geology and petroleum engineering are internationally known. In addition, the university has produced a number of artists and writers; and the University of Oklahoma Press, under the direction of Savoie Lottinville, a former Rhodes scholar, exerts a stimulating influence that extends beyond the state. George Lynn Cross, president, once jokingly observed that his was a university of which the football team could be proud.

Oklahoma's athletic and scholastic laurels aren't confined to the University of Oklahoma. The Agricultural and Mechanical College at Stillwater has not only had a powerful effect on the state's agricultural and livestock progress but has played an important role in cultural activities. Proudly, an A. and M. official showed me a copy of a Paris magazine of art criticism discussing the work of six American artists with reproductions of their paintings. Two of these six artists were from the A. and M. faculty, J. Jay McVicker and Dwight E. Stevens.

Probably the most important man in Oklahoma, year after year, isn't an oilman, a rancher, a politician or a big shot of any kind. It is the farmer, for farming—although oil pays almost half the state taxes —is still the backbone of Oklahoma's economy. Perhaps there never was nor could be a typical farmer, because farmers are individuals right to the bone marrow, but Ray Anderson, who, when I was there, lived near the town of Slapout, deep in Western Oklahoma, is a good example of what can happen to a man with a liking for a particular plot of ground.

During the dust storms of the early thirties, he saw his crops wither and creep back into the ground. He saw his horses die in the fields, their lungs clogged with dust, and he herded his cattle into a corner of the barnyard and shot them, one by one.

While a sizable chunk of the country was blowing away, and one third of the county's people were moving on, bound from nowhere to nowhere, he stayed on the land, managing somehow to feed his wife and family. For one thing, he didn't have any place to go—but, more than that, he liked the land. He always counted on next year.

In 1953, with the dust storms only a nagging memory, Anderson owned a 3900-acre farm worth a lot of money. He had cash in the bank. He had three trucks, a comfortable eight-room house, 300 head of Hereford cattle, 150 Hampshire hogs, a home freezer filled with beef, chickens, peas, roasting ears, peaches and strawberries. He was even thinking of buying an airplane.

Sometimes, in the evening, he liked to stand on his land, look out toward Kiowa Creek, listen to the lonely night sounds, and wonder about the crops still in the ground. "That's part of living on the prairies," he said, "you're always thinking of next year, never looking back; it's always next year's crop."

Arkansas

by CLYDE BRION DAVIS

To a good many Americans the state of Arkansas is merely an irregular rectangle on the United States map, just west of the Mississippi River, supported at the bottom by the state of Louisiana and
held down at the top by the state of Missouri; a sort of backwater
from the rushing stream of national traffic, quietly growing quaint
characters and more fantastically quaint legends. Or at least that is
its reputation.

To other Americans Arkansas is simply a vast, calm sea of growing
cotton—swelling white-crested bolls from horizon to horizon; or the
acrid sting of powder smoke in the misty dawn while swift-winging
mallards swoop in over the Grand Prairie rice fields; or the scream of
a tortured reel when a ten-pound bass pounces upon the lure in a
mountain lake; or the sad cry of night birds where ghostly cypress
knees lift above melancholy swamp waters. Or the intoxicating
aroma of lush, lush spring with honeysuckles embracing rail fences
and the dogwoods abloom and the flames of redbud trees quivering
with urgency and the fragrance of honey-locust trees humming with
the wings of a million wild bees, and the wooded hills echoing the
extravagant ecstasy of redbird, thrush and warbler.

Arkansas could be a barefoot farmer plowing his reluctant pink
acres with one ribby mule. Or a chorus of Negro voices singing at
twilight. Or mountains of bauxite tailings from mines that produce

practically all of the nation's aluminum ore. Or a vista of the wide, gray Father of Waters and a sturdy, squat tugboat, gnomelike descendant of the rococo old side-wheelers, wrestling its string of barges against the Mississippi current. Or hundreds of monuments honoring the Arkansas men and boys who died fighting the men and boys of Illinois, Pennsylvania and New Hampshire in the dreadful years of the Civil War.

In my boyhood I knew numerous elderly men who had taken part personally in that cataclysmic conflict, lending emphasis to the fact that in Arkansas the romantic past was not at all remote.

Even today in parts of the Delta region life goes on much as it must have before 1861. And in parts of the Ozark Mountains the march of years has changed conditions but little since the first moccasined frontiersmen moved west along the ridges from Kentucky and Tennessee and built their cabins beside sweet springs.

True, there is a growing awareness throughout the state that calendar leaves have been fluttering down and that the clock is ticking on. Preachers of progress are winning converts in the sleepiest of backwoods communities. But even today, if you get off the excellent main highways, you will find much the same atmosphere as when General Albert Pike wrote his stirring lines to the tune of *Dixie:*

> *Strong as lions, swift as eagles,*
> *Back to their kennels hunt these beagles!*
> *To arms! To arms! To arms in Dixie!*

The beagles, of course, were those blue-clad invaders from the North, many of whose bones went to dust in Arkansas soil. Of the earlier times, before Arkansas gained statehood in 1836, of the times of exploration and settlement, there are but a few relics surviving.

At the site of Arkansas Post (Poste Aux Arcansas), named by de Tonty for the Arcansas Indians, first colonized by the French and by Germans sent in the 18th Century by John Law, evil genius of the "Mississippi Bubble," all that remains is an ancient well. The "Petit Roche" of the Sieur Bernard de la Harpe, who in 1722 was seeking a legendary huge rock of pure emerald on the Arkansas River, still rests as a monument to his disappointment on the south shore of the river at Little Rock, almost as sacred to Arkansans as is Plymouth Rock to Massachusetts.

Then there is the Arkansas razorback. We can ignore the literal-minded Arkansans who scornfully deny his existence. Of course there are razorbacks. Otherwise, why are the University of Arkansas football teams called the Razorbacks?

The razorback is a sort of Arkansas symbol which might be likened to the British unicorn. He can lick many times his weight in wolves and run faster than a deer. While tall at the withers for a hog—say about ten hands—he is so thin, stories say, that he can squeeze through cracks in the Ozark lime rocks only three inches wide.

When a razorback wishes to travel he takes to the air like a flying squirrel, only better. He doesn't climb a tree to take off; he merely runs into the wind until he hits 60 mph, then flips on his side and soars like a glider. Utilizing hillside thermal updrafts, the Arkansas razorback climbs to 5000 feet. Ground observers undoubtedly have sighted him and reported a flying saucer in the neighborhood. I suppose it's possible that *all* flying saucers reported are merely Arkansas razorbacks on tour.

I have never seen a razorback. But neither have I seen a unicorn or a flying saucer. And I have little patience with those who sneer at the razorback as a fictional character. I think that question is highly irrelevant and immaterial. Are Hamlet and Huckleberry Finn less important just because they happen to be fictional characters?

The state of Arkansas is cut into two broad divisions—the hill country and the alluvial plains. The hill country lies roughly in the form of a crescent, with the high plateau of the Ozark Mountains running east and west along the Missouri border. The Boston Mountains, an extension of the Ozarks, drop south of the Arkansas River to join the Ouachita (pronounced Wash-i-tah) Mountains, which roll on east to Hot Springs National Park. The remainder of the state is delta country, sometimes as level as a billiard table.

Today's Arkansas traveler, if he arrives by air, will land at Little Rock, the capital and metropolis; if he comes by automobile or train, he inevitably will be drawn there. It is so near the center of the state that it might have been placed there with calipers.

Across the Arkansas River is North Little Rock, a chauvinistic community of about 50,000 which refuses to be absorbed by its bigger sister. Its original name was Argenta, because of a hole in the ground alleged to be a silver mine. But when it developed that the mine had no silver they dropped the name in disgust.

In the section along the river called "Little Dixie," or "Black Bottom," is the town's largest concentration of Negroes. The unofficial name of Washington Avenue is "Saturday Street" because Saturday brings happy throngs to the stores, hot catfish cafés and honky-tonks.

Park Hill rises sharply on the north limits of North Little Rock, one of the finest residential districts in either city. In Park Hill some genius discovered a method of making concrete look like weathered wood festooned with vines, and there are not only rustic vine-clad foot bridges but gigantic concrete toadstools that serve as bus stations. Another piece of studied quaintness is a replica of an old grist mill, complete with water wheel, which grinds no grist and serves no useful purpose except maybe as a trysting place for young people in the coolth of the evening.

North Little Rock used to have a reputation as a very tough town. But I was told that the police have cleaned up the place.

Little Rock itself is one of the most attractive small cities in America, with broad, clean streets, excellent hotels and shops, fine public buildings and parks and friendly people. Clerks and cashiers in stores and restaurants smile at a customer and say, "You all hurry back," or "Come back soon," and automobile drivers, believe it or not, are courteous even to pedestrians.

Little Rock, like most of the mid-South, takes religion seriously. Most faiths advertise with electric signs and some imposing neon crosses flame out against the smokeless sky. The sky is smokeless because all Little Rock uses natural gas.

Out on the Pine Bluff road there's a church obviously named for the motel trade; it is *The Dewdrop Pentecostal Church.*

Little Rock, of course, is in the midst of a region where people put some thought to names, particularly for their children. They often do quite well by the boys, but Arkansans love their little girls especially and adorn them with lovely and original names like Miladeen, Carutha, Florentine, Charlene, Loucrecia.

Speaking of names, I remember a girl reporter's interviewing an Ozark woman who, from the salubrious mountain air and water, was hale and hearty on her 105th birthday. The girl asked the old lady how to spell her Christian name, which she pronounced "Pishie," and the old lady said, "Well, I don't rightly know, but I got a picture with my name printed on it." So a great-granddaughter brought a lithograph from the bedroom and it was *Psyche at the Spring.*

Progressive Arkansans, who would be willing to trade the state's distinctiveness for more prosperity, do not like that kind of story. They also profess a distaste for folklore.

Curiously, however, they do not mind the original folklore tale of the Arkansas Traveler. The traveling gentleman, you may recall, pulled up his horse at the cabin of a surly squatter who couldn't repair his leaking roof when it was raining and the roof didn't need repairing when the weather was clear.

In Little Rock, one of the first things a visitor hears mentioned is the Territorial Capitol Restoration, which covers half a block on the edge of the downtown retail district.

I was escorted through the dozen or so buildings of handmade brick or hewn logs, including the territorial capitol, the first Little Rock office of the *Arkansas Gazette* and the home of Lieutenant C. F. M. Noland, who rode horseback to Washington with the Arkansas Constitution in 1835.

The restoration is realization of a dream of a native Little Rock woman, Mrs. James Fairfax Loughborough, who in 1939 persuaded the State Legislature to establish a commission with herself as chairman to engineer the project. At that time the historic buildings were in a sad state of disrepair. Some were Negro houses of prostitution and the block had been condemned as a fire hazard. Mrs. Loughborough restored and furnished the buildings with period pieces.

While 1835 does not seem particularly ancient when compared with many landmarks in the East, these buildings definitely hold an aura of romance. Thousands of visitors from all over the United States go through the Restoration each year and express their delight.

I was particularly interested in the fact that Sam Houston, following his strange resignation as Governor of Tennessee after the split with his bride of a week, had come to Little Rock on one of the most Gargantuan drunks in American history and no doubt roared along this ancient brick sidewalk stark naked after consigning his sombrero, boots and every stitch of clothing to the flames of his campfire.

Here Davy Crockett was entertained before and after his famous Little Rock shooting match, won, he later confessed, by surreptitiously poking a bullet in the hole made by his adversary's shot in the very center of the bull's-eye.

Here, also, must have walked fabulous General Albert Pike, who used to go goose hunting with a cannon loaded with BB shot and who gained wide fame as a lawyer, not only through his remarkable skill, but because he paraded to county courthouses behind a uniformed brass band.

Little Rock is proud of being the only state capital with three capitols—the Territorial Restoration, the "Greek Doric Temple" at Markham and Center Streets and the present capitol. The "Temple" housed the first state government and saw wild disorders during carpetbag days when, at one time, Arkansas had two governors, each with his own army.

Of course most Arkansas travelers go to Hot Springs. It's the oldest and one of the most famous spas in the Western Hemisphere, glittering right in the middle of the verdant Ouachita Mountains. Here is one region of great natural beauty which actually has been improved by the white man. The chain of lakes in Hot Springs National Park—Lake Catherine, Lake Hamilton and Lake Ouachita—were formed by dams. They range in length from twelve to fifty miles, enhancing the mountain scenery and providing year-round game fishing, bathing beaches and aquatic sports.

It's about sixty miles from Little Rock to Hot Springs by the old road. It's a scenic drive, but I sensed there was something wrong. Miles passed before I figured out what it was; there was nothing to look at but scenery—no patent-medicine signs, no cigarette billboards, no shaving-cream poetry. A state law prohibits roadside signs in Arkansas, practically repudiating our American civilization. What possible pleasure can a motorist gain from a view of a green lake sparkling in the lap of a pine-clad mountain unless it is seen framed between billboards advertising miracle detergent?

Several times our road crossed the new four-lane superhighway, which cuts the time between Little Rock and Hot Springs and eliminates most of the head-on collisions between tourists anxious to get to the horse races and tourists anxious to get away from the horse races.

Hot Springs is a focal point in Arkansas, but I really don't believe it is *of* Arkansas. It's a resort city. If I were set suddenly down in Hot Springs and told I was in California or Florida, I would not question it. Well, there are few places as green in California and there are no mountains in Florida, but you get the idea. The buildings and streets look scrubbed with soap and water and the sunshine is intense upon them.

Hot Springs boasts 300 hotels, apartments, rooming houses and motor courts; forty-seven hot springs flowing a million gallons daily, at temperatures from 102 to 147 degrees Fahrenheit, running mostly into eighteen bathhouses which each year give better than half a million baths.

Bath House Row is quite impressive, glistening behind lush greenery. Mostly the buildings tend toward the temple type of architecture, ranging from the Greek through the Moorish and almost but not quite to the Frank Lloyd Wright.

The hillsides of Hot Springs hold many fine residences with broad, landscaped lawns. Some of these, I was informed, belong to notorious Chicago and New York characters who have found sanctuary there. A couple of mansions reputedly built by Frank Costello and Owney Madden were pointed out to me.

We were late arriving at the Oaklawn track and the great grandstand was jampacked and already the concrete area before the parimutuel windows was littered with the discarded tickets of unrealized hopes.

We had only general-admission tickets and I spoke to an usher. He looked at me narrowly and then said, "Cap'n, if you all wants seats, go on down three aisles and see a boy name of Louey. Call 'im Louey like you know him and slip him a little. You know. Then y'all ask 'im about that block of four seats he's got."

So we went down three aisles and I grinned at the usher and said, "Hi, Louey. How you doin'?" and put out my hand. He gave me his hand doubtfully, but brightened when he felt the transfer of material goods and I asked about that block of four seats.

"Well, Colonel," he said—the transfer had promoted me several grades—"I guess you all know about those four seats, don't you?"

"How do you mean?"

He shrugged. "Well, they belongs to a party that ain't been here for three, four days. I dunno. Sure enough looks like they ain't coming today, but if they shows up you all have to get out."

We took a risk, and the owners did not appear.

It was a beautiful day with just a few shreds of white clouds drifting across a brilliant sky, and I don't know how any track could have a more beautiful setting than Oaklawn's mile ellipse snuggling between the high, green Ouachitas.

I am not a horse-race addict, but it must be admitted there is something to the pageantry and excitement of a race meet. One of my companions had a couple of lists of selections and apparently knew what she was about. When the two handicappers picked the same horse, she conservatively split a two-dollar ticket to place or show, and she was more than breaking even.

But when the bugle blipped out assembly for the sixth race and eight four-year-olds minced out in parade, my eye fell upon No. 7, a beautiful, long-legged beast named Andros, the best-looking horse I had seen all afternoon. There's a Greek island named Andros with a temple dedicated to Bacchus, and Bacchus was an interesting god. What more could I want? I plunged two bucks right on the nose of Andros. Andros ran last.

A couple weeks later Andros vindicated my faith by winning one of the big features of the season at greatly lengthened odds. However, I did not see that one.

About as far southeast of Little Rock as Hot Springs is southwest, is the town of Stuttgart, nationally famous as the duck capital of America. Stuttgart is in the Grand Prairie, as flat as the flattest of western plains and mostly treeless. For nearly a century this was cotton country—gigantic plantations operating both before and after the Civil War on a system of virtual feudalism. But at last cotton and nothing but cotton, year after year, exhausted the once rich alluvial soil and most of the land reverted to pasture.

Early in the 20th Century, however, a farmer discovered that the Grand Prairie subsoil held water on the surface and he experimented successfully with rice. Since then rice has become the second most important crop in Arkansas with an annual cash value of more than $50,000,000. Rice brought prosperity back to the blighted Grand Prairie. And it also brought wild ducks—by the million.

Ducks have become such an important byproduct of rice that the fame of Stuttgart rests on the former instead of the latter. The call letters of the local radio station are KWAK.

Each fall Stuttgart is invaded by duck hunters from all over the United States. They come by car, with or without trailer, train and plane, bearing prized fowling pieces of every description, decoys and often dogs. They fill every hotel, motel and tourist home; they camp out in tents and they live in their trailers. A goodly number of the hunters, of course, are Yankees, but Stuttgart doesn't mind *this* invasion, and as a matter of fact, turns the occasion into a festival, even roping off Main Street for outdoor dances.

When not blasting away from the duck blinds in early morning (some blinds are actually steam-heated), most duck hunters would rather talk than anything. Like golfers, they love to replay each shot.

Wearing their colorful garb, they congregate everywhere, recounting their adventures and misadventures, and arguing the merits of various shotguns—the pump gun, the autoloader and so on. If the truth be known, however, an occasional native grandpappy will go out at dawn with an old-fashioned hammer gun and get as many ducks as the engraved thousand-dollar pieces.

The climax of the Stuttgart duck festival is the annual duck-calling contest with a three-day barbecue, everything free to all comers. It is held in November for the so-called world's championship. Aspirants come from afar, the imperious callers who employ only hands and vocal organs and those who use store-bought aids. As the visiting Anatidaean virtuosos practice the conversational nuances of mallard, canvasback and teal, the jingle of Stuttgart cash registers helps to soothe native nerves.

About 40 per cent of the land under cultivation is now devoted to cotton and of that most is in the Delta region. Blytheville, up in the northeast corner of the state in Mississippi County, is the cotton capital. And Blytheville is one of the fastest-growing communities in Arkansas, especially busy on Saturday when the streets are filled with plantation people, black and white, buying and selling and pleasuring around the hot catfish stands and barbecue pits. The real carnival time comes in October, when the annual cotton-picking contests are held.

Historically, the Negro and cotton have been associated together, and the Negro population of Arkansas still runs approximately 25 per cent, heavily concentrated in the Delta country. In the north and west through the Ozarks and Boston Mountains there are so few Negroes that you might drive for a hundred miles without seeing one. On the other hand some cotton communities are entirely Negro.

In recent years Arkansas has lost nearly 10 per cent of its Negro population through the attraction of high wages in the North and West, and the desire to escape racial discrimination. Yet many a poor Arkansas sharecropper comes back disillusioned and bitter.

There was Remmie Dunlap who lived with his wife and children in a sharecropper cabin on a bayou in the lower Arkansas River valley. Remmie was back in Arkansas after several years of working in a Detroit auto factory, and he was glad to be back. His cabin was unpainted, he had no plumbing or electricity. But he had a garden and chickens and pigs and there were plenty of fish in the bayou.

He sat down on the tongue of his dish-wheeled wagon, took off his hat and rubbed his bald pate. "No, sir," he said, "I didn't like Dee-troit at all. Them Dee-troit colored folks is mighty biggety, they got no use for Southern niggers. Calls me Lynch Bait on account I come from Arkansas.

"All I does in this big factory is hold a nut while a white man, he screws in a bolt a million times a day and come night I stand up in a bus far as to Pine Bluff maybe, where we live in a great big brick house and climb up steps and steps to where Magnolia's got washing hanging all over the place and no fresh vegetables on the table and no dandelion greens and no fresh catfish and no fresh air even."

The last time I had ridden on a cross-country bus in Arkansas it was definitely Jim Crow with a painted line separating the rear or Negro section from the front. But the bus which I rode this time from Fort Smith to Little Rock had no such line or sign. It's true that the eight or ten Negro passengers automatically gravitated to the rear, and I don't know whether the driver would have said anything otherwise. He certainly said nothing to the young white men who moved to the rear with a couple of Negro soldiers and chatted with them.

About halfway to Little Rock there was a thirty-minute meal stop. In the restaurant an arrow pointed to the rear with a sign, "Colored waiting room and lunch this way."

The Negro passengers, men and women, started back but were stopped by a white waitress who said, "That isn't very clean back there right now. Why don't you people just eat up here?"

From the town of Crossett (home of the gigantic Crossett Lumber Co.) in Ashley County near the Louisiana line, swing westward through the magnificent shortleaf pine forests to what is known as the Coastal Plain of Arkansas. This country is devoted to general farming and livestock, but it also includes the rich oil and gas fields around El Dorado and Smackover (producing some 30,000,000 barrels of oil annually) and the great and happy watermelon region.

Watermelons grow big and sweet here. They market approxi-mately 3,000,000 a year and they tell about a heavyweight champion that tipped the scales at 198 pounds and was shipped to a movie actor in Hollywood. Asked why, for goodness' sake, they hadn't sent it to one Elwin Charles Roe, the leading citizen of Ash Flat, Ark., who used to throw a baseball for the Brooklyn Dodgers, or even to General Douglas MacArthur, who was born in Little Rock, the answer was, "If Preacher Roe wants a watermelon he can raise it his-self and General MacArthur is a Republican."

When I think of Arkansas watermelons I always think of my brother's experience with a sterling character of the Ozarks. Passing a ten-acre patch of magnificent melons, my brother stopped and asked the farmer how about getting one.

The farmer said sure and plugged half a dozen until he found one he judged had reached the exquisite perfection of ripeness.

When my brother asked the price the farmer stared at him and said, "My God, mister, you don't think I'm *selling* watermelons, do you?"

Then the farmer explained that watermelons to him were *social* fruit. His ten acres were devoted to sociables, parties and good will.

"It's this way," he said. "I'm right proud of that melon you got. But do I sell it to you for money it's no different to you than sending to Montgomery Ward for a pair of gum boots. But do I give it to you and you're welcome and you eat it and you say, 'Dad burn, I never see such a scrumptious melon,' you'll feel friendly to-wards me even if you never see me again and I'll feel friendly to-wards you because I know you feel friendly to-wards me."

Speaking of pleasant Arkansas crops, mistletoe grows pretty much over the state. It's a parasite, of course, and appears in clumps high in hardwood trees. And it is regarded largely as the property of small boys who harvest it for Christmas money. The method of harvest is probably more fun than any other known to man. The boys shoot it down with .22 rifles.

Up above the Coastal Plain in Pike County, just where the Ouachita Mountains peter out, is the belly of an ancient volcano, the only igneous rock in the state. Here, in 1906, a poor farmer named John Huddleston was out fixing to plant his turnip greens when his eye fell on a crystal glittering in the sun.

"Well," said John Huddleston, "there's a nice diamond; it's about time something was turning up."

He took the crystal to a banker in Murfreesboro and the banker laughed. "Diamonds don't grow like that, John," he said, "but it's kind of pretty and I'll give you four bits for it."

John scorned the offer. He scratched around the turnip patch and found several more of the crystals and, although it's a "fur piece" from Murfreesboro to Little Rock, John Huddleston took his crystals to a jeweler in the capital. The jeweler examined the crystals and then exclaimed excitedly, "Man, do you realize what you've got here?"

"Sure enough," said John Huddleston. "They're diamonds, ain't they?" And they were—sure enough.

John Huddleston sold his scrubby eighty acres for what he considered a fortune—$36,000. And in the next twenty years mining operations took about 50,000 white, yellow and brown diamonds from that stony hollow. Most of the diamonds were industrial grade, but some were of fine jewel quality. One of more than forty carats is valued at $75,000, according to the Howard Millars family, which now maintains the diamond crater as a tourist attraction.

The Millars charge visitors $1.25 admission to the area and allow them to keep any diamonds they find. Such visitors are said to have found more than 800 diamonds, some of them of jewel quality.

As an Arkansas friend remarked: "One tourist is better than two bales of cotton—and he's easier to pick."

Arkansas has produced pearls of great price as well as diamonds. There are several factories on the lower White River that cut pearl buttons from fresh-water mussel shells, and, in the course of years, numerous pearls have been found in the river mussels at the Pearl Ann button plant at Clarendon where my father used to have a sawmill. Some of these pearls are worth several thousand dollars.

Arkansas people are much interested in a neighbor named Winthrop Rockefeller. Mr. Rockefeller, the tall, athletic son of John D. Rockefeller, Jr., has established residence at Petit Jean (pronounced Pettet Gene) where he has purchased some 800 mountain-top acres for the avowed purpose of raising Santa Gertrudis beef cattle.

Winding west and north from Petit Jean, one comes finally to Dardanelle, the southern terminus of the Dardanelle & Russellville Railroad, which has two and a half wonderful steam locomotives of the 1880 vintage. They used to have four but a wandering Hollywood property man hauled one out to the West Coast for use in historical movies. They committed cannibalism on the third to get parts to keep the other two running. These last have been slightly modernized—the original diamond smokestacks have been replaced by plain, unromantic-looking stovepipes.

One lean, overalled engineer was out working on his charge with a huge monkey wrench. He drawled sadly, "They been wonderful old engines in their day, but now you got to be a blacksmith and a steamfitter and a regular genius to keep 'em running."

On up into the picturesque Ozark country are the two great man-made lakes—Norfork and Bull Shoals. Norfork was raised by the dam on the north fork of the White River. It is fifty-four miles long and is populated by the biggest bass, large- and small-mouth, that I ever heard of.

Naturally, fishing is mighty popular in both Norfork and Bull Shoals Lakes, to say nothing of the summer float trips on the White River where one may drift lazily with the current in boat or barge on anything from one-day trips to a week or more.

You see a lot of the Ozarks running west to Eureka Springs, and you see a lot of the Ozarks right in Eureka Springs. There are towering peaks heavy with hardwoods and pine. In the spring there is the mingled fragrance of dogwoods, wild plum, crab apple and honeysuckle.

Eureka Springs is a town that never has had a circus, because there's not a level spot big enough to pitch a tent on. Spring Street climbs up the valley in a series of sharp S-turns. There aren't many cross streets, but climb sharply up one of them and you may find the book store of genial and erudite Otto Ernest Rayburn, who writes books and articles about Ozark folklore. He holds that the real Ozark hillbilly, like the mountaineer of North Carolina and Tennessee, speaks a pure Elizabethan English.

I am not entirely convinced. I never heard any Ozark citizen say "God's bodykin," or speak anything like a Shakespearean character. True, a good many words of Saxon origin and onomatopoeian nature are used casually in the Ozarks, especially by the ungodly. But so are they in Montana, Texas and on Third Avenue, New York.

Jesse and Frank James and Cole Younger used to hibernate occasionally in the Arkansas Ozarks, and there are stories of their unfailing courtesy toward the fair sex and their reverence toward preachers. Mr. Rayburn has a story about Jesse's marksmanship. At a party (maybe a church sociable) Jesse pasted an inch square of paper on a tree, strode away twenty paces, whirled suddenly and blazed away with a six-shooter in each hand. He fired eight times and every bullet was in that inch-square paper. Inasmuch as a .45 bullet is practically half an inch in diameter, there couldn't have been much left of that target after the first four or five shots.

Well, Eureka Springs is a strange town in a strange country. Near the top of the mountain is a Catholic Church which one enters through the belfry. Down the canyon is the Basin Park Hotel with the mountain rising so steeply in the rear that each of the seven floors has a ground entrance.

Eureka Springs is a health resort with sixty-three springs gurgling out water alleged to restore youth, vigor and ambition—which one needs if he's to walk those steep streets.

Beyond Eureka Springs, Route U. S. 62 covers some very rugged country, and there's the inevitable Inspiration Point with its inspiring view.

The highway passes close to Pea Ridge, scene of the Civil War's greatest battle west of the Mississippi. Even today histories vary as to who won the battle, but on both sides there were about 26,000 men engaged on March 8, 1862, and approximately 2500 casualties, including three Confederate generals killed. It was here that the great General Albert Pike brought in his brigade of Cherokee Indians recruited from Indian Territory on promise of plenty of Yankee scalps. But the Cherokees never had heard artillery before, and when the big guns opened up the Indians remembered that the fishing season was on and went back home.

Of course fried chicken is an Arkansas institution, and just outside Springdale, at the A. Q. Chicken House, I had fried chicken that was the answer to a fried-chicken fan's prayer. I know it isn't scientific, but I have a theory that it takes a native of Arkansas or Missouri (preferably a Negro) to achieve the heavenly, succulent, golden, crusty-sweet tenderness that makes fried chicken a food for the gods.

Fayetteville is a thriving city, the seat of the University of Arkansas. It's an old town and had rough times during the Civil War, changing hands several times. But it's not typical of the popular conception of Arkansas. As a matter of fact, Washington County usually votes Republican except when Fayetteville's favorite son U. S. Senator J. William Fulbright is running.

I visited the beautiful Fine Arts Center and saw an exhibition of paintings by faculty members and some of the work being done by students. All of it, strangely, was decidedly *avant-garde*. I was puzzled at first that these frank abstractions and nonobjective canvases should be in Arkansas. I wondered whether trouble might be in the offing if some legislative committee visits the Fine Arts Center and sees the taxpayers' money going to teach Arkansas boys and girls how to produce polychromatic doodles. But I don't know. Art is comparatively new to Arkansas. Perhaps it is natural, then, that they should turn to new forms.

Yes, Arkansas is changing. Even the various accents from the Ozark "thar" to the Delta "theah" are leveling off, especially among the young people, to plain "there." Radio, television, the movies, the wars and easy travel are having their effect.

But today's Arkansas traveler will find Arkansas *fundamentally* unchanged. Despite this age of standardization, he will find there a delightful distinctiveness. And, so far, happily, it is not the studied quaintness of some Western dude ranches or New England resort spots.

Arkansas automobile tags are inscribed "The Land of Opportunity." Well, there are opportunities, and aplenty. But I believe a more apt characterization might be simply "The Friendly State."

Louisiana

by JAMES STREET

She's the strange sister of the family, this state of Louisiana—the Frenchy one, never quite accepted in the household of the South and yet never denied, because she is so rich and so different, and so much fun.

She was named for France's fourteenth Louis, a genius and a rake; she's an archipelago of races, languages and religions, vociferously American, pugnaciously Southern and working hard to brew her potpourri into a democratic gumbo.

Most American states are two or three states, geographically and culturally; this dominion of pine and palm, red hills and black bottoms is a dozen.

Therefore, generalizations are dangerous. But we will gamble a few, this being a land where gambling is a man's heritage and Lady Luck is an old courtesan behind a carnival mask, choosing her lovers without regard to race, creed or future condition of servitude.

Louisiana is the Quebec of the United States, split across the middle by Arkansas fundamentalism and bursting with Texas big talk.

The Old South keeps his right eye on Louisiana in envy and contrition, winks at her with his left, and never can bring himself to believe that she, too, is one of his daughters. Yet she is the original Dixie, named for the *dix* bills which, like picayunes, were legal tender in the incubative days and called dixies by the helling Kentucky flatboatmen who really made the first Louisiana purchase with blood, brawn and raw whisky.

The nation thinks she's Catholic, but actually she's Protestant. The nation remembers her Huey Long who wanted to be President and forgets her Zachary Taylor who was. She's the Pelican State although possibly half of her people never have seen a pelican. She's the Creole State although many Louisianans never have seen a Creole and one good brother in the hill country defined a Creole as a Catholic albino.

She's a cuisine mecca for gourmets, but most of her folks eat corn bread. She's the Mississippi River, but the Red River is her backbone. She's New Orleans. That's as silly as saying that California is Los Angeles or that Pennsylvania is Philadelphia.

She's Mardi Gras and a hang-over, but the Sabine Valley rancher in cowboy boots and ten-gallon hat prefers the Texas State Fair at Dallas. She's a lazy Cajun drowsing by a lazier bayou while 80,000 hysterical partisans scream at a football game, for Louisiana takes her football as seriously as Columbus, Ohio—well, almost, anyhow, and that's saying a heap.

She's a cypress swamp, a lurking place for alligators and snakes, brooding in the foreboding shadows of parasitic Spanish moss. Now wait a minute, stranger. Those are oak trees. Cypress is rather rare these days because it is so valuable. There hasn't been a recorded death from snake bite within the memory of most men, and the alligators now are shoes and pocketbooks, much to the disgust of trappers who used to catch them barehanded and kill them with knives.

And that gray cowl on those trees is neither moss nor parasite. The Choctaw Indians called it falling hair. The Spaniards called it Frenchman's wig and the French called it Spaniard's beard. Somewhere along the line it was misnamed Spanish moss. It is an air plant (*Tillandsia usneoides*) and a cousin to the pineapple. Shred one of the strands and you will find a tiny, tough thread. The threads are used to stuff mattresses.

Spanish moss also is good for poems, ghosts and myths, ranging from Evangeline to John Henry to Huey 'ygod Pierce Long who, like Hitler, refuses to stay put, but comes back when the moon is dark and stalks the swamps and tall timber, shouting his battle cry: "Share the wealth! Every man a king!"

One visitor will say Louisiana is a mansion. Bless his romantic heart! Another will say she is a shanty. Bless his sociologic soul! They both are right—to a measure. Nevertheless, the average Louisianan, if there is such a thing, lives in a small town or on a small farm. His house is comfortable, his stomach full. He prefers beefsteak to frog legs.

His teen-age daughter wears jeans and his little son totes a brace of cap pistols, just like kids the country over. He pays very heavy state taxes, except on his land, so his children can have free lunches at school and he can ride on paved roads and retire, maybe, on Louisiana's old-age pension.

If a typical Louisianan (again a generalization) lives north of the Red River, which bisects the state from northwest to southeast, we will call him Lee Johnson. He is a Baptist or Methodist and boastful that he is Anglo-Saxon. He traces his ancestry to the Eastern seaboard, the southern part of course, thence to Tennessee or Mississippi. Grandpa was a Confederate veteran. Hero, naturally. As a Southerner, I wonder if none of the Confederate deserters ever had young'uns.

Anyway, Lee wears khaki on the farm or in the factory because it is comfortable and easy to wash. And before any interlopers—down here they are called the bleeding hearts, bluenoses, yellow-bellies and a few ungracious epithets—get any funny ideas, let me hasten to report that Lee Johnson has been to school. He has Sunday clothes, shoes and maybe an automobile. He dresses up for church, funerals and to go to town on Saturday. His parish may be dry by local option, so if he wants a drink he buys from a bootlegger.

The collar of Lee's shirt usually is open and the sun has reddened his neck. Hence, the sobriquet of redneck. It can be an endearing term when applied endearingly by friends, but strangers are cautioned to avoid it. For, as a rule, Lee Johnson resents being called a "redneck" because his skin is red just as much as his Negro friend resents the word "nigger" because his skin is black.

He is the Southerner of a thousand stories and a thousand legends; friendly, hospitable, his inherent shyness hidden behind his taciturn reserve or disguised completely by his exaggerated big talk and unbecoming boastfulness. He is not as quick to anger as the myth makers say, but don't push him, brother. Just don't push him.

However, if a typical Louisianan lives below the Red River— except in Lake Charles' southwest section or New Orleans' southeast

section, which are separate provinces—we will call him René Le-
Blanc.

He is a Roman Catholic and speaks a French patois that baffles
linguists. His ancestors came from France via Acadia, now Nova
Scotia, or directly from the mother country during the French Revolution. René and his kith are lumped together under the colloquial
term of "Cajuns" (Acadians) and have leavened into one of the largest and most exciting ethnologic families ever to come from the
American melting pot.

René LeBlanc, the bayou man, must not be confused with the
Creole. (We will meet him later in New Orleans and environs.) René
is the counterpart to Lee Johnson, up in the piney hills. He is volatile,
prolific—repeat prolific—as thrifty as a squirrel, as eager as a chip-
munk. He farms, traps, works the swamps, and fishes.

He and Lee are not cronies although their children mingle in college. Lee is inclined to look askance at René, and René probably
feels sorry for Lee. It is a matter of conscience and pride, for Lee's
pride is a bit stiff while René's is an asset to be used only when
needed.

If Lee gets drunk, he hangs his head the next day. If René gets
plastered, he brags about it and maybe throws in a few Gallic fibs
about his amorous triumphs. Lee is a Nordic, in the broad sense,
and René is a Latin, yet they live together under one government,
in peace and usually in harmony.

Also, they both are Democrats by heritage and rebels by choice
on all things except one: the constant and baffling Negro question.
For Louisiana is roughly one third black, or shades thereof, and René
and Lee, miles apart in so many ways, melt together instantly on
this issue.

They believe firmly, belligerently firmly, in segregation and what
is loosely called white supremacy. It is more than tradition. It is a
faith, the substance of things accepted, the evidence of things long
seen.

Here, as elsewhere in the South, the Negro story is snarled in mores
and fears and social taboos. If you want to squabble about it, they
will squabble and swap platitudes with you while a Negro brings
strong black coffee and rich white milk, and somehow they blend.

Uncle Remus and John Henry are gone, and Simon Legree never
lived, but the legends linger on.

Surely no state is more myth-ridden than Louisiana and she has quit trying to dispel the legends. Now she sells them to tourists. Her folks collect a pretty high tariff on romantic fantasies and use the take to buy tractors, combines and historical novels about their moon-dipped past.

For every year, hordes visit her fabulous New Orleans and quaint Cajun country (see guidebooks) to laugh and love or carp and whine, then to go back to their cornfields and city shops, a little wiser, a little poorer, but either confirmed Louisiana addicts or Louisiana critics, in any case connoisseurs, after a week, of a culture that baffled Mark Twain and fascinated Audubon and Lafcadio Hearn.

And this old state, like the rivers that green her mantle and muddy her feet, just keeps rolling along, producing most of the nation's domestic furs, sugar, rice and tetraethyl, and a lot of our oil, salt, timber, paper, sweet potatoes, strawberries, sulphur, cattle, cotton, fish and fun—and Hadacol, a patented elixir which, when I was there, was spending several millions a year to advertise "A Better Tomorrow" by drinking a tonic of 12 per cent alcohol seasoned with vitamins.

The Indians started it all and didn't have a chance. Many of them belonged to the Muskhogean nations and often settled their wars by playing a ball game or a sort of bowling contest called "chunky." We can remember them by the word "chunk," meaning to throw out, which is exactly what we did.

Spaniards were the first tourists. One legend says Alvarez de Pineda found the Mississippi River in 1519, and it's a fair bet that Hernando de Soto really did visit the country in 1541 or '42. After de Soto, a few more Spaniards piddled around here awhile, but didn't like the setup. And for more than a hundred years Louisiana was left to herself, her alligators, her pelicans, and her Indians who played ball games.

The French were smarter than the Spaniards, and in 1682 La Salle and fifty men came all the way down the Mississippi from Canada and claimed the whole valley as Louisiana, from mountains to mountains. To René Robert Cavelier, Sieur de La Salle, it was as plain as the cross hilt of his sword: whoever controlled the mouth of the Mississippi could control a continent. Great day in the morning! Fifty-one *voyageurs* and the richest empire of all times. Where are your monuments, dead men? Where are your struck coins?

La Salle, the first Louisianan, was assassinated in Texas. Oh, well. At least Huey Long was assassinated at home.

England, already on the Atlantic seaboard, and Spain in Florida finally got hep that the Mississippi was the key to the whole she-bang and began reaching. But France sent out the brothers Iberville and Bienville and on March 2, 1699, Frenchmen sailed into the mouth of the river—to stay.

The next day was Shrove Tuesday and they found a little bayou and named it Mardi Gras, which means Fat Tuesday. They got the name bayou from the Indians and it means a sluggish stream, any-thing from a creek to a small river.

That fall the English showed up in two ships; Bienville met them at a bend in the river and convinced them the French had a large force upstream. The English turned back, a strange thing for Eng-lishmen to do, and on that day at that place the bayou country was sealed off as a Gallic land. The bend still is called English Turn.

It may not look good in print, but Louisiana really got going in a gigantic promotional scheme of land speculation. John Law was the brains behind it. Mr. Law was a Scotsman who proved that several million Frenchmen could be wrong. He organized the *Compagnie d'Occident*, sometimes called the Mississippi Company or just plain John Company. The French government nodded approval while the company convinced gullible Frenchmen Louisiana was a paradise.

They sent out settlers and sold stock back home and soon the whole thing blew up, and France almost did, in that incredible fraud known as the Mississippi Bubble. However, the settlers were in Loui-siana and it was a matter of root, hog, or die. They rooted.

Survival was the first problem, and then women. There were not enough women. Governor Jean Baptiste Lemoyne, Sieur de Bien-ville, wrote the John Company that his men must have wives. "They are running in the woods after Indian girls," he reported. Some were caught and the Louisiana potpourri began stewing.

First came the delinquent girls, direct from a house of correction in Paris. Some took husbands. The others never got around to it. Next came the casket girls, *filles à la cassette*, so called because their possessions were in small chests shaped like caskets. The casket girls were ladies, in a sense. The correction girls were just females. So the potpourri stewed a little more, and the folks multiplied.

The French crown took the colony back from the John Company, and Louisiana had her feet on solid ground. The land was rich and she poured produce back to France—cotton, sugar sirup and rum.

Things were humming when England and France squared off for the French and Indian War. England won, France transferred Louisiana to Spain and the dons took over after trickery and bloodshed.

Now here came the Creoles, one of the most misused names in the American language. The word is the French form of *criollo,* a West-Indian Spanish corruption and kin to the English word "create." It came into use in Louisiana with union of the French settlers and the Spanish newcomers, and meant anything, including humans, born in the New World of Old World stock.

It started as an adjective. Hence, there were creole whites, the native-born descendants of original French and Spanish families, and creole Negroes, native-born descendants of the first Negro families.

Gradually, however, the troublesome word became a noun and was capitalized and here the white and Negro Creoles parted. To the white Creoles, the capitalized noun referred only to themselves. But to Negroes the word applied to their light-skinned kinsmen, mostly octoroons.

This is still the situation. So unless you know your way through the Louisiana labyrinth of color, caste and custom it is best to duck it except as an adjective, i.e., Creole cooking, Creole ways, and so forth. This does not apply, incidentally, if you like to argue and fight.

Actually there are few real Creoles in Louisiana today. They live mostly in and around New Orleans in clannish family groups, very close and quite conservative.

They often are called aristocrats and that's all right, if the word fits an American vocabulary. But their aristocracy stems from local prestige and tradition and not, as a rule, from Old World aristocracy.

The Creole melting pot was simmering when down came the Cajuns, first in trickles as exiles from Acadia where England had taken over, then in substantial groups until about 4000 came in. They were French rural stock and headed for the open lands of Bayou Teche, big enough to be a river in most states and approximately 100 miles west of New Orleans. The city Creoles accepted them as peasants and were happy to have them settle the bayous and swamps, near enough to be useful, yet far enough away never to be troublesome.

The Cajuns dug in like crawfish, learned more from the Indians than from the Creoles and claimed the bogs as their place to breathe and breed in their own way. They built skiffs called bateaux to navigate the bayous and chipped their canoelike pirogues—light enough to float on a fall of dew—from cypress logs to travel the swamps.

Soon after the United States was established, Spain buttered up the little seaboard republic by recognizing the Mississippi River as the western boundary of the United States, and to top it off, gave us the right to export through New Orleans, duty free.

That did it. Americans, feeling their oats and sowing them in a new freedom, poured into the Mississippi valley, loaded a few jugs of Monongahela whisky aboard their flatboats and started drifting way down yonder to New Orleans.

Buckskins and Kentucky rifle-guns. Long knives and tall men and taller tales. "I was raised with alligators and weaned on panthers' milk. Git out'n my way!"

The Creoles blanched and hid their daughters. Spain tried to slam the door, but it was too late. Americans were on the levees and they dug in, rightly aiming to stay a spell. They did.

> *I came from Alabama, wid my banjo on my knee,*
> *I'm gwyne to Louisiana, my true love for to see——*
> *O! Susanna. O! Don't you cry for me——*

Napoleon was hacking his swath across Europe and Spain ceded Louisiana back to France and the Louisiana Purchase was set up. The greatest buy in all history, $27,267,622 for a fan-shaped area extending from New Orleans to the Rocky Mountains and Canada. It cost about four cents an acre!

The United States took over on December 20, 1803. The Creoles mumbled in their pointed beards. The Americans whooped it up, and the Cajuns didn't give a whoop. English was made the official language.

On April 30, 1812, the territory of Orleans became the State of Louisiana and that same year the first steamboat came down the Mississippi to New Orleans.

The War of 1812 plunged Louisiana back into strife and settled her American status once and for all. The state's seacoast in those days was a haven for pirates, including Jean Lafitte and one Dominique You, a legend-covered gent who had been a cannoneer in Napoleon's army. Yes, these Frenchmen and the Creoles were critical of America in the way of so many Americans until the shooting starts.

Great Britain reasoned then as many Europeans have reasoned since: that the United States was filled with bickering factions and would collapse within if the proper peg were pulled. New Orleans was the peg. England tried to pull it. It didn't work.

A British army that had defeated Napoleon was landed south of New Orleans and a glorious thing happened, a national miracle. They got together—the Creole planters and the Barataria pirates, the Indians and the Negroes. Andrew Jackson and his Long Rifles were welcomed by the same men who, a few years before, had scorned the American flag and American ways.

The English were routed on January 8, 1815. Legend long since has draped the Battle of New Orleans in tinsel—the glamour of Jean Lafitte, the vengeance of Dominique You. The fact is that a large but confused invading army was defeated by a small, smart American army, well entrenched and beautifully handled by General Andrew Jackson.

Some romanticists insist the golden age of Louisiana then set in to last for forty-five years. This, however, is a matter of values. Her cane and cotton lands were so rich that field slavery was profitable. The traffic soared and slaves poured in, many of them down the Mississippi, sold down the river to the sugar plantations, to the salt mines of the Cajun country. The Cajuns themselves did not own many slaves. They were peasants and asked only to be left alone to tend their little farms and rear their broods under the eyes of their priests.

Manor houses bloomed and folks who were not so much back on the seaboard suddenly became somebody out here, their linen immaculate, their dueling pistols primed, their honor an intangible thing—trigger-happy and deadly. Each new nabob tried to outdo the others while slavery and foolish husbandry exhausted the earth.

During this era of silver doorknobs and sillabub, two unrelated events took place that affected Louisiana, in the long run, far more than all the promenades and minuets put together.

Down in New Orleans, around 1830, a group of bored students, fresh home from Paris, got together for a little binge. It was Shrove Tuesday and tomorrow was Ash Wednesday, the beginning of Lent. So they went out on the town. One legend says (and this one sounds plausible) that they rounded up a few courtesans, painted or masked their faces and they all went out on a hooray, parading the streets. It was a Fat Tuesday all right and this was the beginning of Mardi Gras, Louisiana edition. Street masking for Mardi Gras began about 1835 and the celebration sort of evolved, picking this from that and that from something else, until today it is one of the world's most famous hoedowns.

About the same time, Captain Henry Miller Shreve, a Yankee riverman, built the first steam snag boat and chugged up the Red River to remove the famous raft, an obstruction of logs and debris that had blocked the river for hundreds of years. He opened the Red River to commerce. The city of Shreveport is his monument and so, in a way, is the Red River Valley.

Audubon came down and tutored children and painted the birds. Sam'l Clemens came steamboating and sounding the river. "Mark ti-re-e-e! Mark twain!" He wrote a piece for a New Orleans paper and signed it "Mark Twain."

Lincoln came down and didn't like some of the things he saw. Sherman came down to be superintendent of the state university.

There also came a Yankee reporter-propagandist who really fired up a rumpus. Some sources insist he was one of the Beecher brothers who had a sister named Harriet Beecher Stowe. The legend that he was Henry Ward Beecher, a reporter in his youth, is pretty flimsy, but he could have been Charles Beecher, who came South, or even Edward, a writing fellow. Anyway, he went up the Red River, then back home and began pecking at slavery. Now, Harriet Beecher Stowe had never been South, but she read and listened, and she had a flair. Uncle Tom's cabin was in the Red River Valley. At least, that's what Mrs. Stowe said.

Louisiana has no monument to Harriet Beecher Stowe. However, at Natchitoches, in the Uncle Tom country, is a monument to a Negro. His shoulders are bent, his neck bowed and his hat doffed. The inscription reads, "Erected by the City of Natchitoches in Grateful Recognition of the Arduous and Faithful Service of the Good Darkies of Louisiana."

Many Negroes naturally resent the monument. Others sort of smile. Some get drunk and ask him the way to go home, and he always shows them. It seems a long ways from the Good Darkey monument in Red River Valley to Dillard University for Negroes in New Orleans.

By 1860, New Orleans was one of the country's great cities and the second largest port. Then one of her Creoles, General Pierre Gustave Toutant Beauregard, gave the command that opened fire on Fort Sumter, and the nation began her spasm.

The Civil War bled Louisiana white and left her with her throat cut and her back broken. After Farragut, an adopted son, ran the forts below New Orleans, the state was subdued inch by inch. General Ben Butler was in command of the Union army. They still call him "Beast" Butler around here.

Butler was succeeded by General N. P. Banks. There came a few second-class battles and a lot of first-rate cotton stealing and Louisiana was through.

Reconstruction, radical Republicans and riots stretched the state on the rack and then, twelve years after Appomattox, the occupation was over and Louisiana was dropped to the ground, limp and bloody. By the turn of the century, Louisiana was breathing again, or rather gasping in that torpor that gripped the conquered and colonized South.

The Louisiana revival came out of the eroded red hills of Winn Parish, the dreary pine stumps, the wasted land of turnip greens and fatback. He was Huey Pierce Long, salesman and lawyer, glib as a shell-game operator, sharp as a meat ax. And no governor of this era, excepting Franklin D. Roosevelt, shook the foundations so hard or was the object of so much affection, the target of so much hate.

A fair-to-middling library already has been written about Huey Long. Louisianans who knew him read the books and shrug and smile. They know it is easier to sell a legend than to kill it, and Huey has become a legend since a young doctor shot him down in 1935.

He was in power only eight years, the absolute boss of a Deep South state, and yet this is the genius John Gunther says might have brought fascism to the United States.

Louisianans who knew the Kingfish, as Long styled himself, tell me that Robert Penn Warren's *All the King's Men* is the novel that comes nearest to catching the dictator's personality and character.

He attempted a dictatorship in the rebellious South and died under the same code he espoused; for he dared impugn the racial honor of an opponent's family, and one of the boys cut him down. The tall stacks may belch smoke and write new laws in the sky. A million looms may hum and tractors snort where mules once mired, but this is still the South, still "white man's country." Huey Long, the master, made the most simple mistake. He led with his right. He charged "Tar brush!" And forgot to duck. And yet the Kingfish never used racism as a club. Only as a dagger.

Huey Long the demagogue was a cause. Huey Long the dictator was a result. It was inevitable that he should come roaring out of the red hills, himself a product of a beaten land, a bewildered people. He knew a frightening thing about democracy: that some citizens are willing to swap a peck of freedom for a pint of scarcity.

Huey Long learned about people by selling shortening, store-to-store. Loud. Vulgar. Flashy. He studied law at Tulane University and completed the course in less than a year. Brilliant. Shrewd. Witty.

Then he began piddling in politics, got beat once, and came swaggering out of the hills, bellowing his political gospel like a bull alligator: Take from the rich and give to the poor. Share the wealth. Every man a king!

The conservatives and some of the liberals, the money interests and some of the intellectuals rose up to meet him. The poor fell in behind him, the Rednecks and the Cajuns. The meek were to inherit the earth and here was their Pied Piper. Huey swung from the floor and Louisiana never knew what hit her.

He was elected governor in 1928. Build roads! Span the rivers! Free textbooks for all children. Make 'em go to school. Build a great university. A new capitol. Abolish the poll tax!

"Who is paying for it?" the businessman asked.

"You are," said Huey Pierce Long.

So he bonded his state to the hilt and began levying taxes. Of course, as always, the poor paid, too, but they got something to show for it; the roads, the schools, the textbooks.

His enemies tried to impeach him and he slapped them flat. The New Orleans machine arched its back, and he broke its back. He reorganized Louisiana until he controlled every thread in the political loom and could dictate elections from dogcatcher to governor. Then he had himself elected to the United States Senate, but did not take office until 1932.

It is hard to believe that he was governor only for four years, that he was senator only for three. He fought Franklin D. Roosevelt and was a serious threat for a Third Party. There is no judging what the man might have done.

He was back home, hand-running his legislature, when a brooding young doctor entered the Kingfish's skyscraper capitol and wounded him fatally with a small, foreign-made pistol as he came down a corridor, striding ahead of his bodyguard. The assassin was shot to a pulp; Long wheeled down some steps, and died thirty hours later of internal bleeding from one small wound. His hierarchy fell apart because some of his henchmen got too greedy and too careless, and a few of them wound up in jail. A reform movement swept the state and outsiders assumed the influence of the Kingfish was dead.

In many ways the state of Louisiana is a temple to Huey Pierce Long; the roads, the schools, the debt, the taxes. Raymond Swing summed him best when he wrote, in effect, that to understand the danger of Long you must understand his good works.

Well, Doctor Jekyll was a good doctor too.

So much for Huey Pierce Long. If you also are interested in Louisiana people and byways, in Cajun coffee and fish fries, then come with me. It won't cost much money if you duck the gambling joints and the slot machines that spin and clatter in so many of the roadside eateries. We will learn first that a parish is a county, that gumbo is a Negro-French word meaning a kind of soup, that *café noir* is black coffee, that *café au lait* is hot milk and hotter coffee, and that a conscience can be a nuisance. Gumbo ya-ya is a gabfest for women. Praline is a kind of candy and a Poor Boy is a foot-long sandwich made of French bread.

We came in the middle way, across Mississippi and the Pearl River and knew at once that we were in Louisiana—the swishing moss, the brooding swamps. A quaint little French village? Nope, but there was Bogalusa, a bustling little industrial city. The stuffed crabs were hot and peppery and the coffee was already getting good. The waitress chewed gum and came from the Midwest.

"*Café noir*," I said.

"Huh?"

"Black coffee."

"Oh."

She was the first person I asked: "What is Louisiana?"

"This is. And whatcha getting at, mister?" It was a dry, harsh tone, much harsher than the moss outside, than the warm February sky. "I just work around here. So whatcha getting at?"

Skip it, sister.

My first hitchhiker was standing on a corner in Covington, where the live oaks seemed to brush the top of my car. He had a shotgun in a leather case and was a big fellow about twenty-two.

He settled beside me and I said, "It doesn't take a shotgun to get a hitch around here, does it?"

"No, sir. Just taking my gun back to Baton Rouge. I like to hunt and might get in a little over there. My name's James Sanford and I go to L.S.U."

"You are big enough to play football, Jim."

"I do. Married too. Married when I was seventeen. Said I wanted my girl for my seventeenth birthday present, and I got her."

We were passing acres of tung trees, whence comes the valuable oil, and Jim said, "Used to call this Bloody Tangipahoa parish. Strawberry capital of the world. Lots of Yankees came down. Then Italians and Hungarians moved in, and the feudin' and fussin' started. Everybody gets along pretty good, though, now."

"What is Louisiana, Jim?"

"It's home," he said quickly, and then he thought about it. "I'm studying horticulture over at L.S.U. I like to make things grow. I suppose, in a way, you can say that I'm Louisiana. That's as good as any."

It was night, and flames spurted from a weird bevy of plants at Baton Rouge, lighting the Mississippi that makes this city a seaport 229 miles from the Gulf of Mexico. The woman behind the tobacco counter explained the flames. "Oil and ethyl," she said. "This is the ethyl capital of the world."

By now I realized that almost every place in Louisiana is a capital of something. The flame lights touched the skyscraper state house and the statue of Huey Long in a park where camellias bloomed, the seagoing tankers and Mississippi towboats. This is the capital of government for about 2,500,000 Louisianans, from the Slavonians and Dalmatians down near The Jump, where the river meets the sea, to the Scotch-Irish of Bastrop, up near the Arkansas line.

Tourists mingled with politicians and oilmen in the hotel lobby, the women chattering in a gumbo ya-ya and the men scowling. They wanted a drink, but it was Sunday and Louisiana's capital is a blue Sunday city by local option.

The visitors had been old-homing, visiting, for a fee, the hallowed plantation homes up the river between here and Natchez, the Audubon country. Some had been south, down the river road, and one couple had been to Carville and the leprosarium where Uncle Sam is trying to conquer a disease that is not half as contagious or as deadly as most people think. This couple was amazed at their discovery that the world's supply of perique tobacco is grown on 500 acres, more or less, down in St. James Parish.

Being an old-home hand myself, having lived in Natchez just long enough to catch the bug, I went down the river road to a twenty-two-room mansion whimsically called The Cottage and where, so long ago, folks sat on the upstairs gallery and watched the steam-boat race between the *City of Natchez* and the *Robert E. Lee.*

The Cottage is owned by Frances Parkinson Keyes. She wasn't at home, so we sought Belle Grove, one of the most fabulous of all plantation homes and one of the most foolish, a deserted, decaying testimonial to vanity. Belle Grove was hard to find, but yonder she stood, a sagging barbed-wire fence, old trees and weeds, and a pink stucco palace of eighty rooms, give or take a few.

There was the levee where Negro children played and cattle grazed, and here was the manor rotting away, for this was death in the afternoon of the South's plantation era. Lizards scurried. Bees droned. No other sign of life except, high up the side of the mon-strosity, was the proclamation: "Kilroy was here!"

Mary Evelyn Dickerson provided an answer to the wearisome myth of the swooning Southern lady and smelling salts. Miss Dicker-son is pretty enough for a dance, soft enough for moonlight, an unscarred gladiator in one of the roughest, toughest political arenas in the world.

What is Louisiana? Why, it's progress and prosperity. She wasn't sure of the amount of the bonded debt. That's not her department.

The sun glistened on the bronze memorial to Huey Long, but there was another statue in Baton Rouge and surely more whimsical; a statue to Hebe erected by the W.C.T.U. Maybe the ladies forgot that Hebe was cupbearer to the gods.

Alexandria is the capital, here we go again, of Central Louisiana, called Cenla by a promotional group that hopes to make the land an oil-rich area and a haven for industry and tourists. And there is no doubt about it, Cenla is one of the best fishing sections in the country. It is a place where rice, cotton and cane grow in adjoining fields, where salt and oil come out of the ground and trees grow fast. Here in the steaming Red River Valley hickory skis are started on their journey to the snow hills, and roe of the paddlefish is sold as caviar.

Here, too, is the spacious Hotel Bentley, built by rich old Joe Bentley because another hotel wouldn't let him keep his dog in his room and insisted on his wearing a coat.

Alexandria is the hub of Louisiana, one spoke going northeast to Monroe, the natural-gas capital, an industrial beehive that feels of Arkansas. Another spoke goes northwest to Shreveport, the state's second city, architecturally modern and an oil-gushing Midas that feels of Texas. A third spoke leads southwest to Lake Charles, a shipping and oil center, and a nugget in the Gold Coast that sweeps around from Brownsville, Texas, to the Cajun country.

Across the Red River from Alexandria and in another world is Winnfield, birthplace of Huey Long, Mecca for his followers and a happy hunting ground for lawyers ever since the parish records were destroyed by fire. The issue in Winnfield the day I was there was the little town's new gymnasium for Negroes. It was better than the one for whites and some folks didn't like it.

The community, built around a square, would fit in Mississippi or Georgia—a Saturday marketplace where woodsmen and farmers shared coffee and conversation while their women shopped in an air-conditioned super market called Jitney Jungle and their children licked ice-cream cones.

"What is Louisiana?" I asked the first man I met.

"Well, around here the big 'uns are getting bigger and the little 'uns are getting littler. Louisiana is like any other place, brother. You work and live and do the best you can."

Then I met Thomas Jefferson Wilder. I would have known him anywhere, the Southerner of long furrows and hot suns, his neck red-burned; proud, friendly and religious. He and his wife had come to town to bring buttermilk and eggs.

"Me and Huey Long were boys together back in the country. Huey was sharp as a brier." He cut his eyes over at me in the humor and wisdom of a hunting man. "No, thanks. I don't smoke. Don't drink, neither. I'm a church man. Testify for the Lord twice a week."

We went out to the farm where he lived in a little white house. Hounds and hogs and flowers were in the yard and electricity pulled his pump.

It was a typical Southern hill farm, once exhausted but greening again through conservation and tender care.

"Look at it," said Brother Wilder. "My pine trees are coming back fast and the topsoil is building up. The Lord's been rightly good to me. Come on, let's go see Aunt Tishy Lowry. She was raised with Huey too."

Aunt Tishy had a framed picture of Huey in her hallway and when we left she said, "You all come," meaning, "Come again."

I didn't ask them what Louisiana is. That was obvious. Louisiana is a turnip patch and a cotton field, cool buttermilk on the gallery and hound dogs scratching in the shade.

From the hills of Winn Parish to the Red River bayous of Avoyelles Parish is a short trip, and yet they are poles apart because Avoyelles has a French heritage and Gallic appreciation of gay living, a swishing skirt, a heady drink and a quick-flip of the cards.

"We live and let live around here," said Alton R. deNux, who was mayor of Marksville and a dentist with a sense of humor. His Honor grew camellias and lived well, a friendly host who, like so many Southerners, used his tongue for three purposes: talk, taste and in cheek.

The parish is a network of navigable waterways where fish and ducks abound. We went down a long bayou in Edgar Coco's fishing boat, laughing and whooping, scaring turtles, wild hogs and a moccasin or so.

It was a wilderness of water and trees, and brooding silence. But all along the way were little yellow flags tied to the limbs that shadowed the water—seismograph markers for oil prospecting. The silence won't be long, now, boys: the Texans are coming!

Far, far down the bayou we met two lonely swampers in bright woolen shirts. A coffeepot, a gun and a few fish were in their boat. They spoke no English, but drank Scotch whisky.

Then to a fish fry where a gaunt Negro woman cooked fresh fish in deep boiling fat. She spoke a strange accent and wore a gay bandanna around her head. The fish was smoking hot, the salad stout, and there were no hush puppies, for most Louisianans, unlike other coastal Southerners, do not eat hush puppies, but prefer French bread.

The black land south, where stock roamed at large, was as flat as one of Aunt Tishy's batter cakes, through the town of Bunkie, which was named for its founder's pet monkey, and into the real

Cajun country. I was on watch for "quaint Cajuns" and "old quaint buggies."

There were Cajuns, all right, some of them dressed in their best. The men could have been straight from Madison Avenue, the women from Fifth. I was too busy dodging big automobiles to see many buggies. Amish buggies are more common in Pennsylvania than Cajun buggies in Louisiana.

Opelousas is the sweet-potato capital, where they have learned that the once lowly Southern 'tater is worth more per bushel than corn. Incidentally, sweet potatoes are those juicy red tubers erroneously called yams in the North. The error has taken hold down here and each year Opelousas celebrates a festival called the Yambilee, a sort of small-town Mardi Gras and maybe more fun.

Come to think of it, Louisiana must be the festival capital of the nation, for almost every city and town has some kind of to-do to celebrate something. These include New Orleans' Carnival, of course, and Hammond's Strawberry Festival, Shreveport's "Holiday in Dixie," Opelousas' Yambilee, Crowley's Rice Carnival, New Iberia's Sugar Festival, Grand Isle's Tarpon Rodeo, and the Cotton Carnival at Tallulah.

The moist, rich rice lands spread wide and over there was Crowley, the rice capital, and here was LaFayette, the Cajun capital where afternoon coffee still is called a *collation*.

The crawfish are running in the first stir of spring and the Cajuns catch them in shallow water, grind the flesh of their tails and steep the tasty concoction in herbs and peppers. The mixture then is stuffed into the hollowed-out chests of the crawfish and cooked into a soup called crawfish bisque. It is too good for a king, good enough only for peasants who know how to turn simple things into good food.

Iberia is the ancient name for Spain, but New Iberia is French and my first host here was A. J. Bowab, a Syrian. He talked of Brahma-Angus cattle, industrial surveys and oil barges on Bayou Teche.

This is the pepper capital and the big spoon of Louisiana's sugar bowl. The only "hills" around here are salt domes, miles wide and 5 to 6 miles deep, and the salt, as mined, is too pure for table use. Oil wells rim the domes, one of which is Avery Island. The island was the property of the Avery family for generations. Then years ago a McIlhenny married an Avery. That McIlhenny invented Tabasco Sauce and his son made it famous.

Today the island is owned by a joint family corporation. The Mc-Ilhennys lease land from the corporation to grow their tabasco peppers and on which is located the sauce factory. They also lease land for their famous Jungle Gardens. Exotic plants of all the world thrive on the gardens' 200 acres, which are sanctuary for thousands of birds, including egrets. Visitors come to see the soap trees from India, the Egyptian lotus, and daisies from the Mountains of the Moon and remain to gasp at the 50,000 azaleas and camellias.

Here also lived two friends who represented the extreme ends of the Louisiana index. One is Matt Vernon, a newspaper editor who went North to study and came back to tell his people about the good things he had learned, and to warn them about the bad things.

In another age, Matt Vernon would have ridden away with Nathan Bedford Forrest without asking why. Now he questions everything and has worked his shoulders stooped trying to mesh the Cajuns' agrarian traditions into the industrial revolution. The bigger the sacred cow the harder he hits; needling politicians and lashing Yankee reformers and Southern jingoes. Mr. Vernon since has sold his New Iberia paper and has moved his battleground to Eunice.

Being Southerners, we quickly got to the Negro question. "Emotional or rational?" he asked. "I can talk it either way."

"Me, too," I said. "But let's try it rational."

"O.K." He slouched back into the ease of a man on his own ground. "The big noise over the Negro question down here is getting behind the parade, pitifully. More progress toward acceptance of the Negro's rights has taken place in the last ten years than in the previous fifty. Just don't weep for us, brother. And don't yell at us."

It was his way of saying to all who cared to listen: "Don't point your finger at us as long as your own fingernails are dirty."

The other friend is Weeks Hall, a bachelor educated in New Orleans and Paris, and a painter until his right arm was mangled in an accident. Mr. Hall, the last of his line, lives in "The Shadows," the most photographed plantation home in the world and an architectural antique.

"What is Louisiana?" Weeks Hall poured bayou coffee into silver demitasses, sweetened it with rock sugar imported from New York and laced it with rum. "She is a romantic yesterday and a rich tomorrow. Texas is taking us."

Mr. Hall, a recluse to the point of phobia, amazed even the amazing Henry Miller, who spent several days at "The Shadows" while writing *The Air-Conditioned Nightmare*. Mr. Hall's apparel usually consists of blue denim trousers and easy shoes, but for special occasions he adds a blue denim shirt. It is most intriguing to hear him, surrounded by cut glass decanters, silver services and priceless antiques, call to his valet, "Lay out my blues." One expects to see him in evening clothes and cummerbund. One sees him in blue denim.

Tourists invade his yard at all hours, and in a futile attempt to offset their depredations he has instructed his yardmen to collect a small fee. However, in the confusion that attends Mr. Hall, he seldom pockets any tourist's tariff, but usually winds up lecturing them on Cajun cooking, French art and the unfathomable ignorance of Yankees.

Now whereas his friend, Matt Vernon, is a Southern realist, Weeks Hall is a romanticist, although, down deep, he is far more aware of political and social problems than he ever lets on. He is a passing breed in the South: Don Quixote in the trappings of Sir Walter Scott, yet versed in Voltaire and Thomas Jefferson.

Mr. Hall did me many honors. The two I prize most are his family's recipe for bayou coffee and an introduction to Dr. Thad St. Martin of Houma. Here is the recipe:

Parch green coffee beans in a skillet over a charcoal fire. Stir a bit of butter and a smidgen of sugar into the parched beans, then store the beans in airtight cans to be used as needed. Grind, and pour boiling water over the grounds in a French drip coffeepot.

Weeks Hall also gave an explanation of the difference between Creoles and Cajuns: "A Creole was an urban emigré, a Cajun was a rural refugee."

And now down to Houma, over the long, flat road where drivers seldom dim their lights, past Morgan City—a shrimp capital—and into the Terrebonne country, which means "good land." However, there is a lot of water.

Louisiana, incidentally, has the fourth longest coastline in the country. The marshes and water make this bright little city a fur-and-fish capital, and, of course, there is oil. Houma is pronounced

"Homer" and this is rather confusing because there is another Louisiana town named Homer.

Dr. Thad St. Martin is a Creole who put aside his medicine kit long enough to write *Madame Toussaint's Wedding Day*. He also is another contradiction in the Louisiana story, for Dr. St. Martin is a non-Catholic Creole who lives in a Cape Cod house on the bank of a bayou.

Mrs. St. Martin has all the charm, elegance and beauty that the song attributes to "Creole ladies with dancing eyes"—or however it goes. The only catch is that Mrs. St. Martin is not a Creole.

It was a lush February night and the St. Martins, and their foster daughter, Miss Cecele Edsberg, sat on their porch and discussed Louisiana. They had been shopping that day in New Orleans, sixty miles away, and Dr. St. Martin, a native, talked dispassionately about "the city," while Miss Edsberg talked impassionately. "It is the most glamorous city in America," she said. "Food, fun, politics —anyway you look at it." Miss Edsberg moved down from Illinois.

Dr. St. Martin smiled, perhaps remembering that, year in and year out, the biggest political issue in New Orleans is not the Long machine, graft or gambling, but everyday garbage collection. The garbage can is the political symbol of the housewife's wrath and the powers fear her retribution far more than ward heelers, Frankie Costello, reformers and smoke-filled rooms.

"New Orleans is a good-time city," Dr. St. Martin said. "It always has been. It has the best cooking in the country. The people work hard, but always find time for fun. Drink and food, opera, carnival dancing, horse racing, fishing, baseball, football—you name it and New Orleans will furnish it if it is practical, possible or profitable.

"First of all, it is a city in every sense of the word; cosmopolitan and blasé, wicked and righteous, mansions and slums. However, there is one side to New Orleans that we seldom read about. It is one of the nation's best medical centers."

So it is. Charity Hospital is one of the largest in the world and the medical schools include Tulane, Louisiana State University, Dillard's Flint-Goodridge Hospital for Negroes, and Loyola's School of Dentistry.

The St. Martins visit New Orleans as a well-to-do Connecticut family might visit New York. So where do they eat in the cuisine capital? On this day they had eaten at Galatoire's because they have known a waiter there for a long time. They had oysters *brochette,* broiled trout and broiled sheepshead, and water-cress salad.

Reluctantly I left the St. Martins' porch and headed for the "City of Sin," which actually is one of the most churchgoing communities in the country and home of the influential Baptist Bible Institute.

The Huey Long highway and railroad bridge over the Mississippi and the marshes is awesome, a steel string that is testimony to man's engineering conquest of the seemingly impossible.

Then there is New Orleans, her head cradled in a bend of the river, her feet in Lake Pontchartrain and her backbone along Canal Street. Call her what you will. I prefer the City of Courage, for no city has overcome more handicaps than this one.

Lyle Saxon called her "fabulous." Mark Twain spoke of her food as being as "delicious as the less criminal forms of sin." One of her politicians said of her wine-women-and-song philosophy that "you can make it illegal, but you can't make it unpopular." And this is the place where the first white women threatened to leave unless the food improved.

A thousand books have tried to explain New Orleans, but she continues to speak for herself; in the jazz music that she gave the world, in the roar of the Sugar Bowl crowd, in the rivets that make her a shipyard and the cranes that make her a port, in the looms that make her a garment center and Mardi Gras that makes her a painted lady for one night and a penitent mother the next morning.

More than half a million people live in the city proper, and this does not include the thickly settled environs. She is a Bohemian refuge for writers and artists and yet she sells fewer books than Dallas.

Now this is a matter of personal taste, but New Orleans is the only city I know anything about where you can drop in at almost any restaurant and get a good meal. The most famous eating places are Galatoire's, Antoine's, Arnaud's and Broussard's.

There is no mystery about Creole cooking. It is the natural consequence of geography and people. The Gulf of Mexico gives New Orleans an incredible variety of fish. So do the bayous and rivers. The land gives rice, used as Irish potatoes down here, herbs, peppers, okra, cushaws, a vegetable pear called *mirliton,* and just about anything else you need. Mix these with an Indian-French-Spanish-Negro taste and there it is.

However, the drinking is something else, for New Orleans, Gallic as she is, really is a hard-liquor city. This is the home of three of America's distinctive drinks: the Ramos Gin Fizz (gin, egg white, sugar, lemon and lime juice, orange flower water, sweet cream and soda water), the Roffignac (whisky, Hembarig, grenadine and seltzer), and the Sazerac, which is whisky, bitters and sugar served in a glass rinsed with absinthe.

Take with caution!

The Vieux Carré, called the French Quarter or simply the Quarter, is the original Nouvelle Orleans and is only a speck in the sprawling city and has become something of a bazaar and side show in this age of the fast tourist dollar. If you enjoy history, relics and romance, the best way to see the Quarter is to walk, provided you can duck the night clubs, the saloons and the girlie shows. However, if time is pressing, rent a carriage for a reasonable fee, listen to the guide and ask him questions, then take a short excursion on the river.

South Rampart is the Negro Broadway and voodoo no longer is prevalent but still is practiced secretly. Basin Street is a business thoroughfare and not a meeting place. Picayune, once a coin, now is a newspaper and the Storyville of jazz and brothels just ain't.

The famous and the infamous have been coming to New Orleans for a long time, and the city has sent out her share of personalities. From here came the galaxy of great jazz players, including Louis Armstrong and Jelly Roll Morton.

The Crescent City is a community of clubs and the most exclusive is the Boston Club, a political and business sanctum of a chosen few. It got its name from a card game called "Boston" and not from the Massachusetts city.

To the average American, New Orleans is known as the home of Mardi Gras and jazz music.

This distinctive music was born of the blues and the blues are of Negro origin. Perhaps it began at funerals, the plaintive wailing of trombones and other loud instruments so often used at burials around here. Anyway, somehow was started that four-beat time that mingled with the hot notes of ragtime, and jazz was born.

The early ragtime bands were "spasm" bands, nondescript units that improvised music in honky-tonks and the red-light district. These included such colorful musicians as "Stale Bread" Lacoume and his cohorts—"Warm Gravy," "Family Haircut," "Whisky" and "Seven Colors." Their instruments were a bass fiddle made of half a barrel, a cheese-box banjo, a soapbox guitar and a few other assorted doodads.

This crazy music, unique, stirring, Afro-American, stuck to its native hearth until about 1914, when talent scouts took Dixieland to Chicago.

Visitors here always want to see a jazz band and are disappointed to learn that the great jazz players now are in the North, for this city, like her Southern sisters, exports talent in droves. Here in everyday living you hear expressions and melodies that become famous up North in a few years.

The tapestry of New Orleans has a rich color, a feeling of hot reds and deep blues. But the tapestry is dirty in spots and frayed around the edges. Nevertheless, this city is one of the nation's original tapestries and you have not seen your homeland until you have seen New Orleans.

She is the Southern jewel, deep in a Louisiana setting and shining bright and proud. Although there are specks of dime-store tawdriness on the gem, she makes no attempt to hide them.

Sooner or later most American travelers come here. They whisper in St. Louis Cathedral, murmur in the Cabildo and shout in the hot spots. They soon fall into the slow tempo of Canal Street and eat and drink more than they should. On every side is dead history and live fun, and yet the most famous product of New Orleans is neither carnival nor coffee, but an eighty-two-year-old woman—the late Mrs. Meriwether Gilmer, known to the world as Dorothy Dix.

Dakota

by JACK SCHAEFER

On old maps, not so old that men living cannot recall studying them in school, it was Dakota Territory, one piece, one area. On present maps it is split by an arbitrary line into two states with the colorless, unimaginative designations: North and South. There are differences between the two parts, man-made, results of years of double statehood and a more or less deliberate fostering of differences. There are people in both states who emphasize differences, people who become huffy if called simply Dakotans and insist upon the North-South distinction. But differences fade in the face of physical fact. Geography predominates. The old maps were right. Dakota is one piece, one place, one area. The very name, common to both states, defies the split. "Dakotah" is a Sioux word meaning "united."

But it *is* two states.

Like stiff-necked members of the same family going their own ways, they have little to do with each other—except when rows develop like the one over the bones of Sitting Bull. It is even difficult to get from one to the other except by automobile—and the surfaced line-crossing highways are few and far apart. Most of the railroads and bus lines and air routes run east-west across the states, not north-south from one to the other.

They are both wild-eyed and individualistic and they are both conservative—in opposite ways.

North, a constant hotbed of agrarian reform, is radical, progressive, upsetting in politics with a habit of electing opinionated men
whom sober folk elsewhere often regard as sons of the wild jackass.
South has had its political eccentrics, but nowadays is politically
settled and conservative. North is restrained and sedate about such
things as business and the daily duty of earning a living. South has
the booster, the promotional, the sky's-the-limit spirit. It saw nothing
blue-sky in its attempt to win the United Nations headquarters. It
prepared a flossy brochure boosting its Black Hills for the site. Neighbors Wyoming and Nebraska lent mild support. Practical North remained aloof.

South has the larger population and more cities, yet its general
impression is more rural. Its capital, Pierre (pronounced Pier), looks
like an overgrown country town. Its capitol is an old-fashioned
domed period piece, full of waste space, with rotunda and wide stair-
ways and wide galleries and small Dickensian offices tucked away in
odd corners. North is more rural by most standards, yet it gives a
more settled, staid, businesslike impression. Its capital, Bismarck,
looks like any small-scale, square-blocked city. Its capitol is a tall-
towered, streamlined structure, very modern and quite functional.

South enjoys the colorful gesture. North thinks more of its dignity.
South has a publicity department. North does not. South goes actively
after the tourist trade. North sits back and lets what comes come.
South's license plates are large, adding to the numbers a picture—in
color—of a state boast, the Mount Rushmore heads. North's are small,
narrow, completely practical, carrying only the identifying numbers.

This publicity difference is not necessarily the result of any special
virtue (or vice) of either state. Nature endowed South with more
tourist attractions and thus South has had a stronger taste of the
money the tourist trade brings.

No. There is more to it than that. It is rooted in the people themselves. South's are apt to say: "Want to see our state? Wonderful!
Come along and we'll show it to you." North's are more likely to put
it: "Looking the state over? Fine. Go ahead and enjoy yourself."

Oh . . . Sitting Bull's bones?
He was killed by Indian police during the Ghost Dance troubles

of 1890 at his camp on Grand River in South's portion of the Standing Rock Reservation which straddles the common state line.

His body, with those of the police killed in the fracas, was taken into North's part of the reservation and buried at Fort Yates. When the fort was abandoned in 1895 and all military graves removed, his was left untouched. North liked the notion of having him there.

But South wanted him too. There were arguments through the years, all futile. North had possession. Then came the Missouri Valley flood-control program. The Oahe Dam reservoir, when completed, would cover the grave. South swung into action.

Legal action first. Early in 1953, armed with powers of attorney from some of Sitting Bull's living relatives, South asked North's Health Department to approve a removal application. North's officials were shocked. Indignant telegrams flew about, some all the way to Washington. Then one night a group of South's stalwarts (names officially unknown) slipped north over the line and opened the grave.

What exactly they found, after 60-some years following a quick unceremonial burial, is their secret. Whatever it was, they took it southward over the line to a site already prepared—a good site, overlooking the union of the Grand and Missouri rivers close by the obelisk in memory of Sacajawea, Indian woman guide of the Lewis and Clark expedition. They buried it again and over the new grave they poured twenty tons of concrete to offset any North reclamation project.

There, for all practical and pointing-with-pride purposes, now lie the bones of Sitting Bull. They rest under not only the tons of concrete but also under a six-ton splendid bust of the old medicine man done by South's blue-sky sculptor, Korczak Ziolkowski.

After the kidnaping there were more indignant telegrams. Finally, Mary Louise Defender of Fort Yates, Miss Indian America, acting as North's special representative, smoked a pipe of peace with South's Governor Anderson and the battle of the bones was over.

So much for North and South. This is about Dakota. One man's view of Dakota; an amateur student of Western history who went West to Dakota and found it all he had thought—and more.

Look at the outline on a map: two rectangular blocks aligned precisely east and west, one above the other. There are straight lines three fourths of the way around. On the north, the Canadian border, the famous 49th parallel. On the west, Montana and the upper part of

Wyoming. On the south, Nebraska, straight most of the way then hitting the Missouri River and following the curves downriver to the junction with the Big Sioux. On the east, up the Big Sioux bordering Iowa, then another straight stretch along Minnesota to pick up Big Stone Lake and above it Lake Traverse and on up the Red River of the North to the 49th parallel again.

The area enclosed is Dakota: 148,000-plus square miles of prairie and plain and Badlands and a shading of hills called mountains and a patch of mountains called hills; a huge chunk of territory averaging more than 350 miles in width and more than 400 miles in height on the map, bigger even than the great bull-shaped expanse of Montana, topped in extent only by Texas and California. By size and, more important, by topography, Dakota is the biggest batch of wide-open spaces in the United States. Only Texas could dispute that—and the wide-open spaces of Texas are of a different, less impressive caliber.

Look now along the North-South division line. Almost exactly in the middle the Missouri, the Big Muddy, cuts across. That is the center of Dakota. It is also the approximate center of North America.

Southward, near Pierre, is a small monument which claims to mark the geographic center of the continent. Diagonals from corner to corner of a standard map will intersect there. Northward, above Bismarck, near the town of Rugby, is a stone cairn also claiming to mark the geographic center of the continent.

But the precise spot is unimportant. Any spot in Central Dakota will do, can be shown to be approximately 1500 miles from the Atlantic, the Pacific, the Gulf of Mexico and the lower reaches of the Arctic Ocean. Dakota, neatly framed around that central area, is the heartland of North America.

"Dakota?" said the man at the airport. "What d'you want to go there for? Nothing but droughts and blizzards and fields of wheat. Probably can't even rent a car to get around in."

He was wrong. At Pierre, where the little plane out from Minneapolis landed, there were two rental cars.

Dakota's history, beginning late, moved slowly in terms of modern development. A whole century—from 1750 to 1850—can be taken in one gulp.

The Sioux, still bow-and-arrow, were unable to stand against the

Chippewa—who had some French guns—and were driven westward and spread into Dakota. The fur trappers, the mountain men penetrated all through the territory, taking out a rich plunder in pelts— and leaving no real impression.

In 1775, in the southeast corner where Yankton now stands, one Pierre Dorion married a Yankton Sioux woman and built a cabin and became Dakota's first permanent white resident. Up in the northeast corner, where rival fur companies out of Canada were having almost pitched battles, the North West Fur Company founded Pembina, Dakota's first permanent settlement.

The 1850's started things moving with a relative rush.

This was the period of freehand carving of territories and states by Congress. Dakota did not yet have its name, but settlers already were trickling into the eastern fringe along the Big Sioux. Land companies were starting townsites in the Sioux Falls area.

The settlers were few in number, perhaps no more than 200, but large in ambition, and they started yipping for territorial status. Congress was unimpressed.

Then, early in 1861, Congress suddenly yielded and gave Dakota its name and territorial status. Scattered over hundreds of thousands of square miles there were exactly 2402 white inhabitants.

That was Dakota in 1861. Within twenty-eight years it was ready to become two states.

"I came out here better than 40 years ago," said the man in the old swivel chair in the little false-fronted office building. "From Wisconsin. Thought I had t.b. and needed this higher and dryer climate. Turned out to be tight belt instead. After a time I went back to Wisconsin and couldn't stand it. Too many trees. Too many people and not my kind any more. Just had to get back to this plains country."

Territorial days—those were wild and woolly in Dakota and in basic ways established the modern character of the region.

The 60's were years of beginnings and troubles, Indian and otherwise. Gold had been found in Montana, and the National Government started a survey for a road northward and built forts along the way. Red Cloud, chief of the Oglala Sioux, perhaps the ablest leader of all the seven tribes, rallied them to resist the invasion. In a series of swift campaigns he forced acceptance of a treaty on his terms: abandonment of the forts and a pledge that all of the land between the Big Horn Mountains on the west, the Platte River on the south, the Missouri on the east and north would be left forever as a permanent Indian hunting ground. That included all of Dakota west of the Missouri River.

And all the while the settlers, the sodbusters, the homesteaders were trickling into Dakota.

The 70's were the years of the railroads and wheat—and gold.

The railroads were first. At last people could get to and into Dakota by rail. But why should they come?

The first answer was wheat.

Oliver Dalrymple is the key name. He had partners but he was the active manager, the man who proved what the black-soil region, the Red River Valley and the adjoining prairie could do. Buying big chunks of cheap railroad-grant land, he launched the original "bonanza farm," 12,000 acres at the one sweep, all in wheat. Investment money poured in. Huge farms transformed the virgin land into a rolling sea of wheat. Fifty to 100 sections in one piece was not unusual and a section is a mile square. Those were the days a man could pack food, sling a rifle over his shoulder, plow a furrow straight out till noon, eat lunch, and plow back in time, if he was lucky, to reach home for supper.

The second answer was gold—gold in the Black Hills!

The Indians knew it was there. They knew, too, what would happen if the white men knew. As early as the 30's white men had penetrated the Hills and found gold. They did not get out with it. A small piece of sandstone found near the town of Spearfish and now in a museum at Deadwood had the following crude inscription scratched on it: *came to these Hills in 1833 seven of us All ded but me Ezra Kind Killed by Ind Got all our gold 1834.* The Indians got him too.

The Hills were part of the area set aside by the treaty with Red Cloud to be forever Sioux hunting ground. In 1874, just six years after the signing, that highly controversial military glamour boy, General George Custer, led an expedition into the Hills. Maybe it had military purposes, scientific too. There were geologists along.

But why were prospectors permitted to go too? And why, when they hit gold near the present town of Custer, were messengers immediately dispatched at speed to make the word public outside?

The inevitable stampede started. A new strike, the big one, was made in Deadwood Gulch. In a matter of months 25,000 people were crowding into that narrow twisting gulley with its mushroom tent town, and other thousands were swarming through the Hills. Names like Wild Bill Hickok, Calamity Jane, Preacher Smith, Deadwood Dick, were adding flavor to the tales running through the country.

With a flamboyant gesture Dakota, the land of golden wheat and gold, was on the maps and on the national consciousness.

The 80's were the years of the cattle boom. Ranching in those days was not only profitable, it was fashionable. Investment money poured in; amateur ranchers too. Young Theodore Roosevelt was one of them. He went west to Dakota for a sample of the robust life and stayed the better part of four years. But easily the most remarkable was a handsome French nobleman from Paris named Antoine-Amedee-Marie-Vincent Manca de Vallambrosa, the Marquis de Mores.

The de Mores enterprises made many marks on Dakota. One was, and is, the little town of Medora, named for his American wife, in the heart of the northern Badlands. This was the site of his most ambitious project. He planned to raise cattle and sheep and ship the meat east. He built a big meat-packing plant at Medora. But he was a poor businessman, and the professional ranchers unloaded poor stock on him. At last he closed the plant and departed for Paris. Only the tall chimney of his Medora plant still stands. And nearby, the chateau he built is now a local museum.

Note that chateau. This de Mores, unlike most of the cattle-boom investors, lived in Dakota. He took part in local politics and cattle associations. He started stage and freight lines. He helped finance newspapers. He hunted with the best, with men like Granville Stuart. He tangled with a grizzly and killed it with a knife. He was straight out of a romantic storybook and he was real.

Then, with the terrible winter of 1886–87, the cattle boom collapsed.

At the time, Bismarck, the new territorial capital, was less than ten years old, but full of bounce. It laid the new capitol cornerstone with a flourish. General Grant was there, and Sitting Bull, and James Bryce, author of *The American Commonwealth*. What particularly impressed this visiting Englishman was a speech in which "it was proved that as Bismarck was the centre of Dakota, Dakota the centre of the United States, and the United States the centre of the world, Bismarck was destined to be the metropolitan hearth of the world's civilization." North, too, had its blue-sky tinge in those days.

And all the while the settlers, the sodbusters and the small independent ranchers, were coming into Dakota, spreading out over the far open spaces.

They came . . . the fiddle-footed and the restless always settling and never settled who would move on or back, leaving shacks to weather away in the endless wind . . . the land-grabbers who would pre-empt and homestead only long enough to prove title and sell out . . . the real-estate operators who would lay out townships and draw pretty pictures of buildings never to be built . . . and the solid whipcord men who would stand stubbornly through the hard years, and their women who would often, in the lean, long years, irrigate the dry land with their tears—and stay and make homes seemingly lost yet held in the immensity of the land.

They came, the land-hungry, from the Midwest and the East and Canada, and as many and more direct from the old countries; primarily nordics: Finns with their constant coffeepots and their "Finlander hells" or steam baths; Russian-Germans, many of them Mennonites, who had emigrated from Germany into Russia early in the century; Scandinavians with their insistence upon homeland cooking, Norwegians most numerous among them; a sturdy sampling of Dutch and Irish and English; even a colony of Icelanders in the Pembina area.

They came—and Dakota wanted them and welcomed them and urged them to come. They came as word spread that in Dakota the land was level with no trees or brush to clear away. During one sample week 9000 immigrants traveled by train through Chicago and more than 8000 were ticketed for Dakota.

Then, beginning in '86, there were several years of continued droughts. The Dakota land boom dwindled and collapsed. And reversed. The fiddle-footed, the quickly dissatisfied, the sell-out homesteaders, the weak willed, began to leave. It was a healthy winnowing process. For the stubborn whipcord men and their women—eccentric and independent and individualistic and stubborn—remained.

Year after year they had been petitioning Congress for statehood and the demand for division had been growing. In 1888 the Republican National Convention wrote a double-state plank into its platform. In 1889, after the new Republican Congress had acted, the new president, Benjamin Harrison, signed the official proclamations. The two documents were shuffled and placed on his desk with the texts covered, only the signature lines showing. Officially at least, no one knows which state was admitted first.

That was Dakota. That *is* Dakota, the real, the enduring Dakota. Dakota today remains, in modern terms, what it became in the territorial days. The past is close and often beckoning there.

"Stand over there and look down," said the man in worn overalls and ancient farmer's straw hat. "See those darker streaks in the grass running on around that ridge? Look like wagon tracks, don't they? Well, they are. That's where one of the old freight routes to Deadwood ran. You can't make out a thing down close by them. From up here they still show darker where the wheel ruts were. Sometimes looking down there you can get the notion it wasn't seventy-five years ago but only last week those wagons were moving along."

That North-South division was made by a political institution, the United States Congress. The real, the sensible, the logical division of Dakota is far more ancient—and is east-west. It was made by the Missouri River.

> *Ah-hah, I'm bound away*
> *'Cross the wide Mizzoura.*

That is not just a refrain from a song. It is a living slogan out of the past, still strong in the present. East of the Missouri is east; west of the Missouri is west.

East-river, west-river: Dakotans constantly use those labels. East-river country is chiefly farmland. West-river country is chiefly rangeland. East-river is shotgun country; west-river is rifle country.

No generalizations are absolute nowadays, but the cleavage cut by the Big Muddy is still distinct. A few old-timers claim they can tell which side they are on just by sniffing the air. A simpler test for visitors is a costume check. East-river has plenty of cowboy boots and wide-brimmed hats always in evidence. The majority are the drugstore variety, the mass-produced-for-the-tourist-trade relatively cheap type. West-river they are everywhere and the majority are forty dollars-plus boots and twenty dollars-plus hats, the true articles, usually battered and weary from years of weather and work. East-river they are worn for show, a form of regional fashion. West-river they are worn as practical working equipment.

Fort Pierre proves the point. Pierre, on the east bank, becomes ever more neat and respectable as more state-capital buildings and modern homes and motels are built. It is reminiscent of many another small city back east. You cross the long narrow bridge to the west bank and definitely there is a different feel in the air. You swing south a short distance, to where the Bad River comes in from the west, and the little town of Fort Pierre drowses during the day, looking much as it did when freighters outfitted there for the long haul to the Black Hills. At night Fort Pierre comes alive as cowboys from the west-river rangeland gather in the surprising number of taverns, and state employees from Pierre cross the river to join them. No doubt Fort Pierre gets a nightlife boost from the convenient fact that the river marks the time line, the shift from Central to Mountain Time, and its taverns can stay open an hour longer than those in Pierre. But it does not need the boost. It has the atmosphere, the tradition. An outlander, visiting those taverns, needs to be wary. He may find himself trapped by the west-river cowboy custom of setting up drinks for the crowd.

Northward at Bismarck it is the same. Bismarck itself, on the east bank, is a neat and respectable small city. You cross the river westward and are in Mandan. The names speak the difference. Bismarck was named by men looking eastward across the Atlantic, in the hope that the honor paid the German Iron Chancellor would attract German immigrants. Mandan was named for the Mandan Indians who once had villages there.

Mandan may fool you for a brief time, what you see of it just passing through. Much of it is of recent growth and has an eastern look. The Northern Pacific built a depot there which is a copy of George Washington's Mount Vernon. But the moment you wander off the main street, the western imprint is clear. Anywhere out toward the outskirts, the land opens and engulfs you with meaning and you suddenly realize this is it—this is the land of the high plains of the west. And just a short drop downriver, again on the west bank, is the site of old Fort Lincoln from which, one day in 1876, with banners flying and band playing, General Custer and his 7th Cavalry rode westward toward a rendezvous on the Little Big Horn.

It is the same almost anywhere along the Missouri. East of the river is east. West of the river is west.

Dakota is where, more distinctly and on a longer frontier than anywhere else in the United States, the west begins.

*"I didn't use to believe those old stories about the blizzards," said
the woman who ran the little six-room hotel. "But in '49 we had a
whole month of them, one right on top the other. I'll have you know
that was something. You could walk right up on the roof of this place
from the drifts. It was ten days at one stretch before the road was
open along here and I got mighty sick of canned pineapple too. But
I'll have you know everybody pitched in and helped everybody else
and those with airplanes dropped supplies around and we didn't
lose a life at all. That's human life I mean. Maybe some Federal aid
did come in—but we paid back every cent of it."*

As geologists can point out, Dakota actually is divided into four
quite distinct sections, neatly balanced: two east-river, two west-
river. Starting from the east, the first is the Red River Valley.

This is a long narrow (in Dakota distance terms) strip running
down the edge of North Dakota and fading out in the Lake Traverse
and Big Stone Lake area of South Dakota. It is the last strip of rich,
welcoming, never-failing farmland along the northern tier of American states before the beginning of the real prairies and plains—and
it is a magnificent strip. It is one of the finest stretches of almost table-
top farmland on the continent.

Tucked into the northeast corner is the sleepy little border town of
Pembina which was not only the first permanent settlement in Dakota but the first in the entire American Northwest. A century ago
it was the rallying center for the famous annual Pembina buffalo
hunts. Now it is a quiet farmers' village, notable chiefly for its quaint
old-fashioned gingerbready architecture.

This Red River Valley was the original home of the bonanza farms
and of hard wheat when Dakota was winning the title of breadbasket of the world. It is still great wheat country, golden in harvesttime. But the huge farms have been broken up into merely big farms
and diversified farming dominates, settled and reasonably sober and
sedate.

It is farmland de luxe, almost untroubled even in the bad years
by droughts and grasshopper plagues. But the Red River Valley is
not distinctively Dakotan. It is shared the full length with Minnesota.
Crossing this river brings no perceptible change. Dakota's half of the
Red River Valley could be simply Minnesota lapping over.

The second section, all the vast remaining expanse of the east-
river country from the Red River Valley over to the wide Missouri,

is the Dakota prairie—that great glacial drift, rolling, treeless sea of soil left in ages past by the recurrent sheets of ice that crept down out of the north and leveled off the high places and filled in the low and, melting in defeat along the edges, created the Missouri Trench for the modern river.

That is Dakota. That is a good half of Dakota and most of it is distinctively Dakotan. It is not all pure prairie, only a mere ninety per cent.

In northeast South Dakota with Watertown, appropriately named, as the local capital is the southern lake region. Dozens of lakes and ponds and stretches of marshland speckle the nearly level surface. On up in North Dakota, a jump westward from Grand Forks, is the northern lake region. And on up further, between and above the towns of Bottineau and Rolla, pushing on over the Canadian border, are the Turtle Mountains. North Dakota calls them mountains. To anyone acquainted with the real mountains of the west, they are hills—a pleasant break in the prairie offering scenery and excellent hunting, but hills.

And it is not wholly treeless; almost every watercourse has its fringing of brushes and shrub growth and often genuine trees. But these are far between in the vastness of open spaces and usually dip below the general ground level so that they are lost in the far view. The effect for nearly countless miles is true treelessness. In fact, a real stand of trees, even along a watercourse, is such a rarity that most of the early prairie homes were sod-walled or built of rammed-earth blocks. Even today a city like Aberdeen, in the heart of the prairie, will boast of the trees, all planted by hand, which line its streets.

The prairie is natural grassland. Buffalo into the millions once roamed there; now the only buffalo east-river are on a state game farm close to the Canadian border. The prairie has been settled, tamed, plowed, broken to harness. That is sometimes hard to believe on the long lonely stretches of the graveled roads off the few good highways where the clusters of farm buildings dwindle to a mile or more apart and unbroken distances pull vision beyond grasp of the mind. But signs of the plow are rarely out of sight and those reminders of the taming—the fence lines—are constant companions.

As you push out into this prairie along any of the main east-west routes that slice across it, a sense of the land creeps in and grows until it dominates all else. The few farm buildings merge into their surroundings, natural objects in a natural world, and there is only the land, apparently limitless, serene, indifferent, enduring the surface scratchings of man, under the great rounded bowl of the sky. You begin to understand the quiet unhurried manner that marks so many Dakotans. The day wanes and ahead the sun drops to the horizon and an unbelievable glory of color claims the sky. The people of wooded or hilly or mountainous country do not know what sunsets are.

This is the section which, with some help from west-river, is now the breadbasket of the world—well, in this cold-war era, of half the world. Wheat is the major crop. Dairying is on the upgrade, but beef is still the real cattle business. The old longhorns which followed the buffalo are long since gone. It is Hereford country with a spotting of Angus and Durhams and mixed breeds.

A recent phenomenon is the annual parade of big combines moving north with the ripening grain. Once it was an annual wave of itinerant farmhands following the harvest; now it is a parade of machines, big and ungainly and flamboyant in red paint and almost frighteningly efficient, cutting and threshing and loading in the single operation. They come north out of Nebraska and Kansas and Oklahoma and Texas, crawling northward with the advancing season. In early August they are moving through South Dakota. By late August they are well up into North Dakota, heading into Canada.

This area, too, this prairie, is the bird-hunter's dream come true. From the beginning it abounded in game birds, waterfowl in the lake regions, grouse and prairie chicken everywhere. By time of statehood it was already well known to shotgun sportsmen. Expeditions in what were called "chicken wagons" roamed the seemingly endless acres. Frederic Remington described one such expedition in 1894, in pictures and text, for *Harper's* magazine. The text was ecstatic. And he knew only the beginning.

For the Dakotans have not been content with their natural bird endowment. Partridges and wild turkeys have been introduced and have thrived. So too have ring-necked pheasants. Emphatically so. In 1898 a Doctor Zitlitz brought two male and four female into South Dakota. There were some later stocking releases, never in quantity. There was no need. The pheasants had taken over. By the 1940's, despite constant slaughter called hunting, they had multiplied past counting. A mathematician in South Dakota recently calculated that during a good season there 15,000 birds are killed every hour. The hunter who fails to get his birds in Dakota is a hopeless dub.

About midway along the main east-west prairie routes are the small farm-center cities: Mitchell with its Corn Palace, built for the annual six-day harvest festival, and decorated anew each year inside and out with scenes and designs actually done in corn and other grains . . . Huron, boyhood home of Chic Sale, which holds the annual State Fair and is the undisputed pheasant-hunting head-quarters . . . Aberdeen, quite a railroad and wholesale distribution as well as retail center, once the home of Hamlin Garland and of Frank L. Baum, the Oz-books man . . . Jamestown, where Maxwell Anderson went to school, home of North's oldest and only private college (there are plenty of state institutions) which offers a structure definitely worth seeing, the Voorhees Chapel . . . Minot, which started as a tent town when the Great Northern had to hesitate there in its push westward to build a bridge, then mush-roomed so fast it was called the Magic City.

You move on along the east-west routes and distance engulfs you again and ahead is the Missouri River. All of them strike almost straight to it.

"Yep," said the man on the next stool at the little café. "Wheat didn't do so good this year. But I put me in sixty acres of soybeans too. First anywhere around these parts. Don't know how I'll make out on price, but the damn things sure grew. I'll lease me some more land next year and put in a section of them."

And so westward—across the wide Missouri. For simple talking purposes this next section begins with the river and covers all the rest of Dakota except the roughly oval island of the Black Hills in the southwest corner.

This is the Dakota plain. This is Dakota's slice of the great Missouri Plateau; Dakota's slice of the high plains of which the Missouri Plateau is only a part. Most of this section is semi-arid. That may seem strange if you consult a map, for the whole area is laced with rivers, tributaries of the Missouri. They strike across at almost regular intervals through the plains with names that are resonant of history: the White, the Bad, the Cheyenne, the Mo-reau, the Grand, the Cannonball, the Heart, the Knife, the Little Missouri, dwarfed only by its big brother, the Big Muddy itself.

When the rare local rains hit (they are apt to be sudden and brief and torrential in their briefness) the water sluices off the dry ground and the rivers rise in flash flood and the floodwaters sweep downstream and in a day or two, sometimes in a few hours, the rivers are low and lazy again. You stand on the bank of one, say the Bad, and make a superior comment to a native about such a grim name for such a mild stream. He merely chuckles and points to a tree, likely a northern willow, behind you. High up, well above your head, are mud marks on the bark. "It was up there for a while last week," he says.

This west-river plain is as treeless as the east-river prairie. It is deeply rolling country and broken country with areas marked by lonely buttes rising sharply in strange shapes. Everything is large scale, stretching the muscles of the mind. You drop to a low level and huge rolling shoulders of land seem to hem you in. You climb to a high level and vision races out a hundred miles and more in every direction and falters in the attempt to find a true horizon. Distances constantly deceive. The eastern mind fumbles them. Driving along, you tag behind a slow car waiting to top a rise ahead and see the road clear before passing—and suddenly realize the summit of that rise is still a mile or more away. . . . Those tiny objects far ahead are a water tower and a grain elevator, symbols of a town. Half an hour later with the speedometer still at seventy, they are still there, slightly larger but still there, far off, marking a town lost in the immensity of the land.

This was horse country and still is (a roundup of wild horses in the Medora area brought in more than 200 a few years ago) and the ability to sit a saddle, Western style, is taken for granted. But the horse is being reduced to certain specialties. Many a rancher and farmer has a small plane, not just for getting places in the Dakota distances, but for routine inspection of his acres and crops and herds. Normal work around a ranch is apt to be done in a jeep. It is a common sight to see a modern cowboy skittering in one along the inside of a fenceline checking the wire or heading straight across country in search of wandering stock. In the really tough areas, however, the horse holds its own—and no jeep has yet learned to ease into a herd and cut out the right animals or the difficult art of carrying a rider with hands free for roping a wayward steer in branding time.

"Ranching?" said the man at the first gasoline station in thirty-seven miles. "Old-style, eh? Nothing dudey and no jeeps. There's some around. Friend of mine has one about the same as it was when his pop was a pup. We'll just let bub here watch the station while I run you out. No. Not your car. Mine. Think I'm stingy with my gas?" That ranch was forty-five miles away.

When rains do hit and before the following sun and the endless wind have done their drying work, the west-river plain sets two traps for those unwary enough to wander off the surfaced or graveled roads even on foot. One is what can be called the ordinary mud, the common mud in the low places where the fine silt of ages of erosion has collected. It is not quicksand; it is mud, unbelievably gooey and often unbelievably deep. The story is still told of the passing stranger who saw a cowboy hat lying in a mudhole and carefully reached to pick it up. Underneath was a man's head. The stranger leaned down and took hold of the man under the armpits and hauled him out. "Thanks," said the mud-dripping cowboy. "Now help me pull up my horse."

The other trap is the gumbo. This has given its name to a whole desolate region north of the Black Hills. Gumbo is a black clayey soil that, when dry, bakes hard with endless cracked wrinkles, and, when wet, becomes an expanse of Gargantuan, gummy flypaper.

And of course, emphatically of course, the Dakota plain has the Badlands.

These are true parts of the plain. They do not rise above its general level; they drop below. They are not upthrusts of the earth's surface weathered into the present formations. They are the results of ages of erosion cutting down into the plain.

South's are out some from the Black Hills, below the town of Wall, the main tourist entering point. North's are along the Little Missouri. Of the two, the southern are the real Badlands, what should be called the Worselands, barren of mostly everything but beauty. The northern are more hospitable, wide spaced, with scattered rich grass-plots between the twisted buttes. But in both, the essential formations are the same type.

They cannot be described, those freakish, unearthly jumbles of ridges and hummocks and sharp cliffs and buttes, of domes and pyramids and cones and weirdly lovely shapes out of an artist's nightmare, striped in the browns and reds and grays and yellows and black of the pressed sand and clay and lignite of which they are formed . . . colors shifting in shade and tint with the shifting light and the play of the shadows. They cannot be described. Many people have tried—and the words limp behind the reality. They cannot even truly be held in mind. No matter how often seen, there are areas that always strain belief, are more weird and wonderful than remembered. Hell with the fires burnt out, General Sully described them long ago. That—or a drunken surrealist's dream of paradise.

"No more coffee?" said the waitress in the little combination bar and restaurant, coming back with the pot the third time. "You don't come from around here. Folks out here like three or four cups with a meal, so we just give it to them."

So at last to the last section, the Black Hills.

They are not hills but mountains, not soaring in grandeur like the Rockies and Sierras but solid and honest mountains nonetheless, seen dark-topped with their superb pine and spruce forests in the distance from far off on the plain all around. Geologists say they are the world's oldest mountains. Certainly they are among the world's most beautiful. And they are one of America's newest playgrounds. They are Dakota's chief tourist attraction and they have been publicized and exploited with unashamed exuberance.

Every town has its museum and special baits. Rapid City has its Hangman's Hill and its Dinosaur Park with life-sized models in cement of the prehistoric reptiles which roamed the region some 40,000,000 years ago. It also has (not tourist bait) a major Air Force base. Belle Fourche (pronounced Bell Foosh) has its Black Hills Round-Up. Sturgis has its Jack Pine Gypsy Tour and Key City Rodeo. Spearfish has the Passion Play, brought to this country by Josef Meier. This is technically the world's oldest; its previous history in Germany traces back to 1242. It is presented in a fine natural amphitheater by a huge cast, including a flock of sheep. It is very impressive, and it is also somewhat ironic; the white man's sacred drama has been deliberately transplanted to a site in the once-sacred hills of the Indians.

Hot Springs has its Evans Plunge, largest natural warm-water indoor swimming pool. Custer has its Gold Discovery Days. Deadwood has its annual Days of '76 jamboree and several nights a week

during the season retries Jack McCall for the shooting of Wild Bill
Hickok. This is one of the most enjoyable regional or folk plays
perpetrated anywhere for the tourist trade. It bursts out of No. 10
saloon to begin with a street chase, then adjourns into a nearby
building where, after the ticket-buying stampede subsides, McCall's
actual trial is re-enacted with surprising fidelity to fact and a
judicious attention to hilarious incident. Alibi Ike usually steals the
show.

Natural wonders are given full play: Spearfish Canyon, many a
person's earnest entry for the longest stretch of sheer winding
cliff-lined loveliness in the West; Custer State Park with its buffalo
herd and antelope preserve; Sylvan Lake; Wind Cave National Park;
Harney Peak; the Needles.

And, of course, all tourist trips lead eventually to Mount Rushmore.
But some lead on, not many miles away, to where that magnificently
mad sculptor, Korczak Ziolkowski, is gnawing away at a project
which outdoes even Mount Rushmore in planned scope and which,
if ever finished, might even outdraw it. He is carving a whole
mountain into a memorial to the great Sioux leader, Crazy Horse.

To see the Black Hills as a whole, climb to the ranger tower on
either of the two peaks, the southern Harney or the northern Terry.
You look out and all around are these mountains called hills, dark-
topped with their forests, reaching, tier on tier, into the distance.

And then, looking northeastward from this far southwest corner of
Dakota, vision gradually focuses beyond the hills themselves. There,
lighter in color, limitless into the horizon, is the plain and you
know that it sweeps on to the wide Missouri and that beyond,
farther beyond, is the great expanse of the prairie dropping imper-
ceptibly across the seemingly endless miles to the Red River Valley.

That is Dakota. It is the least-known section of the United States.
It was one of the last frontiers and retains many frontier aspects.
It is still thinly populated in modern terms—not like the desert and
mountain states with concentrations of people in between raw
rough unused regions, but fairly well spread out and thinning
gradually from east to west. There is only one city in the 50,000
bracket, Sioux Falls; only three in the 25,000, Fargo, Grand Forks
and Rapid City; only a dozen in the entire territory which edge
past 10,000. There were no surfaced roads clear across until the
1930's. There are towns today which have declined with the coming
of the automobile, enabling people to live out more easily on the

land. There are ghost towns in which only a few lonely people still keep vigil. There are areas in which the population has dwindled with reversion of farmland to grassland and only a few relics of what were once homes remain. There are still big tracts set aside as Indian reservations. Except in the Black Hills there are no streams of tourists along the highways. Those who do come are easily absorbed into the wide-open accessible spaces.

And all this is an asset. Dakota as a whole still has an uncluttered, unsoiled air, a simple freshness, untainted by the stale weariness of most older overrun regions. The land, not what man has done with it, still predominates.

It is a rare and rewarding place for those interested in Western history. No other section offers the story of Western development with quite the same rounded completeness. Dakota has had every aspect and in abundance: the fur trade, the buffalo, the river traffic, the wagons westward, border trouble with the British, Indian wars, freighting and stage lines, the cattle empire, the open range giving way to fencing, the cattle and sheep wars, homesteading, town settlement, countyseat fights, capital rivalries, railroad surveys and rail-building races and station-site troubles, gold rushes, mining camps, the impact of new land and independence upon immigrants, the transition from territory to state. Its history is recent, close, the markings still plain. Historic sites, well preserved, dot the whole expanse.

Its people have an invincible friendliness, not pushing and back-slapping but honest; not the standardized "friendliness" calculated to bring patrons to dude ranches and sell drugstore-cowboy outfits and tourist curios, but the friendliness of people still stubborn and independent, still accustomed to relying upon their own resources, still sociable and neighborly, still able to be gullible, to have faith in their fellow men. It is sincere first-name country from the first handshake.

Dakotans still look at the land about them and at the sky overhead. They have absorbed the feeling of the open spaces, that there is room enough and there is time enough.

Nebraska

by MARI SANDOZ

Nebraska has been known as the Tree Planters' State, the Bug Eater, Flower, and Cornhusker State, and now finally, by legislative action, it has been named the Beef State. But long before any of these were coined it was called Quivira, the land that is yet to be found.

Back in my childhood in Nebraska, when our father shot a soaring eagle out of the sky, he liked to stroke the handsome shining head and talk grandly of Coronado.

"That Spaniard was right," Old Jules would tell us. "Here's another of the golden eagles he was looking for."

Father always laughed aloud at his joke about the early gold seeker and his land of Quivira, with a river six miles wide, fishes big as horses, and great canoes with golden eagles at their prows —a place where even common people supped from jugs and bowls of gold.

Yet perhaps none of it was too far from the truth, not even the six-mile-wide river. The old Missouri could spread out mightily in those days, and certainly more fabulous canoes than any Coronado had hoped to find churned their fiery way up the current and down, carrying more tangible wealth than even he dared dream of.

But it was a long time from Coronado to the Beef State's prize steaks on the platter, whether golden or plain. For a while the region was known as part of the Great American Desert and then as a very broad and dangerous stretch that must be crossed by the strings of emigrants hurrying West like ants before the winter.

By the time I was old enough to know these things I had spent a lot of time with the rolls of maps my father kept handy for the homeseekers he located at twenty-five dollars apiece, including the necessary surveying for the section of free land. Even before I could read I liked to spread them out on the floor while I let my baby brother cry and the bread dough sour. Nebraska really did look like a large section of a hackberry leaf, as an old Indian once showed me—a giant tilted leaf whose midrib was the bordering Missouri River. The veins of the leaf were the long streams flowing through the state toward the Big Muddy: the broad, flat-watered Platte, the Republican of such deceptively moderate and stable appearance, and the deep-canyoned, crystal-clear Niobrara that ran so swiftly past our home southwest of Rushville, in northwest Nebraska. Once, when father was in a good mood, he elevated the west end of the map to show us how tilted the state really was, rising from 800 feet above sea level in the southeast corner up past us to the Pine Ridge and the Wildcat Range of the western border, a climb to 5400 feet in around 450 miles.

It was this gradual climb toward the Continental Divide, with water and grass all the way westward—the direction the white man seems to move over the globe—that made the state the world's great path of empire. Sometimes my father and the old frontiersmen talked into morning light about those days that gave Nebraska more miles of migration on and along its waters than on any comparable stretch of earth. If I kept very quiet in the woodbox I could stay up to listen until I fell asleep.

This was how I learned that, when the first white men came to Nebraska, all its Indians lived in round houses of earth or skin, round because all the great things were round: the moon, the sun and the dwelling place of the Great Powers around the earth's horizon. Therefore the villages must be round, and their dwellings. When the Indians were put on reservations and sickened from tuberculosis, they believed it was because the houses were square, unholy. I recall one of the old Sioux who used to pick potatoes before mechanization came in. All his family had died of the coughing sickness because, he said, they had slept in a cornered log shack. He would never cross our doorstep but often sat outside on the woodblock for hours, visiting over his pipe.

The first pale-skinned men who came riding were drawn by a scent stronger than roasting buffalo ribs to a starving Indian—the rich, heady musk of the gold rumored in Quivira. Others came through the region following the secondhand stink of gold in furs and hides, and later the lure of the actual metal. But most of the emigrants who cut the deep trails through Nebraska, dropping their broken wagons, burying their dead, were drawn by a sweeter, a more enticing fragrance—free land for the homeless, and the independence that land can give.

"You can't think what the words 'free land' meant to a poor European," a man my father located back in 1888 told me. "Me and my brothers had lost our jobs in the hard times and were fighting with street gangs over the village cats for soup. Then we found a letter in a newspaper from a Herr Sandoz in America, telling of the free land in Nebraska, and perhaps a tourist pass on the railroad from New York. An uncle offered to borrow the money to send me to see. I wrote and the answer came." The old man looked at me quizzically. "It told about the land, and the need in the new country for wives. Old Jules was having wife trouble."

"No complaint about mail service?" I asked.

"That came later, all the years my brothers and I knew your father. He ran me off his place with a gun once because he thought I did not help get the mail service. But he had run me off before that because I would not join his mob that hung a troublemaker who was burning out the settlers and shooting into their houses."

I was silent. I had often thought of that, and of the time when father, a crack shot, had fired at a neighbor not fifty feet away. The bullet went over the man's head because I had struck the stock of the .30-.30 down as I saw father's finger tighten on the trigger.

"He was a violent man," the old settler added, "but he was the first in the wilderness, with no sheriff, no law except his gun. He settled over a thousand homesteaders on good land. Many who stayed got rich. He gave us trees to plant, plums and berries to content the women. Even after our fight, when the cowboys turned cattle into my corn and scared my young wife, Old Jules came to visit with his rifle, and shot target at tin cans nailed on posts. They were there twenty years, old and rusty, but nobody came to make me more trouble."

I nodded, thinking of all the men and women who went out to the world's wildernesses, seeking homes, land.

The people of Nebraska have grown conservative, some even reactionary, perhaps through the loss of young blood to the East. Lincoln, the capital, was long supposed to have the greatest concentration of DAR's for its size. Yet we fostered William Jennings Bryan, Populism and Senator George Norris, and no politician who has made a speech against the northwest wind of the Nebraska Panhandle, and faced the squinted, cynical eyes of the natives, can ever feel too sure which way we may jump next. Nebraska was long included in the Bible Belt, yet we calmly put a bayonet into Crazy Horse, the most modest and ascetic Sioux leader, this after he had surrendered all his weapons for the promise of peace and safety for his people. People from Nebraska occupy positions high and far. General Alfred M. Gruenther, Platte Center, was Supreme Allied Commander in Europe; the former Lincolnite, John M. Allison, was Ambassador to Japan. Some Nebraskans sit alone in Dannemora and Alcatraz. We have had a few pretty cool murderers, reaching from old Chief Blackbird to the recent killing of teen-age girls by young hoodlums, as elsewhere now. On the other hand we grew a most noted jurist, Dean Roscoe Pound, formerly of Harvard Law School.

Even now there are schools with one pupil, movable schools on skids, and pupils too far from any school at all, and yet Nebraska developed the nation's finest prose stylist, Willa Cather.

And if you are a man and want to live to be as old as possible, settle on a farm or in some small Nebraska town—where the average life span is the longest in the nation.

Much of this prairie state was long-grass country, "lightning country," the Indians called it, from the fierceness of the lightning-set prairie fires that sometimes burned for weeks, until they ran into the broad Missouri or were put out by rain, or by wind that turned them to feed upon their own ashes. Nebraska lies in the heart of the largest single piece of arable-grazable land in the world and contains, as one might expect, much fine corn ground and great stretches of wheat land. It also has several oil-rich regions, a 250-mile stretch of well-grassed sandhills geologically unmatched anywhere, a Toadstool Park of select badlands, and some rocky, craggy ridges that are higher and more montane than most of the mountains of the East. In much of the state you find yourself reaching for a blanket toward morning.

There are thousands of lakes here, the larger man-made, one 105 miles around, with fishing, boating and regattas, and the lovely deep blue of the far Nebraska sky in their depths. And there are handsome parks in all parts of the state, and forest and game reserves. Nowhere are the songs of the meadowlarks finer, the wild flowers and the sunsets more magnificent, than on the higher reaches of the state, and in the winter blizzard nothing stands between you and the North Pole save a barbed-wire fence with the posts all down.

"There is no place like Nebraska!" the University rooters sing lustily. Yet for some reason most of the first hundred thousand emigrants marched right through the region, up past Chimney Rock and on westward, until it seemed that nobody would ever stay. Our first white-man highway was the spreading Missouri, but the Platte, flowing the length of the state from west to east, became the real path of empire across our prairie. Its course was followed by the fur men, then by the various Overlanders seeking homes and safety and gold; by the Pony Express for a few profitless months, and by the telegraph and the first transcontinental railroad, until the broad river valley lay worn and bald, bare, it seemed, of every living root.

The first coast-to-coast auto road, the Lincoln Highway, followed the old ruts along the Platte, and the first transcontinental air mail. Today fine trains, high-speed buses and the planes that overtake the sun carry the ambitious up the Platte, though now they are headed for Hollywood, Reno, Yucca Flats or the uranium fields. Those going by car found a straight uncrowded free throughway here long before the East thought of one, and with the hypnotic menace of straight white pavement for hundreds of miles.

When the first heat of the Overlanders had cooled a little, weary emigrants began to spill off like golden grain sifting from a creaking wagon, leaving little settlements to sprout up all along from the Missouri westward, their main drags always headed into the sunset, even today.

Beyond the reach of a handful of troops at Fort Kearney there was no law except that of the fast draw, the belly knife or the ambush. With the danger from animals, Indians and finally outlaws, the most peaceful went armed, particularly the youths who had hit for the frontier for one reason or another and ended up choring for the horses around the stagecoach stations. Usually they were no better fitted to carry guns than the young malcontents today.

From the ranks of such young horse tenders at Nebraska stations rose both Wild Bill Hickok and Buffalo Bill Cody, the two most glamorized figures of the old Wild West. Both are still widely advertised as killers—Hickok of white men, Cody of Indians.

The two Bills went West beyond the law as youths now dream of getting beyond gravity. James Butler Hickok, called Duck Bill around the stage station until he grew the flowing mustaches that covered his long upper lip and made him handsome, went West because a man he knocked into a canal wasn't coming up. At Rock Creek station, he did a real piece of killing. He shot McCanles, the former station owner, for whom he had worked as a stock tender, and was the first man tried for murder in the new county. But this was only shooting a Carolinian, surely a Reb in July, 1861, not horse stealing, and so all Hickok got was the name of Wild Bill, from his wild account of how he killed his victim. But by 1866 he was ready material for the nation's postwar appetite for violence, and in Eastern print the name Wild Bill became a steppingstone to the title "Prince of Pistoleers." Yet Hickok still had to shoot buffalo along the Republican River to pay his gambling debts and buy the fancy dikings of the frontier dude. Today small boys and girls know a Wild Bill very unlike the man who was headed for oblivion and blindness until Jack McCall, also a former trail employee in Nebraska, salvaged him for the hero worshipers with one foolish bullet.

Bill Cody worked westward on the Overland trail and became a meat contractor for the railroad through north Kansas. He had an efficient crew to kill buffalo while he cut a handsome and picturesque figure around the frontier saloons. With his long shining hair, his big hat and his fringed buckskin he looked the romantic hero of the Wild West that the East was building up as an escape from its own drabness. A Broadway publicity man saw Cody, and made him the showiest showman of all time. But Bill was broke much of his forty years in the business and had to return West periodically to his ranch at North Platte.

Because violence and murder were the true golden coin after the Civil War, as they are in any postwar time, Cody was advertised as a killer, but only of buffalo and that other creature marked for extermination—the Indian. Yet no Western contemporary believed he killed even one Indian. As Luther North, of the Pawnee Scouts and a former partner of Cody's, once told me, "Cody wasn't reckless. He'd never hired Indians for his show if he had killed their relations."

Although Buffalo Bill was buried in 1917 he is still very much alive, not only around North Platte and up at Cody, Wyoming, but in the movies, on radio and TV, and in print. No real biography has appeared so far, perhaps because his is the story not of a man but of a dream, a wish fulfillment.

Although Nebraska has no gold mines, it has many stories of buried treasure; say around Nebraska City, at Maguire's Slough, in Knox County, and, my favorite, in Fly Speck Bill's cave. The Speck, nicknamed for the thick scattering of tiny dark freckles across his boyish face, was quietly hanged, but not until he had supposedly buried $300,000 in bullion stolen from the Sidney-Deadwood Gold Trail. Seems he stole this not too far from the spot where the Sioux were forced to sell the whole clutch of the Black Hills for a temporary meal ticket. The sale included the world's richest gold mine, the Homestake, from which the stolen bullion apparently came. One site given for Fly Speck's cave was across the Niobrara from our house, and I can recall many diggings around there. Once when some new treasure seekers came, Old Jules went over, his usual rifle across his arm. The men sprang out of their hole, hands on guns at the approach of what seemed an old mountain man, ragged beard, muskrat cap and all.

"What name you travelin' under?" father asked mildly, as was customary in a region where many had left their names behind with their pasts.

The men holstered their guns at Old Jules' combination of French accent and old-West etiquette. Later he brought them home to supper, as he did everyone. They thanked father for his generosity about the diggings.

"Hell, it ain't on my land!" he replied, laughing.

The gold seekers looked around our poor shacky house, at our bare feet, our patched clothing, and mother's gnarled and workworn hands and tried to pay for the good meal of grouse and homegrown trimmings. They were coldly refused. We were never poor enough to dig for gold on other people's land, or to accept pay for a meal.

It has been said that if you see one Nebraskan alone he will be squinting at the sky. See two and they will be talking about the weather, particularly its unhappy extremes: the deadly winter blizzards, summer scorchers, great floods of the Republican and Missouri regions, the sudden gully washers and hailstorms, the occasional dust storms and killing droughts. One October day can be so lovely it stops the heart, and the next the wind will drive the tumbleweeds like great herds of dark awkward sheep running before the wolf. A May day that is mellow and heavy with the sweetness of wild-plum and chokecherry blooms can bring you a blizzard to ruin the eastern apple crop and clean you out of cattle, or cost you an eye through snowblindness, as a May blizzard did me, back in my child-hood.

Question a Nebraskan and you may be told that swift and unpre-dictable weather changes are what keep a man watching his trail or even that they help him see the interdependence of all things, unconsciously expressing the rudiments of Indian religion as it matured on these Plains.

On the obvious and practical level, every Nebraska tribe had weather men and women and special ceremonials to bring rain, the sun, and so on, long before the white man stuck his bearded face over the horizon. In dry times we try a little rain making ourselves, from prayers to cloud seeding, but it may be years before we are as successful as one old Pawnee rain maker my father knew in the drought of the 1890's. For ten dollars he would bring an inch of rain to the surrounding fields; for twenty he made stronger medicine and guaranteed a soaker. Money was hard to come by, but one group of settlers in east Nebraska finally got twenty dollars together and threw in a jug of whisky. The rain maker went into his ritual and dances with genuine fervor. The sky darkened and the crowd cheered as the rain began to fall. But it turned to hail, enough hail to pound the whole country into the ground.

Nebraska, in a migratory flyway, has set up several sanctuaries for waterfowl, a large one north of Oshkosh, and another of 70,000 acres in Cherry County. The entire lake region is dark with flocks in the fall, the winding traceries of black that are thousands of sand hill cranes going south, the V's of geese, the clouds of ducks added to all the mallards hatched in the region. Father made expert hunters of his sons, and my sisters are good too. Even I learned to take a sound lead on mallards coming in fast on the north wind, although my lot was mostly the plucking and the cooking. I do remember pulling my first Canada goose out of a flock along the last pink rim of the west. The soft warm neck falling over my arm as I ran home with it made me want to cry.

Sound conservation has increased Nebraska's small game and

brought back the deer and the antelope and even varmints, the coyote and the bobcat, but never the buffalo. Anyone who grew up around the Sioux and the old hide hunters must be convinced that Nebraska was once the richest of buffalo ranges, with its excellent waterways, the thick seedy June grasses and the later bluestems that stood more than man-high and could always be tromped out of the deepest snow. The great herds moved like vast dark shadows over the prairie, deer bounding away at their approach, antelope fleeing in droves, while plovers, curlews, prairie chickens and the great black ravens rose everywhere before the thunder and shake of the earth as the buffalo neared. Wild turkeys kept out of their way and flew in heavy whirring clouds through the golden sun of evening to their roosting groves in the breaks that the heavy-shouldered buffalo liked to avoid. The elk and moose usually kept to broken timbered slopes too. The bighorn sheep was all through Pine Ridge and the Wildcat range of the Panhandle and eastward, his great head dark against the clouds as he looked over the swift waters of the Niobrara striking the roiling flank of the Missouri like an arrow from the west.

No gun roared anywhere then, and no stink of powder offended the nose. True, wolves and sometimes mountain lions pulled down any straggling buffalo, and half-naked brown men crept up on the herds, stampeding them over the sheer bluffs of the upper White River country and along the Niobrara. With the women and children to help, they drove the buffalo into pits or into gully or canyon surrounds.

The white man's lead and powder worked faster, and when the herds were only white bones on the prairie or piled in ricks like tardy snowdrifts along the railroad tracks, the longhorns came trailing out of Texas, climbing from one stream to another to the Union Pacific railhead. Angry men stood at their homestead lines, rifles or old muzzle-loaders across their forearms, but the new outfits spread over the public domain, laying verbal claim to the waterways and reinforcing their claim with armed range "protectors" to keep the settlers out.

The next move was into the real long-grass country, the sand hills of Nebraska, a vast egg-shaped region 250 miles long, with the deep Niobrara River canyon cutting around their northern boundary. Inside a low, choppy, windtorn border the hills rise in long, blue-hazed ridges that look like those of a sand bar when seen from a plane high up—sand ridges blown in upon an old lake bed that is black, heavy and generally water-impervious. Long valleys lie between these hills, one reaching over 200 miles.

The hills have many fine stretches of meadow, the wetter in wild hay and timothy, otherwise in alfalfa and bluegrass or even rye and corn to be hogged down by cattle. Strips of buckbrush lie along the foot of the ridges, or long sweeps of blue or yellow wild flowers and mats of bull-tongue cactus with great satiny yellow-green blossoms. Higher up are the fine waxy spikes of yucca bloom and the slender white gillyflowers, with nests of prairie roses that are as large as your palm to sweeten the air as you ride by.

The ridges are generally covered with range grasses, all except the highest, most exposed tops where the wind scoops blowouts for itself. Children were taught that these were always cupped out from the northwest—knowledge that could help them find their directions even in a blizzard. I once reached home that way, a long time ago.

These sand hills are the finest natural reservoir in the world—a great greenish-dun sponge that soaks up every drop of moisture from rain or snow and holds it in water tables and in the two thousand lakes. In most of the region the water works slowly southeastward until, with the lowering altitude, springs begin to ooze and flow as if a giant foot pressed on the great sponge, starting a dozen clear, constant streams that furnish water and power and delight to all those along their paths.

Once the Spade outfit claimed a bear-shaped region 150 miles long through the sand hills, mostly free land, but few settlers dared file within their fences. President Theodore Roosevelt, himself an old rancher, ordered the illegal fences down and sent troops to carry out his orders when the cattlemen defied him. I recall something of the long trials that followed. My father, the locater, the old hunter who knew every section corner, was the star witness. I recall a strange man, plainly not a homeseeker, at our place a long time during those tense days. Once when he was shaving in our kitchen I saw a holster under his arm, not worn openly over goat-hair chaps like the cowboys riding through.

"Secret Service man," father said shortly when I dared ask about this.

I recall mother's worried face, and then father's picture in the Omaha papers when the Spade owner went to the penitentiary for land fraud.

"Whole country be run over by homeseekers now, come spring," father said, bringing home a new surveying outfit. He was gone day and night for the next few years, locating the land-hungry.

Yet the sand hills are still sparsely settled. Cherry County alone is the size of Rhode Island and Connecticut together, with a total population of around 10,000. There are around 300,000 head of cattle, which makes it the world's leading county in beef population. It was in Valentine, the county seat, in 1884, that my father saw his first man killed, with at least fifty men standing around, and no hand was lifted against the murderer. To Jules, the young medical student come west from the orderly little republic of Switzerland, this was a shocking occurrence, to be told and retold many times.

But the people of the sand hills are still the independent and co-operative sort who survive in new regions. Most of the men have leathery faces and wind-scabbed lips, their eyes sun-squinted, foreheads white under the big hats—the tall, lean-hipped men of the cow country everywhere.

"They growed 'em long as potato sprouts in the cellar, reachin' fer the sun," an old cowman said when we talked about Pat Hooper, all the Hoopers. The family had come into the hills before the last Sioux alarm. Pat is well over sixty now, slouch-shouldered in the saddle, with the long face, the lined cheeks and bleached eyes of the years he was one of the head punchers of the region. But he can still send a loop with what seems the speed and precision of a bullet. His kind still top off the outlaw bronc that has never heard of the ten-second limit in rodeo contests. Men like Pat have squeeze chutes now for the branding and dehorning, and perhaps planes to cover the range, with every alfalfa patch a landing field, the windmill tails the windsocks.

Fleeing criminals still hit for the broken sand hills. The ranches are often five, even ten miles apart but there are radios everywhere now, and telephones to rally swift turnouts against a bad man as for the first iridescent smoke sign of a prairie fire on the horizon. The outlaw is hunted by Winchester-armed men in cars and jeeps and from the air. The sandhillers have no locks on their doors and they intend to keep them so.

There are, however, some who remember less peaceful days, the days of the cattleman-settler troubles. D. J. Cole was a boy when his father was shot down between the plow handles on his homestead.

"But my mother was not the woman to be run out, not even by murderers," he told me, his voice quiet.

Mrs. Cole stayed and her son grew up a typical native of the hills, pleasant and soft-spoken, his eyes grave in their nest of sun wrinkles —a man as much at home in the saddle as in the halls of the state capitol.

Although about fortieth in the country by population, Omaha, by geographic and financial position, is a big city, second only to Denver in the whole region between Chicago and the West Coast. It wields a commensurate influence—a one-newspaper town, but a moneyed town, the center of the cattle business, packing more beef than any other place on earth. Omaha long had a cowboy mayor, the old trail driver who traveled under the name of Jim Dahlman, his own, Murray, left behind in Texas.

Omaha has spread to take in the old Mormon Winter Quarters and its monument to their pioneers who wintered there in 1846-7, many in holes in the frozen ground, and to the 600 who died. And it was early Nebraska ranch owners like Swan, Paxton and Creighton who organized the Union Stock Yards, which now handle over two million dollars of livestock each market day.

Their Stock Yards 400 Club is a take-off on the more pretentious goings-on uptown. The club meets in the office building that stands like an upended tall red shoe box in the middle of the vast acreage of stock pens and baled hay. But many members have a prominent part in the flossier doings, too, particularly in Ak-sar-ben, Omaha's big social and publicity circus of the year, with a king in satin knee breeches, a middle-aged king, as is inevitable in a man of importance. His queen, however, is selected for more pertinent qualifications: youth and beauty.

Omaha has its detractors, naturally. The state's one race disturbance occurred here, one that left the courthouse with great slabs of pavement torn up all around, and there have been charges of gangsterism and corruption, particularly political. But thanks to its location and hotels, it remains very popular for conventions and celebrations. The city took the lead in the Golden Spike Days, commemorating the transcontinental railroad, complete with Lucius Beebe and what was rumored as a prearranged bit of local color— a shot from Beebe's Colt in the Fontenelle bar. Like much of the shooting of the old days, it left no corpse, but, I hope, a nice realistic stench of genuine black powder.

Although one mayor banned *Idiot's Delight* for a while, the Omaha Community Playhouse has given many stars their start. On Sundays packing-house workers mingle with the local Bohemians and the mink-coaters inside the rosy marble walls of the Joslyn Memorial for music and art. I recall seeing a couple there once, stocky, middle-aged, whispering together in their own tongue. They were plainly in their awkward best attire, and looked very scrubbed yet with a hint of the fertilizer vats of South Omaha about them. But they stood transfixed before Grant Wood's *Stone City*, their broad faces alight with wonder and that glow that deep recognition brings. Perhaps they had been very homesick for a little white church somewhere back in Lithuania.

Come to think of it, for all the booming industry and the making and breaking of senators, there is a kind of innocence about Omaha. Approached from almost any direction in the spring, the residence streets and many in the business sections, too, have a kind of village air, the buildings set back on neat terraces, fronted by tumbles of bridal wreath. It spills white and foamy down slope after slope of the hilly city, and makes a kind of pale mistiness along the side streets in both directions, while from far away somewhere there is a hint of the purple and the fragrance of lilacs.

Kansans have something of the righteous self-assurance of the Abolitionists who came West; South Dakotans figuratively push their big hats back with the dash of old Deadwood. Nebraskans often seem a little uncertain, a little apologetic, perhaps because they are less one thing than many. There are still traces of the old French traders and river men along the Missouri River towns—faces with the roguishness of the old *voyageur* and the strong dark hair of the Indian. And sometimes only a warmth of nature and an oblique sense of humor will reveal the Indian, with the hair perhaps blond and the eye as blue as a Niobrara harebell.

Many of our towns were started by companies of settlers from the East and from Europe too; Germans, Irish, Swiss and so on, and many Scandinavians. In Nebraska the Johnsons far outnumber the Smiths, and a candidate with a Swedish name is almost a shoo-in at election time. But it's only in the name now, for the characteristic faces, the general build and coloring that set these stocks apart until recently are disappearing, even from the so-called clannish Czechs in towns like Wilber, Loma, or sections of Crete.

The Bohemians have been recognized as a tough, hardy lot from the first one to settle in Nebraska Territory, who apparently walked clear to St. Joseph, Missouri, for his groceries. One young woman drove the cattle of a relative all the way from Wisconsin to Nebraska, afoot, and in my childhood I knew a man and wife, immigrants from Prague, who had pushed a wheelbarrow with their few household goods clear across Nebraska to our region for a homestead.

I recall many fine strong faces among these people, some with the red-brown eye that I've seen only among Czechs, a few northern Italians and an occasional Yorkshireman. The eyes are unchanged, of course, but they look different now. When I stopped off at our Czech centers to ask about the old-timers, I discovered that they are either dead, moved away, or somehow look like the usual older people on television quiz shows. I asked for one fine salty old character who had never learned passable English. He was pointed out to me, getting into a convertible with golf clubs.

"Oh, it's him, all right," I was told.

"Looks like he's been to California," I remarked.

"No, he's slicked up some since we got TV out here. Watches it all the time, evenings."

I remember the fine gray handle-bar mustaches, a neat side part to the whitening hair, an underslung pipe with a metal lid, and bib overalls big enough to turn around in. Now he was clean-shaven, in a loud shirt, maroon slacks and sandals, his hair in a thin white crew cut. All the proportions of the man seemed changed, his face and his figure.

But I was certain I knew two Czechs who would never change. Old Anna Pavelka wouldn't. She had worked as a girl in the Red Cloud home of Willa Cather and was the original of her Antonia. Anna had the earnest face, the sweep of cheekbone, the deep-socketed eye, the husky upper arm. But Anna Pavelka was eighty-six and died the week I was to hunt her up. That left me with the most typical Czech of all, the complex mixture of intellect, temperament and practicality, of the volcanic and the charmingly witty and placid that is the essence of our Czech settlers. This was Professor Orin Stepanek, of the state university. Born in Crete, Nebraska, on, as he always insisted, the wrong side of the tracks, he had the sturdiness of many of his people, with tawny skin, the breadth of planed cheekbone, a fine intensity of eye under coal-black brows, the expressive shoulders and hands, the fine incisive vocabulary, the rich imagination. Although a dynamic teacher of Slavic languages, Continental literature and the cultural approach to life, the carpenter that his father was could not be entirely denied. In his basement he upholstered furniture, and at his table one ate the finest of Czech liver dumplings and roast pork with sweet cabbage.

Yet there are still a few naturals for Willa Cather's Farmer Rosicky left. The spiritual daughters of her Antonia are still there, too, but in slacks and lipstick, perhaps with prize-winning 4-H beeves.

Lincoln always impresses me with its shining cleanness. New buildings, new fronts or at least new sandblasts make the wide streets, overlooked by the white capitol tower, seem even more open to the sun.

The German-Russians brought their onion-top churches to this city of colonial descendants. Often, too, you see Mennonites from a nearby settlement on the streets, the people who brought secret palmfuls of winter wheat to America. Crosses of that wheat are the parents of the fields from mid-Nebraska out through the Panhandle, where the wind runs in bright waves over the golden tablelands and around the black oil derricks.

Although Lincoln treated bank robbers to a $2,000,000 bond and currency haul, it has often been called the Holy City for its many churches and its former ban on saloons and Sunday movies. But war and new industry have changed many things. Every year around a quarter million visitors to the state fair can see the $10,000,000 capitol, built pay-as-you-go into the depression years, and the museums of the Historical Society and the University. The latter has perhaps the world's largest mammoth, standing some fourteen feet high, and many similar exhibits, mostly from the vast fossil beds of the Panhandle and Lincoln County.

There is a natural division across the state at the 100th meridian, where the altitude goes up and the rainfall down—the old arbitrary boundary between corn and cattle culture, the walking plow and the lariat, the old Bible Belt and the land of the gamblers. To be sure, the gambling was less often at poker and roulette than a staking of time, property and life against the violences of nature, the Indians, Western bad men and the range wars.

Now there is more security west of the 100th. Most of the water for the reservoir-fed portion of our million and a half acres under irrigation comes from there. The spreading agro-industrial region is richest along the North Platte. Scotts Bluff, the high country's last rampart against the river that cut this wide valley through the table-land, looks benignly over a lush checkering of irrigated fields and the booming town that is its namesake. Scottsbluff is not only a booming city but a good city. I saw young Japanese, Sioux, Mexican and mill-run young Americans laughing together at the hamburger joints and along the streets. I mentioned this to a mother of teen-agers.

"Oh, we don't have to worry much about our young people here," she said. "Everybody keeps a friendly eye on them—all like good relatives together." She was from the East and could not know that this was very much like the attitude toward young people in the Sioux villages camped in the shadow of the Bluff a hundred years ago.

Up north, off the old Black Hills trail, lies Wild Horse table, named for the herds that once dotted the western reaches of the state and ran like swift shadows over the prairie, their manes and tails a dense cloudiness about them in the wind. They had increased to fabulous numbers since they first came with the Spaniards, here where their prehistoric ancestors, beginning with the fourteen-inch Dawn Horse, once roamed before the Ice Age. I remember our last mustang from these parts—a fox mare so wily she remained in no corral if she could get her nose to the top. Not even the broncobusters breaking Powder River outlaws ever got their ropes on this one. I was still a small girl when she died, but I knew that an era passed with her.

In our northwestern section lies the heart of the state's unpubli-cized scenery. Here is the heading of the Niobrara Valley that cuts clear across northern Nebraska, deep and timbered, moodily golden in the October sun. Beyond are the sheer bluffs and buttes of the White River country, and then Pine Ridge standing dark against the sky.

This is the region of the Sioux and Cheyenne last stands. Wounded Knee is just over the Dakota line. At Fort Robinson, Crazy Horse was bayoneted, and two years later the Dull Knife Cheyennes preferred to die fighting on the January snow rather than return to the hated

Indian Territory. They were pursued over the bluffs for thirteen sub-zero days, until not even one woman was left to run with a child on her back.

And here Dr. Walter Reed, later to conquer yellow fever, was post surgeon and had Old Jules under his care for eight months after he crushed an ankle in a well accident and lay on the prairie for days.

Trade with the Sioux reservations over in South Dakota helped build up the Nebraska border towns from Chadron to Valentine, and the Indians added picturesqueness to their streets. But now, with the Government's withdrawal from the reservations and the accelerated unlanding of the Indians, these towns are swamped by Sioux seeking a livelihood, housing, schools, relief. Signs saying "No INDIANS ALLOWED" have gone up everywhere, the first discrimination in openhearted western Nebraska.

I saw one of the old Sioux on a bus last spring. He looked at me in the quiet way they have and after a while he overcame his reticence and sat down beside me.

"You Sandoz? Straight Eye daughter?" he asked, unfolding a little clipping about my taking a turn around the state.

"Yes," I said, and then I knew who he was, an old friend of my father's, one who had been in the Wounded Knee troubles.

"Me"—poking his thumb toward himself—"me been Lincoln," he said in his awkward English. "Show nephew how do medicine dance."

"How are you people making it?" I asked him, falling into the old local words.

The old man's thin braids stirred a little over his dusty calico shirt. "Bad, very bad," he said.

After a while we talked of old White Eye and Ghost Bear and other friends of my father's. Dead or gone down into sadness, he said, as he looked out over the green alfalfa and winter-wheat fields, the big barns and farmsteads and the ribbon of white highway running where his father had chased buffalo such a short while ago.

With good Sioux manners and even some exuberance, the old man looked into my face. "Indian buy drink now, all over. Drink beer."

"Yes, I know," I said, as I dug out my cigarettes. He took the package, his hand shaking a little in eagerness, and together we smoked in silence, in the good Sioux silence of friends, and when I got off to change buses, I held out my hand. "Don't let the young people forget the old ways of honor," I wanted to say, but I couldn't.

He took my hand, and then the other with his left, the left that is nearest the heart. As the bus started away, I looked after the old man in his mended shirt, sitting, face straight ahead, the thin gray hair hanging down under the old black hat.

I must not forget Mirage Flats, where my father filed the first claim, sank the first well. The Flats is now a fruitful irrigated region, and Walgren's Lake, the reputed home of Nebraska's most persistent sea monster, is a playground. But here on Mirage Flats was the country school where two of my brothers and I learned to speak the tongue of our native land. Here, at ten, I wrote my first short story under the direction of a young teacher who regretted the isolation that our foreignness and our father's feuds and tempers thrust upon us. The story was published in the junior page of a newspaper. I showed it to father and he locked me in the cellar. A Sandoz did not even read fiction, father told me, and she certainly did not write it.

As always, Old Jules' temper soon cooled and he took me quail hunting, but it was understood that the gate to writing was permanently closed. I was, however, already a fence jumper. Years later, the hour he was dying, Old Jules forgot his long opposition.

"Why don't you write my life sometime?" he said. And I did.

New regions seldom applaud the worker in the creative fields. For years Nebraska's interest in art was largely confined to the excellent Indian work displayed in the museums in Lincoln and more recently out at Scottsbluff and in the Hastings House of Yesterday, the latter with the largest collection of High Plains historical material under one roof. But the last twenty years have seen a sprouting of painters out over the state, as though rain had suddenly come to a desert.

Perhaps, among outdoor men, the urge to paint is stimulated by the swift, subtle flow of blue hazes against the Nebraska hills, the yellow-greens, the tans, russets and mauves of the rolling prairie, the patterns of the contoured fields, and the unsurpassed sunrises and sunsets over it all.

Whatever the reason, from Wyoming to the Joslyn, ranchers, farmers, truck drivers, bankers, a café owner, an office worker in South Omaha, a hog breeder—and the professionals, of course—all paint and often achieve shows.

"It's paint rags 'stead a pliers in my old ditty box now," a gnarled cowman replied when I wondered about the easel beside him in the jeep out on the range. "My boy down to the university drug me to look at some pictures Fair time. I seen right away I could do better."

This is my Nebraska, this and the brooding times of evening, when one can sense the recent passing of the buffalo and the Indian, and of all those footsore hopefuls who toiled up the Platte and onward to build the Western empire. And of all the hopefuls who did not go that far.

Once, over twenty years ago, I took Carl Sandburg through the new state capitol. Slowly, silently he saw it all, from the magnificent rotunda to the parapet high up under the crowning statue of the Sower. A long time he gazed out beyond the town, to the spreading horizon in every direction. And when we were down and outside again, Sandburg looked up at the tall white spire a long time too.

Finally he spoke: "You know, this building growing out of the Nebraska corn lands, that's an American tall tale."

Kansas

by DEBS MYERS

The state of Kansas was born of conflict and came of age with a Bible in one hand and a rifle in the other. During its seven years' existence as a territory and a hundred years as a state, it has known guerrilla war, drought, flood, dust, blizzards and grasshopper plagues, has taken these calamities defiantly in stride, put their bitter lessons to everyday use, and has built a sprawling farm empire that sends beef and bread across the world.

For many years Kansas was a spawning ground of gaudy characters and a venturesome kind of progress; few states have produced as many saints and scoundrels, hypocrites and heroes. A country editor named William Allen White once wrote: "When anything is going to happen in this country, it happens first in Kansas. . . . Sooner or later, other states take up these things, and then Kansas goes on breeding other troubles."

Today, with the lean years only a prodding memory, Kansas has become staid and prosperous—a symbol of orthodoxy and starched respectability.

In view of the state's colorful past and sizable achievements, Kansans often wonder why they are regarded in so unflattering a light by so many people. Most Kansans wouldn't willingly live anywhere else; yet they realize that to much of the nation Kansas is viewed almost as an island unto itself, strong in quiet, neighborly virtue, but increasingly barren of the ferment that produces challenge and conflict of ideas.

In this threadbare conception, Kansas is considered as 82,158 square miles of flat and cheerless prairie, producing little except wheat and tedium. And the more than 2,000,000 people of Kansas (if you would accept this same misconception) are uniformly austere and melancholy, tortured by heat, dust, cold, tornadoes and their own consciences.

How much of this is true? Fortunately, very little. The landscape is varied and so are the people. Far from being a flat and monotonous plain, Kansas rises nearly 3000 feet from east to west. The eastern part of the state is rich in hills, trees and water; the ground is lush and rolling. It is an area of small towns, farms, orchards and valleys. The western section of the state (closer physically to the public conception) is a vast, almost treeless land. The farms are large, and the population is spread thinly over prairies which stretch as far as a man can see. Yet to the people who live in Western Kansas the land is good; the brooding immensity of the plains offers expansion and opportunity.

There are fundamental differences between the people of Eastern and Western Kansas. In Eastern Kansas, many of the people are spiritual descendants of the New England Puritans. They are cautious and frugal. Their farms are small and their crops diversified. A farmer outside Topeka said: "My grandfather gave me the best advice I ever got. 'Don't let your farm get so big you don't know every cow and clod on it. And every time you make a quarter, squirrel away a nickel.'"

In Western Kansas the farms and the stakes are bigger. Wheat is the crop that counts and the fortunes of the countryside ride with the abundance of the harvest. The people are used to boom-and-bust. This is a land for taking a chance, riding a hunch or a piece of ground into a fortune or a prat fall.

This too was once the stomping ground of Wild Bill Hickok and Bat Masterson; a region noted for its cattle drives, garish pleasures and sudden death. Today the people in Western Kansas have outgrown their wild-and-woolly past; like other Kansans, they trust in the Bible and in their own horse sense. But deep inside is a strain of maverick, hard to fence in.

To understand Kansas you must understand its violent beginning. In 1855 it was a territory fighting a preview of the Civil War, a struggle to determine whether Kansas would enter the Union slave or free.

In this same year, at North Elba, New York, a slavery-hating fanatic named John Brown received a letter from five of his sons who the year before had emigrated to Kansas. In this letter the sons told Brown of the wrongs done them by the proslavery border ruffians.

That night, after hours of prayer, Brown opened his Bible and read: "And the Lord said unto Saul, go out and slay the Philistines."

"I then saw the light," Brown later said, "and while my wife and I were kneeling in prayer, I heard the voice of the Lord saying— 'John Brown, go to Kansas and slay the border ruffians.'

"The next morning, in obedience to the command of Almighty God, I started out to save Kansas."

Just what Brown saved in Kansas is still a matter of controversy. Some Kansans regard him as a murderer and horse thief; others think him an idealist, patriot and martyr. Perhaps he was something of all these things; certainly he was a symbol.

In leading a war of retribution against the proslavers, Brown fanned a flame that swept Kansas. Farm homes were burned and families driven into the fields. Towns were attacked and looted. From New England, following John Brown, came hundreds of fighting abolitionists, determined to shape the new state in the image of their own zealous conscience. When President James Buchanan offered a reward of $250 for the capture of Brown, the fiery old abolitionist countered with an offer of $2.50 for the person of Buchanan. When the proslavers from Missouri continued to raid across the border, Brown said: "To make them permanent settlers, I will have to drive them into the ground, like fence posts."

Kansas became known as Bleeding Kansas.

In 1859 Brown left Kansas to set off a slave insurrection in the South, was captured at Harper's Ferry, Virginia and hanged for treason, a lonely, unrepentant old man. ("I hold myself accountable to God.") But he planted his bootprints deep in Kansas history.

In 1861 Kansas went into the Union as a free state, and three months later its people answered Lincoln's call for volunteers to defend the Union.

Many of the New England abolitionists settled in Kansas. They were men and women of stern religious conviction and a passionate insistence on personal morality. The heritage which they left Kansas resulted sometimes in a narrowing of personal freedom; during the 1920's, for example, there was a legal ban in Kansas on Sunday movies and the sale of cigarettes.

Meanwhile, other Kansans of less astringent piety turned to political and social reform, a prairie brand of protest which had repercussions across the land. The combination of the two made Kansas for many years an incubator of ideas, symptoms and portent.

Abolition, Prohibition, Populism (an early-day brand of political radicalism), the Bull Moose (when insurgents led by Theodore Roosevelt split from the Republican Party), the guarantee of bank deposits, the blue-sky law regulating investment companies—these were some of the ideas which came whanging out of Kansas and had their effect on millions of people. But many of the beliefs which long dominated the state have gone. Kansas has lost its zeal for political, economic and moral reform. Even the state prohibition law, in effect since 1881, was repealed in 1948 by a majority of 60,000 votes. (This invalidated William Allen White's prediction that Kansans would "vote dry as long as they can stagger to the polls.")

Today most Kansans are fundamentally orthodox and proud of it. This orthodoxy applies to their religion, politics and living habits. The rambunctious human juices which flavored John Brown, William Allen White and other vital, picturesque figures have been distilled into a less exciting amber that produces people with a great deal of solid character, but very few characters. William Allen White commented on this when he wondered what had happened to Kansas' "rugged Shakespearean characters."

Part of the answer to that question lies in the state's current prosperity. As a breeding place of ideas and curious personalities, Kansas was poor and sometimes hungry; a state with a patch on the seat of its pants, driven by short rations and pride into a restless quest for better living. In those days complacency was akin to shiftlessness; to get ahead a man needed imagination as well as drive and patience.

Today full stomachs have appeased much of the old hunger for experimentation. Well-fed and well-to-do, Kansas is still building and still acquiring, but, mostly, it is interested in defending what it already has. The spirit of challenge in many parts of the state has given way to a searching for conformity. There are thoughtful men and women, born and bred in Kansas, who fear this is leading the state into a creative rut. Most Kansans aren't worried over this; they

IOWA   Abundance—here symbolized by Mrs. August Rettig, of Middle Amana, and a sampling of the soil's rich yield.

MISSOURI   (*center spread*) A stretch of rich Missouri River bottom land, glowing with the glorious colors of fall.

NEBRASKA Scotts Bluff from the air, looking out over the high and exciting tablelands of Western Nebraska.

look at their thriving farms and cities and feel that if this is a rut—well, it certainly is a pleasant one.

And, after all, Kansans are inclined to say, there can't be much wrong with the creative processes of a state that has produced so many distinguished citizens who have made their imprint on the times. But when Kansas boasts of these notables, the skeptics nod wryly and ask: "Uh-huh, but how many of 'em stayed in Kansas?" There is a feeling on the part of some Kansans that the state's itch for conformity has chased many of its young men and women to greener, less-confining pastures, where the challenging in mind and spirit could find elbow room and compatibility.

Kansans themselves are to blame for many of the public misconceptions about Kansas. From the beginning, perhaps from an overflowing of Puritanical zeal, they have taken a curious pride in muffling their virtues and preaching their shortcomings: Their summer winds were the hottest, their winter winds the coldest, their droughts the driest and their grasshoppers the hungriest. Today, for the first time, Kansas is taking off its hair shirt and beginning to brag a little. As more and more Kansans see other parts of the world, they realize there are plenty of blessings which begin at home.

Actually, the Kansas climate is like the climate in most plains states. There are stifling hot summers and pleasant summers, there are cold winters and mild winters. The yearly mean temperature is 54°. As far as tornadoes are concerned—well, Kansas has its share, and often they are rip-roarers, but there are many thousands of Kansans who never have seen a tornado. To most visitors, and to a lot of Kansans, the biggest irritant in the Kansas climate is the nagging wind. Some people cuss and rail at the wind, and others accept it calmly; either way it is an inevitable part of their lives. With a degree of candor rare in the attitude of newspapers concerning the weather in their own communities, the *Wichita Eagle,* on April 15, 1880, commented on the Kansas wind in what conceivably may be the most forthright weather story ever written:

"It may as well be asserted here and now that Kansas as a paradise has her failings, not the least of which is her everlasting spring winds. If there is a man, woman or child in Sedgwick County whose eyes are not filled with dust, and their minds with disgust, he, she or it must be an idiot or awful pious. From everlasting to everlasting this wind for a week has howled and screeched and snorted until you couldn't tell your grandfather from a jackass rabbit."

In Kansas, every man is his own weather prophet and the moods of the people are governed by the turning seasons. In the summer, when Kansas has the appearance of a grandmother's quilt patched with gold and green, there is an urgency about men and women as they watch the sky; for the harvest and their hopes are hitched to the wind, the sun and the rain. In the autumn, if the harvest has been good, a festive confident feeling is apparent in the people; they seem to reflect the strength that has come from the bone marrow of the land. This quiet rejoicing finds an outlet in the dozens of farm expositions held across the state.

I visited the fair and festival held each fall in the town of Norwich. Here the people of the countryside come, togged in their Sunday best, and the glut of the land is visible on every side.

There are rows of potatoes, watermelons, pumpkins, squash, carrots and roasting ears; showcases filled with cakes, pies, candy, biscuits and cheese; there are displays of dahlias, marigolds, zinnias and woolflower; exhibits of needlepoint, spinning, lacemaking and wood carving—all part of the productive energy of a people proud of their craftsmanship. There is the din and warmth of carnival: the pied-piper wheeze of a merry-go-round, the shrill excitement at the bingo booth, the muted conversation of farm boys and girls walking the streets together.

The talk is the talk of the countryside:

"The missus just can't pass up a rummage sale; this time she buys a pan, a lampshade and a corset, and she was mad as all get-out when I says, 'Honey, why don't you wear 'em all at once?'"

"The old man insisted on them bringing the body of his boy back from the soldier cemetery in France; he said if there was rain falling on that grave, he wanted it to be Kansas rain."

A parade, led by the Norwich American Legion Post, comes down the street. There is a float decorated in green and covered with red-tissue poppies; it bears a sign: "We must not forget." Next comes a long line of riders on horseback, then more floats. On one float there is a boy with a telescope peering at a placard which reads: "Christian homes, honesty and truth." There are bands with bare-legged majorettes, and boys on decorated bicycles.

At the horse show, held at the high-school football field, are riders and riding clubs from the towns of the region: Wichita, Anthony, Kingman, Belle Plaine, Zenda, Rago, Harper and Cheney. The names of the contestants reflect an ancestry which stretches across the ocean: Stuchal, Dunkelburger, Lichlider and Helmburger.

The master of ceremonies sits on a chair atop a truck and twangs his words through a microphone. He mingles advice to the riders with homespun humor: "Why don't you give that ornery horse an aspirin? Maybe he's got a headache"; "Take that horse down and bring him back fast—if you need to, step on his carbureter"; or "Let's give the younger riders a hand, folks; doggonit, this younger generation can't mess things up worse than us old folks."

There are contests on the horses' gait and training, and relay races; and there is a square dance, in which the riders solemnly wheel their horses to the hillbilly music of a phonograph record entitled *Hell Among the Yearlings.* A man calls the dance for the riders:

> *All to your places, straight up your faces,*
> *Let out your bellyband, stretch your traces,*
> *Circle eight, hands around.*
> *Line up your pardner and line up eight,*
> *Hook those rowels in that old crow bait.*
> *Riding Old Paint and Leading Old Ball,*
> *Get home this summer and not next fall.*
> *Grab your pardner by the craw*
> *And swing her clear to Arkansas.*

The horse show ends and slowly the people drift back to the town of Norwich and to their homes across the countryside; the carnival banners are being taken down and the exhibits hauled away. In the autumn sun the town seems comfortable and secure, sure of itself and sure of the land. It is late afternoon now, the carnival din is hushed and the sun is slanting long shadows toward Sand Creek back of town aways; on the prairie the sun is a long time setting.

Traditionally, the farms and small towns like Norwich have been the backbone of the Kansas economy, but with the flow of new industry into the state during the past decades the bigger towns have broadened their trade areas and their influence. The biggest, richest, fastest-growing town in Kansas is Wichita. Wichita is located in the Low Plains of South Central Kansas, the blending ground between the rolling hills of Eastern Kansas and the flat treeless plains of Western Kansas. It grew up as a cowtown and collapsed with the shifting westward of the Chisholm cattle trail, became prosperous again as a farm town and went into a tailspin when the bottom fell out of farm and real-estate values. Today it makes its money not only from farm products and livestock but from varied industrial production, from the manufacture and maintenance of airplanes and from oil.

In Wichita, as elsewhere in Kansas, the churches play an important role in community life. There are citizens who devote from three to five nights a week to church functions: prayer meetings, pie suppers, Bible study, choir practice, missionary meetings, youth assemblies.

A businessman told me: "I've been attending the same church for about fifty years. I was baptized in this church; I met a lot of my closest friends there; I courted my wife in the church when we both sang in the choir; I've raised my children in the Sunday school and one of my sons grew up in the Sunday school with the girl he later married. Now they're starting their children over the same route."

One hundred and seventy miles northeast of Wichita is Topeka, the capital of Kansas since statehood, and a city which never has lost its leisurely small-town flavor. People here are rarely in such a hurry they lack time to stop on a street corner and visit. From surface impressions, Topeka is a town that doesn't know the meaning of jangled nerves, yet it is the home of the Menninger Foundation built by Drs. William Menninger and Karl Menninger into the largest training center for psychiatrists in the world. (Dr. Karl recently psychoanalyzed Kansas and found it suffering from a "feeling of inferiority . . . an apologetic manner . . . a tendency to join in a bantering ridicule. . . .")

Topeka was once a ferry point on the Kaw River for the thousands of '49ers heading for the California gold fields; today the Kaw bisects the city. In the bottomland, adjacent to the river, are meat-packing plants, flour mills, wholesale houses and small industries. In the northern part of town are the Santa Fe shops, covering 565 acres. In the western part of the city is Washburn Municipal University and close to the university is the Menninger Foundation.

As political center of Kansas, Topeka has produced public figures who have made their mark on the state. Men like the late Charles Curtis, part Indian and one-time jockey who was vice-president under Herbert Hoover; Arthur Capper, former governor and former

United States senator; and Alfred M. Landon, former governor who was the Republican presidential nominee in 1936.

In addition to Topeka and Wichita, there are numerous other important towns in the state: Kansas City, second-largest town in the state, a meat-packing, hay-market and grain-storage center which zealously defends its separate identity though there is no discernible dividing line between it and Kansas City, Missouri; Hutchinson, fourth largest town in Kansas, a salt-mining and milling center; Coffeyville, a farm and industrial town, where eight persons were shot to death in 1892 during a raid by the notorious Dalton gang; Arkansas City, an oil shipping and refining center, where oil-rich Indians from Oklahoma used to splurge and play; Dodge City, once the most famous cowtown in the West and sometimes called the "buckle on the Kansas wheat belt"; and Abilene, also renowned years ago for its frontier wildness and known now as the boyhood home of President Dwight D. Eisenhower.

And there is also, in the south central part of Kansas, close to the Oklahoma border, a rustic little town named Medicine Lodge. In appearance and behavior the town is typical of the countryside—quiet, peaceful, knowing its place in the sun and satisfied with it; but in the 1890's Medicine Lodge kicked up a squall that echoed through the nation. At that time it was the home of two of the most remarkable of all Kansas figures: Sockless Jerry Simpson, the spokesman of a rag, tag and bobtail creed of political prairie-shakers known as the Populists, and Carry Nation, the hatchet-wielding saloon-smasher. Simpson was a political radical and religious skeptic; Carry Nation distrusted all politicians and was a religious fanatic. There is no record that these two ever came to grips; if they had, the smiting and bellowing would have been awful to behold.

Today Simpson is almost forgotten; Medicine Lodge is conservative, predominantly Republican, but there are many persons who remember Carry Nation, most of them with affection. Mrs. Riley MacGregor, the wife of a Medicine Lodge lawyer and legislator, recalls Carry Nation. "I lived next door to her as a little girl. She was good to me and good to other children. I think she was a kindly, misunderstood lady."

Medicine Lodge had its first glimpse of Carry Nation in 1889 when her husband, David Nation, became minister of the Christian Church. At the time Carry Nation was forty-three years old, a chunkily built woman with a determined jaw, who sat in the front pew of the church while her husband preached, giving him brusque instructions on when to raise or lower his voice and when to gesture: "Louder, husband," or "Husband, point your finger at the congregation."

When she thought that the Reverend Nation had talked enough, or when she felt that he was giving a dull performance, she would step into the aisle and say: "That's enough for today." On those occasions when the Reverend Nation ignored her and continued speaking, she would stride to the pulpit, bang shut the Bible, give him his hat and point toward the door.

As a child Carry Nation had been sickly and subject to visions, and at an early age she decided she was a confidante of the Almighty. Her first husband had died of alcoholism.

As she grew older, she grew more emotional, domineering and meddlesome. If she saw a young man smoking a cigarette, she was likely to snatch the cigarette from his mouth and slap his face. When she found a boy with his arms around a girl, she flew into a frenzy, warning the girl that this is a sinful world overrun with vultures. If she noticed a girl exposing a few inches of ankle, she delivered a lecture on morality. But all this was only a warmup; the hatchet-wielding, the wrecked saloons, jail, headlines and vaudeville were still ahead.

Within a few years Carry Nation was the leader of the temperance forces in Medicine Lodge. She frequently arose in prayer meeting at the church, listed the names of the saloonkeepers in town, and demanded to know why officials permitted them to operate in violation of the state law. When she met on the street a man who was known to operate a saloon, she made it a custom to bar his pathway, point a finger and say: "How do you do, maker of drunkards and widows?"

One Saturday afternoon in 1899, Carry Nation and her little band of temperance workers marched down Main Street and dropped to their knees in prayer in front of a saloon owned by a man named Mart Strong. Then, while an assistant manipulated a creaking hand organ, Carry Nation flourished her umbrella high above her poke bonnet, and led the singing of her favorite temperance song:

> *They who tarry at the wine cup,*
> *They who tarry at the wine cup,*
> *They who tarry at the wine cup,*
> *They have sorrow, they have woe.*

This was the beginning. Within a few months, she closed every saloon in Medicine Lodge. She next moved on the saloons in nearby Kiowa, then on her third raid, she made a shambles of a saloon in Wichita, destroying in the process a voluptuous oil painting entitled *Cleopatra at the Bath*, the work of a young Wichita artist named John Noble, who later made an international reputation.

Carry Nation became a national and then a world figure. In 1911, feeble and broke, she died in a hospital at Leavenworth, Kansas. During her life she had instigated scores of riots, been arrested more than twenty-five times, been beaten up a dozen times, scandalized both her enemies and friends, appeared as a temperance lecturer on theatrical platforms, including burlesque, and had helped to bring about national prohibition. Today there is a liquor store only one block from the yellow-brick house in which she lived in Medicine Lodge; and in 1948 her home town went resoundingly wet.

Not long ago a crowd of followers made a sober pilgrimage to her home and dedicated it as a W.C.T.U. memorial. The furnishings include her original bar-smashing hatchet, her old rocking chair and desk and the satchel in which she carried bricks to shatter saloon mirrors.

Jerry Simpson, Medicine Lodge's other famous product, was of a different cut of jib. He was a Great Lakes sailor who had come to Kansas in 1878 at the age of thirty-six and acquired a farm outside Medicine Lodge. His cattle died in a blizzard and he was forced to sell his farm. He then became town marshal of Medicine Lodge at a salary of twenty-five dollars a month. He was a spare, wiry man with a drooping mustache, who borrowed books on history and theology from the Medicine Lodge ministers and then buttonholed them on the street corners to argue about what he had read. In 1890, partly as a joke and partly because it was hard to find anyone to accept the nomination, the Populists persuaded Simpson to run for Congress in the seventh Kansas district. The Populists were not believed to have a chance, and Simpson took the nomination with the wry observation: "Wouldn't it be a hell of a joke if I got elected."

In his campaign Jerry Simpson became the symbol of the unrest sweeping Kansas, of a contagious, singing, foot-stamping crusade that singled out Wall Street as a money-grabbing Old Nick to be overthrown, and called on the people to raise less corn and more hell.

Simpson proved to be a curious, compelling figure on the hustings; to his enemies he was a rube and demagogue and to his followers he was a folk hero who spoke their minds and hopes. "The price of corn is so low that our farmers burn their corn," he told the crowds, "and by the light of that burning corn they read the history of their long injustices." "My opponent wears fine soft silk hosiery. I have no money with which to buy silk hosiery. The facts of the business are I have no socks at all save the natural buff my mother gave me." He illustrated this point by hitching up his pants legs and showing his bare shanks.

Admirers sent socks to Simpson by the hundreds, including a knitted sock four feet long, which Simpson's followers mounted on a pole and carried in their parades. Simpson's opponents called him uncultured and cited as proof a letter in his own handwriting in which he had misspelled the name of Medicine Lodge. "Again I plead guilty," Sockless Jerry said, "and I tell you further I wouldn't give a tinker's dern for a man who can't spell a word more than one way."

Simpson was elected to Congress and served three terms. He became known throughout the nation as an odd, incorruptible figure challenging and disturbing the people's conscience. He wanted a better deal for the prairie farmers and he said so in words that made headlines. Kansas was the seedbed of the Populist movement and Sockless Jerry was the prophet.

With the return of good times, the Populist party disintegrated and the Populists disappeared from public life. Sockless Jerry made his last political race in 1898 when he ran again for Congress and was defeated. Seven years later he died, refusing religious ministration and comforting himself on his deathbed by telling friends: "Populism never will die—it is a cumulative indignation which shall come again and again."

The Populist decline was accelerated by William Allen White, a young, obscure country editor in Emporia, Kansas. In 1896 White wrote an editorial entitled "What's the Matter with Kansas," which had repercussions across the land. In those days, when Kansas was a ragged shadow of its present prosperous self, White concluded there was only one thing wrong with Kansas: the Populists. Drive the Populists from public life, he urged; put an end to the careers of "old human hoop skirts" like Jerry Simpson and give Kansas a chance to win back its self-respect.

Under the Populists, White said, Kansas had become "poorer and ornrier and meaner than a spavined, distempered mule." With flailing sarcasm, White wrote: "Whoop it up for the ragged trousers; put the lazy greasy frizzle, who can't pay his debts, on the altar, and bow down and worship him. Let the state ideal be high. What we need is not the respect of our fellow men, but the chance to get something for nothing."

This editorial projected White for the first time into national attention and into the receptive arms of the Republican Old Guard. In later years, however, White became a Republican liberal—on occasion even a political heretic of sorts, who lambasted his party between elections and returned to the fold on election day. As time mellowed his memories, White revised his opinion of the Populists. He considered them "probably sowers of seeds, but a mighty unpromising looking band of sowers." He later wrote: "The rumps of seedy farmers sticking out of the courthouse windows, as the Farmers' Alliance met, cast the shadow of a great twilight . . . Being what I was, a child of the governing classes, I was blinded by my birthright."

White was born in Kansas and, in the minds of many persons, was the most typical Kansan who ever lived. He was kindly, neighborly, practical, idealistic. He had wisdom, warmth and an instinctive feeling for what was in the minds of people. He made the Emporia *Gazette* a spokesman for the small-town conscience. White was a friend of many of the important men of his generation, he exerted a wide influence on the issues of his time; yet as an editor he insisted, first and last, that the *Gazette* be a local newspaper, concerned primarily with the affairs of Emporia.

In directing the *Gazette*, White never forgot the advice given him as a student at the University of Kansas by a poet-professor named William Herbert Carruth: "You know it's vastly more important than many pious prayers and tons of highfalutin aspirations to get a street in a country town made wide enough so that two loads of hay going in opposite directions still leave it possible for a woman to drive a horse between them without getting hay wisps on her buggy top."

This interest in intimate, day-to-day events of his own town helped shape White's character. He knew his town better than any man, and knowing Emporia, he knew a lot about America.

White has been dead since 1944, yet his memory has a vital, unifying effect on Emporia. In street-corner controversies, in meetings of the city officials, wherever men and women gather in Emporia to pool the community wisdom, his words are recalled and used to settle issues. Today in Peter Pan Park, donated by Mr. and Mrs. White to Emporia in memory of their daughter, Mary, there is a bronze bust of White—a memorial to the man who made Emporia famous.

Emporia is a quiet, friendly town, as much a part of the prairies as the bluestem pasture grass in the Flint Hills beyond the city's edge. It has two colleges and twenty-eight churches.

In appearance Emporia is pretty much what you would expect the home town of America's most famous country editor to be—a place of comfortable, middle-class homes set back on streets, lined with elm and maple trees, of men sitting on their front porches with slippered feet propped on the porch rail, neighbors trading small talk over the back fence, of parks thronged with children.

The *Gazette,* owned by White's son, is operated by veteran staff members who learned the business under White's direction. White's office, just off the news room, is unchanged from the day he left it. There are autographed pictures on the walls from men who have helped to shape the events of the times: Theodore Roosevelt, Mark Hanna, Herbert Hoover, Robert M. LaFollette, William Jennings Bryan and Alfred Landon. Also on the wall is a note White received on his seventy-fifth birthday from Franklin Roosevelt: "Congratulations on reaching the three-quarter mark. I hope that during the next 25 years you will be for me all the time instead of only three and one half years out of every four. I think that in a quarter of a century the firm of White and Roosevelt might be able to bring the four freedoms to at least this nation of ours."

Of the many things written about White, many townspeople think he unintentionally summed up his own life best when he wrote an editorial years ago describing the life of a typical country editor: "He has given all his life to his town; he has spent thousands of dollars to promote its growth; he has watched every house on the townsite rise and has made an item in the paper about it; he has written up the weddings of many of the grandmothers and grandfathers of the town; he has chronicled the birth of their children and their children's children. The old scrapbooks are filled with kind things he has written. Old men and old women scan these pages with eyes that have lost their luster, and on the rusty clippings there fall many tears. In this book many a woman reads the little verse below the name of a child whom only she and God remember. In some other scrapbook a man long since out of the current of life reads the story of his little triumphs in the world; in the family Bible is a clipping—yellow and crisp with years—that tells of a daughter's wedding and the social glory that descended upon the house that one great day."

During the years Kansas has put up with much: grasshoppers, chinch bugs, border ruffians, windstorms, drought, floods, rascals and fanatics.

In the 1930's the dust came; stifling winds of forty-five to sixty miles an hour rooted the crops from the ground and blew them away, leaving a grayish blanket on the fields. The crops which escaped the wind crept back into the ground. Clouds of dirt blotted the sun and airport radios sent out the laconic warning: "no visibility, no ceiling." People wore dust masks to protect their noses and throats and made wry jokes about gophers digging their homes in the air. During the middle of a dust storm, Kansans said, Lady Godiva could have ridden her horse down the main street of some Kansas towns without even the horse seeing her. An old man walked the roads wearing on his back a sign which read: "Beware. The Lord is wrathful."

In parts of western Kansas dunes of gray dirt piled up where there were once plowed fields; farmers lost crop after crop and some of them said to hell with it and moved away. Most of them stayed with the land; they had a grim patience and, besides, there was no place to go.

Today Kansas once more is covered with grass and grain; the old miseries are only nagging memories now. Across the Kansas prairie at harvesttime, great combines clank through the knee-high wheat and into the bins of the combines pours a stream of yellow kernels that means bread for the world's bellyache.

Outside Wichita, a farmer named Sam Barner shielded his face from the sun with a big hand and watched the flailing reels of a combine chew the wheat into spears of rubble. Barner had worked on his farm most of his life; he had known good times and despair.

"We've seen about everything there is to see," Barner said, "and still we're alive and full of beans. I guess a lot of folks think we're mighty set in our ways, and I guess we are. But we insist on working out things for ourselves in our own individual way, and with all this talk about individualism going on in the world, Kansas may come up one of these days with some ideas, agitation and answers that will make a powerful lot of sense."

Barner sifted a handful of grain through his hands and looked at the long rows of wheat glistening and bending in the sun. "When that day comes," he said, "people are going to forget all this stuff about Kansas being stodgy and conservative and cautious because things in Kansas are going to be popping hotter than hog grease on a griddle."

Minnesota

by GRACE FLANDRAU

The train, smooth and fast and filled with the chill of the air-conditioning, rushed northward toward Minnesota. I had asked, as usual, to be told the exact moment we crossed the border, although the much-bored conductor insisted it would look the same on either side. But there *was* a difference, and I felt it, when we did cross.

The scene outside the car windows, however, needed none of the sentimentality of the native's return to make it beautiful. This was southeastern Minnesota, a flawless farming country, silvery under the spring sky and touched with the delicate expectancy of spring. The greens brighter for the blackness of the rich plowed earth, the willows a mist of yellow, the wide, grandfatherly old oaks foolish with tasseled buds. A place of gently rolling hills and groves and wild fruit trees tumbling down the slopes; of well-painted farm buildings and serene cattle, 4-H to a cow, standing dreamily at the barnyard gates. Where such names as Blooming Prairie, Belle Plaine, Elysian, Harmony and the tender Sleepy Eye speak for the feeling of the early settlers.

Although this is the oldest part of the state in point of settlement, it is still wonderfully free, just here, from the untidiness of advancing urbanism. But as we traveled north, more towns appeared. Soon we were near the one-time village Will and Charlie Mayo put on the map of the world. Rochester—where the Mayo boys worked in their father's dispensary, drove him on his rounds, learned their first anatomy from the skeleton of an old Sioux. Gradually, too, the country became more chasmed, more picturesque. Gradually we approached the Mississippi.

It came into view, not magnificently as seen from across the valley, but glimpsed, lying quiet and swollen with spring floods over the lowlands. Then it made its turn below St. Paul, a modest group of skyscrapers appeared and we bumbled across the trestle into the city.

At first, levees and river seemed strangely quiet to me. Then I remembered it was still too early for much water-borne traffic. But there was something wrong about that too. No Minnesota spring could produce an evening as warm and humid as this. Where were the invigorating airs the early travelers wrote about? The astringent cold that cured your sore throat? I'll tell you where. They were just around the corner and by morning they had turned it, bringing a blizzard with them. A "good old Minnesota blizzard" is the loving local term. And that, too, was as it should be. I was glad to be home again.

When, as sometimes happens, Minnesota is spoken of as Mid-western, Minnesotans are likely to remark rather firmly, that it is not a Middle Western, but a Northwestern state. It is a big state—larger than all of New England, with Maryland and New Jersey thrown in. Of mountains there are none, and the tall bluffs along the rivers give to the country above an exhilarating sense of height. Worth noting, too, is the fact that because of its great length from north to south, it lies in two distinct "Life" zones so-called, the Canadian and the Transitional. A fact which accounts in part for the immense variety of plant and animal life, and of birds.

All in all, it is appropriate that *minne,* the Siouan word for water, should be included in our name. (The suffix *sota* means, not the sky-blue of the advertisements, but turgid or whitish.) On three sides we are mostly bounded by water. On the east by the Mississippi and its tributary from the north, the beautiful St. Croix. And farther north and east, for 150 spectacular miles, by Lake Superior, no less. On the west, is the Red River of the North, almost the only river of importance in the United States to flow due north.

The most remarkable boundary is the chain of wilderness lakes and rivers, streams and portages along the Canadian border, in many parts accessible only by canoe, on foot, in motorboat or hydroplane. Yet at a time when the Pilgrims had hardly ventured far enough inland to lose the sound of the sea, it was a fairly well traveled route along which Frenchmen carried on their dramatic, wicked, venerable fur trade. Today, for sportsmen, poets, naturalists, wildlifers and just anybody who wants to get away from it all, it is the most favored region in Minnesota.

There are also, in good round numbers so dear to Chambers of Commerce, our ten thousand lakes, plus the largest number of marshes, swamps, sloughs, fens, muskegs and bogs (lovely words) of any state in the Union. And finally, there is the three-way divide from which our waters rush off—some north to Hudson's Bay, others east to the Atlantic, the rest south to the Gulf of Mexico.

There is also the weather—to which the more vigorous aspects of our personality are attributed. Minnesota's melodrama in four acts.

There are the blue, arctic Minnesota winters: snow, light, and dry and deep on roofs and lawns, slipping in a dazzle of white mist from the suddenly released branch of the evergreen that grows in every yard. Snow falling in soft, big flakes, or fine and hard, driven before terrible winds to blot out the world in days-long blizzards.

(There are the tales heard as a child, of men and women lost and frozen a few feet from their doors. Of the great-uncle who, snowbound in a deserted cabin, made a saw out of a piece of barrel hoop, sharpened a clasp knife and hacked off a piece of each of his frozen feet. And on the fine-drawn face of the man who so often told the story, a shadow whose meaning the child in some way understood: the question, whether he would have had the courage to do the same, and the fear, indeed the certainty, that he would not.)

Winters with everyone on skates, and on toboggans; curling, ice boating, playing hockey. Skiing, which is now the leading winter sport, was at first popular only among the Scandinavians.

The brief and boisterous period which follows is known as the Minnesota spring. It's a time, too—and somehow it makes them the more touching—for the gentle woods flowers, the crocuses and snowdrops, the blood root, anemone and violets. For the full white bloom of the wild plums and crab apples; for the lilacs and jonquils and for the lovely wild orchid which is Minnesota's flower—the pink lady's-slipper, or its sturdier cousin, the green-brown jack-in-the-pulpit.

Then the yards gay with bridal wreath and syringa and Minnesota's summer comes in with a bang. Of this season it must be said at once that while there are a great many "sparkling, winelike" days, there are not a few dog days, of which the less said the better. Nor can we, I'm afraid, ignore the Minnesota storms; on a single night in a single county where I once visited, there took place, in one corner, a cloudburst, in another a cyclone, and in between a thunderstorm in which seven cows were killed.

> From the half
> of the sky
> that which lives there
> is coming and makes a noise.

So sang the ancient Chippewa poet. And how right he was.

With the final act comes the redemption—the Indian summer, Minnesota's matchless fall when all its violence is distilled into color. Skies wildly blue, air crisp and ozone-scented. The thinning brilliant underbrush alive with ruffed grouse and quail and pheasant. Deer step the highways, wild ducks in unequaled numbers and varieties rock on all the waters. The beaver, mink, otter, muskrat and all our countless fur-bearing animals thicken their coats, and up in the northern swamps the squaws bend the wild rice over their birch-bark canoes and beat out the grain.

Also, throughout the state, the weather doesn't differ greatly except that in some places it is colder. Caprice, too, plays a part. For all the time-worn quip, "the coldest winter I ever knew was the summer I spent in Duluth," the day I recently spent there would make the third circle of the Inferno pleasantly cool. And almost anywhere it can be sixty in the morning, eighty at noon, near freezing in the evening.

Which brings us to a gray-eyed young Norwegian farmer beside whom, on a broiling day in Montevideo, Minnesota, I watched a parade. "Yes," he said, "I guess it gets hotter and gets colder here than most places. But it don't get monotonous. My brother out on the Coast says the weather there is always the same. He says it gets monotonous and he's coming home." Monotony is not, in fact, regarded favorably in Minnesota, nor is it, as we shall see, a condition that generally obtains.

A river beside which one's childhood is spent, even if it is the Mississippi, is likely to be taken pretty much for granted. Certainly it meant little to me until the day I stood, a small, scared pupil before a violin master of the Paris Conservatory. He was a sensitive, irascible man, cloistered in his own country as only a Frenchman of that time could be, and had endured me with pain till he learned where I was from. The effect was startling. *"Le Mee-see-see-pee!"* Never, but never, as a boy studying his geography, had he expected even to *see* a native from those shores, much less that one should be his pupil! Jean Jacques Rousseau was in his head, Paul and Virginia and all the virgin rivers, the exotic forests of the world. Next day his delicate little son was permitted a glimpse of me, but cautioned, I am sure, not to come too close.

The Mississippi was the highway that brought the modern world to the Northwest, from the day in 1823, when the first small steamboat staggered upstream to dock at the brand-new military post across from where St. Paul now stands. Soon an excited river traffic began, which by mid-century had built up a kind of climax, not only in numbers but in the nearly lunatic enthusiasm of the travelers. The beauties of woods, waterfalls, gardens of wild flowers; of the "sparkling, winelike" days; the sight of the buffalo and, in St. Paul, of the Chippewa lounging picturesquely about the streets, sent a rush of indescribably purple prose to tongue and pen. Settlers poured in from more easterly states and in countless thousands from overseas: from Ireland first, then Germany and soon from all the Scandinavian countries—workers and peasants who were glad to pay any price in toil and privation for independence and the right to own their own land.

As late as 1930, Norwegian was heard in parts of Southern Minnesota as often as English. In the town of Northfield, the Norwegian college of St. Olaf was founded, now famous for its magnificent *a cappella* choir. And where one of its professors, Ole Rölvaag, wrote his great novel *Giants in the Earth.* In the farming village of Scandia, some thirty miles north of St. Paul, on a certain summer day each year, throngs of handsome, well-dressed people from all over the state come back to celebrate an anniversary—the founding, in 1850, of one of the very first Swedish settlements in Minnesota. The Danes were fewer, but their dairying skills have had far-reaching economic effects. As has the Scandinavian predilection for co-operative enterprise.

In my childhood, Anglo-Saxon Minnesotans tended to regard the foreign-born and their progeny, especially those on the farms, as beings from a different planet. And indeed, there was some difference in dress and appearance. Now all that is changed. Everybody wears the same kind of clothes and looks the same in them. Along the leafy streets of the old river towns are handsome houses occupied for generations by the same families, persons quite as distinguished as, and indistinguishable from, any in the cities.

Everywhere, too, even in the big cities, one is still relatively near the wilderness, the almost unchanged wilderness the early settlers knew. Near the duck pass, the trout or small-mouth-bass stream, the camp in the deep woods, where on a path springy with fallen pine needles the young and as yet fearless deer love to stand and stare into your face as long as you stare into theirs: or, at your approach, a half dozen balls of feathers ricochet out of the brush, and the mother grouse scolds and drags her pretended broken wing to fool you. And where at night, on the shining lakes, the loons make those sounds literary people love, so inadequately, to describe.

To see Minnesota at its most moving and when it is most itself is, to me at least, to see it in the growing time of high midsummer. And to set out, as I did one year, up the beautiful valley of the Minnesota, a river which flows across Southern Minnesota from the west and empties into the Mississippi. This is a rich and beautiful farming country and the Germans who settled here gave nostalgic German names to their towns. In their part of the valley, German was spoken for many years, German ways predominated. However, aside from occasional polka dancing in the streets, to the music of German brass bands, this is no longer true.

(Indeed, the idea that the various racial groups in Minnesota retain the customs of their forebears is an illusion. It is true that for a national festival they may put on the old costumes, dance the old dances to the old tunes. But it is not a part of their daily living. When the girls, for instance, are being themselves, it is in their smart ready-made dresses, with their beauty-parlor hairdos. In the blue jeans in which they lead their 4-H calves or panda-faced lambs into the judging ring. When they preside over their classrooms or dance in their strapless evening gowns at their university or high-school proms. Americans, and in a hundred ways, making the most of it.)

It was hot that day, in the valley, especially so in the pleasant town of Le Seuer, of which I remember only a superlative corn- and pea-canning factory which featured such surprising items as field thermometers perpetually taking the soil's temperature, and radio-telephone conversations between the head office and, for all I know, the peas themselves. And, too, the presence in this Minnesota town of large groups of Bahamians and West Indians, who would later move on to harvest other crops.

My objective was the town of New Ulm to which I had once been taken as a child. Of that occasion, however, I remember nothing but the sound of a cannon, fired not in war but at a cere- mony in honor of Charles Eugene Flandrau and the winning of a battle many years before.

This lovely valley was once a part of the Sioux lands, and one often wonders what these primitive Americans understood of the treaties by which they bartered away their homes and hunting grounds. At any rate, when a summer came in which they found themselves not only without land, but without the food, money or goods promised them, they rose and savagely murdered over a thousand white men and women and children.

Flandrau had been Associate Justice of the Supreme Court of the territory, and later of the state. He was living in the valley when the massacre began, and was elected commander-in-chief of the defenders at New Ulm, where about 1500 women and children had taken refuge. The gallantry and brilliance with which he won the three-day battle make it one of the most moving episodes of our frontier history.

Modern New Ulm is a solid, prosperous town, with pleasant, shady streets and yards bright with flowers. Here is a Flandrau State Park and a commemorative monument. But it was a small bronze plaque, identifying the building where the women and children awaited the outcome of the siege, that moved me most. That and an incident which occurred when Flandrau was evacuating a village to the advancing Sioux. The departing settlers had poisoned a barrelful of whisky and left it in the square. It was one way of fighting Indians; but Flandrau, the last to leave, pulled the plug and drained away the poisoned liquor.

I married into his family long after he died, and I wish I could remember, of that one day I saw him, more than the sound of a cannon.

Farther up in the valley is the gay and friendly town of Monte-video, which we found in the throes of its annual fiesta, the streets crowded with tall, well-boned men and women, and hordes of sturdy, bare-armed children. This celebration, in the weird Amer-ican way, is dedicated to Uruguay, and Uruguay responds by send-ing an official representative. The hotel swarmed with pretty queens, girls mostly from other farming communities and named, like the goddesses of old, for the products of the earth—corn, flax, soybeans and all the rest. Although less poetically, there were also a Boxcar and an Overall queen. Less poetic, too, was the booming voice heard above the bands and the singing in the streets, of the radio loud-speaker, talking endlessly of prices, crops, livestock, and of remedies for all kinds of livestock ailments.

There was also a reception, given by the widow of one of Minne-sota's thirteen Scandinavian governors—fourteen, if you count Harold Stassen who is half Scandinavian—Mrs. Theodore Christianson, at her farm some miles distant. On one side the pleasant, reconstructed farmhouse overlooks the bluff above the river, on the other it faces an endless, sunlit sweep of land, carpeted now with growing grain. And the look of the country, or perhaps the purity of the air—the ethereal lightness of air without dust and without humidity—seemed suddenly to reveal a quality of my state I had vaguely felt but never before defined.

The quality of newness. Of skies that had not had to look down through all the ages upon human suffering; of an air not yet heavy with human sighs. A newness which is not felt in the actual wilder-ness but only, by contrast, in those places to which human beings have recently, and in not too great numbers, come.

It seemed to me that unconsciously, it was felt by the people who were there that day, and of whom there was hardly one who did not point to an island in the river, or a spot along the shore, or upon the bright country above, as the place where his forebears had "taken up" land, and where he or one of his parents had been born.

One of these, a vigorous man with keen, friendly gray eyes, invited me to breakfast. "Will eight o'clock suit you?"—the hour set late, I felt sure, on my account.

He is a farmer and a power in the agricultural affairs of the region—a man who is extraordinarily well informed but who is also quite impassioned. So that such phrases as "those fellows in the cities," "Wall Street," "those bankers"—men who, he believed, had no relation to droughts, floods, frosts, but did have too high prices for what you bought, low prices for what you sold—had a way of erupting violently. "I've only got two men now, maybe in a couple of years I won't have any. If they don't want collectivized farms"— this on a note of the horror felt, I suppose, by most land-owning men —"they better take care of the farmers."

But there is in him, too, still another man. The one who belongs to the soil. We drove slowly past his fields, stopping to look at the barley, the tufted bright-green rows of soybeans, striped in between with the black, black earth—the perfect pattern of a fashionable modern fabric. And, crowning it all, there was his flax—the deep blue of flax in bloom. A lake of color more like a mirage than a lake. A blue that eludes you, as if the massed green stems had only been breathed upon by color. A blue like no other in the world and that reaches less into your eyes than deep into your heart.

Now, as you continue westward, you begin to be aware of something different. There are times when, over a hill or through an opening in the vista, you see too far. You see nothing but light. You are in the midst of nowhere, a shining emptiness, a vast floor, flat and wide as the sea, spreading away to and beyond the whole circle of the horizon. And no sound but the hum of wind along the telegraph wires, the liquid call of a bird or a human voice at once loud and nearly extinguished by the immensity into which it falls. The West, the Prairie, the great valley of the Red River of the North.

You must see the prairies where they are perfect, or you will not see them at all. There must not be the tiniest rise or fall of the earth, or your new sense of dimension will be lost. It must also be away from the centers of activity—out where the great farms are, and where the occasional groups of grain elevators, the straight march of the telegraph poles, the rare, thin lines of planted trees are merely perpendicular lines that accentuate the total flatness.

The low, wooded course of the Red River of the North is scarcely noticeable in these wide vistas. Here, in summers long past, the wild grass grew tall as a man, and the hooves of the buffalo were stained red with the juice of the wild berries. And yet even after Jim Hill brought in his railroad, the soil was considered valueless by everybody but him. Possibly, too, fear of the winter with nothing to stop the sweep of the winds, or to mitigate the heat of summer, may have held back the pioneers. Perhaps it is still only a place for the strong. But from those who are not, something also may be learned.

So there was the delicate-looking man who stood so long beside his weedy flax field, under some compulsion to talk. Sometimes it was about his pioneer grandparents. How their money had run out back on the Mississippi, so they had walked the remaining 300 miles, his mother, then twelve, barefoot and driving the cows. When they did arrive, nothing here but empty prairie, the sod hut, the meager hand tools. "I couldn't have done it," he would repeat, accusing himself.

Or else it was his own hard life he dwelt upon. Six hundred acres to farm and he couldn't get help or pay for it if he could. He had suffered a back injury, too, from which he could not recover. Lightning had recently burned his barns. You needed sons on a farm, and he had none. "I don't know, maybe they had it better then than we do."

Sometimes he didn't talk at all. His tractor chugged softly in the potato patch, in the grove of trembling, silver aspens a meadow lark repeated a clear melodious phrase. And I felt that his thoughts were not really on what he said, but were concerned with what a human being wants; what he needs to be happy; why he lives at all. He, too, a Norwegian, with the something they have that is a little remote and dreamlike in their pale eyes.

It seemed strange, now, to turn eastward—as if one had come to feel that any movement should still be toward the west. Strange to see hills again, and shady towns, and normal-sized farms; to motor hour after hour between undefaced green walls—the second growth now replacing the virgin forests which once covered most of the state.

Blue lakes were everywhere in wild profusion, and wherever a dirt road leads back from the highway, there would be signs bearing such names as K'Mon Inn, Nip Inn, Step Inn and similar whimsies. I was relieved to see them there, having got the impression from one of those most dedicated of pessimists, a Conservation officer, that our Minnesota lakes were beginning to dry up.

Throughout this northerly half of the state are the great state and national parks and forests, the experimental stations for the study and preservation of wild life, the reforestation projects in which Government and lumber companies collaborate in planting new trees.

Here, too, are the reservations where the Chippewa, once the lords of it all, mostly live. And where, in the town of Walker, we paid a visit to one of the state's most distinguished citizens—Ed Rogers, county attorney, and a three-fourths Chippewa Indian. And it was gratifying to hear Indians discussed sympathetically, but without sentimentality. They must be assimilated into American life as other races and peoples have been, but this cannot happen, he believes, while they remain on reservations. As long as they are together, "they'll just be Indians." I should have liked to ask what that is. But one answer is to be found in the translations of their songs by a Minnesota woman who is one of the nation's great authorities on Indian music and poetry, Miss Frances Densmore. And how like any girl was the young Chippewa who sang:

> *What are you saying to me?*
> *I am arrayed like the rose*
> *And as beautiful as they. . . .*

In this region, too, you will get a notion of Minnesota's summer hysteria: in the motor launches, whose interiors are a forest of fine-stemmed rods held tenderly between the owners' knees; at the camps where nothing but fishing is thought of, and on the lakes where nothing else is done.

Strange, too, that here, where such delicious fish as trout of all kinds, wall-eyed and northern pike, and a dozen others abound, the local menus should be largely given over to lobster tails from South Africa, shrimp from Japan and other embalmed delicacies from remote parts of the world.

Often, in Northeastern Minnesota, beside the remote beauty of green forest and blue water, of small, pine-ringed fields ripening on lonely-seeming farms, and quiet ponds where water lilies lie open in full bloom and the wicked pitcher plants wait with their traps set for unwary flies—beside all this organic, surface life, you are aware of something else. You see how the roots even of the tall trees clutch only the surface of bare rock, and you walk on what you learn, with a kind of dreamy satisfaction, is the oldest of all granites. And near the town of Ely, you come upon a softly jade-colored stone known as Ely Green, perhaps the very oldest substance known to man. Two and a half billion years, estimates the latest authority.

Nor is this all. For in this region is Minnesota's greatest geologic spectacle, the open-pit mines of the Mesabi Iron Range. Vast sunken amphitheaters, huge gaping earth wounds bleeding strange and subtle tones of red—rust red, blue or brown or purple reds, and the violent orange of water sometimes lying in the pits. And looking down into them from the observation platforms, you seem to see no men at all, only cranes that whirl, great steel jaws that bite into the red earth, trucks that seem to be self-propelled along roads that spiral around the walls of the pits, and small grublike vehicles which rise nimbly up the steep runways to the trains which, night and day, rumble down to the great docks at Superior and Duluth.

Duluth I remember from childhood with a kind of enchantment. A perpendicular city, a toy town, built straight up and down like a city in a fairy tale. Its air heady with the freshness of the gigantic lake beside which it seemed so precariously to be perched.

Well, it is anything but a toy city now. And yet something of that wry magic remains. It still climbs its steep escarpment and for twenty-four miles along the top looks out over a breath-taking blue void of sky and water. The sense, too, of excitement and urgency still exists, and by some is attributed to the climate: "Nine months of winter and three of poor sledding." A libel.

I'd like to touch upon another subject of which Duluthians are very, very tired. Namely, bears. In Duluth, one hears, bears occasionally stroll into restaurants or are found by startled homecomers in the back yard playing with the children. Even more fascinating is an event reported in the publication *North Country*.

Two men, it seems, went out one morning in their motorboat to take a turn around the harbor. There was also present a large bear, out for a swim.

When the boat loitered too near him, he, deciding he preferred to ride, promptly climbed in and the two gentlemen promptly climbed out. The boat, unguided, tore wildly around the harbor with the bear calmly seated in the stern.

Apparently a boat captained by a bear is news even in Duluth, and brought the citizens flocking to the water front. Finally the bear, bored by it all, resumed his swim. I think I should like to live in Duluth.

Little Falls is a town on the Mississippi, in the center of the state—a farming and a vacation region that was once the richest part of our pinelands; a place that has always had—for me, at least

—an air of incompleteness, as if the forests ought still to be there. It is also a part of Minnesota greatly loved by one of her most celebrated sons—Charles Lindbergh.

Just outside Little Falls is a park dedicated to Lindbergh's father, the Minnesota Congressman Charles A. Lindbergh. There is also the small house where Lindbergh spent the first seventeen and most formative years of his life. In his book, *The Spirit of St. Louis,* he writes with simple and moving artistry about his childhood here, of the tales he heard from his parents and his Swedish grandparents.

He writes about being trapped in a Minnesota blizzard, and about the time his barnstorming plane was forced down in a Minnesota swamp. You recognize the fields he plowed, learn how often, in Washington, father and son talked of the summer when they would return to the Minnesota farm.

In the Lindbergh house are a few mementoes of a boy's childhood: toys, agates, the claw of an eagle and the jawbone of a large pike. But what is of most interest to us, I think, is that this man, who is a symbol of the modern world of flight, should have seen and heard Minnesota's early settlers.

Seventy miles south, also on the Mississippi, we come to Minnesota's urban phenomenon—the Siamese but *not* identical twin cities of St. Paul and Minneapolis.

St. Paul, which had a few years' start, grew steeply up and down her hills and bluffs along the Mississippi. Minneapolis was born on the high, level plateau across the river with all the vast, empty West as her front yard. At her back were the falls which stopped navigation, a geographic circumstance that made St. Paul a great transportation center but gave the power of the river to Minneapolis. The nucleus of population in both cities came from the eastern seaboard. But soon Germans in large numbers settled in St. Paul, as did the gifted, generous, always intensely human and therefore incalculable Irish, while an influx of able, hard-working, hardheaded, forward-looking Swedes made Minneapolis one of the largest Swedish cities in the world.

There is a much-quoted pronouncement to the effect that St. Paul is the last city of the East, Minneapolis the first city of the West. And perhaps it has, or did have, an element of truth. Anyhow, St. Paul was delighted to accept it as a tribute to what she liked to consider her superior gentility, while Minneapolis was quite as satisfied to be the first city of the West, or more accurately, the Northwest. In many ways she still is.

Both are interesting and distinguished cities. Minneapolis, the expansive extrovert, is bigger, more luxurious, has more amusements, stays up later at night, and possesses, perhaps, a more youthful and venturesome spirit. St. Paul is the more cautious and reflective introvert, but one who has known how to make her caution pay.

The Minneapolis names most widely known have for generations been connected with the city's great flour-milling industry. Indeed, it is said that ambitious explorers who like to think themselves first in some remote jungle are not a little annoyed to find the sarongs worn by native women made of flour sacks stamped with the simple legend Pillsbury's Best.

One of the town's cultural delights, incidentally, is a superb Chinese bronze and jade collection—assembled by Alfred Pillsbury and given to the Institute of Art. Another remarkable collection in the Institute, acquired by another Pillsbury, consists entirely of gold objects of great beauty and antiquity. This collection is also Chinese and is one of the very few of its kind in the world.

I suppose a state university—no matter what city it is in—belongs less to the city than to the whole state. In this way, the extraordinary university in Minneapolis *is* Minnesota. I felt this especially when I returned, with the memory fresh in my mind, of so many far-off towns and farms and lonely lakes, and all that variety of peoples whose sons and daughters are, in this university, unified in more ways than in the learning they receive.

It is particularly appropriate that the Mayo Foundation should be a part of the university. No story is more essentially Minnesotan than that of the Mayo brothers. Their diagnostic and surgical genius and organizing ability brought them world-wide fame and yet, with a kind of ingrained unpretentiousness and also a stubborn wisdom, they refused to leave their Minnesota village, but brought the world to them. And now, a great medical building on the campus of the university is called in their honor the Mayo Memorial. A far cry indeed from the skeleton of an old Sioux.

I have left St. Paul to the last because, for reasons not always clear even to me, I think it is the best. On a late August afternoon, just touched by a portent of Indian summer, I walked about the city. I went up onto "the Hill," and along Summit Avenue, once the city's finest street. The shadows were blue under the immense overarching trees; the sunlight yellow as honey on the broad asphalt. And between the mansions once built and now abandoned by the town's plutocracy, there lies spread before you the whole wide, shining valley of the Mississippi.

I stopped to look at the narrow brownstone house in which Scott Fitzgerald lived as a boy, and recalled the pale, handsome and somehow haunted face of the young man I knew only before his explosion into fame. A writer who died just as his vision was reaching the stature of his enormous talent.

I passed the house where Sinclair Lewis spent some of the many restless years after he left his native Sauk Centre. (Incidentally, when I visited Sauk Centre shortly before, I found no one who could point out the place where Lewis was born.) I recalled a visit Lewis paid in St. Paul, some time after *Main Street,* to my brother-in-law, Charles Macomb Flandrau, for whose *Viva Mexico* Lewis had unbounded enthusiasm. He had turned up, unexpectedly, at Flandrau's house in St. Paul, and that night they dined with me. Afterward, Lewis embarked on an interminable monologue made up of imaginary conversations in the American idiom. Flandrau, high-strung, easily bored and not unaccustomed to the center of the stage himself protested angrily, "If you don't stop *talking* I shall leave this house." Lewis, smiling indulgently, went right on. Whereupon Flandrau flung out of the room and into the quiet street. Next morning, pale and shaken, he appeared at our door. "He found me. He talked *all night.* I'm locking myself in here until he is out of Minnesota." Some months later, when *Babbitt* appeared, much of the dialogue had a strangely familiar ring.

It was a relief to leave an avenue so full of echoes and go down into the older town, where the narrow streets have kept something of the old flavor, even though the buildings which flank them have undergone alarming face liftings. Here the former residence streets are mostly a jumble of rooming houses or houses made over into shops and warehouses. On one such street, however, the chaos resolves into a broad, well-tended lawn surrounded by a beautiful wrought-iron fence, and the sturdy, gray-stone mansion is a historic residence. It was built by Alexander Ramsey, who came out in 1849 to be first governor of the Territory of Minnesota.

One of the handsomest of St. Paul's more modern buildings is the courthouse, where a magnificent Carl Milles statue—believed by many to be his finest work—is to be seen. The remarkable setting in which it is placed is a loggia of blue-black marble, three stories high and relieved by touches of bronze and a dim, gilt and mirrored ceiling. At the far end stands the colossal statue of an Indian, carved in veined, cream-white onyx and holding in his hand a pipe of peace. The tall, proud figure is imbued with a nobility which, you are made to feel—by I do not know what magic—is not his alone, but is or must become a part of all men. A summons, stern as it may be prophetic, to a future of which no man need be afraid.

This sense of the future brought to my mind the motto inscribed on the first Great Seal of Minnesota—*I wish to look beyond.* Many Minnesotans, I believe, would feel that it sums up the history and very spirit of their state.

Whether it is truer here than of any other part of America is less important, I think, than that they should feel it to be. That there should be a place, loved in childhood, where, as the Hindu poet wrote of his native valley, the fragrances are sweeter, the moonlight softer than in any other.

> *Blessed am I that am born to this land*
> *And that her best gift to me*
> *Is that I love her. . . .*

Iowa

by PAUL ENGLE

Iowa is the heart of the Heartland.

Its greatest single force is dirt—fat dirt; out of its soil each year more wealth is produced than in all the gold mines of the world. Gently the land rises and falls, not flat, not broken into steep hills, but always tilting its fertile face to the sun.

When a military highway was needed from Dubuque to the Missouri border in the early days of the mounted dragoons, a farmer was hired. He yoked up ten oxen to a long sod-breaking plow and headed south. Day after day they moved, ahead of them the untouched grass and grove, behind them a lengthening furrow of black dirt. No sound but the man's yell to his animals, and the silken, tearing rip of the plow splitting that sod for the first time ever. It was natural for Iowa to use for its military road only the peaceful oxen and the plow. For this is an abundant land.

And when a few years ago the Soviet Union sent the first group of agricultural experts to America to find out what free men working on their own land could raise, it was natural that the Russians should come first to Iowa. And when the Red farmers arrived they were given, in once "isolationist" Iowa, a wealthy welcome, told everything they wanted to know, shown all the methods and secrets of production. They went to the First Presbyterian Church in Jefferson and held hymnbooks, probably for the first time in their lives, watched 4-H boys demonstrate how to kill corn borers, and 4-H girls bake sweet rolls. They lifted their arms at the right time in the Iowa song for the line "That's where the tall corn grows," and they saw their first real drugstore with a soda fountain and ate "Tummy Busters. Eat Two and Get a Free One—49 cents plus one cent tax." For this is an abundant land.

Iowa is the middlest of the Middle West. Its life and people are balanced and solid. It is a country of the small town, the average comfortable life. There are no great fortunes and there is no poverty. But it has the highest standard of living for its area in the world and it has a quarter of all the best land in America.

Look at the map of Iowa, the Missouri wavering down the west side and the Mississippi down the east. Jutting eastward is a fine round pot belly, the broad Mississippi bending around it like a belt. For this is an abundant land.

Iowa carries nothing to excess save its virtues and its weather. It has always been the place of the sensible medium, and of the peace that goes with it. The only Quaker President, Herbert Hoover, came from a little Iowa town. There has never been a war on Iowa soil, or a battle of any consequence. One massacre by the Sioux of a few white settlers. John Brown trained his men at a Quaker settlement, where they did strange calisthenics and drilled with wooden swords. One of his men was censured for hugging girls, which was as violent an act as any of the group committed in Iowa. When the time for fighting came, Brown left his peaceful settlement, where the Quakers had assisted him without knowing his wicked purpose, and went off to bloody Harpers Ferry. Iowa men marched off to Vicksburg, but the Civil War never came to their state.

When my grandfather rode with the Fifth Iowa Cavalry in the 60's, he chased the Sioux in Dakota Territory but never caught up with him. Inkpadutah, the leader of the Sioux who massacred thirty-two men, women and children at Spirit Lake, realized that Iowa was too peaceful for such wild goings-on, and fled west.

Kentucky was the Dark and Bloody Ground, but Iowa has always been the Bright and Bloodless Ground.

Of the Missouri River the old saying is: too thick to drink, too thin to plow. But Iowa is just right to plow, no waste land, no swamps, no mountains, no large forests. Glaciers scoured off the soil from other states and dumped it on this lucky land, giving Iowa its long reaches of loam. After grass had grown and died for centuries, sink-ing its roots so deep that prairie fires couldn't burn them out, the soil became as rich as the side of a fat hog.

Then the settlers came, and the sod-breaking plows, with their great oak beams to hold the point of the plow down against the tough buck of the roots, and the great crops began to spring up. France had its Field of the Cloth of Gold, but Iowa still has its Fields of the Cloth of Green.

The common shape of Iowa landscape is the little valley, with tiny streams everywhere like veins meshing a marvelous body. And along all of the streams, wooded slopes with willow, elm, maple, hickory, black walnut. The streams are everywhere, the dark rivers with the silt of fields: Raccoon, Coon, Wolf, Catfish, Mosquito, Polecat, Opossum, Pike, Turkey, Skunk, Cedar, Crab-apple, Squaw, and Five Barrel Creek, so called because dragoons found five barrels of whisky buried near it. And most lyrical of all, in the high hills of northeastern Iowa, the Tête de Mort (call it Teddymore), proof that the French once were here, and that a band of Dakotahs was killed by Sac Indians and scalped and thrown over a cliff.

There is no soft nonsense about the seasons in Iowa. Winter is a savage season; blizzards out of the west rattle the teeth in your skull. Frost goes deep in the fallow ground; snow piles up and when the ice comes, impenetrable, squirrels scamper over it hungrily. But then will come the incredible May morning when the sun drips a gold life on the land, seeds jump in delight under the plowed fields, the sprouted corn turns the countryside into tufted quilts, and the pigs squirm out into the light of day ("Sows opened weak on the Chicago market" says the radio report) and calves jump stiff legged around the barn. The air itself has the quality of food and breathing is nourishment. The pastures glitter with green.

Then summer overwhelms us. We can hear the crops growing, the corn up an inch a day, the pigs grunting their growth as they crunch their food—more elaborately planned and mixed than that of any child (buttermilk, yeast, fish, soybeans, sugar, corn, limestone, cobalt, acetate, zinc carbonate, linseed oil, rolled oats, fish liver, manganese sulphate, vitamins, antibiotics, riboflavin, and many others). The porkers have had their "one-shot wormer" and are busy hanging bacon on their slick sides. The whole state turns into a skillet, frying human, animal and plant life. Midnight differs a few degrees from intense noon. Corn grows tall and men grow limp. People droop by night and drop by day. But everything flourishes.

Autumn is the Iowa season. All of the winter's frozen rest, the spring plowing, the summer cultivating, move toward the final act of harvest. The land browns, oats ripen, corn begins to dent, hay is cut, the alfalfa for the third time. As the long corn leaves turn brittle the air itself turns crisp and tree leaves burn the branches for a while before falling. It is a season truly called "the fall." Things come to earth, the crops to barn, the kids to school. The delirious activity of summer slows down, as the urgency of jobs to get done before it's too late falls away.

Between summer and autumn come the county fairs, with their rows of Jerseys, Guernseys (with the highest butter-fat content in their milk), of Holsteins (the largest producers of milk in bulk), the mouse-colored Brown Swiss with their calves looking like heavy-boned fawns, the glistening flanks of Black Angus beef steers, polished and combed, or the ruddy Herefords with their white faces. And there is usually a single hog litter totaling a ton. The wildly carved running horses on the merry-go-round carry children to the same sweet and brassy tunes. The exhibits of farm machinery are fantastic, the prize squash, pumpkin, corn, startle the eye with their size. And of course there are the formidable yet delicate and fluffy cakes with blue and red prize ribbons on them, the prize pickles, canned beans, enough to shatter the stablest stomach. Along the race track where the horses are jogging with their light sulkies and the old-time horsemen with their legs straddling the shafts, families are engaged in that most typical, most delightful Iowa activity—consuming food.

What people come? Farmers with their families, faces tanned but a sharp white line around the neck where the shirt collar kept off the sun, with the deliberate walk of men accustomed to plowed fields and bumpy pastures. They watch the fat-steer judging and the heavy draft-horse judging, look at the machinery, take a suspicious glance at the Kewpie doll stands and the jaded girlie shows, but mostly they talk, talk to other farmers they haven't seen in a coon's age. (What's the age of a coon?) Everywhere clusters of men arguing weather, crops, prices (today's prices are mentioned in the tone of voice one uses coming home from a funeral), politics, the Government (in the tone one uses for a difficult uncle you don't really want around but whose wealth might be needed later on).

The women are here, too, and the kids; it's a family affair, something for everybody, the home-convenience exhibits for the ladies and the Ferris wheel for the screaming kids. But town people are here too, especially the ones who grew up on farms and moved away. They've changed some, they walk a little faster and gesture more abruptly, but they still like the smells of the barns and the bawl of the calves and the leathery tang of harness being soaped for the afternoon's first trotting heat. You can take the boy out of the farm but you can't take the farm out of the boy.

Across the top of the Great Seal of Iowa is the motto: Our Liberties We Prize and Our Rights We Will Maintain. And to prove that those rights will be maintained, a soldier with rifle stands in the foreground, a plow and a great swirling flag behind him. To a surprising extent, they are maintained, although now and then there is a little uncertainty as to just whose rights are meant. A few years ago the body of a GI was refused burial at a Sioux City cemetery, although he had died protecting his country's liberties, because he was too much a 100 per cent American, a real Indian. But this is rare. It is a matter of pride that the first case to come before the Supreme Court of Iowa Territory gave freedom to a Negro slave. And this same regard for human liberty came up a century later when a Negro Army officer stationed at a radar base near Waverly could not find housing for his family, although an apartment was available. When the other tenants heard about it, they petitioned to have him as a neighbor and welcomed his family with a celebration.

There has always been a sense of the just in Iowa. More than a hundred years ago when the defiant Sac Chief Black Hawk was presented to Andy Jackson in Washington he looked him in the eye and said simply, "I am a man and you are another."

Even obscenity gets a fair hearing. A few years ago the ladies of Dubuque were frightened by the appearance of comics, reprints, pocket books near schools. Hearings were held and the naughty evidence was introduced, such fiction as that of Erskine Caldwell, Richard Bissell (Dubuque's own, author of *A Stretch on the River* and *The Pajama Game*), and the usual popular novels, along with some gruesome comics and a history of art which charmingly proved that the female nude had interested more artists than had bowls of fruit or happy children. But in the end, the decision taken was the moderate, middle one to be expected of Iowa people: the chance of censorship was worse than the chance of indiscriminate novels being read. One argument of real power in a state essentially rural-minded was that the corset sections of mail-order catalogs contained more photographs of undressed models than any of the books being questioned.

When the Russians came to Iowa they expected to find the fields full of people. As they were driven along the roads between the luxuriant corn and oats and alfalfa, with the yards and pastures full of hogs and cattle, they kept asking, "But where are the workers?" Usually they were told that a man and his wife and children, with an occasional hired man, farmed the place. One of them exclaimed, "By you one man—by us a hundred!" What he did not realize was that this staggering production of food by a few people was done by the same class of farmers the Soviet had murdered in the early 30's. They had never seen a husking hook fastened to a glove. They kept asking at the agricultural college at Ames who was their *boss* in Washington, and could not believe that the college operated independently of the Federal Government. When they asked Guy Stover, Jr., a farmer near Reinbeck, who told him what to plant, he replied: "Nobody tells me what to plant. Nobody. I can let the whole farm grow up in weeds if I want to and nobody can say a thing."

They ate meals of roast beef, vegetables, ice cream, angel-food cake, salad, milk, all of which came from the same farm. They discovered that small-town newspapers in Iowa were thicker than Russia's national dailies. They had their first experience of motels, a dime store, golf, a country club. They discovered, as the Charles City *Press* put it, every reason under the sun why the Iowa farmer produced twenty times as much food as the Russian farmer, except the main one, the freedom under which the Iowa farmer operates.

The Russians came in the hope of learning how to feed their people. That was natural, for men and women have always come to Iowa with hope. In the 1850's came a group of Germans calling itself The Community of True Inspiration, who believed that God still spoke directly to man. They settled between Iowa City and Grinnell and built seven little Amana villages in the medieval manner, the families living close together in the communities and going out to work in the fields. They had the wisdom to realize that the Lord could best be served with good land rather than poor, and took up 26,000 acres of rich bottom soil and wooded hills along the Iowa River. They ate in communal houses (five times a day, in leisure and abundance, with excellent grape and dandelion wine brought out to those working in the fields at noon). All property save clothing

and furniture was held in common. Each adult received a tiny sum
known as "year-money" for odd expenses, the least-skilled worker in
the hog house receiving the same housing and maintenance as the
most responsible farm head. God was worshiped not in churches but
in houses without cross or decoration and no music save the unac-
companied human voice grandly ringing out the hymns written by
their own brilliant prophet Christian Metz.

They flourished in their isolated, abundant and devout life until
the wicked world came to them by newspaper, paved road, car,
radio, and the young people began to yearn for the things they saw
others having, like bicycles and Sunday baseball. They voted to dissolve the old communal-property idea and to form a corporation in
which everyone worked for a salary. Each adult was given one share
of Class A voting stock; when issued in 1932 a share was worth
fifty-four dollars—today it is worth many times that. Houses are
painted, cars are everywhere, television aerials rise as high as the
native hickory and oak trees.

Again Iowa released the energies of people who came to her.
Working with odd items from local shops, George Foerstner and
others created a little freezer. And now in the cornfields at Middle
Amana, where oxen loafed not long ago and daily prayers out of the
early 18th Century were uttered in praise of God and in disparage-
ment of weak man, there is a bright new factory from which more
home freezers are sold than from any other plant in the world.

Iowa has always believed in bringing together the holy and the
useful. Dutch who would not conform to the established church in
Holland came in 1847 to found the town of Pella, where every May
the old Dutch clothes and the wooden shoes come out, and there is
dancing in the street. Why shouldn't they dance? They're in Iowa
raising tulips, and raising the hem of their long dresses, oh so slightly.

And the French came to start their own idealistic community at
Icaria on the Nodaway. Property was held in common, but alas, not
the zeal for work. A dance hall was built, however, with plenty of
zeal and native wood, but soon there were only individual men and
women working their own lives.

The Hungarians came after the failure of the 1848 revolt against
Austria. But they were aristocrats full of zeal to build a New Buda in
northwestern Iowa, and what the land needed was a sharp plow, not
an edged sword.

The Norwegians came to northeastern Iowa, in the handsome hill country, to settle the town of Decorah and found Luther College. Some crossed the frozen Mississippi in the depth of winter, proving the stern devotion of a faith that could build log cabins in a wilderness and a hundred years later produce blond, unbeaten football teams with Viking names.

Naturally, the Mennonites came here to build their fine farms, with that same combination of hard work and solid faith. Around Kalona they wrestled with some hard questions: Was it right to drive an automobile? (Most drive buggies; a few, cars with the chrome painted out.) Was it proper to use a tractor with metal tires but not with rubber tires? Would pickles tied to the feet cure a child of convulsions? Should the preachers forbid turkey roasts, ice-cream suppers, imposing weddings, laces, corsets, Christmas trees? The men in their beards, the women and children in their black bonnets and high shoes, come into Iowa City to shop, and to peer quietly at the naughty world. And then go home to work their rich farms with their old simplicity.

The Czechs came to Spillville in the northeastern country, where Anton Dvorak came to write his music in the peaceful valley where his native language was still spoken. And signs across part of Cedar Rapids today are in Czech, and the Sokols do their fine gymnastics and the kolaches are made with prunes or poppy seeds. Once a Czech girl named Jaroslava Holobulova graduated from Coe College at the top of her class.

But most amusing of all the peoples who came to Iowa were the English younger sons who settled in Le Mars in the northwest to learn farming in the 1880's. They brought to Iowa their own sporting ways; cricket practice was held on Broken Kettle Creek, and the Le Mars cricket team beat St. Paul. Polo was played against Cherokee and Council Bluffs. But the polo ball proved more attractive than the humble pumpkin, and the younger sons left the plow in the furrow and rode into town to "paint the place a rip, staring red."

But the purpose of these gay British boys, since the place was Iowa, was to learn how to raise food. A visiting newspaperman wrote about them: "The young men who make up this community are . . . graduates of Oxford or Cambridge. On one farm I met two tall and handsome young farmers whose uncle had been a distinguished member of Parliament. The last time I had seen them was in a London drawing room. This time they tramped me through the mud and manure of the barnyard to show me some newly bought stock.

They were boarding with a Dutch farmer at three dollars a week in order to learn practical farming. . . . Another young farmer had been connected with a Shanghai bank. There was a brother to Lord Ducie, not to speak of future baronets, viscounts, and honorables . . ."

But real liberty had its price. One of the Englishmen wrote that he could no longer stand the Iowa attitude: "The other evening on the closing of the House of Lords (as they had named a saloon), I was standing with four or five friends talking when the deputy marshal comes up and requests me in his usually suave manner to 'cheese this racket.' Liberty is constantly jammed down your throat here, but it seems to me an exploded theory, when an officer can do what he likes with your right of speech." Discouraged by equal parts of being told to cheese it and of hard work, the younger sons gave up their western ghosts and left.

The English were the gayest of all the Iowa settlers. More solid were the "Hook-and-Eye Dutch," who refused to put up the tops of their buggies because the sun was no harder on them than on the horse.

But no matter what their origins, Iowa people believed in education. With the lowest rate of illiteracy in the United States, it is natural that one of the country's largest manufacturers of fountain pens should be the W. A. Sheaffer Pen plant, at Fort Madison, and that one of the finest state-wide newspapers should be the Des Moines *Register*, unique today in having an editorial page with generous convictions and the courage to express them. Iowa believes, with the mixture of idealism and practicality which has always distinguished the people of Iowa, that personal freedom is nothing but old-fashioned right, and every man's due.

The Cowles family is a solid example of what human character can mean to a state, through its many gifts to colleges, the foundation it has endowed, and through dramatizing in the pages of the *Register* the fact that a nation's security lies as much in its ideals as in its bombs, and that liberties must be prized, even at the risk of offending subscribers.

Even in liquor, Iowa has chosen the medium way. Knowing the strong temperance feeling among the people, and yet suspecting that, since it was mentioned in the Old Testament, drinking might be here to stay, the state compromised. Under the fancy that a man would remain soberer if he took a bottle home, where there was no one to observe but the kiddies, all bars (save for beer) were outlawed. State liquor stores were set up without advertising or decoration. Some dramatic things have happened as a result.

Because of a fear that liquor purchases might be criticized by their neighbors, many people in the first year drove to the next town to buy where they might be unrecognized. On the way, they would pass the cars of those from the next town hurrying over to *their* liquor store to buy in secret. One enterprising newspaper, the Eagle Grove *Eagle*, discovered that, on the basis of gross liquor sales, Eagle Grove and nearby Clarion had exchanged populations. Any action connected with the naughty word "liquor" is news.

The demon rum even lurks behind innocent beef cattle, and caused one governor embarrassment. At an Iowa State Fair, the governor accepted the grand-champion baby beef, only to discover that it was owned by the Storz Brewing Company of Omaha. He gave it away for charity. And at the Waterloo Cattle Congress he agreed to pose with the grand-champion bull, a colossal animal, and then found that it belonged to a Milwaukee brewer named Pabst. It's a delicate thing when the governor of the state producing the finest fat cattle can't be photographed with a baby beef or giant bull without first sniffing them for fumes of alcohol.

But in the long run, Iowa's system works out for the average best. It returns an annual profit to the state of several million dollars, so that drinking might be called patriotic. At the same time that those who loathe the spectacle of public bars are spared that hideous sight, their neighbors who like a nip are allowed to buy all they wish.

Realizing that the surest way to produce a balanced people was to educate them, the first General Assembly to meet in Iowa founded a university. Later came the first law school west of the Mississippi. And since the state believes that fertility in the arts should try to equal fertility in the soil, it was only natural that the University of Iowa should have been the first in America to bring all the creative arts to the campus, boldly and with honor to the artist. Students were encouraged to write plays, novels, poetry, short stories, compose a string quartet or a symphony, to paint in oil or gouache or water colors, to carve in wood or stone or metal, or to act in plays.

At Iowa, the creative artist is equal to the scholar: Philip Bezanson of the University Music Department composed a piano concerto which was conducted by Dimitri Mitropoulos with the New York Philharmonic Orchestra, and the soloist was John Sims of the Music Department; and in the same field house where the Iowa basketball team won the Big Ten championship two years running, Mitropoulos conducted the Berlioz *Requiem*. University of Iowa painters and sculptors exhibit in the finest shows in the country; more poets from the University of Iowa were represented in the *New Campus Writing* one year than from any other institution. Tennessee Williams wrote some of his first plays at the superb University theater. Some thirty novels have been published out of the Fiction Workshop.

Iowa's congenial attitude toward the arts has had some remarkable effects on the personality of the state. In Des Moines the state capitol is so extreme an example of ornate decoration that it has the complex beauty of the grotesque (the people, however, seem to love it). Across town, out Grand Avenue with its 19th-Century big houses covered with gingerbread, is the new municipal Art Center, designed by Eliel Saarinen, the 20th-Century architect from Finland. On the walls may be an exhibit of modern art; its variety and abundance will amaze you.

Go to one of the most congenial cities for art in America, Cedar Rapids. At Coe College there has been a long-term exhibit of the most advanced art from the Solomon R. Guggenheim Museum in New York. For fifty years Cedar Rapids has had its own art association and for many years its own symphony orchestra. It was not chance that Grant Wood painted his first oils here; dozens were bought locally long before he became famous. (I remember the time he painted on a canvas—for a startled eighth-grade art class I belonged to—the sound of a piece of music, following the sound over the curves and whirls with his brush.) It was in the country around Cedar Rapids that he found the neat and formal landscape for his paintings. Here were the artificial-looking trees, which he had seen first on his mother's china, trees rounded by the steady wind before Wood rounded them on his own imagined hills. Here he saw the patterned corn, the young sprouts lined across the fields like knots tied on a quilt. Wood painted the birthplace of Herbert Hoover at nearby West Branch (settled by the same Quakers who had befriended John Brown in the bloody days). With his instinct for order, which he found in the cultivated and controlled Iowa landscape, he cleaned up the field beyond the little white house. When a resident of West Branch saw the painting, he remarked gratefully, "Well,

Grant, that's the house all right, and we sure thank you for mowing them weeds."

So it is natural that in Cedar Rapids there should live Marvin Cone, the country's leading painter of all the shapes and richness and variety of wooden barns, and all the intricate, many-doored interiors of haunted houses. For he, too, has found in the Iowa scene a pattern and a pride.

Every summer at the county fairs one sees the letters "4-H" everywhere. They stand for Head, Heart, Hands, Health, and are an effort not only to make better farmers out of the young people but to give them better lives, to improve the style of clothes worn by the girls and the style of public speaking used by the boys. Some of the finest baby-beef steers in the world are owned by 4-H boys and girls, who feed them, brush them, keep records of costs and diet, tend them like pets, and then compete at the fairs, selling them for the fanciest prices, often over a thousand dollars for one animal. Girls compete in the same ring with boys and sometimes beat them. It's a fine sight to see a young girl leading a Black Angus curried to glossy brilliance or a Hereford to a glowing ruddiness; and at times a tearful sight when a creature which has been pampered and worked over for a year is sold for slaughter.

When the 4-H members take part in a contest, there is no public posturing in bathing suits. The *healthiest* boy and girl from each county are chosen, and compete in a state-wide and then a national contest. For the girls, there is no mere beauty contest, but one for the best groomed—in clothes each has made—but many of these girls would brighten a bathing suit too.

The Iowa farmer has come a long way since the frontier grace at meals:

> *Mush is rough,*
> *Mush is tough,*
> *Thank Thee, Lord,*
> *We've got enough.*

His problem is no longer getting enough mush, but producing too much beef, pork, corn, wheat. When nearly everybody else in America has been increasing his income, the farmer's has dropped by 30 per cent. He was urged to raise as much food as possible, and the wars exaggerated this. But suddenly, just when the farmer had bought more machines to produce more food, there is too much food. Corn is sealed in round metal bins outside every town in Iowa. Too many hogs go to market (you can't let a hog wait, and you can't tell it to stop eating; when it's ready for market it's got to go), and the price is down to half what it was not long ago.

Now the farmer is traditionally "agin the Guvment," but of late years he has turned, kicking and screaming most of the time, to that same Government which he has cussed out with such pleasure. He doesn't want controls. The old phrase "independent as a hog on ice" is a wonderfully and miserably accurate description of the farmer's position. A fat hog sliding across the ice is the least independent thing in the world. The farmer wants to be his own boss, he doesn't want anyone telling *him* what to do, but he finds the market a mighty slippery place. He looks at his corn-fattened beef cattle, or his hogs, and knows he will get barely his cost back, and maybe not that. So he looks toward that suspicious and remote city called Washington. He wants to remain individualistic, but he doesn't want to go bankrupt. When the same situation rose in the early thirties, the farmers overturned milk trucks, brought guns to auctions and forced the sale of foreclosed farms for a dollar. These people were called "sons of wild jackasses."

The result is a mild schizophrenia on the farms. Leave me alone but help me. The younger farmers accept the curious combination of the individual going his own way (my father, born on a farm, used to say that a real country was one where a man could go to hell the way he wanted to) and the Government stretching out a long, helping arm from Washington.

The state grows with the times, too, for recently industrial production surpassed agricultural. New factories are coming in, many small and specialized ones to the smaller towns. The big cereal plants, the agricultural machinery factories, the Quaker Oats in Cedar Rapids where entire boxcars of grain are picked up and rolled over on their sides, an aluminum factory on the Mississippi, all expand the state's income and alter its rural character.

Even in fighting, Iowa men have struck a balance. In 1870 two men fought until they were, as the old account says, a mangled mass. Both were arrested, whereupon each said that it had all been for fun, just to see whether a man from Kentucky could beat a man from Maine. The loser even argued that the winner should not be fined because, after all, he had won.

The famous Iowa 34th Division of World War II fought from North Africa to Sicily to Italy to Germany, still looking after those plain rights. Yet Buffalo Bill, born down at Le Claire on the Mississippi, had to leave Iowa for a more violent life.

Iowa balances a furious physical climate with a congenial human climate, for the hearts of the people are as abundant as the land around them. Graced from the beginning with a fullness of food, they have made abundance and creativeness an integral part of their rights and liberties. If there is hope anywhere in this wicked world or in these many states, it is certainly here, exploding like popcorn in a pan. (Of course Iowa raises more popcorn than any other state). When a farmer falls sick at harvesttime, neighbors move in with fifteen corn pickers and gather his crop in a day. When the young writers, musicians, painters, sculptors of the United States want a sympathetic community as an alternative to New York, here is a university welcoming them not merely as students but as artists. When Marvin Cone needed a year away from teaching so that he could paint without distraction, businessmen (those same maligned businessmen of whose stony hearts we read) put together a purse of money and told him to spend it anywhere he wished. And he painted more in one year than in any other five.

Suddenly, those outrageous seasons no longer matter in the face of the life, the people, the hope. They become rather a source of pride that one survives them, a source of that very abundant fertility which hard work meets halfway, between heaven and earth, between the two great rivers.

Missouri

by PHIL STONG

"I'm from Missouri" is a phrase heard not only in every one of the other forty-nine states—but also in London and Rome and Vienna and Timbuktu. Even before the rise of Harry Truman, Missourians got around.

When "You'll have to show me" follows the first phrase, do not be fooled by the humorous quotation marks in the Missourian voice. And do not—repeat not—believe that it is a request for information. It is a demand for supporting evidence on whatever you are saying or trying to sell. If you can't produce it, God help you.

If you have heard the dubious legend about the origin of the phrase—that Missouri miners, arriving late at the silver rush in Colorado, had to be shown how to dig silver—forget it. Missourians never arrived late anywhere where diggings were good, or asked any questions when they got there.

The only thing riskier than trying to show a Missourian something is to confuse his home state with another. Kansas Citians are especially dangerous—I'm married to one, and I shudder when someone assumes that Kansas City is in Kansas, and then says, "Well, there *is* a Kansas City, Kansas." The answer will be a languid question, "Is there?" Certainly it's disingenuous, but it states the Missouri faith —that there is nothing like Missouri, that Missouri is a body of land completely surrounded by inferior, benighted, pitiable, unimportant territory.

It was in St. Louis that Johnny done Frankie wrong, and W. C. Handy dreamed up the bluest of all blues; and it was no rhyme-dictated accident of Tin Pan Alley that the cowboy in *Oklahoma!* sings "Ev'rythin's up to date in Kansas City," for Kansas City has always been Oklahoma's shopping and good-time town.

From the days of the freighters and the Santa Fe and Oregon Trails and the Pony Express, Missouri is still "home" and "back East" to large sections of the West and Southwest. Indeed, it is only in Missouri, say the Missourians, that "Texans don't dare to brag." Too many of them started out from here without a longhorn or an oil well to their names.

As the oldest state completely west of the Mississippi, Missouri views all of western America with the eyes of a worldly-wise grandmother, amused, uncritical, faintly patronizing—and above all, well satisfied with her own racy past—the memories of lovers —of dashing fellows from France and Spain; Virginia cavaliers, Bostonians not too godly to hurry to a land boom; earnest, idealistic Germans fleeing a Germany already, in 1830, hostile to democratic ideals; roistering boatmen from New Orleans and Cincinnati; woodsmen in coonskin caps, trappers and miners and priests and outlaws —good, bad, but very few indifferent, among these men who poured across the last great river into Missouri in the surge of America across the continent.

For many, Missouri was the jumping-off place to the wilder West. For others of the merchant's temperament, it was rich enough and wild enough and far enough west to be a stopping place—there was more money to be made in outfitting the wagon trains of the gold-and-silver seekers than in going with them. The rich Black Prairie of north Missouri appealed to the Southern planters, the Ozarks looked like home to the Kentucky mountaineers, and the rivers—not only the giant Mississippi and the Missouri, but the wonderful web of smaller streams, attracted everybody.

Many a westward traveler, approaching the dusty plains and deserts between him and the Pacific, looked at this wealth of water and unpacked his wagon. Shovels meant for mining went into the rich black dirt of north Missouri farms. Trees cut from the thick woods along the rivers made a snugger home than huts of sod or adobe. This was a new land fresh and wild as anything farther west—but pleasant and hospitable to human beings. It caught and held its lovers, as it still does—especially in October.

Wherever they are, Missourians get homesick in October. At our house in Connecticut, it is not the calendar, or the starting of the furnace, that heralds the month, but my Missouri wife looking wistful, staring out the window at the first color in the trees. "I wish we could get some black walnuts," says Virginia, "or run out to Grandview for some apples—Ben Davis apples, not these big vulgar Baldwins they have here—and some cider, real old-fashioned cider from Independence, no Yankee water added."

"No real old-fashioned worms taken out, either," I usually say, though it never gets me anywhere. Everybody knows that Missouri worms are harmless—they only add protein to the cider.

But there comes a time when you have to go to Missouri in October and see for yourself.

Missouri is larger than all New England, I found—by 3000 square miles. It is also younger, warmer (though sometimes colder in the winter), richer, brighter (especially in October), racially far more complex, lazier, friendlier, more shiftless and more gracious. It is less raw, less righteous, less ambitious than most of the other Midwest states. In its 132 years it has reached a mood like its autumnal weather, a golden leisure of the spirit, a readiness to laugh but not to disapprove. I saw no frantic struggle for a future here, but no fear, either. "Ev'rythin's up to date in Kansas City," as the song says, and everything's booming in St. Louis, growing in the northern prairie, resting in the Ozarks.

A good place to start is at Jefferson City, the capital, and a good time is the one we picked—early twilight of the first day in October. The lights were coming on and there were two bridges over the Missouri River, the one we were driving on and the one below, traced by golden blobs of lamplight on the water.

This is a proper entrance to the Missouri scene, over a river and into a town, for settlement followed the many-fingered rivers in this state and the townspeople everywhere are not so much train meeters as river watchers. Up the Missouri, past Jefferson City, have come many strange craft: French pirogues and Creole flatboats, gaudy passenger steamers—flaunting their gilt and mahogany and New Orleans-French cuisine by day, meekly tying up by night because the Missouri is even more capricious, dangerous, and violent than the Mississippi—barges and tugboats and latter-day excursion steamers, now, alas, vanished from the inhospitable waters of the Missouri—rather, from its shoals and snags, for water in depth is what the Missouri has always lacked.

In Jefferson City and all other river towns, we learned, jet planes score the heavens with their vapor trails, and few Missourians will gawk skyward. But let a tiny feather of wake show in the river or someone yell, "Boat coming!" and people will come running to the riverbank.

Over the river and into Jefferson City we came, and turning left, saw the State Capitol on its lighted hill, with Ceres from Roman myth on top, four hundred feet above the river, looking down at the American Titan, Thomas Jefferson, on his rostrum in the center of the great stairs leading to the portico. The elegant structural lines of the building derive from Renaissance Italy, the columns from Corinth, Greece, and the building material, a luminous off-white marble, from Carthage, Missouri.

The famous murals of one of Missouri's most gifted sons, of a famous Democratic family—that stormy petrel of the art world, Thomas Hart Benton—may be seen in the Capitol's House Lounge, perhaps the most fiercely attacked and fiercely championed paintings in 20th-Century America. They dare to show Missouri through the clear, cool, sardonic, but affectionate eyes of the native-born artist.

No pioneer mothers show their muscles here; no pie-faced airborne angels lead the prairie schooners westward; there are no scrolls or scales of justice or flaming swords or smoking cannon. This is Missouri "social history," with plenty of wild Missouri action. In one panel Frankie is shooting Johnny—in the seat of his pants. In others, slaves are auctioned, Holy Rollers are baptized in a river, politicians shout, women roll pastry and change diapers, a judge dozes on the bench of a courtroom complete with cuspidor—at which many have fired and some have missed.

Fine black plumes of smoke go up from paddle steamers and chunky 19th-Century locomotives, from tar-and-feathering bonfires and factory chimneys, rolling from panel to panel like a Wagnerian motif. But smoke is strangely absent from one object—the fat cigar jutting like a small, sinister torpedo from between the fat fingers of Boss Tom Pendergast of Kansas City.

This dormant cigar and the large, sleepy face of its owner brought down the heavens on the head of Mr. Benton. Democrats cried that

he had cruelly libeled Mr. Pendergast, and Republicans objected
to the preservation of the Pendergast features in any light at all.
"Paint 'em out," went the cry. "Run Benton out of the state." But
the pay-off was a victory, not only for the artist but for the wry,
realistic humor of Missourians. After sixteen years, the murals are
still there, and will be till the Renaissance palace enclosing them
falls off its bluff into the Missouri River.

Columbia is, in its own unabashed phrase, "the Athens of
Missouri." It has not only the oldest state university west of the
Mississippi but Christian College for women, founded in 1851 by a
stubborn Missourian because the state university, of which he was
then president, would not admit his female offspring. Here also is
Stephens College, five years younger than Christian but possibly
more famous because it has had Joan Crawford as a student and the
late Maude Adams as professor of the drama, and operates its own
riding stables, a country club with chauffeur service to shuttle the
girls to and from the campus, and a flying field for pupil pilots. It
also offers charm courses and jaunts to Florida in aid of "social
graces."

Columbia is the heart of "Little Dixie." Jefferson City, across the
Missouri, was held by Union forces throughout the Civil War; but
Columbia was, by and large, a Johnny Reb town. The largest of its
old homes have the true pillared porticoes of the South. The waitress
is likely to call you Mistuh Man or you-all, and the food she brings
will be either fried chicken or ham and beans, with corn bread—or,
if you squawk for it, beef; but it is better not to squawk. This is
not beef country—Missouri cooks almost invariably overcook it. But
if you say so, the waitress' eyes will fill with tears and all the
Missouri diners within earshot will give you an icy stare.

Columbia on an autumn afternoon is a charming town to drive
through slowly, as we did, down quiet residential streets under a
golden rain of falling leaves, out Boon's Lick Trail, past the women's
colleges, then south around the stadium and back to the sunlit
campus of Missouri U.

You will want to explore the School of Journalism, oldest in the
world (founded in 1908). The daily *Missourian* is published here,
with an overpowering staff of several hundred students and with
its own presses, linotypes, photographic laboratories, press services
and engraving rooms.

Floyd Shoemaker, secretary of the State Historical Society of Missouri sat at his desk in the M. U. Library Building.

"The first appearance of 'Show me' in print," he explained to us, "was in a song published in 1898, *I'm From Missouri and You've Got to Show Me*. But in the colloquial speech it runs much farther back. Maybe one of your Connecticut Yankee peddlers ran into it in trying to sell his wooden nutmegs. I'm willing to bet with you that some outsider coined it, some high-binder, shellgame, crooked foreigner who met his match here in Missouri.

"Not that we wouldn't have used it first if we'd thought of it. We don't mince words about anything, not even ourselves, here in Missouri. You know about the Boone County man, not so very long dead, who spent years writing a biographical dictionary called *The S.O.B.'s of Boone County?* He always said, 'I'll never finish it. Every time I go into Boonville or Columbia, I get new material.' And yet —I knew him—let an out-of-stater make cracks about Missouri or Boone County, and he rolled his sleeves up fast."

Mules seemed at this point a more pacific topic.

"Mules?" Mr. Shoemaker's voice softened. "Those marvelous creatures. The best little, smartest little, toughest little beasts in these United States. Go over to the School of Agriculture experimental farm and hear about them from experts."

At the school on the edge of town, we heard the voice of the tractor loud upon the land, and saw the glitter of every modern machine that man has invented to do his farming for him. The prospect for the mule looked bleak. But soon we found that his little candle still burnt in this heartless, mechanistic world. Professor L. A. Weaver, chairman of the Department of Animal Husbandry, and his assistant, John M. Kays, looked at each other, smiled, sighed, and told us about the Missouri mule.

"He's strong," said Mr. Weaver, "and smart. *Too* smart for many human beings. He is easy to take care of, healthier than the horse, and he feeds himself. He won't drink when he's too hot, and in a barnful of oats he'll eat just as much as he needs, where a horse would founder."

"Horses are dumb?" I asked.

"At least nervous. The mule is a great relaxer. You can see that when he rolls—and he rolls every chance he gets. He is happily at home in the universe—or at least in Missouri; and the horse, like man—non-Missourian man—is an anxious, ambitious, miserable fellow."

"Some non-Missourians appreciate him," said Mr. Kays. "Carolina tobacco planters buy him, and the Greek and Spanish governments. But there aren't enough of him left. Here in Little Dixie we used to raise mules by the thousand."

I said with a feeling that I was hitting below the belt, "Have you any at the School of Agriculture farm?"

They both said quickly, "We always keep a pair."

"For old times' sake?" I asked.

"No," said Mr. Kays. "For mud and ice. Here in Missouri we have every kind of weather there is—and for some of it nothing is any good except the Missouri mule."

This is Daniel Boone—or rather, Boon—country. Except for Boone County, named at a later, more educated time, the *e* is missing. You follow Boon's Lick Trail (now U. S. 40) from Columbia to Boonville, an Old South town with Classic-Revival mansions and a sunny cobbled street leading to the river wharf which was once the heart of Boonville business.

Here is Kemper Military School and its formal red-brick campus —the oldest military academy west of the Mississippi, founded in 1844. It is distinguished also by its good nature in answering questions about its worst pupil, Will Rogers, who hit the campus in 1897 out of Indian Territory in a ten-gallon hat and high-heeled red-top boots with spurs, coiled ropes draping his luggage. Colonel H. C. Johnston says, "Will Rogers was here for a year and a half, doing second- and third-year high-school work. His version of his stay here —that he spent one year in the guardhouse and the other in fourth grade—was wrong on both counts. He was an erratic student, but an indefatigable prankster." Of himself in the elegant Kemper uniform, Will later said, "One of my kids saw a picture of me and said, 'Mamma, I knew Daddy had been everything, but I never knew he was a bellhop.'"

The first land battle of the Civil War was fought four miles from Boonville on June 17, 1861, the Virginians of Little Dixie being even quicker on the trigger than the Virginians back in Virginia. It is said that there are only two Republican families today in all of Howard County, and none in Boonville. Some Republicans landed here from the river but they went south into the Ozarks or west into the Great Plains. Occasionally a good Democrat went West too. In the Boonville law office of Judge Roy D. Williams you can see the notice posted in 1826 by a Howard County saddle maker, offering a reward of one cent for the capture of his missing apprentice, Kit Carson. This was not an evaluation of young Kit's abilities but a kindly effort to help a young Southern gentleman without capital find richer hunting grounds out West.

Driving east from Howard and Boone counties, you traverse the last of Little Dixie, Callaway County. It has been known as the Kingdom of Callaway since 1861, when four hundred old men and boys, armed with one log painted to resemble a cannon, bludgeoned a promise from the leader of the invading Union militia to stay out of the Kingdom if they in turn would disperse their "forces." The agreement was kept and all was quiet in the Kingdom for the rest of the 19th Century.

In the twentieth, however, two earth-shaking events have taken place. Native-born Henry Bellaman wrote the best-seller *King's Row* about Callaway County, with too much candor to please his neighbors—and Winston Churchill appeared with President Truman in Fulton in 1946 to accept a degree from Westminster College (enrollment that year, 233) and to make his "Iron Curtain" speech, whose rumblings are still heard on world seismographs.

From the lilies and languors of Little Dixie you roll suddenly into a brave fresh old world—Missouri's Rhineland, settled by German intellectuals in the 1830's. The road to Hermann runs south from U. S. 40 through the woods, walnuts and oaks and hickories, to the Missouri-Rhine, then over the bridge and into a fairy-tale German town, swept, scrubbed and dusted from its gabled roofs and medieval balconies to the cozy cobblestones in the steep streets. Here German is often spoken. Hermann predates both World Wars, and during the Civil War its people supplied the extra liberal pressure needed to keep Missouri officially in the Union.

They paid for their abolitionism—but not too much, as you can see when you pass the courthouse. For there is the famous "artillery" of Hermann, which saved the town from the army of Confederate General Marmaduke—one cannon. Six old men were left in town when the young men departed to join the Union Army, and they dragged their one cannon from hill to hill, firing one shot from each, till General Marmaduke thought he was surrounded. He caught up with it in time, however, and rolled it into the Missouri River, but the townsfolk fished it out and put it in its present place of honor.

In firing a salute to Hermann's fiftieth anniversary, in 1886, this venerable blunderbuss outdid itself and slightly burst asunder. "It's looking sort of frail," said a Hermannite standing near us as we looked at it, "but that's all right. We shan't be needing it again." German Hermann, Missouri, is still a morning town—full of sunny faith in the future of Missouri and America.

Out of old Germany you follow a long, gently curling road southwest toward another province of old America, the Ozark Highlands, the world of the hound-dog, the hilltop cabin and fiddle music at moonrise. Presently we were rolling along a peaceful road that climbed over wave after wave of hills, each one higher than the last. The sun at our right was going down, and only the ledges at our left burned with autumn color. From the last high shelf, in the warm dusk, our road turned right and downward, to the shores of Lake Taneycomo and the pillared front of old Hotel Rockaway.

Here the fishermen come in, with catches of jack salmon and bass and yellow cat and with the ambling stride of luxuriously tired sportsmen. Here you can eat your good dinner in peace and quiet, or by cocking an ear you can listen to Ozark conversation. It is slow and mild, as by this time you will expect in Missouri.

"You ever think that li'l ol' houn'-dog of Jim Bacon's would take the prize?" (There was a spur-of-the-moment hound show hereabouts today.)

"I want to get some water-ground meal at Kissee Mills before I leave."

"Can't. The water's over it, and old John Hires has gone to Colorado."

"I don't care how many damn dams and new lakes they make, give me old Taneycomo." Then sadly, "Wonder what will happen to Taney when the new lake fills up?"

Lately through the Ozark Hills, one of the last redoubts of natural man, with their sweep of wild and carefree uplands and their 19th-Century calm, their coonhounds and foxhounds and leaning cabins and tarantellas to fiddle music, there is heard the swelling roll of thunder on the left—a warning of the end that is coming to this way of life. It is the thunder of water, not gushing in its age-old mountain chasms but dammed and released by man, guided into valleys and over the roofs of towns, stocked with fish and outboard motors, and calling in the outside world.

Look at Forsyth, or rather, look *for* it. Not long ago it was a little

Ozark town sleeping in the sun since 1837, apparently world without end. Now its streets and homes are under water and the hallways of its ancient courthouse are filled with mud. It is part of the bed of Bull Shoals Lake and nothing can save it. There is a new town of Forsyth on higher ground, with a "modern"-style courthouse, paved streets, sewers, a $75,000 golf course, boat docks and stone bathhouses.

There will be more ducks, they say, when the big lake rises, and more fish. My guess is that there will be fewer ducks because there will be more hunters; perhaps fewer fish, too, per fisherman. The new sportsmen will be a different breed, the kind who will like the glittering new eight-story "Fishermen's Apartment Hotel" (*sic*).

But the old spirit is not dead yet. We stopped at a group of tourist cabins and found a note tacked on the open office door: "Cabins 1, 5 and 8 ready. No. 9 will be to fix. Look around, take one, and we will be back about four o'clock." That's the authentic voice of Ozark hospitality.

The trip from the Anglo-Saxon world of the Ozarks to Old France in eastern Missouri is like interplanetary travel, and also like a short cruise between centuries, made not by rocket ship or time machine but by a day's drive from Taneycomo to the Mississippi River. No rocket would do. For the full flavor of this part of the state, you need a good slow automobile, a bright October day, and the kind of soul that takes easily to transmigration.

Two hundred miles of the Ozark uplands lie before you like a Persian rug flung carelessly over the top of the world, here rucked up into gleaming ridges and there smoldering in the shadow of the valleys. It is also, my wife kept saying, like a giant spice chest spilled under the sun, cinnamon and nutmeg and cloves and cayenne. The truth is that it is like nothing I have seen anywhere, not even October in New England. There are red and black oak, hickory and maple and yellow pine, hawthorn and sumac and the rare smoke tree. The hillsides are so steep that plants on the north and northeast exposures are of the Appalachian family, while those on the south and southwest belong to Texas and Oklahoma and New Mexico. For Missouri is a meeting point not only of human history but also of East and West, botanically speaking. We made the two hundred miles last as long as possible.

Under all this fire lies water, rumbling through the earth, gushing, swirling and bursting in spray, through cracks in the mountain porphyry and granite to form the "sinks" and pools and rushing rivers of this Big Spring Country. Among hundreds of giants, Big Spring, near Van Buren, is largest of all; its average flow of 252,000,000 gallons a day would supply water for the city of St. Louis. It must be dazzling at midday, but in twilight, as we saw it, it is pure magic. Deep in its own state park, at the end of a lonely, twisting road, one comes upon it, a smooth wide torrent of unearthly blue sliding out of a ledge of rock at the foot of a high, darkling cliff.

We drove on to Poplar Bluff, where the Ozark upland ends on the rim of the alluvial plains of the Missouri delta. Here, in the delta, the cotton blossom doesn't blow in October, but the fields are dotted with the last white fluffs of cotton bolls clinging to the stem. Up and down the sunny aisles go the gleaners of all ages from six to sixty, for when the machines have finished, the human hand and eye take over. There are flashes along the ground of white goose wings, and in the air a strong exultant honking. The geese's work was done last spring, and pleasant enough it was too—the eating of delicious bugs and weeds between the cotton plants. Now the birds are honking at the autumn sun. If cotton is "a lazy man's crop," it is a lazy goose's too.

From the Delta we proceeded to New Madrid (pronounced *Mad*rid) in the southeastern corner of Missouri, where we took El Camino Real, the much-traveled road to St. Louis, and found ourselves in a new kind of country, and in another century. The life of this 200-mile road, since the Spaniards hacked it out of forest and swamp in 1789, has been a procession of violence: invaders invaded, butchers butchered, Indian heroes and Indian villains, the tramp of early miners toward Missouri silver—and lead and other minerals— the scuffle of Spaniard against Frenchman, and Frenchman against Englishman, and in the end, the footbeats of a brand-new breed, the Americans, who came to stay.

Four flags have been carried along this road, and the priests of many faiths have walked here: Catholics in dusty cassocks, German Lutherans, Anglican vicars of George III, Defender of the Faith, Wesleyans and Baptists and Scottish Covenanters. There was witch- craft here and religious frenzy, martyrdom and atheism.

On this Royal Road—now U. S. 61—you arrive at Cape Girardeau, where the Cherokees crossed the Mississippi on their "Trail of Tears" from Georgia and Tennessee to exile in the Indian Territory

now called Oklahoma. Not far from here is the hilltop grave of Major
Louis Lorimier, the French-Canadian adventurer who worked first
for Spain, then for Britain, then stirred up the Indians against the
new republic, but finally yielded to the accomplished fact of the
Louisiana Purchase and became a good American. Beside him lies
his "consort," Charlotte Pemanpieh Bougainville, under her epitaph,
"noblest matron of the Shawnee race."

Missouri cemeteries, like Missouri homes, often sit high over the
rivers—"to watch the boats come in."

From Cape Girardeau north, the road runs for ten miles between
walls of roses, then it bends northeast through uplands toward the
river, skirting an astonishing intruder on Missouri soil, the 18th-
Century Illinois-French town of Kaskaskia. Its twenty-odd square
miles were suddenly cut off from Illinois by the capricious Mississippi, and the Illinois town now sits on the Missouri shore like a
pearl in an oyster, or like a cinder in the eye—depending on which
state is doing the talking.

Four or five miles ahead, El Camino Real comes to another kind
of island in Missouri—the ancient and beautiful 18th-Century town
of Ste. Genevieve, awash in the 20th Century, quiet in its place and
perfect in its time like a Pompeii where the lava only burned the
calendars and stopped the clocks. Ste. Genevieve, dating from
1735, is the oldest permanent settlement in Missouri west of the
Mississippi. (Kaskaskia is older, but it was east of the river when
founded.)

In many of the oldest houses of Ste. Genevieve, the original families
still live today among their exquisite possessions—inlaid furniture
from old-time Paris, harps and Pleyel pianos and music boxes still
tinkling with schottisches and waltzes popular in France a century
or more ago.

This town lives by the Angelus, ringing out from the parish
church in Du Bourg Place at six A.M. and noon and six P.M. There
are processions on all holy days, and on New Years' Eve masked
celebrants go singing La Guignolée and stopping at every house for
wine. We saw a procession ourselves, that October afternoon, of
very small children with bent heads and prayerful hands winding
into the very large church—an incredibly large church for a town
of about 3000 people.

Du Bourg Place is bordered by the old houses and pink-walled
gardens of the first families of Ste. Genevieve, each one a temptation

to the curious visitor. And best of all, if your face is clean and you have a civil tongue in your head, you will be freely welcomed to these houses. There is no French *hauteur* in French Missouri—only French *politesse*, heightened and warmed by pioneer hospitality.

In the famous Philipson-Vallé house the Henry Rozier family still lives, descendants of Ferdinand Rozier who arrived here in 1811 with a young man named John James Audubon and set up a mercantile business. But as a businessman M. Audubon turned out to be a fine bird painter, and the partnership dissolved. From the walls of this house the Rozier and Vallé ancestors look down on the same chairs they used to sit in, and *grand'mère* Odile Vallé, of blessed memory for her charities, can smile on the unchipped, untarnished fittings of her tea table, on the old brandy in her fine French glasses, and, best of all, on her young descendant, Hank Rozier. In the houses of Ste. Genevieve, life has a golden continuity such as I have seen nowhere else in the nation. "It's cozy," said my wife, and the word did not sound condescending.

Against the walls of these old gardens we saw beds of coppery chrysanthemums, always a French favorite, and here and there the last fall blossoms of an almost vanished beauty, the old General Jacqueminot Rose.

Up the hill again one goes to the Old Cemetery, the last home of all the Vallés and Roziers and other fathers of the town—and of an unnumbered group of nameless passengers who died in a steamboat explosion just off the Ste. Genevieve shore, who sleep together in a sunny hollow, aliens and of unknown faith, but welcome here among the angels and the crucifixes.

St. Louis is the largest city on the Mississippi, almost twice as big in population as New Orleans. But many of its citizens seldom see the river to which the city owes its birth. Although St. Louis stretches for miles along the crescent-shaped shore, its 20th-Century growth has been inland, a steady fan-wise expansion toward the west.

One of its monuments, Carl Milles' sculptural group, *The Meeting of the Waters*, has misled more people than perhaps any other symbolic art in America. Facing the Union Station, it is the only bit of St. Louis remembered by millions of travelers who spend an hour or two between trains in this great railroad center. But the Missouri and Mississippi Rivers meet about twenty miles northeast of this statuary, as the crow flies, in a no man's land of swamp and tangled willows beyond the city limits.

Although named for a saint, St. Louis early became a center for free-thinking French intellectuals, followers of Voltaire and Rousseau and Diderot, and admirers even of Thomas Paine and Thomas Jefferson, regarded by the devout as infidels. (They were devout Deists.) Of the huge library of Auguste Chouteau, the celebrated fur trader and early pillar of the city, one fourth of the titles had been proscribed on the Catholic Index of that day.

In the spring of 1804, with the threat of Puritan rigor approaching from American rule (the Louisiana Purchase had been signed in Paris the year before), there was a sad day when the Spanish flag was lowered in the Place d'Armes, and the French flag was raised for one night before the alien Stars and Stripes should be run up. And that night, among other noises in the rebellious city, rang the cry, "God shall never cross the Mississippi!" There are persons in Iowa and Kansas who say He never has, so far as Missouri is concerned.

At any rate, the state has never had a Blue Law on its books, in spite of the influx of *les Bostonnais*, as the French St. Louisans scornfully called all Americans. Far more welcome were the "good" Germans who poured in after the German Revolution of 1848, bringing their arts and crafts, their cobblers, beer and music, and above all their zeal for freedom.

St. Louis, to the eye of the visitor, is old and new, beautiful and ugly, with formal parks and monuments, rows of "town houses" fashionable in the 1870's, and sudden vistas down short private streets barred by private gates, under the shoulders of the roaring business district. Here the ten-story Wainwright Building, though dwarfed now by others, still claims prestige as America's first and model skyscraper. Here is the courthouse of the long-drawn-out miserable trials of the Dred Scott case. There is the Art Museum, left over from the World's Fair of 1904. And yonder is Washington University, founded by the grandfather of T. S. Eliot, who some-where in the waste land of his pre-British past harbors a memory of St. Louis, Missouri.

One of these streets is the *Back Street* of St. Louisan Fannie Hurst; there on South Broadway Eugene Field was born and played with his gingham dog and calico cat; those iron "galeries" stem from the French West Indies; that planter's punch you have drunk from Jamaica to Bermuda and back originated here, in the old Planter's

Hotel; in one of these houses the American Winston Churchill was born, to write *Richard Carvel* and *The Crisis,* and in due time to reply to his British namesake, who was worrying about the duplication of names, "You, sir, had better insert your middle initial, since I, having been born in 1871, owned our name unchallenged for three years." That's how the "S" (for Spencer) was introduced into the most celebrated by-line of our times.

The American Churchill's attitude befits a St. Louisan—proud, dignified and reasonable. These are friendly people, kindly toward newcomers who do not offend by acting either brash or stuffy. Though St. Louis is a city of successful businessmen, there is little shop talk after hours, and anybody who throws his wealth around had better go back where he came from—which will certainly not be St. Louis. In spite of its 20th-Century sedate elegance, this city has not forgotten where *it* came from—its youth as a hard-living, hard-fighting river town.

At night, when the theaters and hotel supper clubs are full, there are still St. Louisans who drive down through the dark, deserted streets for a glimpse of the quiet river. The levees are still there. We saw them, sloping up from the water's edge, their cobblestones moon-pricked and cut by shadows from the empty, leaning warehouses which once held all the water-borne riches of this midcontinental river valley. On a night in late October, the levees hold in their very silence the ghosts and echoes of the past; of rafts and pirogues and stern-wheelers, and boatmen and river pirates and black men straining at bales of furs and cotton, and at crated china and pianos for the city's overlords.

In the last century three Missourians have emerged to world-wide fame. The first, in time as well as in genius, was Mark Twain of Hannibal.

No lions whelped in the streets of Florida, Missouri, on the November night in 1835 when Samuel Clemens was born; but Halley's comet flashed over it, not to be seen again until the April night in 1910, when he lay dying. Now the 200-odd inhabitants of Florida are content with the single claim to fame that, for the first four years of his life, Sam Clemens lived in their town.

Hannibal, on the river, thirty-five miles northeast of Florida, considers itself, rightfully, the wellspring of his legend. Here is his world, the "little white town drowsing in the sunlight," from which he drew the rich strands of his Missouri novels, from which he embarked for

Life on the Mississippi, and which sent him into the world as a not-so-Innocent Abroad.

That white frame house beside the stone museum on Hill Street is the Clemens home—or, if you like, Tom Sawyer's home. The fence beside it is marked "Tom Sawyer's fence," but whether Sam ever painted it himself cannot be proved. It is a neat respectable house, in which Jane Clemens brought up her family after the neat respectable way of her Tennessee and Virginia forebears, only once bursting forth at Sam, when he was brought home half drowned from swimming in forbidden Bear Creek: "I guess there wasn't much danger. People born to be hanged are safe in water."

Across the street is the "Becky Thatcher House," the home of Becky's prototype, Laura Hawkins. It houses now one of the finest bookshops in Missouri, and upstairs, the restored rooms of the Hawkins family. To the young Sam, this house stood for all that was elegant. It is much more richly furnished than his own. The mirrors and polished-mahogany candlesticks and prism-hung table lamps gave him his first inkling that beauty as well as usefulness could be considered in setting a domestic scene. In the bedroom of the child, Laura, lingers a breath of Becky Thatcher's charm for Tom. Her blue silk dress, her cambric nightgown and her petticoat are laid across her small four-poster, and her long stockings on the chair are of the softest white lisle.

Up the Hill we drove—it is called Holliday's Hill now, but of course its true name is Cardiff—and sat on the warm stones near the Memorial Lighthouse, where once stood the house of Mrs. Holliday. In *Tom Sawyer* she was the Widow Douglas, who kept a lamp burning at night in her window to guide the paddle steamers. From here you can see the bluffs where Tom and Huck climbed, and Jackson's Island, where Huck and Nigger Jim hid out before starting their long trip down the Mississippi on a raft.

There have been changes in the river, some made by its own whims, and others, like the Mark Twain Bridge, by man. But down there at the water's edge a few small white grasshopper figures were diving in the warm fall weather, and any two of them might have been naked young Sam Clemens and that other river rat, Tom Blankenship, better known as Huckleberry Finn.

No boats came along while we were there, but they still do sometimes—a tugboat with its string of barges, or occasionally the last of the stern-wheelers, the *Gordon C. Greene* of Cincinnati. When this happens, the cry goes out through Hannibal, "Stee-eee-eeeamboat a-comin'," just as it did in Mark Twain's day, and the people all go hurrying, not seeing his ghost among them.

Westward from Hannibal and the river, you drive through a rich and smiling country, the farmlands chosen by the canny Southern planters, where the Black Angus cattle grow fat, the houses and barns are freshly painted, and the towns rest complacent in the shadow of huge trees.

You drive toward another shadow, at first no bigger than a man's hand with a pistol in it, but spreading darkly out of history over the whole countryside, into legend and ballad, and a world celebrity that surpasses Mark Twain's own. For this is the country of Jesse James, that dark figure which sprang from the dragons' teeth of the Civil War and grew, even during his thirty-five years on earth, larger than life and only half as natural. The gallant guerrilla, the avenger of the attempted hanging of his stepfather by Union Kansas raiders, the Robin Hood defending the poor, the handsome, brave and chival-rous hero—that is what the world by short memory has made of the outlaw Jesse James.

Here in Northwest Missouri, he was born, and robbed the trains and banks, and finally hid and died, shot down for the $10,000 price on his head by a man who posed as his friend. Through this country-side he was hunted, and saved by respectable citizens from justice. He actually slept in more houses than George Washington allegedly slept in, says Homer Croy, his biographer, and the fact is a matter of pride to descendants of the householders—the otherwise decent men who lied for him.

The Robin Hood aspect of the legend rests, so far as I can find out, on one incident supposed to have happened in the Ozarks. The story is that Jesse and his brother Frank and Cole Younger, having lunched at a widow's home, learned that she expected the mortgage holder on her house to arrive that day and set about foreclosing. The James brothers gave her the $800 she needed, then rode away and ambushed the mortgage holder and took the money back at gun point. This proves (to some) that they were not only philanthropists but humorists.

Chivalry? The James boys never gave their victims an even break, and Jesse often finished off a wounded and helpless trainman or bank employee out of sheer ill temper.

Then what can you do about this monstrous evil legend? When the oldest inhabitant in one place has told you, "The James boys weren't so bad. Lots of people sympathized with them," you can go, as we did, from one crime scene to another, to Otterville and Osceola, Savannah and Lexington and Liberty—only a partial list of towns in Missouri that drew their attention between forays into many other states. And you can visit the house where Jesse James was born and the house where he was killed. Between the two there is not so much as a hair's breadth in comfort or culture or pleasantness.

The birthplace at Kearny, near Excelsior Springs, is a weather-beaten log house clinging to the frame ell added in 1893. The door into the original kitchen is only five feet high. The fireplace, damaged in the bombing that killed Jesse's half-brother and tore off their mother's arm, has now fallen in. In the front wing you can see the sampler worked by this strange, hysterical woman in her girl-hood, before she met and married the Baptist minister, Robert James, who fathered Frank and Jesse and then sensibly went away and died in California before his sons set off on their blazing orbit.

There is nothing here of Home Sweet Home.

The other house sat for years after Jesse's death on a high terraced street inside St. Joseph, hoodooed perhaps more by its decrepitude than by its history. It rented in those days for eight dollars a month. Finally someone bought it and hauled it out to Highway 71, where it now stands near a Jesse James Tourist Court, a filling station and a hot-dog stand. Signs beside the road say, "Stop! This is the Jesse James House. See the Bullet Hole." For a price, of course.

The bullet hole is there, all right, in the wall of the mean front room, though it looks as if it had been made by an atomic weapon. The loving hands of tourists picked and chipped off souvenirs till the management covered the gap with glass.

There is a "blood" stain on the floor which, the guide explains, must be periodiocally renewed, so many pilgrims walk over it. The bed is said to be the original on which Jesse's bleeding body was laid; it does not look comfortable. Neither does anything else in the house, and the cramped proportions of the rooms preclude any possibility that Jesse and his family ever enjoyed domestic luxury from his many robberies.

You can see a picture of Jesse here, taken as he lay dead on a wooden plank, and it will dispose of the fable of his beauty. He had black hair and a lightish beard, a pug nose and high, flat cheekbones.

Even so, the picture is probably less forbidding than his face in life, for the lids are down over his cold, terrible blue eyes.

The James legend aside, St. Joseph is now Missouri's third largest town and a place so relaxed and with so little boosterism that its city limits have not changed since 1909. Its most interesting antiquity is the Pony Express stables on Penn Street (rebuilt in the 1880's), which St. Joseph hopes to turn into a museum.

The St. Joseph *Gazette* once employed Eugene Field, whose conversation probably paid him better than his verse. Both here and in Kansas City later, he had unlimited credit and drinks on the house at all the best saloons, for as long as Gene Field sat talking in a bar, the place was crowded.

If you want to see where he courted his bride, you may still drive "in those leafy aisles, where Cupid smiles, in Lover's Lane, Saint Jo."

Missouri's third world celebrity is Harry S. Truman, of Independence and Kansas City.

Sue Gentry, of the Independence *Examiner*, said, "The most emotion I have ever seen the town show was on the night the Trumans came home 'for good.' The town was glad to have them home. But it also meant that the shooting was over. The newspapermen, who swarmed here for nearly eight years—'like the locusts of 1856,' as some old-timers said—have gone to greener pastures."

So have the cordons of Secret Service men—the city police do what little guarding is necessary, mostly against autograph seekers—to the delight of a certain newsboy. For one whole summer he had tried to collect for his papers at the Truman house, but "Those men would never let me in." He got a check by mail, of course, as soon as Mrs. Truman learned about it.

The former Summer White House in Independence is the family home of Mrs. Truman, a large, comfortable Victorian house with gables and jigsaw work and several porches. "Of course he had to have a porch at the White House," said a passing policeman to us. "They *lived* on those porches here, and Washington's just as hot as Independence in the summer."

Mrs. Truman is a member of the esteemed Wallace and Gates families in Independence. Her people made Queen of the Pantry flour, a favorite of Missouri cake bakers, who are famous in their own right. "Mrs. Truman and her mother have never been the 'running-in' kind of neighbors," we were told, "but they could always be counted on in time of trouble." The former First Lady goes to the same grocery store and the same hairdresser she has always patronized.

As for the former President, he drives regularly to his office in Kansas City. Once in a rare while he walks on a downtown street alone, and someone will stop and turn around and say, "Why, I believe that's Harry Truman." That's how easy it is to retire from the floodlights of the world theater into the shadowy wings of one's own Missouri town.

If you have planned well for October in Missouri, you will be in Kansas City toward the end of the month. That is when you can visit the American Royal Livestock and Horse Show, greatest spectacle in the state, and see this "Gateway to the West" at its glittering finest. There will be cowmen in the best hotels and night clubs, and their wives and daughters will be buying smart clothes in the shops, side by side with oil heiresses from Kansas and Oklahoma. For just as St. Louis faces the East Coast and Europe, this town looks squarely westward. And do not believe those British novelists who put a silly, dowdy American woman in their books and say she comes from Kansas City. There are more handsome and distinguished-looking women here, on Petticoat Lane, than on any other street I have seen, including Park Avenue and the Waldorf's Peacock Alley.

Over the foundations of its rough-and-ready past, and the morass of Pendergast politics and corruption, Kansas City has held up a crest of high-style urban civilization. Where St. Louis is sedately luxurious, this town is rich but cheerful. In the Hotel Muehlebach, in the magnificent Kansas City Club, in the exclusive River Club—built in 1950 on the summit of Quality Hill overlooking the Missouri and the Kaw rivers—you see people paying for their fun, but *having* it. There is more talk between tables here than in St. Louis, livelier dancing, better eating; and fewer signs of that common malady of the successful—guilty conscience.

Listen to the trenchant voice of Thomas Hart Benton, in *An Artist in America,* written some years after he fled from Paris and New York to make his home in Kansas City: "There is a difference between the precious gentility of the West and that of the East. Your western people are very friendly even when the desire to be of a superior quality runs them into affectation and pose. . . . The better part of the male gentility of the western cities seem to be secretly aware that the antics of a pink coat are not exactly in harmony with the substance of western life. . . . This basic uneasiness keeps them quite human and I must say that, so far, I have not met a really complete ass among them."

This from Mr. Benton is a staggering hyperbole of praise.

The American Royal Livestock and Horse Show, which draws exhibitors and spectators from all over the United States, has its own immense pavilions—six acres of floor space—clinging to the bluff at Twenty-third Street.

In spite of Mr. Benton's aversion to pink coats, there are hunters and steeplechasers shown here that probably cannot be matched in England, and the jodhpurs and hard hats and gentlemanly stocks worn by both sexes, are overwhelming. There are splendid Western saddles, too, and five-gaited horses—out here riders believe that the horse himself should do part of the work—and every other kind from the brewers' big brown Clydesdales to midget ponies.

The cattle and sheep and hog shows take place in the daytime, and draw the working farmer, the livestock broker and the packer. They also draw me, a onetime farmer. For this is the biggest and best livestock show in America—maybe in the whole world.

Also there, in the flesh, are the Missouri mules, the clean-boned "pulling machines" with the trim, pointed ears. And they are never alone in their stalls. These mules are pets—working pets, of course, but closer to the human race than any horse. Ed D. Frazier, veteran mule breeder of Drexel, Missouri, explained it this way: "If we don't stay around here, our mules droop, they don't show well. So mother and the kids and I spell each other. Sure, we sell them, but we sort of hate to. You know, the Rhode Island Democrats wanted me to *give* them a mascot, free for nothing. But I wa'n't that good a Democrat. Besides, you don't just give a Missouri mule away. He's a character and you want to know who's going to handle him. I just told those Yankees they'd have to show me cash and proof they'd treat him right. He's still right here in Missouri where he belongs."